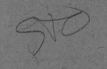

8-16-76

Introduction to international economics

The Irwin Series in Economics

Consulting Editor
LLOYD G. REYNOLDS   *Yale University*

Introduction to
international economics

DELBERT A. SNIDER, Ph.D.

Professor of Economics
Miami University

 Sixth Edition   1975

RICHARD D. IRWIN, INC. Homewood, Illinois   60430

Irwin-Dorsey International   London, England   WC2H 9NJ
Irwin-Dorsey Limited   Georgetown, Ontario   L7G 4B3

Sixth Edition

First Printing, March 1975

ISBN 0-256-01653-4
Library of Congress Catalog Card No. 74–24445
Printed in the United States of America

For Helen, Suzanne, and Chris

Preface

The present edition of this book is the result of the most extensive of the five revisions that have been made. Attention is called especially to the following major changes:

1. The pure theory of trade is divided into two parts. The first part, covered in Chapters 2–4, examines the theory in the context of pure competition and centers on the Heckscher-Ohlin factor-proportions theorem. The principal revision introduced in this discussion relates to the specification of capital as consisting of human as well as material components, with the implications that follow for resolving the Leontief Paradox.

   The second part is devoted to trade under imperfect competition, which is recognized as falling outside the scope of the Heckscher-Ohlin theorem. The focus of the discussion is on technological-gap and product-cycle trade.

2. In the section devoted to international factor movements—Chapters 7 and 8—the influence of imperfect competition is again introduced, with the primary emphasis on the activities of multinational firms.

3. The principal changes in Part Three, dealing with international monetary relations, consist of analyzing the collapse of the Bretton

Woods system, describing the monetary developments that followed, and discussing the reform proposals submitted by the "Committee of 20" in June, 1974.
4. The final part of the book, on economic development, has also been revised to place greater emphasis on the specific contributions of trade and factor movements to the growth of developing countries, including the various policy issues connected therewith.

My indebtedness for the analysis and ideas contained in this book is too extensive to cite. I cannot refrain, however, from mentioning the special debt to G. C. Hufbauer, whose empirical work on the theory of trade is heavily drawn upon, in particular in the discussion of trade under imperfect competition. In addition, I am grateful to Dr. Hufbauer and the National Bureau of Economic Research for permission to reproduce data contained in Table 4, page 157, of G. C. Hufbauer, "The Impact of National Characteristics and Technology on the Commodity Composition of Trade in Manufactured Goods," in Raymond Vernon (ed.), *The Technology Factor in International Trade* (New York: National Bureau of Economic Research, 1970).

Finally, I wish to thank Ms. Nancy Roderer for outstanding efficiency in typing manuscript, and to my wife for her patience and aid.

February 1975   DELBERT A. SNIDER

Contents

xi

List of tables and figures

Introduction

1

The significance and scope of international economics

 The daily lives of most of us are largely confined to activities in our home communities. We are aware of the local economy, for this is the immediate provider of the goods and services we consume and the source of our employment opportunities. Most of us are also conscious, however, that the local economy is only a small part of a much larger national economy. Aside from personal services, by far the greatest portion of the goods and services we purchase are not the product of the local economy: the meat on the table may come from Texas via packing plants in Chicago, the clothing in the wardrobe from manufacturers in New York, the fruit in the bowl from Florida and California, the car in the garage from Detroit, and so on. At the same time, our jobs yield products which more than likely will be consumed outside the local economy.

The complex of interrelationships among the thousands of local communities, bound together through a vast volume of exchange of goods and services and the movements of people and capital, constitutes the national economy. Awareness of the national economy is sharpened by the presence of a federal government whose influence is felt, through its taxes, spending, and regulations, in every nook and corner of the country.

We live and work in a local economy and a national economy; but we also live and work in an international or "world" economy. Just as national economies are composed of local and regional parts, so the world economy is composed of national economies. The world economy is "looser" than the usual national economy, in the sense that the national members of the world economy are not as closely interrelated and interdependent as the local and regional parts of the typical national economy. However, for many national economies external economic relations are of paramount importance. And for nearly all countries, participation in the world economy could not be withdrawn without extremely serious adverse consequences which would be felt at every level in every community.

THE SIGNIFICANCE OF INTERNATIONAL ECONOMIC RELATIONS

There are different ways of assessing the significance of international economic relations. The broadest measure is the volume of economic transactions among countries. The principal international economic transaction is the exchange of goods and services among countries. Recent data on the volume of world merchandise trade are presented in Table 1.1. In addition, there are annually billions of dollars of service transactions—shipping and passenger transportation, insurance, tourism, and so on.

Besides trade in goods and services, an important second category of international economic relations consists of the movement of capital, in the form of loans, grants, and investments, and of persons who migrate across national boundaries. Later, we shall call these "factor movements" and identify the significant role they have in the world economy.

Aggregate data conceal the position of individual components. In

TABLE 1.1
WORLD MERCHANDISE EXPORTS, SELECTED YEARS

Year	Value (billions of dollars)	Quantum Index* (1963 = 100)
1938	23	38
1950	61	45
1958	108	71
1968	239	151
1972	412	211

* Excludes trade of centrally planned economies.
Sources: United Nations, *Statistical Yearbook* and *Monthly Bulletin of Statistics*, various issues.

the case of trade and factor movements, the position of different countries varies by wide margins. The best single indicator of how important international trade is for a particular country is the proportion of its national income accounted for by its exports or consumed in the form of imports. The latter proportion—the ratio of imports to income—is called the *average propensity to import.* The average propensity to import ranges from a high of nearly 50 percent for the Netherlands to a low of 3 or 4 percent for the United States.

However useful the figures on the trade of the world and of individual countries are, they do not fully reveal the significance of international economic relations. For some countries, existing populations could not be sustained, or, if so, only at severely reduced standards of living, in the absence of international trade. A prime example is the United Kingdom, whose population of 27 percent and area of 3 percent that of the United States would not permit her to provide anything like her present standard of living out of domestic resources alone. By importing foodstuffs and raw materials in exchange for highly manufactured goods and international services, she is able to maintain a relatively high standard of living.

For most of the countries that take advantage of the benefits realizable from geographic specialization on a worldwide basis, the internal economy is integrally tied into the world economy. External and internal economic conditions and relations are not separated into compartments that can be sealed off from one another without vitally affecting the content of each. They are, rather, different components of the same organic whole. As a consequence, it is not legitimate to conclude that, for example, if the imports of a given country are 15 percent of its national income, the latter would be affected only to this extent if trading relations with other countries were cut off. Imports may be a vital, even though, quantitatively, a relatively small, proportion of the total national economy. An analogy might be the role of, say, steel output in the total national production of the United States. Steel has a much greater significance for the economy than the ratio of steel output to total production would indicate. Just as, for instance, a strike in the steel industry can create a "bottleneck," slowing down overall production, so a cutting-off of the external trade of a country could cause a bottleneck effect on its national economy.

The above remarks are applicable, though to a much lesser extent than for most countries, even to the United States. Having a vast territory, rich in a wide variety of resources, and possessed of a huge internal market, America, unlike a country such as Great Britain, could maintain its present population at a relatively high standard of living even though economic contact with the outside world were completely cut off. Nevertheless, the American standard of living would be significantly lowered and its potentiality for continued growth and development reduced, perhaps seriously, were the United States to become economically isolated. Americans would have to forego or drastically reduce the consumption of such items as coffee, tea, and cocoa, the domestic supply of which is now totally imported, and of numerous other consumer goods which are now imported in large quantities. More important, notwithstanding the wide variety of raw materials found within the United States, there are many strategically important minerals and other primary products for which she is largely or entirely dependent on foreign sources —such as crude rubber, tin, asbestos, chromite, jute, nickel, and newsprint. Indeed, there are only two metals (magnesium and molybdenum) used by U.S. industry for which it is not partially or wholly dependent on foreign supplies. In general, as compared to the beginning of this century, when the United States produced some 15 percent more raw materials than she consumed (excluding foodstuffs), by mid-century she was using 10 percent more materials than she produced.

It might be correctly argued that, were the United States cut off from all foreign supplies, she should be able in most cases physically to replace them by increased domestic output of the same or substitute commodities. But this argument misses the real point. It is not so much a question of physical incapability of producing at home what is now imported, though in some instances, such as certain minerals, this may be the case, but rather that the real cost of the home-substituted output would be so much higher than the real cost of imports. The chief consequence for the United States of economic isolation, in other words, would be a lowering of the standard of living.

On the export side of the American economy, production and employment in many important sectors depend significantly upon foreign markets. The export of agricultural commodities such as rice, cotton, wheat, tobacco, soybeans, lard, and dried fruits usually amounts to from 20 to 40 percent and more of U.S. production of these commodities. From 15 to 30 percent of the domestic output of such industrial goods as machine tools, tractors, textile machinery, printing machinery and equipment, office appliances, motor trucks and coaches, and oil-field machinery and tools are exported.

In general, we may conclude that for nearly all countries—with the exception of those that are in a primitive state of economic development and those, like the Soviet bloc countries, that deliberately minimize external economic relations on political grounds—international trade is a highly significant and integral part of the national economy. Adam Smith long ago enunciated a principle that has since become famous and accepted everywhere as a fundamental economic maxim: when production is organized on the basis of specialization, total output is much greater than it would be if production were carried on by self-sufficient, economically isolated production entities. The volume of international trade—the result of geographic specialization—is eloquent empirical evidence of the seriousness with which Adam Smith's principle has been accepted.

IMPLICATIONS OF ECONOMIC INTERDEPENDENCE

The economic interdependence of countries in the world economy carries with it unavoidable problems. Very few countries can escape the repercussions flowing from economic developments originating outside their borders or can ignore the external reverberations of their own policies. Public consciousness of these interrelationships has been sharpened by the world energy crisis and the shock to the economies of oil importing countries set off by the oil embargo.

But the interconnections among national economies extend far beyond those relating to particular commodities. For example, the inflation currently plaguing the United States is a worldwide phenomenon, and it is extremely difficult for any one country to solve the problem through its own efforts alone. Like unemployment, inflation tends to spread among major countries, the transmission channels provided by trade and capital movements. The ability of a country to pursue independent monetary and fiscal policies to combat either inflation or unemployment is accordingly circumscribed.

Many other basic problems are worldwide in scope and call for international solution rather than a series of separate national measures. As the world's population continues to expand and nature's store of resources dwindles from usage, the threat of widespread starvation in the poorer countries and of increasing austerity elsewhere looms larger. Even if crises of catastrophic proportions are avoided, the problem of the two thirds of the world's population living at a near-subsistence level will continue for a long time to challenge the world economy.

POLITICAL ASPECTS OF INTERNATIONAL ECONOMIC RELATIONS

Up to now the discussion has centered on the economic aspects of international relations, and this indeed will be the focus throughout. But a word is in order at this point on other, closely related facets of the world economy. International economic relations are conducted within a framework of national and international law, institutions, and practices which influence, and are influenced by, economic relations. Political influences and effects are the most obvious, and probably the most important, of these extraeconomic aspects.

The international economy is a reflection of the political division of the world into separate, sovereign states, each of which has its own set of institutions and policies. National boundaries constitute obstacles in various ways to international economic relations. The most obvious of these obstacles are tariffs and quantitative restrictions on the movement across national frontiers of goods and services and limitations on the movements of persons and of capital. Less direct but nonetheless potent barriers exist by reason of separate national monetary systems, giving rise to the complex problems of international monetary relations. The not infrequent use of economic measures as instruments of political policies adds to the special difficulties which beset foreign trade and factor movements.

The vitality of the forces underlying international economic relations is attested to by the large volume and continuing growth of these relations notwithstanding the obstacles encountered. Evidently, the benefits of trade and factor movements are great. Recognition of this fact has led to an increasing degree of international cooperation to reduce the barriers to economic relations among countries. Various agreements and institutions relating to trade and investment and monetary arrangements have considerably changed the environment within which international economic relations are conducted. Nevertheless, as compared to interregional relations within national boundaries, international economic relations are subject to a special set of restraints.

On the other side of the coin, international political relations are strongly influenced by economic relations. Politics may be defined in terms of *power* relationships, while economics deals with the use of scarce resources. A major ingredient of power is command over resources. The dominant power position of the United States and of the Soviet Union are the most obvious examples of the relationship between command over resources, actual or potential, and international politics.

The economic strength of a country, however, depends upon more than the mere physical inventory of its resources; it also depends upon how efficiently its resources are employed. International economic relations provide the opportunity significantly to increase the efficiency of resource use. There is, therefore, a strong motive for countries to construct an international political framework within which economic relations with other countries are fostered. Friendly and stable political relations promote economic relations; beneficial economic relations encourage friendly and stable political relations.

The mutually supporting interconnections between international economics and politics are most sharply brought out by regional movements toward economic integration, of which the European Common Market is the outstanding example. The Common Market in Europe had its origins in the desire to achieve political integration. Rather than approaching the latter goal directly, European statesmen concluded that it would be more feasible to proceed indirectly via the route of economic integration. The thinking was that if countries become closely tied together economically they can hardly avoid parallel political cooperation. Whether this is an entirely valid conclusion remains to be seen, though the presumption in its favor is stong.

THE TASKS OF THEORY

Economics has its ultimate justification in providing guidelines for rational and intelligent policy making. The prime prerequisite for fulfilling this function is to find a satisfactory explanation of observed phenomena—the why's and wherefore's in the case at hand of international economic relations. Unless the causes and effects of international trade and factor movements are known, the bases for policy formation, which requires prediction of the effects of various measures, would be extremely weak and shaky.

More specifically, the major and basic questions in international economics which need to be answered are as follows:

1. Why do international specialization and exchange and, parallel to this, international movements of labor and capital, occur?

2. What determines which commodities and services and factors of production will be exported and imported by each country and in what quantities?

3. What economic effects follow from free international trade and factor movements? In particular, how are the efficiency and structure of national economies and the distribution of real income affected?

Part I of this book is devoted to finding answers to these questions, calling for an examination of the so-called "pure theory" of international trade.

Part II is devoted to what might be called "deviations from the pure model of international trade." This would be an unnecessarily formidable title, however, for what are, after all, rather commonplace phenomena. As in all sciences, the pure theory of international economics makes certain simplifying assumptions; one is that there are no artificial barriers erected by governments to the free flow of goods and services from country to country. In actuality, however, this assumption is unrealistic. National governments impose tariffs and quotas against foreign goods and sometimes even interfere with the export of home-produced goods and services. The reasons for and consequences of such actions are an important part of international economics.

A third major part of international economics has to do with the *mechanisms* rather than the substance of intercountry economic relations. Especially important in this connection are international monetary relations. Since each country has its own monetary system, what are the instruments for making payments from one country to another? Where and how does a country obtain the means of making international payments? What are the causes and the effects of an imbalance between a country's current international payments and current international receipts? A description of institutional arrangements, as well as a theoretical analysis, is required to answer these important questions, and both are provided in Part III of this book.

A related task of international economics, also undertaken in Part III, is to analyze the processes that bring the national economies of different countries into a set of balanced international relationships. In view of the political right of each country to determine its own policies and the consequent possibility of conflicts in national economic policies, the problems of keeping equilibrium relationships internationally or of restoring such relationships, if disturbed, are of prime importance.

Finally, in Part IV we discuss the international economics of the special problems of less developed countries.

RECOMMENDED READINGS

PETERSON, PETER G. *A Foreign Economic Perspective.* Washington, D.C.: U.S. Government Printing Office, 1971.

United States International Economic Policy in an Interdependent World. Papers submitted to the Commission on International Trade and Investment Policy. Washington, D.C.: U.S. Government Printing Office, 1971.

The student is well advised to become familiar early with the following principal primary sources of international trade and monetary statistics.

Prewar Data

LEAGUE OF NATIONS, Geneva. *International Trade Statistics.*

————. *Review of World Trade.*

————. *Industrialization and Foreign Trade.* 1945.

————. *International Statistical Yearbook.*

————. *The Network of World Trade.* 1942.

Postwar Data

FOOD AND AGRICULTURAL ORANIZATION (FAO), Rome. *Yearbook of Food and Agricultural Statistics.*

————. *Yearbook of Forest Products Statistics.*

INTERNATIONAL LABOR OFFICE (ILO), Geneva. *Yearbook of Labor Statistics.*

INTERNATIONAL MONETARY FUND, Washington, D.C. *Balance of Payments Yearbook.* Issued annually, with loose-leaf sections issued more frequently.

————. *International Financial Statistics.* Issued monthly. The best source of current data on trade, exchange rates, production, and other economic and financial conditions for the principal trading countries of the world.

UNITED NATIONS, NEW YORK. *Demographic Yearbook.*

————. *Monthly Bulletin of Statistics.*

————. *Commodity Trade Statistics.*

————. *Yearbook of International Trade Statistics.*

————, jointly with the INTERNATIONAL MONETARY FUND and the INTERNATIONAL BANK FOR RECONSTRUCTION AND DEVELOPMENT. *Direction of International Trade.*

————. *World Economic Report.* Economic surveys are also made for various regions of the world—Europe, Latin America, and Asia and the Far East.

U.S. DEPARTMENT OF COMMERCE, Washington, D.C. *Foreign Commerce Yearbook.*

————. BUREAU OF THE CENSUS. *Historical Statistics of the United States, 1789–1945.* 1949.

————. *Statistical Abstract of the United States.*

————. *Survey of Current Business,* monthly. Best source of current data on the international economic and monetary transactions of the United States. Special supplements are occasionally issued on particular subjects, such as *Balance of Payments of the United States, 1919–1953* (1954).

————. *The United States in the World Economy.* 1949.

————. *Foreign Commerce Weekly.*

STUDY QUESTIONS

1. See how many of the items which you consume that you can separate out according to their origin as provided by the local, national, and international economy.
2. Identify the major categories of international economic relations.
3. Define the average propensity to import and assess its significance as a measure of the importance of foreign trade to a country.
4. What is meant by the statement in the text that cutting off foreign trade would have a "bottleneck" effect on national economies?
5. Why is the cost, rather than the physical capability of producing goods and services, the critical consideration in determining a country's imports?
6. How does the existence of separate national states affect the world economy?
7. Distinguish between international political and international economic relations.
8. Give some concrete examples of the mutual interrelationships between international political and international economic relations.
9. Review the basic questions with which international economics as a field of study is concerned.

part one

The theory and
empirical foundations
of international trade
and factor movements

2

The pure theory of international trade: The proximate causes

The so-called "pure theory" of international trade seeks to explain the underlying causes and major effects of the international exchange of goods and services. The theory is based on certain simplifying assumptions, and relates to "real" economic variables, abstracting from any independent influences which may be produced in actuality by monetary factors. (The role of monetary factors is considered in Part III of this book.)

An examination of the actual pattern of international trade would reveal its tremendously varied and complex character, embracing thousands of goods and services moving among countries in a crowded network of trade channels. Not only is the nature of the products entering into foreign trade highly diversified, ranging from unprocessed raw materials and agricultural goods to sophisticated manufactured articles, the economic and social conditions and structures of the participating countries display marked variations. Relatively undeveloped agricultural economies as well as advanced industrial economies, centrally controlled as well as free enterprise economies, competitive market structures as well as monopolistic market structures—these and various combinations thereof are all represented in the world of trade.

15

The task of theory is to distill from the mass of real-world relationships the dominant, central forces which broadly determine the general pattern. In view of the variety of conditions under which trade occurs, it is not surprising that a single, comprehensive trade theory of universal applicability is difficult, if not impossible, to find. For example, the principles that underlie trade among market economies may have little relevance to the trade of centrally controlled economies. Products produced and exchanged in competitive markets are not subject to the same analysis as those traded in monopolistic markets.

Traditional theory focuses on the causes and effects of international trade in the context of competitive markets. Although a significant fraction of actual trade is not conducted in this framework and, therefore, requires a different approach, the competitive market model nevertheless is extremely useful, both on its own account and as background for other models. Accordingly, in this and the following chapter we shall examine the traditional theory and subsequently discuss the modifications and extensions which noncompetitive markets require.

BASIC ASSUMPTIONS

Since we shall be discussing in this and the next chapter the theory of trade in the context of a particular institutional and behavioral framework, it is essential at the outset to specify the characteristics of the latter. It will be assumed that trading countries have a free-market form of economic organization, with production decisions made by profit-maximizing, private business firms, each operating in purely competitive markets. The assumption of pure competition implies two especially important characteristics of the economy: each firm is a "price-taker," unable to influence the price of its product or the prices of productive inputs it hires, all prices being determined by market demand and supply; and each firm produces a product that is identical to the products of the many other firms in the given industry. Government, it is assumed, pursues a policy of laissez-faire, interfering with market operations neither domestically nor internationally.

It shall further be assumed that whereas internally in each country both final products and productive factors (labor and capital) move without impediment or cost—thus creating fully integrated markets with single prices—internationally only final products can be traded with equal facility as internally, productive factors being immobile. The costless freedom of product movements internationally results in a single world price for any given traded good, while the immobility of labor and capital implies the possibility of continuing international differences in wages and the rate of return on capital. (Later, however, it will be shown that under certain restrictive conditions the effect of trade is indirectly to equalize factor prices internationally.)

The above, plus additional assumptions in particular cases to be specified when appropriate, no doubt impress the reader as highly unrealistic. So they are, in the sense that they are a poor fit with observed reality. As indicated earlier, however, theory, by its nature, cannot be simply a catalog of real-world details. The test of a theory ultimately lies in its empirical reliability as a predictor. While the model to be developed below is not applicable to the trade of centrally controlled economies or, without amendments, to trade conducted in monopolistic markets, it is relevant to a large portion of world trade.

THE PROXIMATE CAUSES OF TRADE

The goods and services available to a country for its use are provided by domestic production and by imports from foreign countries. Some products—indeed, normally the majority—are practically excluded from trade, the source of supply being confined to domestic production. Nontradables include bulky goods, the transportation costs of which are very high in relation to their value, and the myriad personal services which by their nature can feasibly be produced and consumed only at the local level. Nevertheless, there remains a vast array of products which enter into international trade and which may be called, for short, "tradables."

The first task of trade theory is to explain why certain goods and services are imported from abroad rather than produced at home. In some cases, the reason is so obvious that no more than a simple statement is required: some goods and services are imported because they are not physically producible domestically. A country without domestic resources of petroleum clearly cannot have available oil and gasoline except through importation from producing countries. The pleasures of the Gallic culture cannot be directly experienced by foreigners except through visiting France—that is, "importing" travel in France.

Absence of the ability physically to produce at home certain goods and services, however, accounts for only a minor fraction of the vast flow of international trade. The great bulk of traded goods and services probably *could* be, in a physical sense, produced by the importing countries. Indeed, frequently the same product that is imported is also produced at home by the importing country, the sources of supply being divided between the domestic economy and foreign exporting countries.[1]

Why does a country import a product that is producible (perhaps actually produced) at home? The answer is readily apparent if we adopt the perspective of private business firms, which in a market economy make the decision to import. A profit-seeking firm is motivated to import a product when it can be obtained more cheaply abroad than at home. This suggests that it is international *differences in prices* which are the proximate causes of trade in standardized products.

The principle that international price differences constitute the immediate basis for trade can even be extended to those products which some countries are physically incapable of producing. In such cases, the domestic costs of production may be regarded as infinite; hence, prices in foreign producing countries are bound to be lower. However, the theory of trade in goods not producible in importing countries is trivial and will be excluded from further consideration. We shall assume instead that all trading countries are physically capable of producing all goods.

Comparative Cost Differences

It is fairly obvious that business firms will seek to import standardized products the prices of which are lower in foreign countries than at home (provided, of course, that the costs of transportation are not as great as the price difference). International price differences, however, are only the surface cause of trade; the objective of theory is to penetrate this surface to arrive at a deeper explanation of trade. The first probe is directed at what immediately lies underneath international price differences. The answer to this search was provided early in the 19th century by the British economist, David Ricardo (1772–1823).

Ricardo is credited with developing one of the most famous doc-

---

[1] Even when a country is unable to produce at home identically the same good available from abroad, often it is capable of producing more or less close substitutes. Such is the case for most differentiated products—different varieties of essentially the same good. However, since differentiated products are usually associated with imperfectly competitive markets, they will be treated separately in a later chapter.

trines in economics: *the principle of comparative costs. The principle states that each country will tend to export those products the comparative costs of which are lower at home than abroad and to import those the comparative costs of which are lower abroad than at home.*

The key concept here is that of *comparative* costs, as opposed to *absolute* costs. The doctrine states that international comparative cost differences are the determinants of trade, absolute cost differences not being necessary. To clarify the meaning of this statement, it is first necessary to draw the distinction between absolute and comparative costs.

Absolute costs are measured in terms of some standard unit. Ordinarily, the standard unit is money. If the cost of good X is \$1 and of good Y \$2, X is absolutely cheaper than Y. By contrast, *comparative* costs are measured in terms of each other, rather than expressed in a common unit of measurement. In the present example, the cost of X, compared to that of Y, is 1:2 (and of Y compared to X, 2:1).

There is no way of determining whether the absolute costs of products, expressed in different national monetary units, are higher or lower in one country than another, unless there is some means of converting all prices into a common monetary unit. For example, if the cost of X is \$1 in the United States and 500 rupees in India, we cannot tell where X is cheaper unless the dollar can be converted into an equivalent amount of rupees. As we shall see presently, the foreign exchange market provides a means of making such conversions.

Comparative costs, on the other hand, can be determined without the presence of a common monetary unit or means of converting different monetary units onto a common base. For example, if X cost \$1 in the United States and 500 rupees in India, while in the two countries good Y costs \$2 and 2,500 rupees, X is *comparatively* cheaper in India, since the cost of X compared to that of Y is 1:5 in India and 1:2 in the United States. Correspondingly, Y is comparatively cheaper in the United States (since 2:1 is less than 5:1).

In investigating the origins of foreign trade we cannot point to international differences in absolute costs, for until trade has actually begun there is no way of identifying or measuring absolute cost differences across national monetary boundaries. But *comparative* cost differences *can* be identified and measured even when countries are in a hypothetical state of pretrade isolation from each other. What needs to be shown is that pretrade comparative cost differences internationally constitute the basis for the emergence of absolute price differences, expressed in a common monetary unit, hence to trade relations.

A very simple model suffices to demonstrate that pretrade differences in comparative costs lead, in a competitive market system, to the price differentials which motivate private firms to engage in trade. For the purpose of the demonstration, a hypothetical example will be constructed, in which at first only two countries and two commodities are assumed to exist. The reader is also reminded of the assumption that purely competitive markets are in operation and that each of the two commodities is internationally standardized in the sense that different units of each commodity are indistinguishable from each other, regardless of the location of their production.

Let the two countries of our model be the United States and Argentina and the two commodities be cloth and beef. Suppose that in pretrade isolation the price of cloth is $4 per yard in the United States and 200 pesos in Argentina, while the price of beef per pound is $1 in the United States and 20 pesos in Argentina. (Since competition is assumed to prevail, the price of a good is the same as its cost of production, so that price comparisons are equivalent to cost comparisons.) This hypothetical information is summarized in tabular form as follows:

	United States	*Argentina*
Cloth	$4.00	P.200
Beef	1.00	20

No comparison of absolute prices between the two countries is possible as yet. It is not legitimate, for example, to conclude that either or both products are absolutely cheaper in the United States because it takes fewer dollars than pesos to buy them, for these currencies are different units of measuring price and there is no established relationship between them. Were Argentina to issue a new currency, converting old pesos into new ones at a ratio of 100 old for one new, both products would then sell for fewer pesos than dollars, even though no change in the real situation has occurred.[2] This has illustrated the futility of attempting direct absolute price comparisons.

Fortunately, however, it is easy to compare relative prices. Based on the hypothetical figures given above, the ratio of the price of cloth

---

[2] France performed precisely the kind of operation referred to in 1960, exchanging 1 new franc for 100 old ones. The consequence was only to lower all prices to 1/100 their previous levels.

to that of beef is 4:1 in the United States and 10:1 in Argentina. Hence, the relative price of cloth is lower in the United States than in Argentina, while the relative price of beef is lower in Argentina than in the United States.

It would not be difficult to show how private traders would have a motive to engage in barter deals, with U.S. cloth being exchanged directly for Argentina beef. But it is closer to reality and more revealing of other important aspects of trade to let money serve its usual function of medium of exchange.

In order for traders to deal in monetary rather than barter terms, a connection between the dollar and peso must be created. The connection is provided if a *rate of exchange* between the two currencies is established. A rate of exchange is the price of a foreign currency unit expressed in domestic currency units. If there were a rate of exchange between the dollar and the peso at which traders in each country could purchase the currency of the other, a direct and absolute price comparison for each good could be made.

Converting Relative into Absolute Price Differences: The Rate of Exchange

One way of establishing an exchange rate is for the governments concerned to agree upon monetary arrangements under which foreign currencies are bought and sold to private traders at some specified price. However, in our present model we want to exclude government and confine ourselves to the assumption that a laissez-faire market price system is operative. In this case, whether or not an exchange rate is established depends entirely upon whether or not a private *market* for foreign exchange develops in which an equilibrium price emerges.

In order for a free-market price for anything to come into existence, there must be some price range over which there are both demanders and suppliers, so that at some particular price the total quantity of the item in question demanded is equal to the total quantity offered for sale (supplied). Now let us see how these conditions are fulfilled with respect to dollars and pesos, given the assumptions made above as to the pretrade prices of cloth and beef in the two countries.

A foreign exchange market in dollars and pesos will tend to develop in each of the countries, but we need observe the market in only one, say, the United States, since whatever conclusions arrived at will be equally applicable to the other country's market. The immediate question, then, is whether there will emerge a market demand and supply for pesos in the United States.

Looking at the demand side first, we observe that private traders will want to buy pesos if they can be obtained at any price (rate of exchange) *less* than 5 cents per peso. Why? Simply because in this case beef is *absolutely* cheaper in Argentina than in the United States. For example, suppose that pesos could be purchased at a rate of exchange of 4 cents. The Argentina price of beef of 20 pesos is then the equivalent of $0.80, compared to the United States price of $1. Traders would want to buy pesos in order to be able to buy beef to import into the United States.

Turning next to the supply side of the foreign exchange market, we note that private traders would be happy to *sell* pesos at any rate of exchange *above* 2 cents per peso. The reason? At any such rate cloth could be exported to Argentina, sold for pesos, the pesos in turn sold for dollars, and a profit realized. For example, if the exchange rate were 3 cents per peso, a yard of cloth costing the exporter $4 would yield 200 pesos which could be sold for $6 on the exchange market.

Combining the demand and supply sides, we observe that there is a common range in the dollar exchange rate on the peso over which there are quantities of pesos both demanded and supplied—the required condition for the emergence of an *equilibrium rate of exchange*.

The equilibrium rate of exchange is the particular dollar price of pesos at which the total quantity of pesos demanded is equal to the total quantity supplied. This is the rate that will in fact tend to prevail under competitive conditions.[3]

We know that the equilibrium rate of exchange in our example must lie somewhere between 2 cents and 5 cents per peso.[4] Where exactly the rate will ultimately tend to settle will be considered later. The main point now is this: at any rate of exchange within the range 2 cents–5 cents per peso, the *absolute* price of cloth is lower in the United States than in Argentina, while the *absolute* price of beef is lower in Argentina than in the United States. Hence, traders are motivated to import beef from Argentina and to export cloth from

---

[3] The ordinary law of supply and demand studied in principles of economics is the basis for this conclusion.

[4] The student is invited to work out the reason why the rate of exchange cannot, initially at least, be outside the range. *Hint:* Assume that the rate is outside the indicated range, for example, 6 cents per peso or 1 cent per peso. Now see whether there would be *both* a demand *and* a supply of pesos at the assumed rate.

the United States. The beginning proposition that comparative cost differences in pretrade isolation become differences in *absolute* prices upon the opening of trade relations is thus illustrated by our example.

A corollary to this proposition is that if relative prices are the *same* internationally in pretrade isolation, no trade will occur. The reader can convince himself that this is the case by assuming the same pretrade relative prices of cloth and beef in the United States and Argentina (say $4 and $1 in the United States, 200 pesos and 50 pesos in Argentina for cloth and beef, respectively) and observing that there is no rate of exchange at which there are both a demand and supply of pesos.

As indicated earlier, we want to know not only under what conditions international trade will occur but also what determines its pattern. In the hypothetical case discussed in the preceding pages, a specific pattern of trade was established: the United States exported cloth and imported beef, Argentina exported beef and imported cloth. Was this an arbitrary pattern of trade or a necessary result of the assumed price data? If it was the latter, what is the general principle involved?

First, the pattern of trade we deduced was *not* arbitrary. Given the assumed pretrade price data, it would not be possible at any equilibrium rate of exchange for the absolute price of beef to be lower in the United States than in Argentina or for the absolute price of cloth to be lower in Argentina than in the United States. In verifying this conclusion, the student need only remember that the equilibrium rate of exchange on the peso must fall within the limits of from 2 to 5 cents.

Cloth becomes the absolutely cheaper good in the United States and beef the absolutely cheaper good in Argentina because each was the respective country's *relatively* cheaper product before the opening of trade relations.

The general principle is as follows:

A country tends to export the product the comparative cost (and price) of which is lower in pretrade isolation at home than abroad and to import the product the comparative cost (and price) of which is higher at home than abroad.

It has been shown that comparative cost differences are the basis for the emergence of international price differences, which are the immediate condition for motivating private traders to engage in trade. It is worth emphasizing again that *absolute* cost differences are not a necessary condition for trade to occur. Suppose, for example, that the United States were able to produce both cloth and beef at lower real costs than those incurred in Argentina, with real costs measured in terms of the physical quantity of productive resources (land, labor and capital) required to produce a unit of a good.[5] One might be tempted to say that in this event Argentina would wish to import both commodities from the United States, while the United States would have no motive to import either from Argentina. Such a conclusion would be erroneous. In the first place, it is not possible for a country only to import while refraining from exporting. It is easiest to see why in terms of the foreign exchange market: there would be a demand for foreign exchange to pay for imports but no supply of foreign exchange provided by exports. When economic relations between countries are confined to commodity trade, as in our present model, exports are the means of paying for imports, so that "one-way" trade is not possible.

More fundamentally, the source of the benefits yielded by trade lies not in absolute real cost differences but in comparative cost differences. Whether or not a country is in some sense absolutely more efficient than another in all lines of production, it is sufficient as a basis of trade for *relative* differences to exist, as reflected in comparative cost differences. In this connection, it is important to note that, unlike absolute costs, comparative costs cannot be lower for all products in one country than in another. If Argentina has a comparative cost advantage in beef relatively to cloth, she necessarily has a comparative cost *disadvantage* in cloth relatively to beef. Likewise, a lower comparative cost of cloth in terms of beef in the United States is equivalent to a higher comparative cost of beef in terms of cloth.

MULTICOMMODITY, MULTICOUNTRY TRADE

For the purpose of arriving quickly at the concept of comparative cost differences as the basis of trade, we employed the simplifying assumption of there being only two commodities and two countries. A "two-by-two" model of this sort has the pedagogic virtue of permitting an unambiguous specification of comparative cost positions and

---

5 In fact, there is no satisfactory way of measuring absolute costs. The classical economists adopted as the measure of costs the amount of labortime required to produce a good. The weaknesses of this measure are discussed below.

the resultant pattern of trade. The question now is whether such a highly simplified model is relevant to an actual world of many commodities and countries.

Multicommodity Trade

First, consider the case of more than two commodities, while retaining the assumption of only two countries. Assume that in pretrade isolation the price (and cost) relationships shown in the accompanying table prevail. The question is, which country has a comparative advantage in which commodities? In a two-goods model, there is no difficulty in finding comparative costs; not so in the present case. The first problem is that different answers are obtained depending upon the pair of goods chosen for comparison. For instance, cloth is relatively cheaper in the United States than in Argentina when compared to beef and also when compared to wheat. But in comparison to either bicycles or tractors, cloth is relatively cheaper in Argentina!

	United States	Argentina
Beef .... $	1.00	P. 20
Cloth	4.00	200
Wheat	0.50	15
Bicycles	20.00	1,200
Tractors	1,000.00	80,000

To resolve this problem, let us calculate the ratio of Argentine prices (in pesos) to the United States prices (in dollars) for each good. The result is:

Beef	20:1
Cloth	50:1
Wheat	30:1
Bicycles	60:1
Tractors	80:1

Now the commodities may be ordered on a scale of comparative costs, from lowest to highest, with the direction measured from left to right for the United States and from right to left for Argentina:

U.S.→tractors—bicycles—cloth—wheat—beef←Argentina

This shows that for the United States tractors have the *least* comparative costs, while the opposite is true for Argentina. We can therefore identify tractors as the good in which the United States has a clear-cut comparative advantage and beef as the commodity in which Argentina has an unmistakable comparative advantage. The United States will certainly tend to export tractors and import beef. But what are we to conclude with respect to the other three commodities?

The answer depends upon the equilibrium rate of exchange between the dollar and the peso. Suppose that the equilibrium rate of exchange is 1.8 cents per peso. Referring to the assumed price data given above, we see that at this rate of exchange beef, wheat, and cloth are all absolutely cheaper in Argentina than in the United States, while bicycles and tractors are cheaper in the United States than in Argentina. If, then, 1.8 cents per peso is the equilibrium rate of exchange, the total value of Argentina's exports of beef, wheat, and cloth is equal to the total value of its imports of bicycles and tractors, and similarly for U.S. exports and imports. Thus, in the scale of comparative costs, the dividing line in this case lies between bicycles and cloth, with the United States having a comparative advantage in the goods to the left of the line and Argentina in the goods to the right of the line.

However, the dividing line is not fixed. Suppose, for example, that at the rate of 1.8 cents per peso the total value of imports demanded by the United States exceeds the toal value of U.S. exports demanded by Argentina. As a consequence, the dollar rate of exchange on the peso will rise until an equilibrium rate is reached. If the equilibrium rate happens to be 2.0 cents per peso, cloth will disappear as a traded item, for its price will then be the same in both countries. Were the equilibrium rate to rise above 2.0 cents, cloth would switch from being an import of the United States to becoming an export along with bicycles and tractors.

In general, the commodities falling in the middle range of the scale of comparative costs have an indefinite status until the rate of exchange is known. However, no matter where the dividing line between exports and imports falls, *the comparative costs of the commodities exported are always less than the comparative costs of the goods imported.* In this most important respect, the multicommodity model yields essentially the same results as the two-country model.

Multicountry Trade

The analysis of multicountry trade follows lines similar to that of multicommodity trade. Again, we may be sure that each country will export those commodities the costs of which are relatively lower at home than abroad and import others that are relatively lower in cost abroad. But which specific goods will be exported and imported by each country cannot be determined in advance without specification of world prices.

	United States	*Argentina*	*Italy*	*France*	*Japan*
Price of beef $1		20 pesos	50 lira	10 francs	40 yen
Price of cloth. $4		200 pesos	150 lira	60 francs	80 yen
Ratio of cloth price to beef price 4:1		10:1	3:1	6:1	2:1

To illustrate, assume the pretrade price data shown in the accompanying table. From the ratio of the price of cloth to the price of beef given in the last row, the comparative cost positions of the countries can be ordered on an ascending scale, as follows:

Comparative cost of cloth in terms of beef
$\rightarrow$Japan—Italy—U.S.—France—Argentina
$\leftarrow$Comparative cost of beef in terms of cloth

This shows that Japan has the greatest comparative advantage of all countries in cloth and the greatest comparative disadvantage in beef, while Argentina is in the reverse position. The countries in between may export or import either commodity, depending upon the world equilibrium ratio of the price of cloth to the price of beef. Suppose that total world demand and supply lead to an equilibrium cloth-beef price ratio of 5:1. Italy and the United States would then join Japan as exporters of cloth and importers of beef, since the comparative cost of cloth in these countries is lower than in the rest of the world. On the other hand, if the world equilibrium cloth-beef price ratio were, say 3.5:1, Italy would still export cloth along with Japan, but the United States would join Argentina in exporting beef. At a cloth-beef price ratio of less than 3 (but more than 2), all countries would export beef to Japan in return for Japanese cloth.

Wherever the dividing line between cloth exporting and beef importing countries falls, all countries to the left of the line would export cloth and all to the right of the line would export beef. Further, whichever good a given country exports, its comparative cost is less than in the world as a whole, while the good it imports has a lower comparative cost abroad than at home.

Multilateral Trade

We have seen that, in the two-country model, equilibrium requires that each country's exports to the other be equal in value to
the imports from the other. Does the same principle apply between
each pair of countries when there are many countries trading with
each other? That is, does equilibrium require that trade be *bilaterally* balanced? The answer is no—fortunately; for there is no reason
to expect reciprocal international demand in a free market to produce such a pattern of trade.

Equilibrium, under our assumption of relations confined exclusively to commodity trade, requires only that each country's total
exports be equal to its imports. A country may fulfill this equilibrium condition even though its trade is unbalanced bilaterally with
each of its trading partners, provided only that the sum of its
bilateral import surpluses is matched by the sum of its bilateral
export surpluses. If this holds for each trading country, we say that
there is multilateral trade equilibrium. To illustrate this point, there
is presented below a hypothetical trade matrix for five countries,
each of which is in bilateral imbalance but multilateral balance.

Exports from ↓ \ Exports to →	Japan	Italy	United States	France	Argentina	Total Exports
Japan	–	80	100	5	5	190
Italy	50	–	80	40	20	190
United States	60	30	–	90	50	230
France	25	65	40	–	15	145
Argentina	55	15	10	10	–	90
Total Imports	190	190	230	145	90	845

The exports of each country listed in the left-hand column are
shown horizontally; the imports of each country listed in the top row
are shown vertically. From the data given, we may summarize each
country's bilateral trade balance as in the accompanying tabulation
(a plus sign indicating an export surplus, a minus sign, an import
surplus).

Each country is enabled to pay for its import surpluses from one
or more other countries with its export surpluses to the remaining

With⟍ Bilateral Trade⟍ → Balance of ↓⟍	Japan	Italy	United States	France	Argentina
Japan	—	+30	+40	−20	−50
Italy	−30	—	+50	−25	+ 5
United States	−40	−50	—	+50	+40
France	+20	+25	−50	—	+ 5
Argentina	+50	− 5	−40	− 5	—

countries. Thus, Japan pays for its import surpluses from France and Argentina with its export surpluses to Italy and the United States, etc.

General Equilibrium

Since there are, in fact, many countries producing many goods and services, very little can be said a priori concerning the *specific* composition and pattern of trade or the international value of any one commodity. Demand and supply, price and cost conditions, and exchange rates are mutually dependent in a set of complex general equilibrium relationships. In the simple model of two countries and two commodities, the composition and pattern of trade can be directly determined from the comparative cost data. In the multi-country, multicommodity model, there is no such simple and direct line of causation. Indeed, as we have seen, the term "comparative costs" loses much of its meaning in this case, except within the context of an already established general equilibrium. With given demand and supply conditions in each country and with given international demand, a particular country will have a comparative cost advantage in certain commodities and a comparative disadvantage in others. Let international demand shift, and the comparative cost situation of the country will change, with some articles formerly exported now being imported or vice versa.

Within the framework of general equilibrium, each traded commodity will tend to have the same price, at equilibrium rates of exchange, in all countries (except for transportation costs), the price being at that point which equates world demand and supply. Whether a given country will export or import a particular commodity depends upon the domestic demand and supply at the prevailing world price. If the quantity demanded at home exceeds the quantity supplied domestically, the excess quantity demanded will be imported; if the quantity supplied exceeds the quantity demanded, the excess will be exported; if the quantity produced at home at the world price just equals the domestic demand, the commodity will be neither exported nor imported. But the domestic equivalent of the world price depends upon the rate of exchange, which, in turn, in a free market, will be such as to equalize the *aggregate* exports and imports of the country.

General equilibrium, then, involves a balancing of numerous interrelated forces, international and domestic. One basic point, however, emerges: with given demand and supply conditions, both at home and abroad, each country will have a comparative advantage in certain commodities, which are exported, and a comparatve disadvantage in others, which are imported. Many commodities will tend to be on the margin between an export and import status, falling to one side or the other or remaining in the middle, depending upon international demand. Some commodities, in which the comparative advantage is greatest, will tend always to be exported, while others, in which the comparative disadvantage is greatest, will tend always to be imported. Irrespective of the exact composition of trade, any imported commodity will have a lesser opportunity cost, measured by the amount of exports required to obtain it, than it would have if produced at home.

RECOMMENDED READINGS

See the list given at the end of Chapter 3.

STUDY QUESTIONS

1. List the basic assumptions underlying the theory of trade under competitive conditions.
2. What kinds of products are practically excluded from international trade?
3. State the principle of comparative costs.
4. Distinguish between absolute and comparative costs.
5. Why is it not possible to compare absolute costs internationally in pretrade isolation, whereas comparative costs can be meaningfully identified?
6. Define the rate of exchange.

7. What is required for an equilibrium market rate of exchange to be established?

8. Show that comparative cost differences lead to absolute price differences in a free market.

9. Prove that absolute cost differences are not necessary for international trade to occur.

10. In what manner must the principle of comparative costs be modified to apply to multicommodity, multicountry trade?

11. Trade equilibrium requires only that each country's total exports and total imports be equal, not that trade be balanced bilaterally with each trade partner. Explain.

3

The pure theory of
international trade:
The underlying causes

We have concluded that in a competitive market system pretrade comparative cost differences among countries account for the emergence of the international price differences motivating private firms to engage in trade. The law of comparative costs informs us that, in a two-commodity, two-country world, each country would tend to export that product the comparative cost of which is lower at home than abroad and to import the product the comparative cost of which is higher at home than abroad. Extended to a multicommodity, multicountry model, the doctrine of comparative costs states that, in the context of a general equilibrium system, each country will tend to export those products at the lower end of its scale of comparative costs and to import those at the upper end.

Although the law of comparative costs yields a highly informative and useful insight into the causes of trade, standing alone it is clearly only a superficial view, for it leaves unanswered the obvious question of what accounts for comparative cost differences. It is the intent in this chapter to delve more deeply into the causes of trade, in an attempt to find the underlying reasons for international comparative cost differences. The assumption of competitive markets and standardized products is continued in this discussion.

CLASSICAL THEORY

When Ricardo formulated the doctrine of comparative costs to explain international trade the prevailing theory was that costs are determined by the amount of labor time required in production. The classical labor theory of value held that if good X requires per unit of output 10 hours of labor, while good Y requires 30 hours of labor, the value (and price) of Y will tend to be three times that of X. Ricardo, applying the labor theory of value, concluded that comparative cost differences are therefore attributable to relative international differences in the amount of labor time required to produce various goods. If in country A good X requires 10 hours of labor and Y 30 hours, while in country B X requires 5 hours of labor and Y 10 hours, then the comparative costs, as measured in labor time, are lower in A for good X and lower in B for good Y. (Note also in this example that B has an *absolute* advantage in both products, though a comparative advantage only in good Y.)

While the doctrine of comparative cost differences as the basis for trade is still as valid today as in Ricardo's time, the explanation of comparative costs in terms of the labor theory of value is *not* generally accepted today for several reasons.

The first reason is the modern rejection of the labor theory of value. While labor is nearly always the largest component of cost, it is rarely the sole component. Output is the joint product of several different factors of production rather than of labor alone. This would not matter in determining relative costs provided that other factors of production were always combined with labor in the same proportions. An American economist, Frank Taussig, writing about a century after Ricardo, believed this to be a sufficiently valid generalization to save the labor theory of value. However, few economists today would agree.

A similar objection to the labor theory of value is its assumption that labor in each country is homogeneous, so that comparisons of the labor time required for the production of various goods yield a true measure of their relative values. In fact, labor (as well as other factors) is not homogeneous; it consists of numerous qualitatively different subgroups, known as "noncompeting" groups. Again, Taussig attempted to circumvent this objection by postulating a similar hierarchy of noncompeting groups in different countries, leaving the *relative* wages of various groups about the same in all countries.

Whether this is true is an empirical question that has not been settled. Until it is, the assumption must be treated with extreme caution.

Finally, the clinching objection to the labor theory of value is that a much better theory, free of the chief weaknesses noted above, has evolved since Ricardo's day. The modern theory of value takes into account on the cost side all factors of production, not just labor alone, and defines cost in terms of sacrificed alternatives instead of in terms of the absolute quantity of inputs required in production. In the minds of most economists today, this concept of *opportunity* cost is much more significant and relevant than the notion of costs as equated to labor time.

There is a second objection to the classical theory of trade: it never really explains why comparative cost differences exist. If it requires relatively less labor to produce a given good in one country than in another, why is this? The answer of the classical economists is vague and general, put usually in terms of differences in economic "climate." But one must be more specific than this if the fundamental basis for trade is to be meaningfully identified. The modern theory at least boldly attempts to identify specific bases of trade.

MODERN THEORY

As mentioned above, in modern thinking opportunity cost is the most meaningful and significant concept of cost, and it is a concept which lends itself readily to analysis of the causes of trade. We have seen that a basis for trade exists if in pretrade isolation comparative costs differ internationally. Cast in terms of opportunity costs, the equivalent statement is that a basis for trade exists if opportunity costs differ internationally.

Different opportunity costs imply different comparative costs. This is because opportunity costs are defined, as are comparative costs, in relativistic terms. The opportunity cost of good X is the amount of good Y that must be sacrificed in order to produce X. Say that the output of Y must be reduced by two units in order to release the resources required to produce an extra unit of X. In this case, the marginal opportunity cost of X is $2Y$. In a perfectly functioning price system, such as we are assuming to exist, the market price and money cost of X would be twice that of Y, so that the comparative cost of X is $2Y$, the same as opportunity cost. Hence, if opportunity costs differ internationally, so too do comparative costs, and the basis for trade is present.

Our objective now is to discover what may account for international differences in opportunity costs according to modern theory.

Equilibrium in Isolation   1924447

It is convenient to begin our search by observing the equilibrium conditions prevailing in each country in pretrade isolation. To keep the analysis manageable at a simple level, we assume that there are only two goods, X and Y. It is also assumed that a perfectly functioning, competitive market system is operative in each country.

In each country in pretrade equilibrium, the marginal opportunity cost of X in terms of Y (and, reciprocally, of Y in terms of X) is at a certain level. (*Marginal* opportunity cost is the *additional* cost of producing one *extra* unit of output.) In equilibrium, the relative market prices of the goods are equal to their marginal opportunity costs, and at these prices the total quantity of each good demanded by consumers is just equal to the quantity being produced.

These equilibrium conditions are easily illustrated graphically, and in a manner that will prove helpful to our subsequent analysis.[1] The basic device used is the *production transformation curve,* familiar to students from their first course in economics, where the curve usually goes under the name of *production possibilities curve.*

As will be recalled, the production transformation or possibilities curve shows the alternative combinations of output which an economy is capable of producing with its given stock of resources fully employed in the technically most efficient manner. The *slope* of the curve at any point measures the *marginal opportunity costs* of production when the output combination is at that point. To illustrate, refer to Figure 3.1.

AA' is the assumed transformation curve of country A. Each point on the curve represents a possible output combination of goods X and Y. At point P, for example, Ox_1 of X and Oy_1 of Y are produced. The marginal opportunity cost of X at point P is measured by the slope of the curve at that point. The slope of the curve is given by the ratio of the vertical to the horizontal distances covered by any movement along the straight-line *tangent* to the curve. In Figure 3.1, BD is the line tangent at point P and has a slope equal to BC/CD. This ratio represents the marginal opportunity cost of X, for it shows the rate at which good Y (measured vertically) must be sacrificed as the output of X (measured horizontally) is increased. Con-

---

[1] The graphical techniques employed in the remainder of this chapter and in the next chapter are extended in a complete graphical model in the Appendix to Chapter 4.

FIGURE 3.1

THE PRODUCTION TRANSFORMATION CURVE

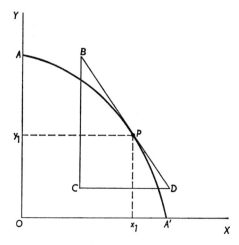

versely, the reciprocal of the slope—CD/BC—measures the marginal opportunity cost of Y, since it shows the rate at which X must be sacrificed as the output of Y is increased. (The slope of the curve is a valid measure of marginal opportunity costs only for very small changes in output, for each point on the curve has a different slope.)

If P is an equilibrium output point, the slope of tangent line BD measures not only marginal opportunity costs but also the *relative prices* of X and Y. For example, suppose that the ratio BC/CD equals 1.5. Then we know that the marginal opportunity cost of X is $1.5Y$ (and the marginal opportunity cost of Y is $2/3X$). For equilibrium to prevail, the price of X must therefore be 1.5 times that of Y.

To determine whether there is a basis for trade, the same procedure as above is followed for country B. The necessary condition is that pretrade equilibrium marginal opportunity costs and relative prices of X and Y are different from those in country A. In diagrammatic terms, the slope of B's transformation curve at the pretrade equilibrium output point must be different from A's if trade is to occur.

Opportunity Cost Differences

If, as we have concluded, trade is in response to pretrade international differences in opportunity costs, the next question to pursue is what accounts for these differences. The clue to the search for the answer is provided by the above discussion. In each country, opportunity costs are determined by the conjunction of two sets of forces: those determining the *shape* of the transformation curve and those determining the equilibrium *location* on the curve. *Differences in opportunity costs, therefore, arise as a result of either differently shaped transformation curves or different equilibrium locations on the curves, or both.* (As we shall see, however, it is possible for differences in one respect to be offset by opposite differences in the other respect.) Our investigation shall proceed accordingly, with the shape of transformation curves being considered first.

The Shape of Transformation Curves

A transformation curve is the expression of the conditions of production in an economy. Its shape (and position) are determined by the amounts and kinds of resources available and, given the state of technology, the technical possibilities of converting the output of one good into the output of another good through reallocating the given resources. It follows that if all countries possessed identically the same quantities and kinds of resources and produced under identical technical conditions, they would have identical transformation curves. Differences in the shapes of transformation curves must therefore be attributed to differences in one or more of these conditions.

Factor Proportions

Let us first consider how the technical conditions of production affect the shape of the transformation curve. Following this we shall look at the influence of resource supplies.

Technical conditions of production are revealed in the *production function,* which is the relationship between factor inputs—land, labor, capital—and output of the good. The characteristic of the production function centrally important for the purpose at hand relates to the proportion in which inputs are employed in producing a good.

Usually a good can be produced by any one of numerous different combinations of factors. This is because, within limits, different factors can be substituted for each other in the production process. However, the rate at which any factor can be substituted for another without reducing output *diminishes* the more extensive the substitution is. As a consequence, ever-increasing quantities of the factor being substituted for another are required to maintain any given level of output as the substitution proceeds.

While the substitutability of factors permits a possible wide range of choice among alternative technically feasible factor proportions, the economically most *efficient* (least-cost) combination depends upon relative factor prices. The relatively cheaper a given factor is, the greater is the proportion in which it is used in the factor mix.[2]

With relative factor prices given, different goods usually have different least-cost factor proportions, owing to different production functions. Accordingly, commodities may be classified on the basis of the factor used in the relatively greatest proportion. For example, if in producing X and Y each in the most efficient manner the ratio of labor to capital (L/K) is always greater for X than for Y at given factor prices, we call X a relatively *labor-intensive* good and Y a relatively *capital-intensive* good.

With the above remarks as background we are enabled to arrive at a fundamental proposition concerning the shapes of transformation curves:

Different factor intensities for different goods give rise to increasing marginal opportunity costs and a concave transformation curve. The same factor intensities for different goods lead to constant marginal opportunity costs and a linear transformation curve.

Figure 3.1 is an example of a *concave* transformation curve—that is, a curve bowed outward as viewed from the origin. Such a curve reflects *increasing* marginal opportunity costs. As shown earlier, marginal opportunity costs at any point on the curve are measured by the slope of the curve at that point. It will be observed that as the output of X is increased (and of Y decreased), the output point moves down the curve to *increasingly steeper sections,* indicating increasing marginal opportunity costs of X. Conversely, as movement occurs along the curve in an upward direction, signifying the increasing output of Y, the slope becomes less and less steep. This, too, indicates increasing marginal opportunity costs for Y, since the latter are measured by the *reciprocal* of the slope of the curve.

Let us return now to the proposition that different factor intensities for goods lead to increasing marginal opportunity costs and a concave transformation curve. To see why, suppose that the output

2 The general principle for achieving the least-cost factor combination is that the marginal rate of technical substitution of factors be equalized with the ratio of factor prices.

of Y, a capital-intensive good, is reduced by one unit. Labor and capital are released from the Y industry (for convenience we assume that these are the only factors employed) and transferred to the X industry. However, the proportion of labor to capital released from the Y industry is smaller than the proportion used in the labor-intensive X industry. This means that there must be some substitution of capital for labor in the X industry, and the extent of this substitution becomes greater the greater is the transfer of factors from Y to X. But capital has a diminishing effectiveness as a substitute for labor, with the consequence that increasingly larger reductions in the output of Y are required to achieve *equal* increments in the output of X as the transfer of resources progresses. Increasing marginal opportunity costs therefore prevails. The same phenomenon, operating in reverse with labor substituted for capital, causes the marginal opportunity cost of Y to rise as its output is increased.

We pause briefly to note an implication of the above analysis: if factor proportions were always the *same* in the X and Y industries, opportunity costs would tend to be *constant*. Graphically, this would be shown by a *linear* (straight-line) transformation curve—that is, a line with constant slope. However, empirical observation clearly reveals that different goods are normally subject to different production functions with respect to factor proportions, so that we may henceforth omit further reference to the constant opportunity cost model.[3]

The preceding discussion points to the conclusion that, owing to different production functions for different goods, transformation curves are normally concave. (The possibility of a curve being convex will be briefly examined at a later point in this chapter.) Since we are considering a given pair of goods, X and Y, does this mean that the transformation curve can be expected to have the same shape in country A as in country B, in the sense that for any given output combination the marginal opportunity costs are the same in the two countries? Even though the transformation curves are concave in both countries, they may still not be of identical shape in the sense indicated, for either of two reasons.

The first possibility is that production functions differ between countries, as well as between goods. If, for example, the production function for X is different in country A from that in country B, and

---

[3] By contrast, the classical theory was based on the assumption of constant opportunity cost. This was the consequence of a one-factor (labor) model, in which case the issue of factor proportions, of course, does not arise.

possibly also different in the two countries for good *Y,* this might well cause different slopes of the transformation curves at given relative output levels.

The second possibility has attracted more attention in the literature. Even if the production function for each good is the same in both countries (though different as between the two goods), the transformation curves will nevertheless be different *if relative factor supplies are not the same in the two countries.* Since relative factor supplies are obviously and markedly different as between countries in the real world, this is a highly relevant proposition in trade theory, deserving elaboration.

Relative Factor Supplies

Suppose that country *A,* as compared to country *B,* has relatively a large supply of labor and small stock of capital. We may then designate *A* as a relatively *labor-abundant* country and *B* as a relatively *capital-abundant* country, irrespective of the *absolute* size of their factor supplies.

Now assume as before that good *X* is a relatively *labor-intensive* product, good *Y* a relatively *capital-intensive* product. This means, as we saw previously, that the proportion of labor to capital is always greater in the production of *X* than in the production of *Y.* As a consequence, the labor-abundant country, *A,* will be able, as compared to country *B,* to produce relatively more of the labor-intensive product, *X,* than the capital-intensive product *Y.* In diagrammatic terms, the production transformation curve of country *A* will be stretched out relatively farther on the *X*-axis and be relatively shorter on the *Y*-axis than the curve for country *B.* This is illustrated in Figure 3.2, where *AA'* is the transformation curve of country *A* and *BB'* is that of country *B.* It is clear from the figure that, *for any given output combination,* the marginal opportunity cost of *X* is lower in *A* than in *B.* Along any ray from the origin, such as *OR* or *OR',* the ratio of the output of *Y* to that of *X* is the same. Hence, at A_1 on *A*'s transformation curve and B_1 on *B*'s curve, the output ratio is the same in the two countries. Similarly, points A_2 and B_2 on the ray *OR'* represent the same output ratio. In these and all other cases, it is observed that the slope of *A*'s transformation curve is less than the corresponding point on *B*'s, indicating lower marginal opportunity costs of *X* in country *A.*

FIGURE 3.2

THE EFFECT OF FACTOR SUPPLIES
ON TRANSFORMATION CURVES

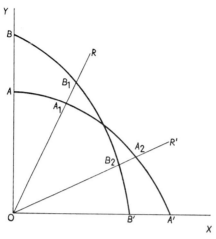

The economics underlying this is as follows: *Because* A *is a labor-abundant country and* B *a capital-abundant country, wage rates, compared to the price of capital, will tend to be lower in* A *than in* B. The principle here is that, other things being equal, the greater the amount of other factors of production available for a given factor to work with, the greater is the marginal productivity of the factor. Under competitive conditions, the price of a factor service is equal in equilibrium to its marginal product. Thus, the marginal product of labor and the wage rate can be expected to be lower in A than in B, while the marginal product of capital and the rental price of capital can be expected to be lower in B than in A. Now relatively low wage rates clearly cause relatively low costs of production for labor-intensive goods, while relatively low rental prices of capital lead to relatively low costs of production for capital-intensive goods. Hence, the relative abundance of labor in country A and of capital in country B imposes a bias in the direction of a comparative advantage for A in the labor-intensive commodity X and for B in the capital-intensive commodity Y.

In summary, *different factor intensities for commodities, in combination with different relative factor abundance, are responsible for concave transformation curves of different shapes.* In concluding this section, it must be emphasized that differences in *both* relative factor intensities and in factor supplies are required to produce this result. If factor intensities are the same for all commodities in all countries, differences in factor supplies (and hence in relative factor prices) will not be a cause of comparative cost differences, since all goods will have the same opportunity cost in each country, though different costs in different countries. In similar fashion, different factor intensities do not lead to comparative cost differences if relative factor supplies (and factor prices) are the same everywhere, since in this case the costs of commodities will bear the same proportion in all countries.

Pretrade Output Points

We noted some pages back that international differences in opportunity (and comparative) costs arise as a result of either differently shaped transformation curves or different equilibrium locations on the curves, or both. Having examined the possible reasons for differently shaped transformation curves, we need now to show the relevance of pretrade locations on the curves to opportunity cost differences.

In what we have come to regard as the normal case of concave transformation curves, the reason for the relevance of locations on the curves is readily apparent: marginal opportunity costs are different at different output points. The same thing is true if the curves are convex (attributable to economies of scale, discussed later). Only in the classical case of constant marginal opportunity costs, reflected in linear transformation curves, are output points irrelevant, since marginal costs are invariant with respect to output.

We have seen that with increasing costs and concave curves, there may be a bias in the direction of lower marginal opportunity costs for certain goods (one particular good in the two-goods model) in one country. Such is the case illustrated in Figure 3.2, where the transformation curve of country A is "stretched out" in comparison to that of country B, as the result of A's assumed relative labor-abundance in conjunction with the assumption that X is a labor-intensive good.

However, the bias imparted by different cost conditions can be either reinforced or counteracted by differences in pretrade output combinations. An extreme instance of the latter effect is illustrated in Figure 3.3, which reproduces the transformation curves of Figure 3.2.

As noted previously, for the same output combination in A and B, marginal opportunity (and comparative) costs of X are lower in A

FIGURE 3.3

OFFSETTING INFLUENCES ON
OPPORTUNITY COSTS

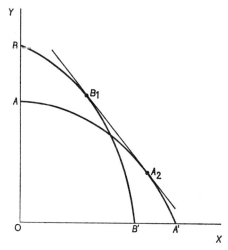

than in B. Suppose, however, that pretrade output is at point B_1 in country B and at point A_2 in country A. In this case, marginal opportunity costs are the *same*, as evidenced by the fact that the line B_1A_2 is tangent to both curves at the indicated output points.[4]

The question to be investigated now is what determines different locations on transformation curves. The question is equivalent to asking what determines the pretrade allocation of resources.

In a competitive market system, the allocation of resources among alternative uses is determined by *demand*. If the demand for good X, compared to that for good Y, is relatively greater in country A than in country B, resources in A will be drawn more extensively into the X industry than is the case for B. If increasing costs prevail, this difference in demand conditions works in the direction of making the opportunity cost of X higher in A than in B, thus counteracting, partially or wholly, the bias on the production side toward lower opportunity costs of X in A. If the pattern of demand were the reverse, the effect would be the opposite: to increase the comparative cost advantage of A in good X.

The pattern of each country's demand is based principally upon the community's consumer preferences or tastes, and the level and

---

[4] The student is invited to demonstrate for himself that different output combinations can serve to *widen* opportunity cost differences. An extreme case—the polar opposite of that illustrated in Figure 3.3—is where different output combinations cause opportunity cost differences even though transformation curves are of identical shape.

distribution of real income. The demand for X may be relatively greater in A than in B because consumer tastes in A more heavily favor X while consumers in B have a stronger preference for Y. Or it could be that X is regarded as a necessity and Y as a luxury, and that the level of real income in A is lower than in B or less unequally distributed in A than in B. In short, demand would have a neutral role in determining comparative costs under increasing (or decreasing) cost conditions only if consumer preferences, real income levels, and the distribution of income happen to be such as to cause the same pattern of relative demand in different countries.

Summary of Modern Theory

It may be useful briefly to summarize the rather extended discussion of the modern theory of trade. Beginning with the proposition that trade occurs as the immediate result of relative price differences internationally, we proceeded to investigate the causes of the latter. Since in competitive equilibrium relative prices in each country equal marginal opportunity costs, our attention turned to the determinants of opportunity cost differences. In terms of the production transformation curve, we sought to explain the possible reasons for international differences in the slopes of the curves at pretrade equilibrium output points.

We found that transformation curves are normally concave, reflecting increasing opportunity cost conditions, owing to the presence of different factor intensities for different goods. But the presence of different relative factor supplies in different countries prevents transformation curves from having identical shapes. (International differences in production functions might also be responsible for this.) The relative abundance of a particular factor imparts a bias, on the production side, toward lower opportunity costs for the good relatively intensive in that factor.

However, actual opportunity costs depend not only upon the shapes of transformation curves but also upon output locations on the curves. The latter we found to be determined by demand conditions. International differences in the pattern of demand may either widen or narrow opportunity cost differences.

In capsule summary, the search for the underlying causes of trade leads to international differences in factor supplies or production functions, in conjunction with the pattern of demand.

The Heckscher-Ohlin Theorem

There is one rather unsatisfying aspect of the modern theory of trade as presented in the preceding pages: it is too general to allow more than a rather vague and amorphous impression of the underlying causes of trade in the real world. Technical conditions of production, as revealed in production functions, resource supplies, and the pattern of demand are all involved.

The mark of a "good" theory is its ability to explain a phenomenon in the most simple terms and with the fewest variables possible. Can the modern theory be simplified in this manner? Two Swedish economists, Eli Heckscher and Bertil Ohlin, attempted to do so several years ago in formulating a theorem bearing their names.[5]

The Heckscher-Ohlin theorem may be stated as follows:

Comparative cost differences are based on relative differences in countries' factor endowments; each country tends to have a comparative advantage in, and to export, those goods requiring in their production the factor in relative greatest supply in that country, and to have a comparative disadvantage in, and to import, those goods requiring in their production the factor in relative scarcest supply in that country.

It will be noted that this theorem is simply a special case of the more general modern theory described in the preceding pages. Of the several parameters which theoretically influence comparative costs, one in particular is identified as having a central role. It is this grand simplification of complex reality that makes the Heckscher-Ohlin theorem a remarkable tour de force.

The assignment of a dominating role to relative factor endowments as an explanation of comparative cost differences is based upon several conditions. Among these conditions, apart from the presence of competitive markets, the major ones are (1) internationally identical production functions, (2) the absence of factor-intensity reversals, (3) no large international differences in the pattern of demand, (4) constant returns to scale, and (5) the proper specification of factor categories. If these conditions hold, the modern general theory of trade leads to the Heckscher-Ohlin theorem as a special case, since the effect of these conditions is to eliminate all determi-

---

[5] Ohlin, basing himself on earlier work by Heckscher, presented a complete statement of the theorem in his *Interregional and International Trade* (Cambridge, Mass.: Harvard University Press, 1933).

nants of comparative cost differences *except* for differences in relative factor endowments.

It is proposed now to examine each of the above conditions under-lying the Heckscher-Ohlin theorem. We are interested both in the reasons for the significance of the conditions and in the theoretical or empirical bases for believing them actually to be present.

Identical Production Functions

In the theoretical discussion earlier in this chapter, it was observed that internationally different production functions for a given prod-uct could be responsible for comparative cost differences, in which case the Heckscher-Ohlin focus on factor endowments as the underly-ing explanation of trade might prove to be misleading.

Production functions are physical input-output relationships, stat-ing the various quantities of output producible through the use of various amounts of factor inputs. Provided that given technical knowledge is applied, a given set of qualitatively identical factor inputs will yield the same output wherever the productive operation is carried on. That is, the physical laws of production are universal. Consequently, production functions can differ internationally only if technical knowledge differs from one country to another.[6]

It follows that the validity of the assumption of internationally identical production functions hinges upon the universality of tech-nical knowledge. In fact, this is clearly not always the case at any given moment of time. Technological changes are frequent in the modern world, and the diffusion of new knowledge often occurs only after a lag. This is especially true of sophisticated industrial processes and gives rise to a *dynamic* theory of trade based on technological gaps. Trade arising from technological changes falls outside the framework of the Heckscher-Ohlin theorem and will be separately examined in Chapter 5.

It is a common observation that over time technical knowledge tends to become a "free good," available to all countries. Especially is this true for the standardized products to which the Heckscher-Ohlin theorem is applicable. Hence, we may conclude that the assumption of identical production functions is acceptable within the context of the Heckscher-Ohlin theorem.

---

[6] For a fuller discussion of this conclusion, see I. F. Pearce, *International Trade* (New York: W. W. Norton & Co., 1970) , pp. 323–28.

Factor Proportions

A second condition assumed to exist by the Heckscher-Ohlin theorem relates to another characteristic of the production function, namely, factor proportions. The theorem requires that commodities be unambiguously classifiable according to their factor intensity. This means, it will be recalled, that if a commodity is classified as, say, labor-intensive, the proportion of labor to other factor inputs used in its production is always greater than for those goods designated as capital-intensive or land-intensive. This condition is critical for the conclusion that relative factor supplies determine comparative cost differences.

It is theoretically possible, however, for factor intensities to switch at some factor price relationships—a phenomenon called *factor reversal*. Factor reversal occurs if at some factor price ratio a good changes from being, say, labor-intensive to being capital-intensive. The reasons for such switching are too technical to be appropriately discussed here,[7] but its consequences for the theory of trade deserve to be pointed out. (It also has other important implications, especially for factor pricing, that will be discussed in due course.) If factor reversal occurs (it may occur once or more than once), there is no longer a definite relationship between comparative cost advantage and relative factor abundance. A labor-abundant country, for example, may have a comparative advantage in either labor-intensive or capital-intensive goods.

Factor reversal is clearly devastating to any theory of trade along the lines previously presented here, and especially to the Heckscher-Ohlin version. It may provide some comfort to note that factor reversal in some cases *cannot* occur, for technical reasons, and in other cases *will* not occur. The probability of factor reversal appears to be significant only when there are large differences between countries in relative factor prices.

Whether in fact factor reversals occur has been studied empirically. One investigation, comparing industries by capital intensity in the United States and Japan, led the author to conclude that factor reversals do indeed occur, convincing him (and some other economists) that the Heckscher-Ohlin theorem is thereby robbed of any

---

[7] The interested reader may consult Harry Johnson, "Factor Endowments, International Trade, and Factor Prices," *Manchester School of Economic and Social Studies*, September 1957; reproduced as Chapter 1 in Johnson's *International Trade and Economic Growth* (Cambridge, Mass.: Harvard University Press, 1961.)

predictive significance.[8] However, later empirical studies, proceeding on a broader base and using different measuring techniques, reach a quite different conclusion. In the words of one investigator,

. . . Some industries appear to be more labor-intensive in one or more foreign countries, and others less so, than in the United States. But few of these shifts could be regarded as clear and significant reversals of factor intensities.[9]

Unless and until more definitive studies contradict this conclusion, we would appear to be justified in accepting the hypothesis of the Heckscher-Ohlin theorem that goods can be categorized according to their factor intensities.

Economies of Scale

Still another aspect of production functions is involved in the assumption of the Heckscher-Ohlin theorem that there are constant returns to scale. Constant returns to scale mean that unit (or average) costs, as well as marginal costs, are unaffected by the scale of production of the individual firm or industry. *Increasing* returns to scale, by contrast, mean that average costs of production decline as the size of the firm or industry increases because of economies of scale.

Economies realized by an individual firm as the consequence of enlarging its scale of production are known as "internal" economies of scale. In some industries, the output of the firm required to exhaust all possible internal economies is so large that only a few firms can survive. In such cases internal economies of scale are incompatible with pure competition and, therefore, fall outside the framework of the Heckscher-Ohlin theorem. The role of internal economies of scale will be examined later in the discussion of imperfectly competitive models of trade.

External economies of scale, on the other hand, are consistent with pure competition, for they depend not upon the size of individual firms but rather upon the size of a whole industry. If, as an industry expands, each firm in the industry finds that its average and marginal costs fall, then it is possible for there to be *decreasing* marginal opportunity costs and *convex* transformation curves. Comparative

---

[8] See B. S. Minhas, "The Homohypallagic Production Function, Factor Intensity Reversals, and the Heckscher-Ohlin Theorem," *Journal of Political Economy*, April 1962.

[9] Hal B. Lary, *Imports of Manufactures from Less Developed Countries,* National Bureau of Economic Research (New York: Columbia University Press, 1968) , p. 80.

cost differences are as likely to be present in this case as when marginal opportunity costs are increasing and transformation curves are concave. However, the explanation of the basis of trade then may differ from that provided by the Heckscher-Ohlin theorem. Instead of relative factor supplies it may be the relative size of industries which account for comparative cost differences. Moreover, a comparative cost advantage may develop, or become greater, as the *result* of trade when decreasing costs prevail. Even if initially comparative cost differences were negligible, once trade opportunities arise each country may develop a cost advantage in particular products in which there are economies of scale realizable through specializing in those products.

While the theoretical possibility that economies of scale are a potentially important cause of trade must be admitted, empirical studies indicate that the phenomenon is of limited significance in the real world. Several empirical investigations have found evidence that returns to scale are generally constant.[10] It would appear, therefore, that the assumption of constant returns to scale is empirically questionable only to a limited extent and may be safely adopted as a general first approximation to reality.

The Pattern of Demand

It was noted in our general discussion of the theory of trade that demand conditions as well as production conditions enter into the determination of comparative costs. The Heckscher-Ohlin theorem assigns a dominant influence to the production side only by virtue of the assumption that the pattern of demand is similar among countries.

On the basis of the general principles determining economic values, the presumption against ignoring demand or assigning to it a subsidiary role is strong. Demand and supply jointly operate to determine price, with no a priori basis for imputing dominance to the one or the other. As we observed earlier, it is quite possible theoretically for differences in the pattern of demand to exert an influence on comparative costs *counter* to that exerted by relative factor endowments considered alone. If such happens to be the case, the explanation of trade according to the Heckscher-Ohlin theorem, of course, requires major amendment.

---

10 See H. Robert Heller, *International Trade, Theory and Empirical Evidence,* 2d ed. (Englewood Cliffs, New Jersey, 1973), p. 67.

As with respect to many other issues, the proper settlement of the role of demand in trade theory can be made only on the basis of empirical evidence. Unfortunately, the available evidence is rather meager. What evidence we have suggests that whereas the pattern of demand tends to be rather similar between countries of similar per capita income levels, it varies widely between countries with large differences in per capita income. Differences in demand conditions are therefore likely to have a significant potential for affecting comparative cost differences only between countries of markedly different levels of per capita income. Even in this case, however, there is no evidence so far available to indicate any tendency for different patterns of demand to outweigh the influence of production conditions. Tentatively, at least, we can accept the assumption of similar demand conditions as empirically warrantable.

The Specification of "Factors"

We come now to the last in the list of conditions underlying the Heckscher-Ohlin theorem. Since the theorem focuses on relative factor endowments as the key determinant of comparative cost differences, a proper specification of the factors of production is essential for the theorem to be meaningful. A *mis*specification of factors can easily lead to the erroneous conclusion that the theorem is incorrect, as demonstrated by certain empirical tests, discussed below.

Traditionally, factors of production are classified into the three categories of land, defined as the productive resources provided by nature; labor, defined as human productive effort; and capital, defined as man-created means of production. While this is a very useful classification for some purposes, it can create serious difficulties as the basis for applying a factor-proportions theory of trade.

The principal problem is that a broad factor category, such as land or labor, includes a wide variety of qualitatively different units. Land, for example, can be fertile or barren, arid or plentifully supplied with water, rich in valuable minerals or devoid of them, etc. Similarly, labor may be skilled or unskilled, professional or manual, well-educated or illiterate, etc. To treat each broad factor category as if it were homogeneous obviously could be very misleading. On the other hand, to separate factors into strictly homogeneous groups would result in a multitude of factor categories, leaving the concept of relative factor endowments operationally meaningless.

With respect to land, the above problem can be resolved fairly easily. For the most part, land is a major factor input only in primary products, such as agricultural commodities and natural resources. The special attributes of land required for the production of various primary commodities are easily identified and the bases of comparative advantage in such products fairly obvious. Thus, countries with a relatively large endowment of "wheat-growing land" (United States, Canada, Argentina, for example) tend to have a comparative advantage in wheat. Even more obviously, comparative advantages in natural resource products—such as petroleum, coal, bauxite, copper, etc.—are clearly based on the relative endowments of known and accessible reserves of these resources.

Because the explanation of trade in primary products is so direct and simple, economists are inclined to concentrate on the theory of trade in manufactured goods, in the production of which land plays a relatively unimportant role. Accordingly, land is frequently ignored, with labor and capital assumed to be the only factor categories.

Putting land aside, we are left with the problem of meaningfully defining labor as a homogeneous factor. It is possible to divide labor into various types—unskilled manual, skilled manual, technical, professional, etc.—and to treat each type as a separate factor. However, there is another approach, which has the advantage of avoiding the complications of multifactor models and, in addition, provides a more penetrating analysis.

The latter approach is based on the proposition that the productivity of human beings is attributable to two separate and distinct sources: (*a*) labor time, and (*b*) human capital.

Labor time is simply the clock-hours spent in productive activity. It is the one element that all labor has in common and that can be measured in terms of the same units. Although it may be true that the workers in some industries or in some countries exert more effort per hour of work than in other industries or countries, it is fair to presume that, on the average, an hour of labor represents the same amount of productive effort wherever the labor service is rendered.

It follows that qualitative differences in labor are the reflection mainly of different amounts of education and training. But these in turn are the consequence of different amounts of "human capital" embodied in the workers. In its most general sense, capital includes any resource that yields a flow of productive services over time. Man-made material means of production—building, equipment, tools, etc.—are easily recognizable types of capital. Less obvious but essentially equivalent means of production are created in the form of the education and training of persons in the labor force, for these attributes, like material capital, increase the flow over time of valuable economic services. Moreover, the process through which human capital is created is the same as that for material capital—the investment of current income saved.[11]

By separating out the element of human capital embodied in workers and placing it alongside material means of production in the factor category "capital," labor time is left as the residual measure of "labor" as the second, homogeneous factor. Accordingly, countries can be classified as labor- or capital-abundant in the proper sense appropriate to the factor-proportions theorem of trade.

Empirical Tests

We have found that the conditions underlying the Heckscher-Ohlin theorem can reasonably be supposed to exist. However, the ultimate test of the validity of a theory is not the reasonableness of its assumptions, but whether it is supported (or at least not contradicted) by empirical investigations.

The first serious test of the Heckscher-Ohlin theorem was made by an American economist, Professor W. W. Leontief.[12] Leontief made use of his well-known input-output table for the United States to determine the capital and labor requirements for a given bundle of exports and for a given bundle of imports. On the presumption that the United States is clearly a capital-abundant country, the Heckscher-Ohlin theorem would predict that her exports would be relatively capital-intensive and her imports relatively labor-intensive. The results of the study indicated the reverse: United States exports as labor-intensive and imports as capital-intensive, thus apparently contradicting the Heckscher-Ohlin theorem. This conclusion has come to be known as the "Leontief Paradox."

Leontief-type tests made by other investigators for other countries have shown mixed results. Some reinforce the inference from Leontief's study that the Heckscher-Ohlin theorem is defective, while others appear to confirm the theory.[13] In general, it can be con-

---

[11] See P. B. Kenen, "Nature, Capital and Trade," *Journal of Political Economy* vol. 73 (October 1965).

[12] "Domestic Production and Foreign Trade: The American Capital Position Reexamined," *Proceedings of the American Philosophical Society*, September 1963; and "Factor Proportions and the Structure of American Trade: Further Theoretical and Empirical Analysis," *Review of Economics and Statistics*, November 1956.

[13] The studies referred to are the first and the last three references in the Recommended Readings list at the end of this chapter.

cluded that these earlier tests do not support the Heckscher-Ohlin theorem.

The failure of Leontief-type tests to verify the Heckscher-Ohlin theorem can be explained on several different grounds. One possibility, of course, is that the theorem is invalid. An alternate explanation is that the tests were inadequate. That the latter explanation may be the correct one is indicated by later tests, which support the theorem. Before examining these later, supportive tests, some of the principal inadequacies of Leontief's and other investigations are worth noting.

The crucial weakness of Leontief's test lies in its treatment of capital as consisting only of material means of production. Such an approach, as observed in our earlier discussion, fails to identify the capital components embodied in labor in the form of education and training, thus ignoring important qualitative differences among various types of workers.

Leontief himself was aware of the objections to lumping different kinds of labor into a single factor category. To resolve the paradox that his tests showed—that the United States, a relatively capital-abundant country, imports labor-intensive goods—Leontief hypothesized that United States labor is three times as effective as foreign labor, so that actually the United States is relatively labor-abundant when the comparison with other countries is made in terms of equivalent units of labor. However, no convincing reasons for accepting this rather arbitrary contention were advanced.

A second weakness of Leontief's test is of an altogether different kind, and one from which no empirical test of the Heckscher-Ohlin can easily escape, namely, the presence in the real trading world of a variety of conditions which violate the postulates of the theory, thereby possibly rendering it inapplicable. Two postulates in particular are relevant in this connection: the postulates of purely competitive markets and of trade uninhibited by tariffs and other artificial barriers. Let us look briefly at the implications of each of these deviations of the real world from the theoretical model.

With regard to market structures, the Heckscher-Ohlin theorem does not require for its validity that pure competition literally prevail. As mentioned before, theory always abstracts from real-world details in order to focus on essentials. In fact, pure competition as a theoretical concept practically never exists in reality. However, in many markets there is an approximation to the results produced by pure competition sufficient to validate the predictions of the theory. Such, for example, is the case for a large number of standardized products heavily traded internationally. On the other hand, a significant portion of world trade is in goods produced and sold in markets so imperfectly competitive as to render the assumption of pure competition unfruitful. In such cases the Heckscher-Ohlin theorem is not applicable or at least requires important modification. In other words, conditions in the real world are so diverse that no one theory has yet been devised to be universally applicable. (Thus, the theory of trade under monopolistic conditions will be considered later in Chapter 5.)

The second postulate of the Heckscher-Ohlin theorem poorly reflected in the real world is the absence of artificial trade barriers. The actual presence of tariffs, quotas, and other barriers to trade results in a pattern of trade different from that which would emerge in a world without such barriers. This does not invalidate the theory, however. On the contrary, the theory of trade *without* barriers is necessary to determine the effects of barriers, as we shall see in due course in a discussion of the theory of tariffs and quotas. While trade barriers do not invalidate trade theory, they do make empirical tests of the theory difficult. For example, on the basis of the Heckscher-Ohlin theorem we would predict that a capital-abundant country tends to import labor-intensive products. If, however, the country imposes artificial barriers to the import of such products that are higher than on other products, an investigation of its actual trade pattern might fail to confirm the theorem.[14]

The presence of imperfectly competitive markets and of trade barriers makes any fair test of the Heckscher-Ohlin theorem difficult. As observed earlier, however, the central defect of Leontief-type tests is the measurement of capital endowment in terms only of the material means of production and the corresponding measurement of labor endowment in terms of the man-years of labor available, without distinguishing among different types of labor. The role of "human capital" is thus left unidentified and unaccounted for. It is therefore quite probable that the failure of early tests to confirm the Heckscher-Ohlin theorem is attributable to the misspecification of labor and capital. This conclusion is reinforced by the results of more recent tests which identify human capital, though indirectly, and which support the Heckscher-Ohlin theorem. Let us briefly examine some of these tests.

---

14 See W. P. Travis, *The Theory of Trade and Protection* (Cambridge, Mass.: Harvard University Press, 1964) for elaboration of the argument that tariffs account for the Leontief paradox.

It is practically impossible directly to measure human capital, since, unlike material capital, it is not traded and priced in markets. However, there are reasonably good proxies for human capital for which data are available. One proxy for human capital is labor skills. More highly skilled labor can be assumed to have a larger amount of embodied capital in the form of education and training. A second, related, proxy for human capital is wage rates. On the grounds that wage rates reflect not only the return on labor time spent, but also the return on embodied human capital, industries in which education and training are important will have high average wage rates. Hence, average rates, by industry, can serve as a proxy for the amount of human capital used.

Various empirical studies show that the exports of countries relatively well-supplied with skilled labor tend to require in their production relatively greater amounts of skilled labor than the production of goods that compete with imports.[15] Moreover, countries with comparatively large amounts of unskilled labor tend to specialize in commodities produced with relatively large amounts of such labor and to import skill-intensive products. To the extent that different skills reflect different amounts of human capital, these results show that countries relatively well-endowed with human capital tend to export commodities that are human-capital intensive. The same general kind of results have been produced by using wage rates rather than skills as its proxy for human capital.

As a specific example of the above approach, a recent study of United States trade may be cited.[16] The study reveals that for both of the two periods covered (1958–1960 and 1968) import replacements in the United States utilized a much lower skill ratio than did exports. The study also shows that wage rates are somewhat lower in import industries than in export industries, though the disparity here was not as great as for skill ratios.

The conclusion that the United States has a comparative advantage in products manufactured with relatively large amounts of human capital is quite convincing. In view of the fact that the United States has a relatively large endowment of human capital, this conclusion is in accord with the Heckscher-Ohlin theorem.

The failure of earlier tests of the Heckscher-Ohlin theorem, based

---

[15] See Donald B. Keesing, "Labor Skills and Comparative Advantage," *American Economic Review*, May 1966, pp. 249–58.

[16] See United States Tariff Commission, "Competitiveness of U.S. Industries," TC Publication 473 (Washington, D.C., April 1972).

on the concept of capital as consisting only of material means of production, together with the later supportive tests based on the endowment of human capital, raises the question of the role of capital in the broad sense—material plus human—in determining comparative advantage.

It is reasonable to suppose that there is a close relationship between a country's endowment of human capital and its endowment of material capital. A high ratio of material capital to labor is associated with high per capita income, which in turns usually is accompanied by large investments in education and training of labor. This suggests that if tests of the Heckscher-Ohlin theorem according to relative endowments of human capital are successful, so, too, should be tests in which a single, inclusive measure of capital—embracing material as well as human components—is used. This expectation has been supported by several empirical investigations.[17]

In general conclusion, the evidence indicates that, provided the factors of production are properly specified, the Heckscher-Ohlin theorem is valid.

RECOMMENDED READINGS

BHARADWAJ, R. *Structural Basis for India's Foreign Trade.* Bombay, 1962.

CORDEN, W. M. *Recent Developments in the Theory of International Trade,* chaps. 2 and 4. Princeton University, International Finance Section, Special Papers in International Economics no. 7, 1965.

HABERLER, GOTTFRIED. *The Theory of International Trade,* chaps. 9–12. New York: Macmillan Co., 1937.

HELLER, H. ROBERT. *International Trade, Theory and Empirical Evidence.* 2d ed. Englewood Cliffs, N.J.: Prentice-Hall, Inc., 1973.

JOHNSON, HARRY. *Comparative Cost and Commercial Policy for a Developing World Economy.* Stockholm: Almquist & Wiksell, 1968.

KENEN, PETER B. "Toward a More General Theory of Capital and Trade," *The Open Economy: Essays on International Trade and Finance.* New York: Columbia University Press, 1968.

OHLIN, BERTIL. *Interregional and International Trade,* Parts 1 and 2 and chaps. 12–14. Cambridge, Mass.: Harvard University Press, 1933 (reprinted 1952). The complete statment of the Heckscher-Ohlin theory.

---

[17] See, for example, P. B. Kenen, "Toward a More General Theory of Capital and Trade," *The Open Economy: Essays on International Trade and Finance* (New York: Columbia University Press, 1968).

ROBINSON, ROMNEY. "Factor Proportions and Comparative Advantage," *Quarterly Journal of Economics* 70 (May–August 1956). A sharp criticism of the Heckscher-Ohlin theory.

STOLPER, W., and ROSKAMP, K. "Input-Output Table for East Germany with Applications to Foreign Trade," *Bulletin of the Oxford Institute of Statistics*, November 1961.

TATEMOTO, M., and ICHIMURA, S. "Factor Proportions and Foreign Trade: The Case of Japan," *Review of Economics and Statistics*, November 1959.

WAHL, D. F. "Capital and Labour Requirements for Canada's Foreign Trade," *Canadian Journal of Economics and Political Science*, August 1961.

STUDY QUESTIONS

1. State and evaluate the classical labor theory of value.
2. Contrast the concept of opportunity cost with that of labor cost.
3. How do differences in opportunity costs imply differences in comparative costs?
4. Review the meaning and construction of the production possibilities or transformation curve.
5. Show how differently shaped transformation curves reflect different cost conditions.
6. Why do pretrade output points have no influence on comparative costs if constant cost conditions prevail?
7. If there are increasing or decreasing marginal opportunity costs, why must pretrade output points be specified in order to determine comparative costs?
8. In what sense can it be said that differently shaped transformation curves exhibit a bias toward a comparative cost advantage in one product?
9. Construct an example in which comparative costs differ even though transformation curves are identical.
10. Factor inputs are usually substitutable but only at diminishing rates. Explain.
11. Clearly explain the meaning of factor intensity.
12. Explain how different factor intensities for different commodities lead to increasing marginal opportunity costs.
13. On what basis may countries be classified with respect to their factor endowments?
14. What effect does a relative abundance of labor have on the shape of

the transformation curve when a labor-intensive good is measured vertically?

15. Through what economic mechanism does relative factor abundance affect relative factor prices and comparative costs?

16. Prove to your own satisfaction that both different factor intensities and different relative factor supplies are necessary for either one to cause comparative cost differences.

17. Specify the principal determinants of pretrade output points.

18. State the conclusions of the Heckscher-Ohlin theorem. What simplifying assumptions does it make and on what grounds?

19. What consequence for the theory of trade would follow from the presence of international differences in the production functions?

20. Explain the meaning of factor reversal and indicate its significance for trade theory.

21. How may economies of scale serve as an independent basis for international trade?

22. Under what conditions can relative demand be expected to differ most internationally?

23. Define "human capital." Why is it conceptually equivalent to material capital?

24. Describe the proxy for human capital used in empirical tests.

25. What is the proper specification of "labor" as a factor of production in the context of the Heckscher-Ohlin theorem?

26. Describe the "Leontief Paradox."

27. State some of the possible principal reasons for the failure of early empirical tests to verify the Heckscher-Ohlin theorem.

4

The economic effects of competitive trade

In the two preceding chapters, attention was focused on the fundamental causes, and the determinants of the pattern, of international trade, within the framework of purely competitive markets. The theory of trade in imperfectly competitive markets remains to be examined. However, before turning to this topic, which will be covered in the next chapter, we pause to consider the important question of what major economic effects are produced by competitive trade.

THE EQUALIZATION OF PRICES AND COSTS

As a prelude to exploring the less obvious and more fundamental effects of trade, let us begin with the observation that, under the assumptions we have adopted, trade results in the elimination of the price and cost differentials which are initially responsible for its occurring. Ignoring transportation costs and assuming the operation of free and competitive market forces, every article entering into international trade must have the same price in all countries at prevailing rates of exchange. This is simply the consequence of there being created a *single international market* in place of the separate national markets in existence before trading relations are begun. The common international price of each traded good will in equilibrium be at that level at which total world demand equals total world supply.

Not only are prices equalized by trade, so too are marginal (and average) costs. For each good price is equal to marginal cost in competitive equilibrium, so that the international equalization of prices carries with it the equalization of costs in the countries producing the goods. This is the reason why with constant cost conditions specialization tends to be complete: the international price of the good, equal to its cost of production in the country with the comparative cost advantage, is below its cost, at all output levels, in the other country, which does not, therefore, produce it. Under increasing cost conditions, however, some of the import commodity may be produced at home, since, at a reduced output level, domestic cost falls to the level of the international price, equal to the cost of production in the export country.

The international equalization of costs and prices as the result of trade raises this apparent paradox: why should a commodity be exported or imported if its domestic price and cost are the same at home as abroad? The solution to the paradox is, of course, that the *reason* why the price and cost are the same is *because* there is trade. Were trade to stop or be reduced below the volume at which the price is the same in all countries, a differential in price would appear and cause trade to start up again or to increase in volume until the differential disappeared.

The Role of Transportation Costs

It is worth reiterating that the equalization of the prices and costs of goods as the result of trade is dependent, among other things, upon the absence of transportation costs. In reality, of course, transportation costs always are present, with consequences for trade which deserve at least brief discussion.

The first point to make is that transportation costs constitute a natural barrier to international trade that cannot be hurdled in all cases. The price of a good to an importing country includes the costs of freight, insurance, and handling. If these exceed the difference in the domestic price of the good abroad and at home, trade does not occur. Many goods and services are practically excluded from international trade for this reason. Bricks, for instance, are produced for highly localized markets because of the cost of transporting them in relation to the cost of producing them.

Where transport costs do not remove the advantages of trade, they quite often exert a determinative influence on the pattern of specialization and trade. Consider, for example, a particular industry requiring various raw materials available only in different geographic regions. Clearly, there will be a tendency for trade to occur, but what will be its pattern? For example, which region will bring all the required raw materials together for fabrication of the finished product? Other things being equal, the location will be where *transport costs are minimized.*

A classic example is the steel industry in the United States. The tendency to locate near the coal supply rather than the iron ore ranges stems from the fact that, per ton of steel, a greater tonnage of coal than of iron ore is used. Similar considerations apply to most industries requiring large amounts of fuel—cement, glass, calcium carbide, etc.[1] In other cases, nearness to the market for the product, differential freight rates (based on the type of material or commodity, the volume of traffic, the type of transportation means available, etc.), and similar elements enter into the determination of the best location of particular industries from the standpoint of minimizing transport costs.[2]

In general, transport costs reduce the volume of trade below the level it would be in their absence and in some instances significantly modify the pattern of geographic specialization.

Factor Price Equalization

One of the most interesting and important effects of international trade is in the direction not only of equalizing prices of goods internationally but, under certain circumstances, equalizing *factor prices* as well.

The most convenient starting point for showing a tendency toward factor price equalization as the result of trade is the Heckscher-Ohlin trade model, described in Chapter 3. It will be recalled that in this model each country specializes in the production of the good which uses a relatively large quantity of the country's relatively

---

[1] See Edgar M. Hoover, *The Location of Economic Activity* (New York: McGraw-Hill, 1948), pp. 32 ff.

[2] For a detailed description, see Hoover, *The Location of Economic Activity*, pp. 32 ff.

abundant factor. The relatively abundant factor is also the relatively *cheap* factor, since a factor's price is equal to its marginal productivity, and relative abundance implies low marginal productivity.

The effect of trade is to reduce the relative abundance of a country's abundant factor and to reduce the relative scarcity of its scarce factor. This occurs even though the *physical* supplies of the factors remain constant. The relatively abundant factor becomes economically less abundant (scarcer) *because of the increased demand for it,* while the relatively scarce factor becomes economically less scarce (more abundant) *because of the decreased demand for it.* These changes in relative factor demand are the direct consequence of the country's specializing in the product in which it has a comparative cost advantage, together with the assumption that different goods have different factor intensities.

Suppose, for example, that country *A* is labor-abundant and capital-scarce, and that good *X* is labor-intensive and good *Y* capital-intensive. As the result of trade, *A* increases its production of *X* (in which it has a comparative advantage) with resources released from the *Y* industry (in which it has a comparative disadvantage). The resources released from the production of *Y* consist, by assumption, of a greater proportion of capital to labor than used in the production of *X*. Hence, for full employment of capital to be maintained (also assumed in the model), the "extra" capital released from the *Y* industry must be absorbed in the *X* industry. The ratio of capital to labor is thereby increased in the *X* industry. It is in this sense that labor becomes relatively scarcer and capital relatively less scarce.

Since a factor's marginal productivity and price increase as its relative scarcity increases, wage rates rise and the rental price of capital falls as *A* shifts resources from the *Y* industry to the *X* industry. The same phenomenon can be observed from another point of view. Since the demand for *X* has increased and that for *Y* has decreased, the demand for the principal factor (labor) used in producing *X* increases, while the demand for the principal factor (capital) used in producing *Y* falls. As far as individual firms are concerned, it is the consequent rise in wage rates relatively to the rental price of capital that induces a substitution of capital for labor to maintain the least-cost combination of inputs. It should be noted that the substitution occurs in the *Y* industry as well as in the *X* industry, since the wage rate is relatively higher in all employments.

The same kind of changes in relative factor scarcities and prices occur in other countries. In country *B,* labor-scarce and capital-abundant, wage rates tend to fall and the rental price of capital to rise as resources are shifted from the labor-intensive X industry to the capital-intensive Y industry.

These changes in relative factor prices serve, of course, to reduce the initial disparity in the international prices of factors. Before trade, wage rates were low in country A and high in country B, with the reverse relationship in the rental price of capital. As the result of trade, wage rates rise in A and fall in B, while the rental price of capital falls in A and rises in B.

Given the assumptions of the Heckscher-Ohlin model, the tendency toward factor price equalization is inevitable. By adopting certain additional assumptions, it can be shown that not only are factor price differences reduced by trade, they are *eliminated,* leaving each factor with the *same* price in all trading countries. The conditions necessary for this extreme result to follow, however, are highly restrictive and never encountered in reality[3]

Even the much weaker proposition that factor price differences are merely reduced without being completely eliminated depends upon the validity of the assumptions underlying the Heckscher-Ohlin theory of trade. We observed earlier several assumptions of the theory concerning which doubt has been raised. One of these assumptions was shown to be especially critical for the theory of trade— namely, the assumption that each commodity is produced with the relatively intensive use of a particular factor resource, and that this factor intensity remains intact at all factor price ratios. So-called "factor reversal," in which a good switches intensity in one factor to another, removes the basis for predicting the pattern of trade according to relative factor supplies. More than this, *factor reversal also destroys confidence in the effects of trade on factor prices.* Instead of being able confidently to predict that trade will narrow factor price differences, with factor reversal present we can only say that, though probably factor prices will be affected by trade, *the effect may be either to widen or reduce differences.*

Regardless of the specific effects of trade on factor prices, depending upon such things as the absence or presence of factor reversal, one general observation seems fairly secure: *trade affects the distribution of income within each trading country.* If a tendency in the direction of factor price equalization holds, in each country the relative and absolute income share of the abundant factor is increased. If,

---

[3] For a description of the conditions referred to, see J. E. Meade, *Trade and Welfare* (London: Oxford University Press, 1955) , chaps. xix–xxiii.

on the other hand, there is factor reversal, the share of the scarce factor may either increase or decrease relatively to that of the abundant factor. But, in any event, some factor owners are very probably adversely affected by trade, while others are benefited. This has important implications for trade policy, as we shall see.

THE GAINS FROM TRADE

The culminating question we must examine are the *welfare effects* of international trade. The ultimate purpose of descriptive, or "positive," economic theory is to furnish the basis for arriving at rational and intelligent judgments on policy issues. This leads into the area of *prescriptive,* or "welfare," economics in which value judgments cannot be avoided. It will be our intent, however, to keep the welfare evaluation of trade as free of value judgments as possible.

The Gain from Specialization

International trade is the result of extending on a wider scale the specialization in production characteristic of all modern, developed economies. Just as specialization within a country increases efficiency and real income, so for the same reasons does specialization on an international scale increase the efficiency and output of the world economy.

World Output and Welfare. The opportunity for the world to reap the benefits of specialization is present whenever the marginal rate at which any pair of goods can be transformed into each other is not the same in different countries. The marginal rate of transformation between goods is indicated by their marginal opportunity costs. Say the marginal opportunity cost of good Y is $2X$. This tells us that an extra unit of Y can be produced with the resources used to produce two units of X, or that an extra unit of X can be produced with the resources used to produce one-half unit of Y. It is in this sense that one good can be "transformed" into another at a rate given by their marginal opportunity costs. We have seen that differences in marginal opportunity costs lead to specialization and trade. Let us now observe how this results in an increase in *total world productivity*.

Suppose that the marginal opportunity cost of Y is $10X$ in country A and $2X$ in country B. Let country A reduce its output of Y by one unit and country B increase its output of Y by one unit. The combined output of Y by the two countries thus remains constant. What happens to the combined output of good X? Country A is able to increase its production of X by ten units. Country B is forced to reduce the production of X by two units. Hence, the combined output of X increases by a net amount of eight units. The "world" $(A + B)$ has available for its use the same amount of Y as before but eight units more of X. It is also possible for the world to have more of Y and the same amount of X, or more of *both* goods. For instance, if A reduces its production of Y by one unit and B increases its output by two units, the combined production of Y increases by one unit and of X by six units (plus ten in A, minus four in B) .

It is to be noted that world production is expanded in the above example without any change in the quantity or quality of productive resources. The source of gain in output is the greater *efficiency* in the use of given resources.

Observe further that the opportunity to increase world output through reallocating resources continues to exist as long as marginal rates of transformation or marginal opportunity costs of any pair of commodities are not the same in different countries. The possibility of further gains is exhausted only when either the countries become completely specialized or marginal rates of transformation have become equalized.

The result of the world's resources being reallocated until marginal rates of transformation are equalized everywhere can be simply put in another way: *the world's production and consumption possibilities are maximized.* It is in this sense that the world's *welfare* is improved by free international trade. As our earlier analysis showed, free trade leads precisely to the reallocation of resources postulated above. Differences in marginal rates of transformation are equivalent to comparative cost differences and in trade equilibrium comparative costs, and, therefore, marginal rates of transformation are equalized. Hence, free trade yields to the world the opportunity of consuming more of all goods or of consuming more of some and no less of others. It would be difficult to find a less ambiguous criterion of welfare improvement.

National Output and Welfare. It is conceivable for the world's welfare to be advanced by trade while the welfare of a particular country is decreased. Since attitudes and policies are usually based on each country's conception of its own national interests, it is important to view the welfare effects of trade from the individual country's point of view.

Let us presume, as the theory of trade informs us, that each country specializes in the production of the good in which it has a comparative cost advantage and exchanges that good for another on terms of trade more favorable than the domestic marginal rate of transformation.

To fix ideas, assume that a country has a comparative advantage in Y whose marginal opportunity cost at home is $2X$, and that the opportunity to trade on terms of $1Y = 5X$ is opened up. This is equivalent to saying that the country can transform Y into X at a lower marginal opportunity cost through trade than in economic isolation. As a consequence, through specializing in Y and trading some of it for X the country's consumption frontier is pushed outward beyond its domestic production boundary. In pretrade isolation, the country's consumption possibilities were limited to its production possibilities; with trade, its consumption possibilities extend beyond its pretrade production possibilities.

To illustrate, suppose that before trade began, the country produced and consumed $100Y$ and $50X$. With trade, the output of Y is increased, say, to 101 units, at the opportunity cost of decreasing the production of X to 48 units. Now the extra unit of Y is traded for 5 units of X, leaving the country with 100 units of Y and 53 units of X for home consumption. Net result: the same consumption of Y as before trade plus three additional units of X. This is not, of course, the only possibility. More of *both* goods would be made available if, for example, *half* the extra unit of Y produced were exported for $2\frac{1}{2}$ units of X, leaving posttrade consumption at $100\frac{1}{2}$ Y plus $50\frac{1}{2}$ units of X.

The above plus all other consumption possibilities with trade as compared to the pretrade situation can be shown diagrammatically, as in Figure 4.1. BB' is the country's production transformation or possibilities curve. Point P is assumed to be the pretrade production and consumption point. The opportunity to trade is shown by the terms-of-trade line TT', the slope of which measures the terms of trade. The equilibrium output point with trade is P', where the transformation curve is tangent to the terms-of-trade line, and therefore the marginal opportunity cost ratio of the goods is equal to their international price ratio.[4] The movement of the output point from P to P' represents the extent to which the country specializes with trade in the production of good Y.

---

4 At the point of tangency the slopes of the transformation curve and of the terms-of-trade line are equal. The slope of the former measures the ratio of the marginal cost of X to the marginal cost of Y, while the slope of the latter measures the ratio of the price of X to the price of Y.

FIGURE 4.1

CONSUMPTION POSSIBILITIES WITH TRADE

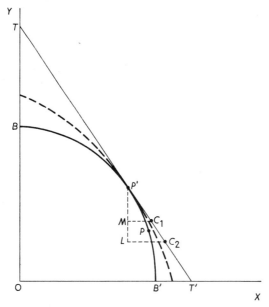

The terms-of-trade line TT' now represents the country's consumption possibilities. If MP' of Y is exported, MC_1 of X is received in exchange, so that point C_1 is reached in consumption. LC_2 of X can be obtained by exporting LP' of Y, bringing the country to point C_2 in its consumption. Any other point on TT' can be reached in a similar manner.

That the country benefits from trade in the same sense that the world as a whole was shown to gain is clearly demonstrated. If the country chooses the combination of X and Y represented by point C_1, more of *both* goods is available for consumption than was true in isolation at point P. (This is shown by the position of C_1 above and to right of P.) The country's welfare can therefore safely be said to have improved as the result of trade. The same conclusion holds even if the consumption of one of the goods with trade is less than in isolation, such as at point C_2. Since C_1, with more of both goods available, is an alternative option open to the country, C_2 must be presumed to yield at least as much total utility to the community as C_1.[5] Two additional comments on the above discussion remain to be made. The first is that the potentiality of gain from trade depends

---

[5] For the use of consumption indifference curves to show the gain from trade, see the appendix to this chapter.

upon the opportunity to trade on terms *different* from pretrade marginal opportunity costs. If, for example, with reference to Figure 4.1 the pretrade output point had been P' instead of P, the country would have been consuming the same quantities of X and Y before trade as after trade. In this case, there would be no point in trading—a conclusion in accord with our earlier analysis which showed that comparative cost differences are a necessary condition for trade to occur.

A second comment relates to the terms of trade. How far beyond its production possibilities curve a country can consume clearly depends upon the slope of the terms-of-trade line. In Figure 4.1 if the terms of trade were more favorable, the line TT' would be less steeply sloped, swinging the country's consumption possibilities frontier further outward on the X-axis. Any given amount of Y exports would thus exchange for a larger quantity of X imports. By the same token, of course, the gain realized by B's trading partners, whose terms of trade are less favorable, would be smaller.

The terms of trade are extremely important, therefore, in determining the division of the world's gains from trade among the participating countries. For this reason, after examining the so-called "exchange gain" from trade, we shall consider what determines the terms of trade.

The Gain from Exchange

The gain from trade discussed above arises out of two sources: the greater efficiency of resource use as the result of specialization and the greater utility enjoyed by consumers as the result of a different set of consumption opportunities. For convenience, we may call the latter the *gain from exchange.*

To isolate the exchange benefits from the specialization benefits, let us assume that for some reason resources are not reallocable, so that each country continues to produce the same "mix" of goods and services after trade as in isolation. The potential gain from specialization is therefore left unexploited. What, then, are the possible benefits from engaging in trade?

Suppose that in pretrade equilibrium the price of good X is $1 in country A and 100 lira in country B, while the price of good Y is $2 in A and 500 lira in B. The assumed situation is as shown in the accompanying table.

		Good X	Good Y
Country A	. . . .	$1	$2
Country B	. . . .	L.100	L.500

Since relative prices, and therefore comparative costs, differ, we know that there is a basis for mutually beneficial specialization and trade. But we are assuming that specialization in production does not occur. Nevertheless, the potentiality for exchange benefits from trade is present because of the differences in relative prices.

In equilibrium, consumers in each country purchase that combination of goods which yields the same marginal utility or satisfaction per dollar's expenditure for each good consumed. Were this not the case for any consumer, he could increase his total utility from a given expenditure by rearranging his purchases until the indicated relationship was established. In terms of our example, then, we see that for consumers in country A the marginal utility of Y is twice that of X (since the price of Y is twice that of X), while for consumers in country B the marginal utility of Y is five times that of X.

Consumers in both countries can obtain greater total utility from a given amount of expenditure by trading on terms of trade anywhere between $1Y = 5X$ and $1Y = 2X$. For instance, let the terms of trade be $1Y = 3X$. A consumer in A exchanges a unit of Y for three units of X with a consumer in B. But prior to the exchange the marginal utility of the unit of Y to the consumer in A is equivalent to the extra utility yielded by two units of X. Therefore, A's consumer is giving up (exporting) a good worth to him the equivalent of *two* units of X, and receiving in return (importing) *three* units of X. In effect, he is gaining a "bonus" of one unit of X by trading.

Looking now at B's consumer, three units of X are given up in return for one unit of Y. But the extra unit of Y has a marginal utility for him equivalent to that of *five* units of X. So he, too, gains a bonus, in his case amounting to two units of X.

Both sets of consumers continue to gain from further exchanges until, as the result of diminishing marginal utility, the ratio of the marginal utilities of X and Y is the same for consumers in both countries. This automatically becomes the situation when the equilibrium relative prices of X and Y are the same in both countries—a condition brought about by free trade.

It will be observed that the exchange gains from trade result from the reallocation of consumption expenditures, whereas the specialization gains from trade flow from the reallocation of productive resources. Even though these are separate and distinct sources of benefits, they are clearly parallel phenomena, each springing from the wider set of feasible alternatives afforded by trade. Maximum benefits are realized if *both* sources of gain are exploited, though either alone justifies trade.

THE TERMS OF TRADE

As indicated above, how the gains from trade are divided among participating countries depends upon the terms of trade.

By the "terms of trade" is meant the ratio at which goods are exchanged. When there are only two goods being traded, as in the model we have been using, the terms of trade are given simply by the ratio of the international prices of the goods. If, for example, with trade at an equilibrium rate of exchange the international price of X is \$1 and of Y \$2, the terms of trade are $1X = \frac{1}{2}Y$, or $1Y = 2X$. In reality, of course, numerous goods enter into international trade, and the terms of trade then must refer to the international price ratios of a country's "bundle" of exports and its "bundle" of imports.[6]

The terms of trade are clearly important to a country, for they determine what quantity of imported goods any given quantity of exports will exchange for. Especially the less economically developed countries of the world are sensitive to their terms of trade. Many of these countries depend upon imports to help feed their people and to provide essential raw materials and manufactured goods. If their terms of trade deteriorate—that is, become less favorable because import prices on the average rise relatively to export prices—their ability to pay for imports with exports is decreased, thereby posing a threat to an already low standard of living.

If one country's terms of trade improve (import prices fall relatively to export prices), clearly one or more of its trading partners' terms of trade must deteriorate. As a consequence, the *division of the gain* from trade among trading countries depends upon the terms of trade, as we shall see later. Further, the possibility is thus raised that each country may attempt to obtain a larger share of the gain from trade through various devices to improve its terms of trade. This

---

6 The terms of trade are usually measured as the ratio of the weighted index of import and export prices. This yields, not the absolute terms of trade (which do not have too much meaning with many commodities involved), but *changes* in the terms as compared to some base period.

prospect of economic warfare will be examined in our later discussion of tariffs and quotas in Chapter 9.

Let us now turn to the question of what determines the terms of trade in a competitive market setting.

Limits of the Terms of Trade

First of all, *the possible range within which the terms of trade can fall is limited by the pretrade marginal opportunity cost ratios* in the trading countries. To understand why this is so, let us revert to an earlier example of trade between Argentina and the United States in cloth and beef. The same pretrade cost situation in the two countries as assumed in the earlier discussion will be retained for the present purpose, summarized as follows:

	United States	Argentina
Cloth	$4	200 pesos
Beef	$1	20 pesos

The pretrade cost ratios of cloth to beef are 4:1 in the United States and 10:1 in Argentina. The terms of trade must then fall somewhere between 1 cloth = 4 beef and 1 cloth = 10 beef, for a very simple reason: *On any terms outside this range, one of the countries would not be willing to trade* [7] For example, on terms of 1 cloth = 3 beef, the United States is unwilling to export cloth for beef, since 4 beef can be obtained at home at the marginal opportunity cost of 1 cloth. On the other hand, the United States *would* be willing to export beef for cloth, but Argentina would refuse to trade, since 3 beef can be obtained domestically at a cost of less than 1 cloth. The reader can satisfy himself that similar situations in reverse apply if the terms of trade are anywhere above 10 beef for 1 cloth.

The Equilibrium Terms of Trade

Within the limits set by pretrade domestic cost ratios, *the terms of trade tend to settle at an equilibrium level at which the total value of each country's imports equals the total value of its exports.* (The

---

[7] To state the point in a different, though equivalent, manner, no equilibrium rate of exchange can be found outside the range of 2 cents to 5 cents per peso. At an exchange rate of 2 cents per peso, cloth exchanges for beef on terms of 1:10, and at an exchange of 5 cents per peso, the terms are 1:4.

equality of imports and exports is an equilibrium requirement only when nontrade transactions—such as loans, gifts, and other capital transfers—are excluded from the model, as in the present discussion.) Should exports not equal imports on given terms of trade, a change in the terms would occur until equality is established. The change in the terms of trade would be brought about through a movement in exchange rates, or in commodity prices, or both.

To illustrate with our United States–Argentina example, suppose that equilibrium is initially reached with the rate of exchange at 2½ cents per peso, the cost and price of cloth at $4, and of beef at 20 pesos. The terms of trade are therefore 1 cloth = 8 beef. (The 20-peso price of beef is equivalent at the assumed rate of exchange to $0.50, so that the ratio of the price of cloth to the price of beef is 1:8.)

Now suppose that U.S. demand for Argentina beef rises, the Argentina demand for U.S. cloth remaining constant. The immediate result is an increase in the rate of exchange on the peso in response to the increased U.S. demand for pesos to purchase more beef. As the rate of exchange on pesos moves upward, the *dollar* price of beef rises, and the *peso* price of cloth falls. For example, at an exchange rate of 3 cents per peso, the dollar equivalent of 20 pesos is $0.60, and the peso equivalent of $4 is 133⅓ pesos, whereas at the previous exchange rate, the prices were respectively $0.50 and 160 pesos. The higher dollar price of Argentina beef reduces the quantity the United States wishes to import, while the lower peso price of U.S. cloth increases the quantity Argentina wishes to import. At some rate of exchange, then, equality between the values of imports and exports is restored, and equilibrium is reestablished. If the new equilibrium rate of exchange is 3 cents per peso, the terms of trade will be 1 cloth = 6⅔ beef, assuming that the prices of cloth and beef remain $4 and 20 pesos, respectively. The increase in the U.S. demand for the import good has therefore resulted in a deterioration in her terms of trade and an improvement in Argentina's terms of trade.

The same kind of result would follow if the assumption that the prices of cloth and beef in the exporting countries remain constant were dropped. Under increasing cost conditions, the Argentine price of beef would rise in response to the greater demand for beef imports by the United States. The cost of beef to the United States thus increases, and her terms of trade move adversely not only because of a rise in the rate of exchange on the peso but also because of the higher peso price of beef. However, to the extent that the peso price of beef goes up, the rise in the equilibrium rate of exchange is moderated, since each performs the same function of reducing the quantity of beef demanded by the United States.

In summary, the terms of trade are determined by the forces of international demand, in conjunction with internal cost conditions in each country and the equilibrium requirement that, in the absence of all economic relations other than commodity trade, the total value of each country's imports equal the total value of its exports.

Reciprocal Demand[8]

The foregoing discussion points to the conclusion that it is the demand of each country for the other's export product that mainly determines the terms of trade. *Import* demand, however, is a function not only of demand for the import good but also of domestic supply of that good. For instance, if the quantity of beef demanded in the United States at a price of $0.60 per pound is 100 million pounds per day, the import demand for beef depends upon the quantity *domestically* supplied at that price. If none is produced domestically—because of complete specialization under constant cost conditions—the entire domestic demand becomes import demand. But if, say, 40 million pounds of beef are domestically produced at $0.60 per pound, the import demand will be 60 million pounds.

A technique for explaining the terms of trade which embodies all the relevant variables—demand, supply, and equilibrium requirements—is provided by *reciprocal demand* analysis.

The reciprocal demand of a pair of countries for each other's export products can be shown through the construction of international *offer curves* for each of the countries.

A country's offer curve represents the quantity of export goods which it is willing to exchange for a specified quantity of import goods on each of various terms of trade. The characteristics of typical offer curves are revealed in Figure 4.2.

OMNA is the offer curve of country *A*, *OPB* of country *B*. *A*'s export good is *X*, measured on the horizontal axis, its import good is *Y*, measured on the vertical axis, while *B*'s export good is *Y* and its import good is *X*. Each point on an offer curve represents the quantities of export and import goods which the country is willing to

---

8 This section can be skipped without loss of continuity.

FIGURE 4.2

RECIPROCAL DEMAND AND THE TERMS OF TRADE

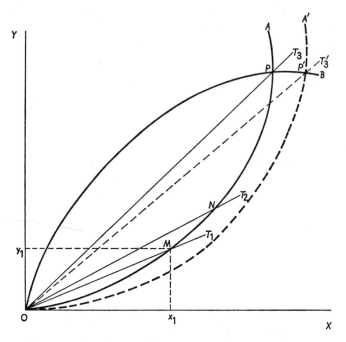

exchange. Thus, point M on A's offer curve indicates that country A is willing to exchange Ox_1 of X for Oy_1 of Y. How much of its export good a country is willing to trade for any given amount of imports is a function of the terms of trade. At point M on A's curve, the terms of trade are measured by the slope of the ray OT_1, equal to Oy_1/Ox_1. On more favorable terms of trade (from A's point of view), shown by a steeper terms-of-trade line such as OT_2, A is willing to offer a larger quantity of its export good in return for a larger quantity of imports (point N). However, as the volume of exports A gives up and imports she receives increases, her terms of trade must become increasingly more favorable to induce her to continue this process. This is why A's offer curve bends upward (and B's curve bends downward).

The reasons for the decreasing willingness to trade without a price inducement as the volume grows are twofold: the relative marginal utility of the import good compared to the export good declines as the domestic availability of the first increases and of the second decreases; and the marginal opportunity cost of the export good increases as its output is expanded, assuming increasing cost conditions.

At some point, these forces may become strong enough to make A unwilling to offer any greater amount of her export good regardless of the terms of trade, though, of course, the quantity of imports desired continues to increase as their price (the terms of trade) becomes more favorable. Such a point is indicated when A's offer curve becomes vertical. If her curve beyond that point turns backward to the left, this indicates that she is willing to offer only an increasingly *smaller* quantity of exports for greater quantities of imports.

Precisely the same considerations apply to country B, explaining the tendency for her offer curve to bend rightward, and perhaps eventually downward.

Equilibrium requires that the amount of X which country A offers in exchange for a given quantity of Y be equal to the quantity of X which country B is willing to accept in exchange for the given quantity of Y. This condition is fulfilled only when the offer curves of the two countries intersect. In Figure 4.2 the curves intersect at P, so that P is the equilibrium point, and OT_3, on which P is located, represents the equilibrium terms of trade.

It can now be shown how changes in reciprocal demand affect the terms of trade. Suppose that A's demand for Y increases, B's demand for X remaining constant. In graphical terms, A's offer curve moves to the right, becoming the broken line OA', indicating that A is willing to offer a larger quantity of X than before for any given quantity of Y (or is willing to accept a smaller quantity of Y for any given quantity of X). OA' intersects B's offer curve at point P', and the equilibrium terms of trade become OT'_3. The slope of OT'_3 is less than that of OT_3, showing that the terms of trade have become less favorable for A, and more favorable for B, as the result of A's increased demand for imports.

Some Welfare Questions

That trade provides the opportunity for the world and for each trading country to obtain a greater quantity of goods and/or to obtain greater total utility from the consumption of given quantities of goods has been demonstrated. However, we have *not* concluded that *every individual's welfare* is improved by trade. Indeed, the probability is very strong that some individuals will in fact be *harmed* by trade unless deliberate steps are taken to avoid it.

One group of individuals adversely affected by trade are those whose tastes happen to favor heavily the goods which his country exports. The usual effect of trade is to *increase* the domestic prices of export goods and to *decrease* the domestic prices of import goods. This follows from the pretrade international differences in relative prices which are eliminated as the result of trade. Unless, therefore, the income of the individual with a strong preference for the export good is increased, he may be worse off with trade than without it. Note, however, that the probability of this kind of ill effect diminishes as the number of goods entering into trade increases, for the chances of having the adverse effects of higher prices on preferred exports goods being offset by the beneficial effects of lower prices on preferred import goods are then greater.

A second kind of adverse welfare effect is suffered by those whose *incomes* are reduced by trade. As observed earlier, trade is nearly certain to cause a redistribution of the national income of each trading country. If the Heckscher-Ohlin theorem holds, it is specifically the owners of the relatively scarce factor whose income is reduced by trade. But in any event, a depressive effect of trade can be expected for certain factor owners.

If some people are hurt, even though others reap benefits, how can it be concluded that the *general welfare* is advanced by trade? There is no objective method of making interpersonal utility comparisons. But modern welfare economics has come up with a resolution of the dilemma thus posed.

The principle appealed to is as follows: the general welfare is improved if those who benefit from trade could compensate those who lose from trade, while leaving the first group with a net gain and the second group in at least a no worse position than before trade. On the basis of this criterion, trade can be said unambiguously to promote the general welfare. Trade increases the real national income of each participating country. Clearly, therefore, everyone *could* have a larger real income, or some people could have a larger income without others having a smaller income. Whether, in fact, the national gain from trade is so distributed as to produce either of these results depends upon whether the machinery possessed by the state for redistributing income (monetary and fiscal measures) is employed to that end.

As a matter of practical policy, there is very little chance that redistributive measures would, or could, assure that in fact no one is harmed by trade. From a strict purist point of view, therefore, we could only say that trade offers *potential* gain to a society. But it is worthwhile to point out that the same thing is true of nearly *all* economic events and actions which we are pleased to regard as contributing to progress, for hardly any economic change occurs without in some respects adversely affecting particular individuals. Economic advancement would indeed be difficult to achieve if every step had to be accompanied by some deliberate redistribution of benefits to compensate those individuals harmed.

RECOMMENDED READINGS

BALDWIN, ROBERT E. "The New Welfare Economics and Gains in International Trade," *Quarterly Journal of Economics,* vol. 66, no. 1 (February 1952). Reprinted in American Economic Association, *Readings in International Economics,* chap. 12. Homewood, Ill.: Richard D. Irwin, Inc., 1968.

HECKSCHER, ELI. "The Effects of Foreign Trade on the Distribution of Income." Reprinted in American Economic Association, *Readings in the Theory of International Trade,* chap. 13. Philadelphia: Blakiston, 1949.

JOHNSON, HARRY. "Comparative Costs and Commercial Policy," *Money, Trade, and Economic Growth,* pp. 28–40. Cambridge, Mass.: Harvard University Press, 1962. An excellent brief summary of the modern theory of the causes and effects of international trade, including the phenomenon of factor reversal.

MEADE, J. E. *Theory of International Economic Policy.* Vol. 2, *Trade and Welfare.* Oxford: Oxford University Press, 1955.

SAMUELSON, PAUL A. "The Gains from International Trade," in American Economic Association, *Readings in the Theory of International Trade,* chap. xi.

———. "International Trade and the Equalization of Factor Prices," *Economic Journal,* June 1948.

STOLPER, W. F. and SAMUELSON, PAUL A. "Protection and Real Wages," *Review of Economic Studies,* November 1941, pp. 58–73.

STUDY QUESTIONS

1. Why does trade eliminate international cost and price differences?
2. What kinds of influences on trade do transportation costs have?
3. Explain the effects of trade on the relative abundance and scarcity of factors of production. What implications does this have for factor prices?
4. How does factor reversal affect the tendency toward factor price equalization as the result of trade?

5. Why does trade nearly inevitably adversely affect some individuals?
6. Distinguish between the nature and sources of the specialization and the exchange gains from trade.
7. In what sense can it be said that the world's welfare is advanced by international trade?
8. What limits the consumption possibilities of an economy in isolation? How are these limits enlarged through trade?
9. How does trade make possible an increase in the total world output of goods with the same quantity of inputs employed?
10. What influences do the terms of trade have on a country's share of the gain from trade?
11. What particular individuals or groups are likely to be worse off with trade than without?
12. Describe the welfare principle that underlies the conclusion that society benefits from trade even though some individuals are harmed by trade.
13. Define the terms of trade. Why are they important?
14. Why do pretrade cost ratios set limits to the terms of trade?
15. What is meant by the "equilibrium" terms of trade?
16. What is the effect on a country's terms of trade if its demand for imports increases? If the foreign demand for its export goods increases?
17. Define the international offer curve and explain its construction.
18. What accounts for the usual curvilinear shape of offer curves?
19. In terms of reciprocal demand analysis, what determines the equilibrium terms of trade?

APPENDIX: A DIAGRAMMATIC ANALYSIS OF INTERNATIONAL TRADE

The theory of international trade can be very succinctly presented with the use of diagrammatic techniques. In the text a limited number of diagrams is employed to illustrate some of the basic relationships in trade theory. In this appendix, it is proposed to extend the diagrammatic method for the benefit of those students who find such an approach helpful in understanding complex relationships

In Chapter 3 it was shown that comparative cost differences, which underlie international trade, are determined by production functions, resource supplies, and demand conditions. The first two of these elements together are responsible for the shapes of production transformation curves, while demand determines the equilibrium location on the curves. Our first task is to show diagrammatically

how production functions and resource supplies generate transformation curves. Throughout it will be assumed that X and Y are the
two commodities each of two countries, A and B, produce; that labor
(L) and capital (K) are the only factors of production and that they
are substitutable for each other, though at diminishing marginal
rates; that X is labor-intensive and Y capital-intensive at all factor
price ratios; that there are constant returns to scale in both industries; and that A is a labor-abundant and B a capital-abundant
country.

Production Functions, Resource Supplies, and the
Production Transformation Curve

The production function for a good can be represnted, under our
assumptions, by an isoquant. An isoquant shows the alternative
combinations of labor and capital which are physically capable,
employed in the technically most efficient manner, of producing a
given quantity of output.

In Figure 4.3, $q_x q_x$ represents the isoquant for good X, $q_y q_y$ the
isoquant for good Y. Each isoquant is convex to the origin, reflecting
the presence of a diminishing marginal rate of technical substitution
(MRTS) between labor and capital. This means that as more of
either input is substituted for the other, increasing amounts of the
substituted input are necessary to keep output constant as successive
units of the other input are withdrawn. The MRTS at any point on
an isoquant is measured by the slope of the isoquant at that point.
Hence, the diminishing MRTS of labor for capital is reflected in the
diminishing slope of the isoquant as movement down the curve
occurs, signifying an increase in the ratio of labor to capital.

It will be noticed that the isoquant for X is drawn so that it
intersects that for Y, lying above Y's isoquant to the left of the intersection point and below to the right of the intersection point. The
significance of this is its indication that X is always relatively labor-
intensive and Y relatively capital-intensive. The least-cost (economically most efficient) proportion of labor to capital to employ is
attained when the MRTS of labor for capital is equal to the ratio of
the price of labor to the price of capital. The latter ratio is represented by the slope of a straight line connecting the two axes. One
possible ratio of the price of labor to the price of capital is given by
the slope of the line $W_k W_L$ in Figure 4.3. At this factor price ratio,
the least-cost combination is shown by the point of tangency between

FIGURE 4.3

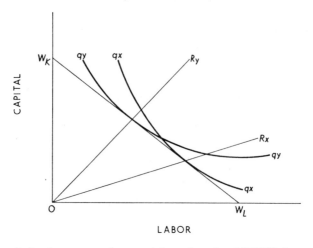

PRODUCTION ISOQUANTS AND FACTOR PROPORTIONS

$W_k W_L$ and the isoquant, for at this point the MRTS between labor and capital (equal to the slope of the isoquant) is equal to the ratio of the price of labor to the price of capital. It will be observed that the least-cost combination for good X requires a larger proportion of labor to capital than for good Y. This is indicated by the steeper slope of the ray OR_y than of ray OR_x, each of which shows by its slope the proportion of capital to labor employed at the given factor price ratio. The student is invited to demonstrate for himself that at any other assumed factor price ratio, X will be produced with a greater proportion of labor to capital than employed in producing Y.

The next step is to construct a so-called "box diagram." Before undertaking this, it is first necessary to explain that for each good there exists a "map" of isoquants, consisting of as many isoquants one wishes to draw. Each isoquant represents a given level of output, so that different isoquants for the same good represent different levels of output. (Under our assumptions, however, all isoquants for a given good have the same shape.) Second, in equilibrium, although the factor proportions employed differ for X and Y, the MRTS of labor and capital is the *same* for the two goods. The reason for this is that in each case the least-cost combination requires equality between the MRTS and the price ratio of labor and capital, so that at any given factor price ratio the MRTS must be the same for the two goods.

We proceed to draw a box diagram, as in Figure 4.4. The dimensions of the box show the factor endowments of the country. The

FIGURE 4.4

THE EFFICIENCY LOCUS

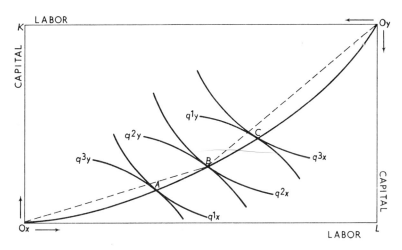

width of the box $(O_xL$ or $O_yK)$ measures the country's labor endowment, the height $(O_xK$ or $O_yL)$ its stock of capital. Factor supplies may be measured either from the lower left-hand origin O_x or from the upper right-hand origin O_y. If the O_x origin is used, labor is measured from left to right, capital from bottom to top. If the O_y origin is used, labor is measured from right to left, capital from top to bottom. Two different origins are designated because the factors are allocated between the X and Y industries. Hence, that part of the labor force used in the X industry (measured from O_x) must be subtracted from the total labor force to give the amount of labor employed in the Y industry (measured from O_y), and the same for capital.

The isoquant maps for X and Y may now be inserted into the box, but to avoid clutter only three pairs are shown. The X-isoquants are drawn from the O_x origin and therefore have the usual shape. But since O_y is the origin for the Y industry, its isoquants are flipped over from their normal position. The location of isoquants in the box indicates the level of output. The farther an X-isoquant is from the O_x origin in the northeast direction, the greater is the output of X; the farther a Y-isoquant is from the O_y origin in a southwest direction, the greater is the output of Y. The level of each good's output is indicated by the superscript of the isoquant. Because of limited resources, assumed to be fixed in amount, the greater the output of either good, the smaller is necessarily the output of the other good. Thus, when the output of X is $q^1{}_x$, the output of Y is $q^3{}_y$, while if X output is $q^3{}_x$, the output of Y is $q^1{}_y$.

The equilibrium requirement that the MRTS of labor and capital be the same in both industries is satisfied only at the points where X- and Y-isoquants are tangent (since MRTS is measured by the slope of an isoquant and at the point of tangency the slopes of the two isoquants are the same). In Figure 4.4 the three pairs of isoquants shown are tangent at points A, B, and C. All the other points of tangency between the isoquants not drawn are assumed to lie on the line O_xABCO_y, which is known as the *efficiency locus*. Hence, whatever the allocation of resources between the X and Y industries, it will be somewhere on the efficiency locus.

It will be observed that the efficiency locus has been drawn to bend below a straight-line diagonal connecting O_x and O_y. This particular shape of the curve is a reflection of our assumption that X is a labor-intensive good and Y a capital-intensive good. The indication that this is the case is given by the different slopes of the rays from the two origins to any point of the efficiency locus. For example, at point B on the locus, the ray O_xB has a less steep slope

FIGURE 4.5

Transformation Curve Derived from the Efficiency Locus

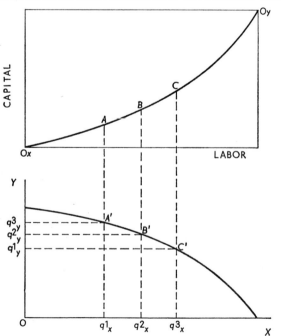

than the ray O_yB. In each case, the slope of the ray measures the ratio of capital to labor. At every point on the efficiency locus (except at the terminals O_x and O_y), the slope of the ray from O_x is less than that from O_y.

Since the efficiency locus shows the various possible maximum output combinations of X and Y, it provides the information required to construct a production transformation curve. The generation of a transformation curve from an efficiency locus is illustrated in Figure 4.5. It will be observed that the downward-bowed efficiency locus has its counterpart in the concave shape of the transformation curve. In economic terms, the different factor intensities of X and Y—reflected in the shape of the efficiency locus—cause increasing marginal opportunity costs, reflected in the concave shape of the transformation curve, as explained in the text.

Demand and Pretrade Equilibrium Output

Now that the transformation curve has been established, we may proceed to determine the equilibrium output point in pretrade isolation. Given the conditions of production summarized in the production transformation curve, output is determined by demand. The conditions on the demand side are shown by a *consumption indifference map.*

With a given distribution of income, a community consumption indifference curve shows the various combinations of goods among which the community is indifferent, in the sense that consumers as a group have no preference for one combination as over against another. Suppose, for example, that the total satisfactions or utility enjoyed by the community from the consumption of 100 units of X and 200 units of Y is designated U_1. It may be presumed that there are numerous combinations of X and Y that would also yield utility U_1. A few other such combinations might be $110X + 180Y, 120X + 155Y, 130X + 120Y$. These and all other combinations giving the same level of utility would lie on the community indifference curve which represents total utility U_1.

Each consumption indifference curve can be expected to have a convex shape, as illustrated in Figure 4.6. The convexity of the curve is a reflection of the phenomenon of diminishing marginal utility, or, in the terminology we shall use, *diminishing marginal rate of substitution in consumption.* The principle involved is that the greater

FIGURE 4.6

A CONSUMPTION INDIFFERENCE MAP

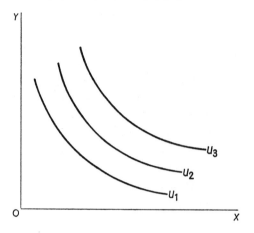

the consumption of one good compared to another, the less is the marginal utility of the first good compared to that of the second good. Hence, the marginal rate of substitution in consumption of X for Y, with total utility remaining constant, diminishes as X is substituted for Y. In a like manner, the marginal rate of substitution of Y for X diminishes as Y is substituted for X. In order, therefore, for total utility to remain constant, increasing amounts of X must be obtained to compensate for successive one unit losses of Y, and vice versa. The convexity of the indifference curve is the geometric expression of this.

If more of *both* X and Y are consumed, the total utility of the community is greater. Indifference curve U_2 in Figure 4.6 thus represents a higher level of community satisfaction than curve U_1, and so on for successively higher curves.[9] The assumption is that the *community seeks to get to the highest level indifference curve possible.*

A community's consumption possibilities, however, are limited. In isolation, consumption is limited to production. In diagrammatic terms, a community in isolation cannot reach an indifference curve that lies beyond its production transformation curve. The highest

---

[9] There are difficulties involved in constructing a map of community indifference curves which we are ignoring. The chief problem is that changes in income distribution —which normally occur as a result of engaging in trade—lead to different community indifference curves, so that there is no uniquely determined set. It is possible to circumvent this difficulty through various assumptions, but for the purpose at hand we may accept the indifference map as given.

attainable consumption indifference curve, therefore, is the one tangent to the production transformation curve. In Figure 4.7, U_3 is the highest attainable indifference curve.

To reach U_3, it is clear that production must be on the transformation curve AA' at the point of tangency, P, with the indifference curve. At this point of tangency, the two curves have the same slope, so that the marginal rate of technical substitution is equal to the marginal rate of substitution in consumption—the condition for an optimum allocation of resources.

In equilibrium, both the marginal rate of technical substitution and the marginal rate of substitution in consumption are equal to the ratio of the price of good X to the price of good Y. This is shown in Figure 4.7 by the price line RR, the slope of which measures the ratio of the price of X to the price of Y. We have thus determined the equilibrium ratio of commodity prices in isolation in country A.

Precisely the same procedures are followed in arriving at the ratio of commodity prices in country B. The only requirement for a trade potential to exist is that the ratio of prices be *different* in different countries. In what follows, we shall assume that the pretrade ratio of prices in country B differs from that in A, specifically, that the relative price of X is lower in A than in B. A's comparative advantage in X may be thought of as the result of her being a labor-abundant country, with X a labor-intensive good, creating a cost bias in favor of X that is not offset by demand.

FIGURE 4.7

Equilibrium Output and Consumption in Pretrade Isolation

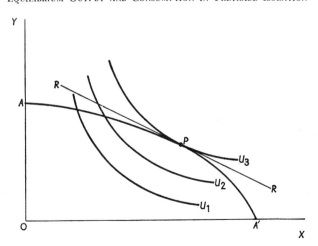

Production, Consumption, and Trade

Reciprocal demand determines the terms of trade between X and Y. The terms must fall somewhere within the range set by pretrade cost ratios in A and B, but in any event the relative price of Y will be lower with trade in country A than in isolation. This is shown in Figure 4.8 by the terms-of-trade line TT, the slope of which is greater than A's pretrade price line RR.

As a result of being able to trade on the terms given by TT, country A expands the output of X until the ratio of the marginal cost of X to the marginal cost of Y equals the international price ratio of X and Y, given by the slope of the terms-of-trade line. A's equilibrium output point with trade is therefore at Q, where the terms-of-trade line is tangent to the production transformation curve. However, A will wish to consume X and Y at point C, where the terms-of-trade is tangent to consumption indifference curve U_4. A is enabled to consume at point C by exporting VQ of X in exchange for VC of Y. The result of specialization and trade is to move A off its highest consumption indifference curve without trade (U_3) to a higher curve (U_4).

The same analysis, with the same general effects is applicable to country B. In Figure 4.9, B's equilibrium output in pretrade isolation is at P', where the highest consumption indifference curve U is

FIGURE 4.8

INCREASED CONSUMPTION POSSIBILITIES WITH TRADE: COUNTRY A

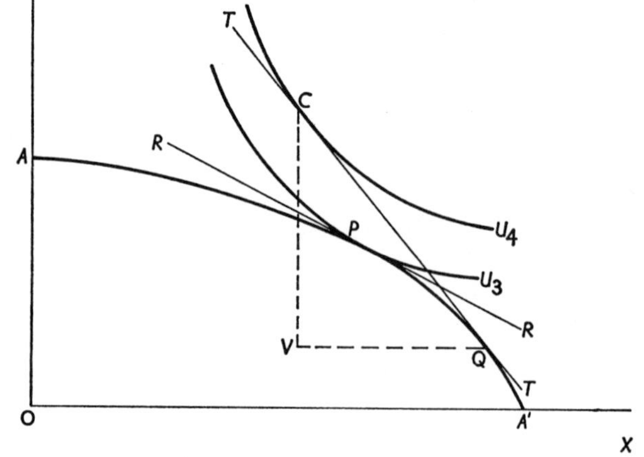

FIGURE 4.9

<small>INCREASED CONSUMPTION POSSIBILITIES WITH TRADE: COUNTRY *B*</small>

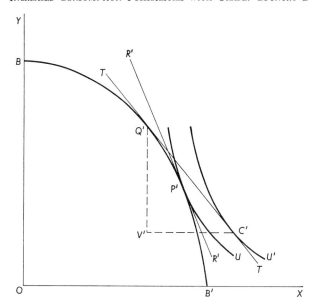

tangent to the production transformation curve BB'. The equilibrium pretrade ratio of the price of X to the price of Y is given by the
slope of the line $R'R'$. $R'R'$ has a steeper slope than RR in the
preceding figure, indicating that the relative pretrade price of X is
higher in B than in A.

Now the possibility of trade opens up, on terms given by TT,
which is of precisely the same slope as for country A. The production
point in B is moved to point Q', where the terms-of-trade line is
tangent to the transformation curve. Consumption, however, is at C',
where the terms-of-trade line is tangent to B's highest consumption
indifference curve U'. This consumption point is reached by B's exporting $Q'V'$ of Y in exchange for $V'C'$ of X.

It will be observed that for TT to be the equilibrium terms of
trade, the quantity of A's export of good X must be equal to the
quantity of X that B wishes to import, and similarly for B's export of
Y and A's import demand for Y. In terms of Figures 4.8 and 4.9, CV
must equal $Q'V'$ and VQ must equal $V'C'$.

The net result of trade, then, is a reallocation of resources in each
country toward the product in which it has a comparative advantage,
and the movement of each country onto a higher consumption indifference curve, indicating a higher level of welfare.

5

The theory of trade in imperfectly competitive markets

Up to this point, we have considered the theory of trade in the context of a competitive market price system. It was noted early in the discussion that in fact trade occurs under a variety of conditions, not all of which by any means permit the application of a competitive market model and the associated Heckscher-Ohlin theorem. The intent of this chapter is to investigate theories of trade relevant to real-world conditions different from those postulated in the previous model.

The first, and major, part of the discussion will be devoted to trade among market economies in which markets are imperfectly competitive. A relatively brief consideration of the trade of centrally controlled, nonmarket economies will conclude the chapter.

TYPES OF MARKET IMPERFECTIONS

As earlier observed, no actual market is *purely* competitive as idealized in theoretical models. However, the extent to which actual markets deviate from the competitive model varies enormously, ranging from close approximation to hardly any recognizable similarity. Pure competition requires, among other things, that, first, a good be produced by so many individual firms that no one firm has a perceptible influence on market supply and price, and, second, that the output of each firm in an industry be undifferentiated from that of other firms in the industry. *Imperfect competition* may arise either because of the fewness of firms in an industry, allowing individual firms to exert an appreciable influence on price, or because the outputs of different firms are differentiated, or because of a combination of both conditions. Accordingly, imperfect competition is classified into the following categories, in ascending order of deviation from pure competition:

a. Monopolistic competition: many firms, with differentiated products

b. Oligopoly: a few firms, with either standardized products (homogeneous oligopoly) or differentiated products (differentiated oligopoly)

c. Pure monopoly: a single firm in the industry

If oligopolistic firms agree to act in concert, they may become in effect a pure monopoly.

THE EFFECT OF IMPERFECT MARKETS ON COST-PRICE RELATIONSHIPS

In perfectly competitive markets, the long-run equilibrium price of a good equals its average and marginal cost of production. In imperfectly competitive markets, price tends always to exceed marginal costs (and usually to exceed average costs as well). This difference in the relationship between price and cost in the two types of market is familiar from principles of economics, but it may be useful briefly to recall the analysis.

Every firm, whether competitive or monopolistic, seeks to produce at the output level at which marginal revenue from the sale of output equals the marginal cost of production, for this is the condition for maximizing profits. The major difference in the situation of competitive and monopolistic firms lies on the revenue side of the equation. Although costs may also differ (one reason for which may be economies of scale, discussed below), let us provisionally assume they are identical for the competitive and the monopolistic firm.

A competitive firm can sell any amount of its product it wants at the prevailing market price, over which the individual firm has no control and no influence. (This is because there are so many firms in the industry, each producing the same standardized good, that no one firm can significantly affect market supply.) Consequently, the marginal revenue of the firm is the same as the price of the good and remains constant at all levels of sales.

In contrast, the marginal revenue of a monopolistic firm varies with the volume of sales, declining as the quantity offered for sale increases, and is always *less* than the market price. This is the consequence of the firm having to lower sales price in order to sell a greater quantity. When price is lowered, it must be lowered on *all* units sold (except under discriminating monopoly, discussed below) and not just the last. Therefore, the additional, or marginal, revenue derived from the sale of an extra unit of output is *less* than the sales price, a loss of revenue being incurred on the other units which would have commanded a higher price if fewer units had been offered for sale.

Hence, whereas under pure competition price, marginal revenue, and marginal costs are all brought into equality at the maximum-profit output level, under monopoly marginal costs and marginal revenue are equated at an output at which price is *above* marginal revenue and marginal costs. These results are shown graphically in Figure 5.1.

In Figure 5.1 (*a*) the competitive firm is confronted with an infinitely elastic demand curve, *D,* indicating that it can sell all it

FIGURE 5.1

OUTPUT AND PRICE OF COMPETITIVE FIRM AND MONOPOLISTIC FIRM

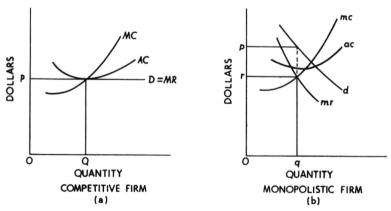

desires at the prevailing market price, P. The firm's demand curve is equivalent, therefore, to its marginal revenue (MR) and the sales price (P). Free entry also keeps average costs (AC) equal to the market price, and, since average costs and marginal costs are equal only at the lowest point on the average-cost curve, OQ represents the firm's most efficient output.

In Figure 5.1 (b) the demand curve for the monopolistic firm (d) falls from left to right, indicating that, in order to sell a larger quantity of its product, the firm must lower its price. Hence, the firm's marginal-revenue curve (mr) lies below the demand curve. The output oq maximizes the firm's profits (equalizes marginal costs and marginal revenue), and sells at price p, which is rp greater than the marginal revenue and marginal costs. Furthermore, since the marginal-revenue curve cuts the average-cost curve to the left of its lowest point, the firm is not using its plant and equipment at maximum efficiency. (And since there is not free entry into the industry, price can continue to exceed average costs, and excessive profits can be realized.)

DISTORTING AND RESTRICTIVE EFFECTS OF MONOPOLY ON TRADE

The difference in the price-marginal cost relationship in competitive and monopolistic markets is the basis for predicting that the type of prevailing market structure has important effects on international trade.

Perverse Specialization

First, it is to be noted that, whereas in perfectly competitive markets prices are accurate measures of marginal costs, in imperfect competition prices misrepresent marginal costs. But it is international *price* comparisons that are the immediate determinant of whether a product is imported or exported (or neither). It is possible in extreme cases for a country to have an apparent comparative cost disadvantage in a given product, as indicated by a relatively high domestic price, even though the true comparative cost—measured by marginal costs—is lower than abroad. If trade were conducted accordingly, there would be *perverse* specialization and a decrease in the efficiency of resource allocation.

Loss of Specialization Gains

In less extreme cases, perverse specialization is avoided, but the potential gains from trade are prevented from being fully realized. To see why, note first that the immediate effect of free trade is to create a single international price for each traded product. In perfect competition, the international equalization of prices carries with it the equalization of marginal costs. It is through the process of equalizing marginal costs that the *specialization gains* from trade are realized. Until marginal costs are internationally equalized, potential gains from trade are not fully exploited. Under imperfect competition, the equalization of prices as the result of trade does not, except fortuitously, bring about an equalization of marginal costs; hence, the potential benefits from trade are stopped from being pushed to their limits. For example, if the marginal costs of a given product are lower in country A than in country B, even though the price is the same, A continues to have a comparative cost advantage in the product which trade has not eliminated.

Loss of Exchange Gains

Just as imperfectly competitive markets tend to obstruct the complete realization of specialization gains from trade, so, too, they may lead to a loss of potential exchange gains. It will be recalled from the discussion in the preceding chapter that exchange gains are derived from exposing all consumers to identical prices. Free trade establishes identical prices internationally under competitive conditions. Some types of imperfectly competitive behavior prevent international price equalization and, thus, prevent the complete capture of possible exchange gains.

A clear case of interference with the enjoyment of exchange gains from trade is the practice of monopolistic price discrimination.

Theoretically, a monopolist could realize the greatest possible amount of profits from a given output by charging each individual buyer the highest price he was willing to pay rather than go without. Fortunately, this type of price discrimination cannot easily be practiced on a large scale within a national economy. In combination with tariffs, quotas, or other types of obstacles to reimportation, however, a monopolist may find it much easier to discriminate in price between the home market and foreign markets.

It will increase monopoly profits to pursue this policy if the elasticity of demand for the commodity is different in the home and foreign markets, for, at any given price, the more elastic the demand, the greater is marginal revenue—that is, the more total revenue will increase as a result of selling an additional unit of the commodity. Suppose, then, that the domestic demand is less elastic than the foreign demand. The monopolist will tend to produce that output at which marginal costs equal total marginal revenue, which is the sum of marginal revenue at home and abroad. But a higher price is charged domestic buyers than foreign buyers in order to equalize the marginal revenue in the two markets. This is shown graphically in Figure 5.2: let D_h be the home demand: D_f the foreign demand; MR_h and MR_f the corresponding marginal-revenue curves; and MC the marginal cost curve. MR_T is the total marginal-revenue curve, equal to MR_h and MR_f summed horizontally. Total output is OQ, at which marginal costs and total marginal revenue are equal, but the output is sold in the home and foreign markets in the proportions OH and OF, respectively; for, with this distribution of sales, the marginal revenue is the same in both markets. But OH supply on the home market commands a price P_h, which is higher than the price P_f commanded in the foreign market by OF supply.

The practice of charging a higher price at home than abroad, apart from transportation costs, is called "dumping" in the foreign market. While foreigners may gain from the lower price charged

FIGURE 5.2

INTERNATIONAL PRICE DISCRIMINATION

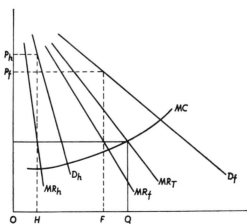

them, domestic consumers are exploited by the higher price which they must pay.

Trade Obstruction: Cartels

Except for the limited possible effect of monopoly in leading to perverse specialization, the other effects discussed above do not *eliminate* the benefits of trade, even though they reduce the benefits. In the final case of monopolistic practices now to be considered, international trade tends to be highly restricted, in some areas even prevented, and to this extent, of course, the potential social benefits of trade are not obtained. The practices having these adverse effects on trade are those associated with international *cartels*.

A cartel is an agreement among firms to follow a set of prescribed policies with respect to their operations. How extensive and detailed the agreement is varies with circumstances in the industry, but, typically, output, pricing, and marketing policies are covered. When a cartel is confined to a national economy, it is simply a form of oligopolistic collusion through which the firms in an industry attempt to achieve a purely monopolistic position. An international cartel, embracing firms located in different countries, is usually less able than a domestic cartel to act like a single firm. More commonly, an international cartel, instead of creating a single international monopoly, seeks to divide up the world market into separate, insulated national or regional monopolies.

The motives for forming cartels are obvious enough: to reap the greater profits joint policies permit and to avoid the well-known uncertainties the interdependence of a few firms in an industry generates. The policies adopted to maximize the joint profits of the cartel members include the principal device used by pure domestic monopolists: the restriction of output, accompanied by the setting of price above competitive, and presumably above noncollusive oligopolistic, levels. A common method of restricting output is through establishing output and sales quotas for member firms. To be effective, this requires that the cartel organization have the power to enforce output limits by imposing sanctions or penalties upon fractious members.

The ability of a firm to maintain a monopolistic price depends upon the absence of competition from rival firms. Free international trade exposes firms to the competition of foreign firms. Indeed, as noted below, this must be counted among the significant benefits of trade. The most common technique of international cartels to avoid competition is the division of the market among participating members. Market allocations may be made on either a product or a geographic basis, or both. An excellent example was the world chemical cartel established in the early 1930s. Major American, German, and British pharmaceutical and chemical firms agreed to divide up the world market, giving each firm exclusive rights to sell designated products in assigned territories. The logical end result of market allocations would be the breaking down of the world economy into virtually isolated economic blocs, bereft of the benefits of trade.

The period between the two world wars witnessed the greatest flourishing of international cartels. Since that time the prevalence of cartels appears to have declined. Perhaps two of the principal reasons for the weakening of the cartel movement are the inherent tendencies for cartels to disintegrate and a change in public attitudes and policies toward them.

The tendency for cartels to disintegrate arises out of the motive of each member firm to circumvent the output and sales quotas and territorial restrictions of the organization to take advantage of the high prices made possible thereby. Of course, once such a movement gets underway, the effectiveness of the cartel is lost.

Public policies toward cartels have generally been less friendly since the end of World War II than previously. The United States has had a long-standing prohibition under the antitrust laws against the participation of United States firms in cartels which affect her foreign commerce. (However, the Webb-Pomerene Act of 1918 permits an association of exporters to restrict competition among themselves in export trade.) It is only more recently that European countries have adopted anticartel policies. Earlier, cartels were generally tolerated and in some countries, such as Germany, officially supported.

That cartels are far from being a dying institution, however, has been painfully brought to the public's attention by the activities of the Organization of Petroleum Exporting Countries (OPEC). During the last quarter of 1973, OPEC succeeded in limiting the supply and quadrupling the price of oil, thereby creating a worldwide energy shortage. From the point of view of petroleum exporting countries, the sharp increase in the price of oil resulted in a sudden dramatic improvement in the terms of trade and the capture of huge monopolistic profits. (It is estimated that at the prices and output levels prevailing in mid-1974, more than $100 billion per year of revenue from oil exports will be received by oil exporting countries.) From the standpoint of the world economy, a shock wage was set off by these developments with multiple repercussions, including the aggravation of inflation, the creation of severe balance-of-payments disequilibrium, the erection of an additional impediment to the growth of less developed countries, and a redistribution of the world's wealth and income. Perhaps a positive effect of the oil crisis has been to raise public consciousness of international economic interdependence and the potential disruptive influence that can be exercised by cartels.

THE EFFECTS OF TRADE ON MONOPOLY

We have seen that imperfectly competitive markets interfere with the processes through which unrestricted international trade under perfect competition leads to a worldwide optimum allocation of resources. This is not to say, however, that trade under imperfect competition yields no social benefits. On the contrary, in addition to the realization, though incomplete, of the specialization and exchange benefits associated with competitive trade, there are special benefits yielded by trade in imperfectly competitive markets. In general, these special benefits derive from the extra competitive elements injected by trade into national market structures.

The greater competitiveness introduced by trade manifests itself most importantly in the increased elasticity of the demand curves confronting monopolistic domestic firms. We recall that in the case of pure competition the firm's demand curve (average revenue curve) is infinitely elastic (horizontal), signifying the absence of any control by the firm over the market price of its product. Under imperfect competition, the firm's demand curve falls from left to right, indicating that price is determined by the firm when it decides on its output. The greater the degree of competition, the more elastic is the firm's demand curve and the' more closely is approximated the competitive social optimum.

Consider the case of domestic firms enjoying some degree of monopoly power when the national economy is insulated from the world economy and then being exposed to a going world market in the *identical* product, with a single world price below the domestic price. Assuming the absence of trade barriers and transportation costs, the domestic price of the good becomes the same as the world price, and the position of the domestic firms is transformed from imperfectly competitive to virtually purely competitive. The reason for this transformation, of course, is that the one previously missing requirement for pure competition under the assumption of a standardized product—namely, the presence of a large number of firms—is supplied by enlargement of the market to include the outside world. From the standpoint of the individual firm, the demand curve is therefore tilted to a horizontal position at the world price, from its previous shape of falling from left to right (compare Figure 5.1). Following the maximum-profit rule of equating marginal revenue and marginal cost, domestic firms now expand their output until marginal cost is equal to the world price. This is the same as the purely competitive equilibrium output, monopolistic restriction having been exorcised by free trade.

It is doubtful whether trade can very often perform such a radical and complete transformation of market structure as described above. However, the usual effect of trade is at least to *dilute* monopolistic elements and move imperfectly competitive markets closer to the competitive end of the spectrum. For example, a national industry, because of economies of scale or barriers to entry, may be dominated by a handful of large firms—the mark of an oligopoly. In isolation from the rest of the world, oligopolistic firms have a strong tendency to coordinate their policies, by agreement if legal, tacitly if not, in order to maintain a secure position and enjoy economic profits. Firms in the same industries in other countries are likely to follow similar practices. If free trade opportunities develop, the market is enlarged to embrace the firms operating in all the countries having such industries. As a consequence, each firm has more rivals to contend within, and each national industry loses all or some of its power to control output and price. This is precisely the main reason international cartels are formed, as discussed previously—to protect national oligopolistic power positions from being eroded by trade. If cartels are outlawed and trade remains unrestricted, the opportunity for the many more firms now in the enlarged market to engage in coordinated action on an international scale is greatly reduced. Correspondingly, the abuses of oligopolistic power are restrained. In short, free trade can be regarded as a powerful antitrust device.

ECONOMIES OF SCALE AS A
BASIS OF TRADE

Other things being equal, imperfect competition leads to a less economically efficient volume and pattern of trade and resource use than are produced by perfect competition. However, other things are not always equal. In some cases, perfect competition is not possible; in certain other cases, it would be possible but less socially desirable than imperfect competition. There are two major situations which necessitate or justify less than perfectly competitive markets. The first, to be considered in this section, arises out of the presence of economies of scale. The second, discussed in the next section, is the result of product differentiation.

Internal economies of scale, reflected in lower average costs of production as output increases, may be realized as a firm enlarges its productive capacity. Economies may be obtained for a variety of reasons: increased productivity through the greater specialization and division of labor a larger output permits, more economical combinations of different factor inputs, the advantages gained from using certain types of equipment which cannot be constructed below a minimum size and output capacity.

Lower average costs because of economies of scale cannot continue indefinitely. After all the sources of lower costs have been fully exploited, increasing returns to scale give way to constant returns and constant average costs. The volume of a firm's output at which average costs have reached their lowest level depends upon the technical conditions of production and varies from industry to industry. In some industries, the lowest average cost output level for a firm is so large that a given market can absorb the total output of only a few firms, each producing at lowest average costs. In cases of this sort, perfect competition, which requires many firms in an industry, is not feasible, so that an oligopolistic (in the limit, a purely monopolistic) market structure develops.

In a competitive industry, long-run equilibrium is not compatible with unrealized economies of scale by the firms in the industry. As long as a competitive firm can lower its average costs by increasing its scale of operations, it pays it to do so. This action, together with the pressure exerted by the freedom of new firms to enter the industry, leads to production at the lowest average-cost output level, at which no further economies can be obtained. In contrast, an oligopolistic firm may find its maximum-profit output to be below the level at which economies of scale would be exhausted and average costs lowest. In the latter event, if the firm were to increase output, average costs would decline until the optimum scale (at which average costs are lowest) is reached.

The presence of unexploited internal economies of scale provides a possible source of comparative advantage and basis for specialization and trade not admitted in our earlier trade model applicable under purely competitive conditions. In contrast to the competitive model, in which larger outputs are accompanied by higher costs, with increasing returns to scale, larger outputs are accompanied by lower costs. Hence, a country may have a comparative advantage in a product because the output of the product is greater than in other countries. The greater output, permitting the capture of scale economies, may in turn be associated with a larger population and/or a higher per capita income. The hypothesis that larger countries tend to have a comparative advantage in industries with economies of scale has been supported by various empirical studies.[1]

Another implication of increasing returns to scale should be noted: a comparative advantage may develop as the *result* of trade. The comparison of costs before trade opens up may show a country as having no advantage in a given product. If there are increasing returns to scale in that product, however, the expanded market trade provides may lead to an increase in output and therewith the development of a comparative advantage.

PRODUCT DIFFERENTIATION AND TRADE

One of the requirements of pure competition is that the products of the different firms in a given industry be standardized. If the products of different firms in an industry are differentiated a market structure of either monopolistic competition (many firms in the industry) or differentiated oligopoly (few firms in the industry) prevails.

In many areas, product standardization is not possible. This is generally the case for personal services and for products in which location enters as a significant attribute, such as the services of retail stores and automobile service stations. In a vast number of other instances, standardization is not inherently impossible but could be achieved only by sacrificing variety. Thus, there is no technical reason why standardized automobiles, soap, clothing, toothpaste, and a myriad of other goods now differentiated by brand could not be produced.

Different varieties of a given product are more or less close sub-

[1] See, for example, Donald B. Keesing, "Population and Industrial Development: Some Evidence from Trade Patterns," *The American Economic Review,* June 1968, pp. 448–55.

stitutes for each other. (Otherwise, they would be regarded as different products.) Yet each brand has some particular characteristics which distinguish it in the eyes of consumers from other brands of the same product. It is to be presumed that, other things being equal, the availability of a variety of brands contributes to consumers' welfare by enlarging choices and allowing each consumer to acquire the particular bundle of product characteristics optimal for him.

Product differentiation is itself a basis for international trade. Trade in standardized products is based on comparative cost differences, with comparatively low-cost goods exported and comparatively high-cost goods imported. But the concept of comparative costs loses its sharpness of meaning when products are differentiated. Consider, for example, a two-product, two-country model, consisting of wine and cheese produced by France and England. If each product were standardized, comparative costs could clearly be identified, and it might be determined that France has a comparative cost advantage in wine and England in cheese. But if, as in fact, there are numerous varieties of wine and cheese, no firm basis for determining comparative cost positions exists, since the things the costs of which are being compared are not identical. Nevertheless, trade is likely to be engaged in, simply because at least some consumers in each country will wish to purchase particular foreign brands of each product in preference to domestic brands of the same product. Moreover, this leads—in contrast to trade in standardized goods—to "two-way" trade, with countries both importing and exporting each product.

Various hypotheses concerning the determinants of the volume and pattern of trade in differentiated products have been advanced. One of these relates to the development of new products and will be considered separately in the next section. For already well-established products, a reasonable hypothesis is that trade will tend to be reflective of different national tastes and income levels. The consumers of a high-income country in which labor time is highly valued are prone to prefer sophisticated, labor-saving types of products. In lower income countries, on the other hand, less emphasis is likely to be placed on time-saving and convenience features. In each case, domestic firms are inclined to concentrate on the types of products most suitable to the home market. This latter proposition is based on the familiarity of domestic producers with the special traits of the home market and the risks associated with attempts to cater to the preferences of less familiar foreign cultures.

The combination of special national preferences on the part of

both consumers and producers tends to restrain trade in differentiated products among countries with greatly different cultures and
income levels but to encourage trade among similar countries.

Trade in differentiated products has two important effects. The
first, mentioned previously, is to enlarge the horizon of consumers,
allowing them to be more selective in their expenditure. The second
effect is to increase the degree of competition to which domestic
producers are exposed. By increasing the number of rivals, trade
reduces the market power of oligopolists, as discussed earlier. By
increasing the available number of substitute varieties of a product,
trade tends to increase the elasticity of demand for each firm's output, thereby reducing the divergence between price and marginal
costs and inducing a closer approximation to pure competition.

Both the above effects of trade in differentiated products must be
counted as socially beneficial.

DYNAMIC FACTORS: TECHNOLOGICAL-GAP AND
PRODUCT-CYCLE TRADE

All the various theories of trade discussed so far have presupposed
the existence of a given and unchanging state of technology. Actually, of course, technology changes, sometimes astonishingly. A technological change may be expressed in new methods of producing
existing goods or in the production of entirely new goods or varieties
of old ones. In either case, the pattern of comparative advantage and
of trade will very probably be affected.

The most obvious effect of technological developments on trade is
produced by the creation of an entirely new product, such as the
electronic computer. Until the technical knowledge of how to manufacture a newly developed product is acquired by other countries, the
innovating country clearly has an "advantage" in, and will export, it
if there is a foreign demand. Such trade is sometimes called "technological-gap trade."

The advantage in new products enjoyed by innovating countries is
not likely to last indefinitely, though it may be prolonged by the
legal monopoly afforded by patents. In the long run, knowledge
tends to be a free good. It is disseminated internationally through a
variety of routes: technical journals, patent licensing, the multinational corporation, etc. Hence, a country's advantage in particular
products based on technological innovation may be temporary,
though, for reasons stated below, certain countries tend to continue

having an advantage in a stream of new products. The ephemeral nature of the advantage in particular technological-gap products is emphasized in the so-called "product-cycle" theory of trade, to which we now turn.

The developmental stages of a new product tend to reflect demand and production conditions in the home market. Innovation nearly always carries with it a considerable risk, and firms are inclined to provide risk capital only in markets with which they are familiar.

Knowledge of the public's probable reaction to a new product and ready accessibility to the specialized labor and equipment necessary for the manufacturing process improve the innovator's chances of success.

Once a new product has been introduced and has gained some acceptance in the home market, its export to foreign markets—especially those with similar tastes and income levels—normally follows. For some time the innovating firms are likely to enjoy a virtually monopolistic position. Sooner or later, however, production spreads to importing countries, with either local firms beginning to manufacture the product or the innovating firms establishing branches or subsidiaries in the importing countries. Production in foreign countries is encouraged as local demand expands, technical knowledge is acquired, and the best manufacturing process has become established. The availability of relatively cheap factors important in the production of the good may be the decisive consideration in undertaking local manufacture.

As production spreads to other countries, the original innovating country is faced with increasing competition and declining exports of the product, not only to other manufacturing countries but to nonproducing areas as well, the latter turning to the newer and lower cost sources of supply.

Finally, the innovating country may itself become a net importer of the product, the original advantage having vanished as the monopolistic position enjoyed at first gives way to foreign competition.

In summary, the product cycle embraces a series of stages, beginning with production and export by the innovating country and ending with that country's importing of the product—or, more usually, some differentiated variety of the product.[2]

---

[2] For a fuller statement and empirical verification of the product-cycle hypothesis, see Raymond Vernon, "International Investment and International Trade in the Product Cycle," *Quarterly Journal of Economics,* May 1966; Louis T. Wells, Jr., ed., *The Product Life Cycle and International Trade* (Boston: Harvard University Press,

Even though the advantages in trade a country acquires from technological developments and innovations may be only temporary for each product, for some countries there is a more or less constant stream of such products, the loss of advantage in earlier ones being accompanied by the emergence of new ones. That is, certain countries appear to have a comparative advantage based on technology and innovation. The United States is a prime example.

Empirical investigations have shown that the manufactured exports of the United States are heavily weighted with high-technology products which are produced by research-oriented industries. Thus, in 1962, the five industries with the strongest research effort—as measured either by research and development expenditure or by the number of highly trained technical personnel as a percentage of total employment—accounted for over 70 percent of United States exports of manufactured goods but less than 40 percent of the country's total sales of manufactures.[3]

Why should the United States apparently have a comparative advantage based on technology and innovation? Several factors are probably involved. One is the high level of per capita income, which creates a favorable market for new products. Secondly, innovations tend to be labor-saving, so that the greatest incentive to innovate is found in high-wage countries. Thirdly, the United States is plentifully endowed with skilled labor, usually necessary, especially in the early stages of developing a new product. Finally, the introduction of sophisticated technological advances may be associated with economies of scale, which, in turn, tend to be realizable mainly in large, high-income markets, such as exist in the United States. The hypothesis that all these factors have an explanatory role is supported by the fact that other countries with similar characteristics—such as the United Kingdom and Germany—have similar type exports.

TRADE OF CENTRALLY PLANNED ECONOMIES

In this last section we turn to the theory of trade in a quite different context, that of centrally planned economies (CPEs). We

---

1972) ; G. C. Hufbauer, "The Impact of National Characteristics and Technology on the Commodity Composition of Trade in Manufactured Goods," *The Technology Factor in International Trade,* ed. Raymond Vernon (New York: Columbia University Press, 1970).

[3] See William H. Gruber, D. Mehta, and R. Vernon, "The R and D Factor in International Trade and International Investment of United States Industries," *Journal of Political Economy,* 75, no. 1 (February 1967).

shall adopt as the prototype of CPEs, socialist economies, such as the Soviet Union, Eastern Europe, and mainland China.

Except for a limited amount of state trade, the trade of market economies is the result of the decisions of private firms and individuals. In centrally planned economies, trade decisions are made by the state. This distinction immediately raises the question of whether conventional theories of trade, such as we have considered at length in the preceding chapters, are applicable or relevant to CPEs. The answer can be formulated at either of two different levels: in terms of a strictly economic rationale or as an explanation of actual experience. At the former level, the basic principles of trade are equally applicable to centrally planned as to market economies. As an explanation of historical experience, however, our theoretical models appear to have little relevance. The bases of these different answers will now be examined in turn.

The Economic Rationale for Trade by CPEs

Trade in market economies is conducted by private firms in pursuit of the profit motive. Since in a centrally planned economy the profit motive, as such, does not exist, does it not follow that CPEs have no reason to engage in trade? This conclusion would be quite erroneous. It will be remembered that trade yields benefits to the whole economy in the form of specialization and exchange gains and not merely to private firms in the form of profits. Indeed, it is the *social benefits* of trade which justify it from a national and world welfare point of view.

Many pages earlier we concluded that the primary social benefits of trade derive from comparative cost (and relative price) differences. The existence of comparative cost differences is independent of the form of economic organization, though the latter is likely to affect—because of its influence on preferences—the pattern of comparative costs. Centrally planned economies are certain to have comparative cost advantages in some products and disadvantages in others. By exporting the former in exchange for the latter, the efficiency of the economy is increased, and the total availability of goods and services is expanded beyond the no-trade level.

In order for an economy to reap the benefits offered by trade, the marginal opportunity costs and the marginal social benefits of the goods it produces and consumes must be known and measurable. In a competitive market economy, the price mechanism automatically performs this function. Suitably modified, a price system can also be employed in a centrally planned economy to determine opportunity costs and to reflect social benefits, as shown by modern socialist economists.[4] In any event, if a centrally planned economy devises a method of efficient resource allocation it will have the basis for determining the optimum volume and pattern of trade with other countries.

The Political Element in CPE Trade

Even though economic efficiency would be as well served by trade for centrally planned economies as for market economies, the attitude of the Soviet Union and similar socialist countries toward foreign trade has historically been negative, though recently some relaxation has occurred. Perhaps the basic reason for the antitrade stance of these countries has been ideological in nature.

Reflecting the general disdain of Marxian thought for "bourgeois economics," Marxist economists have not accepted the theoretical principles of trade as expounded by western economists. The theory of comparative costs has been described by some Soviet economists as "a pseudoscientific, reactionary foreign trade theory disseminated by bourgeois economists . . . to serve as a theoretical basis for the western discriminatory foreign trade policies towards Socialist countries."[5]

On a more pragmatic level, the socialist countries have been fearful of the political implications of the economic dependence on foreign countries which extensive trade relations would create. This fear has been especially strong, of course, with respect to trade with nonsocialist economies. (Hence, the bulk of Soviet trade has been with eastern European countries of similar ideological persuasion.) The desire to be economically independent of the rest of the world is expressed in policies of *autarky*. However, whether or not autarky has been a theoretical goal of the Soviet Union, it is not a practical operating principle. More realistically, the Soviet Union has tended to minimize its participation in foreign trade but not to strive literally for economic self-sufficiency.

It is to be noted that the Soviet Union's aversion to trade with

---

[4] See, for example, Abba Lerner, *The Economics of Control* (New York: Macmillan Co., 1944) .

[5] Quoted by J. Wilczyski in "The Theory of Comparative Costs and Centrally Planned Economics," *Economic Journal,* March 1965, p. 66.

western countries is not entirely unilateral. Western countries, the United States in particular, as part of "cold war" politics, have restricted both imports from and exports to the Soviet bloc countries, though in recent years a progressive relaxation of these restrictions has been occurring.

A third reason for the limited participation of the eastern socialist economies in foreign trade arises out of a mixture of economic and political considerations. Contemporary centrally planned economies generally are characterized as highly growth-oriented. Typically, such countries, like developing countries, place great emphasis on building a domestic industrial base. Industrialization is regarded not merely as economically desirable but as an expression of nationalistic pride. To accomplish industrialization, domestic production of manufactured goods is favored over the importation of foreign goods, even though the latter are cheaper. In market economies, imports are restricted through tariffs and quotas and domestic industries stimulated by a variety of subsidies. In centrally planned economies, the same objectives are pursued through direct state controls over trade and the planning process. In both cases, from a "liberal" point of view, the policies are uneconomic and irrational. But, from a more objective point of view, it can be argued that, given industrialization as a national goal, with value placed upon it, it is rational to bear the costs of less efficient use of resources to achieve the goal, provided that the marginal social utility gained is worth its marginal costs.

Finally, centrally planned trade has no doubt been obstructed by deficiencies of the planning process itself. As mentioned earlier, the efficient allocation of resources requires the accurate determination of opportunity costs in relation to social benefits. The only established way of doing this is through the application of the principles of a price system. Although there is evidence that the principles are beginning to be tentatively applied, accurate social costing and pricing have doubtfully yet been achieved. An inevitable side-effect of inaccurate accounting is the absence of a rational basis for integrating trade relations into the overall plan of resource allocation.

Notwithstanding the above constraints, the foreign trade of centrally planned economies has not been negligible and in recent years has been expanding at a more rapid pace than the trade of market economies. A significant part of CPE trade has been of an *ad hoc* variety—imports to fill unplanned shortfalls in domestic production, exports of unexpected domestic surpluses. However, with the easing of East-West political tensions and the introduction of more sensitive accounting procedures and allocative mechanisms, a greater integration of trade into overall planning can be envisioned.

RECOMMENDED READINGS

COMMITTEE FOR ECONOMIC DEVELOPMENT. *A New Trade Policy Toward Communist Countries.* New York, 1972.

EDWARDS, CORWIN D. *Economic and Political Aspects of International Cartels.* U.S. Senate, Subcommittee on War Mobilization of the Committee on Military Affairs, 78th Cong., 2d sess Washington, D.C.: U.S. Government Printing Office, 1946.

———— ET AL. *A Cartel Policy for the United Nations.* New York. Columbia University Press, 1945.

GRUBER, WILLIAM ET AL. "The R and D Factor in International Trade and Investment of United States Industries," *Journal of Political Economy,* February 1967, pp. 20–37.

HOLZMAN, F. D. "Foreign Trade Behavior of Centrally Planned Economies," *Industrialization in Two Systems: Essays in Honor of Alexander Gerschenkron.* Edited by H. Rosovsky. New York: John Wiley, 1966, pp. 237–65.

HUFBAUER, G. C. "The Impact of National Characteristics and Technology on the Commodity Composition of Trade in Manufactured Goods," *The Technology Factor in International Trade.* Edited by Raymond Vernon. New York: National Bureau of Economic Research, 1970, pp. 145–211.

JOHNSON, HARRY G. "International Trade Theory and Monopolistic Competition," *Monopolistic Theory: Studies in Impact.* Edited by R. E. Kuenne. New York, 1967.

KEESING, DONALD B. "Labor Skills and Comparative Advantage," *American Economic Review,* May 1966, pp. 249–58.

STOCKING, GEORGE W., and WATKINS, MYRON W. *Cartels in Action.* New York: Twentieth Century Fund, 1946. Case studies of some important cartels.

UNITED NATIONS, DEPARTMENT OF ECONOMIC AFFAIRS. *International Cartels.* 1947.

VERNON, RAYMOND. "International Investment and International Trade in the Product Cycle," *Quarterly Journal of Economics,* May 1966, pp. 190–207.

WILES, P. J. D. *Communist International Economics.* New York: Praeger, 1969.

STUDY QUESTIONS

1. Define "pure competition." What condition with respect to the number of buyers and sellers would create a monopolistic element?

2. Why, in competitive equilibrium, is the price of each commodity equal to its marginal costs of production? Why is this not true under monopolistic conditions?

3. Show how monopoly, through preventing the equalization of price and marginal costs, leads to an uneconomic allocation of resources, both internally and internationally.

4. What is meant by "perverse specialization"? Under what conditions is it possible?

5. Show how imperfect competition could result in a loss of specialization gains from trade. In a loss of exchange gains.

6. What is the economic basis for international monopolistic price discrimination?

7. Define "cartel" and describe some of the policies cartels follow.

8. Show how international trade tends to reduce monopolistic power.

9. How may economies of scale provide the basis for comparative advantage?

10. Why does the concept of comparative costs lose its sharpness of meaning when products are differentiated?

11. Illustrate how product differentiation is a basis for trade.

12. Why is trade in differentiated products likely to be greater among countries with similar cultures and income levels than among those greatly different in these respects?

13. What kinds of benefits does trade in differentiated products yield?

14. What is meant by "technological-gap" trade?

15. State the product-cycle theory of trade, identifying the various stages of production and trade.

16. What accounts for the comparative advantage of the United States in high-technology products?

17. Show why the economic basis for trade does not depend upon the operations of a free market economy.

18. Explain the reasons for the limited participation of centrally planned economies in international trade.

6

A survey of world trade
and its empirical bases

The theoretical bases of international trade have been examined in the preceding chapters. In capsule summary, we concluded that, in the context of competitive markets, differences in relative factor endowments are the central determinant of the pattern of trade, while in imperfectly competitive markets such things as economies of scale, product differentiation, and technological gaps provide the explanation of trade. In this chapter it is proposed to examine the actual pattern of world trade, followed by a description of the empirical bases of trade.

THE COMMODITY COMPOSITION OF TRADE

It is of interest to decompose total trade into major types, for the relevant theoretical explanations vary accordingly.

Table 6.1 shows the percentage distribution of world trade among manufactures, foodstuffs, and raw materials. The first point of interest to note is the recent dominant importance of trade in manufactured goods, accounting for approximately two thirds of total trade. The data also indicate, however, that this dominance is a relatively recent phenomenon. Before World War II, manufactures

TABLE 6.1

COMMODITY COMPOSITION OF WORLD TRADE,
PREWAR AND 1970
(percentages)

	Prewar	1970*
Manufactures.	40	64
Foodstuffs	25	15
Raw materials	35	18
Other, unclassified	2	2

* Total does not equal 100 percent because of rounding.

Sources: League of Nations, *The Network of World Trade* (Geneva, 1942), pp. 23–24; General Agreement on Tariffs and Trade, *International Trade 1970* (Geneva, 1971), p. 22.

accounted for only about 40 percent of trade. The trend in recent decades has been in the direction of an increasing fraction of trade in manufactured goods and decreasing shares of food and raw materials. Undoubtedly the basic explanation for this shift in the composition of trade is the increase in real income, especially of the developed countries (which account for the bulk of world trade, as noted below), together with the higher income elasticity of demand for manufactured goods as compared to primary products. In addition, the growth of trade in raw materials has been restrained by the development of synthetic substitutes by industrialized countries.

It is quite possible that the historic trend in the composition of trade is in process of being broken. The recent emergence of world-wide shortages in foodstuffs and natural resources is leading toward a reemphasis on trade in these products, with relative increases in their prices enlarging their share in the value of trade. The so-called energy crisis and the accompanying multiple increase in the world price of petroleum is the most obvious example, though the prices of other natural resource products may well follow a similar upward course over the coming years.

THE SHARE OF TRADE BY COUNTRIES

Tables 6.2 and 6.3 present data on trade from a different perspective: according to the participation of different types of national economy. The latter are divided for this purpose into three categories: developed market economies, developing (that is, less developed) economies, and centrally planned economies. The domination of world trade by developed market economies is striking.

Moreover, of developed market economies a mere handful ac-

TABLE 6.2

DISTRIBUTION OF WORLD EXPORTS BY TYPE OF ECONOMY
(percent of total exports)

	1953	*1959*	*1965*	*1969*	*1973*
Developed market economies . . .	65.0	65.4	68.9	71.0	79
Developing market economies . . .	25.5	22.3	19.5	18.1	21
Centrally planned economies . . .	9.5	12.3	11.7	10.9	*
	100.0	100.0	100.0	100.0	100.0

° Data for centrally planned economies not included.
Sources: United Nations, *Yearbook of International Trade Statistics,* table A 1969; International Monetary Fund, *International Financial Statistics,* June 1974, p. 36.

counts for the lion's share of world trade. The United States, Canada, Japan, and the nine members of the European Common Market together conduct approximately 60 percent of the world's trade, and close to three quarters of the trade in manufactured goods. The basic reason for such a high degree of concentration of trade is easily perceived: the capacity to export and the ability to import are both functions of the degree of economic development.

Not only do the industrial countries account for the greater part of world trade, they also carry on a disproportionate part of their trade among themselves, as the data in Table 6.3 show. Perhaps this is not surprising, in view of the previous comments on the relationship between development and trade.

COMPOSITION OF TRADE BY TYPE OF ECONOMY

We may now combine the characteristics of trade by type of commodity and of economy, as in Table 6.4. It is not surprising to see that the exports of industrial countries consist predominantly of manufactures, while the exports of less developed countries are largely primary products.

TABLE 6.3

THE PATTERN OF TRADE AMONG ECONOMIES BY TYPE,
ANNUAL AVERAGES, 1962–72
(percentage of totals)

Exports from \ Exports to	*Developed Market Economies*	*Developing Market Economies*	*Centrally Planned Economies*
Developed market economies	76.7	19.1	3.8
Developing market economies	73.6	19.8	5.4
Centrally planned economies	24.1	15.0	60.7

Source: World Bank/IDA, *Annual Report, 1973,* table 2, pp. 84–85. Because of various minor discrepancies in classification the percentages do not sum to 100.

TABLE 6.4

Trade by Type of Commodity and of Economy, 1970
(in billions of dollars)

Exports from \ Exports to	Developed Countries	Developing Countries
Developed countries:		
Manufactures	110.4	32.2
Primary Products	37.6	6.6
Developing countries:		
Manufactures	9.1	3.0
Primary Products	30.7	7.3

Source: General Agreement on Tariffs and Trade, *International Trade 1970* (Geneva, 1971), p. 22.

Two slightly more subtle points are of interest. The first is, contrary to what one might expect, industrial countries furnish more primary products to each other than they import from other areas. The second, related observation is the asymmetry in the position of less developed economies. On the one hand, their manufactures imports are overwhelmingly furnished by industrial countries, while they furnish less than half of the primary product imports of industrial countries. In short, less developed countries as a group are much more trade-dependent upon developed countries than the reverse. No doubt this asymmetry helps explain the perennial complaint of developing countries that they are in a vulnerable position in the world economy. One aspect of this vulnerability relates to the terms of trade. It is frequently alleged that the less developed countries as a group suffer over time from deteriorating terms of trade— that is, a decline in the prices their exports command, compared to the prices they must pay for imports. Unbalanced trade-dependence lends credence to the allegation, though there is little objective evidence to support it.

THE IMPORTANCE OF TRADE TO INDIVIDUAL COUNTRIES

Aggregate data conceal the position of individual countries, for whom the importance of trade varies widely. Perhaps the best single quantitative indicator of the role of trade is the average propensity to import, defined as the ratio of imports (M) to national income or gross national product (Y) —that is, M/Y. The ratio of exports to income is an alternative measure, but since in the long run it is imports which directly contribute to the economic welfare of a country, while exports constitute the social cost of imports, the propensity to import is the more meaningful measure of the importance of foreign trade to a country.

TABLE 6.5

IMPORTS AS A PERCENTAGE OF THE GROSS NATIONAL
PRODUCT IN 1970, SELECTED COUNTRIES

United States	4.0	United Kingdom	17.9
U.S.S.R.	2.1	Italy	16.2
Japan	9.5	Canada	17.5
West Germany	15.9	Netherlands	42.9
France	12.7	Belgium-Luxembourg	42.0

Source: U.S. Tariff Commission, *Trade Barriers*, TC Publication 665, vol. 1 (Washington, D.C., April 1974), pp. 75–76.

Table 6.5 shows the average propensity to import of a selected number of countries. The most salient feature of the data is the tremendous difference in the propensity to import between countries in the highest and lowest ranges. The very low ratio for the United States and the Soviet Union and high ratios for such countries as the Netherlands and Belgium-Luxembourg suggest that, at least for countries with a high per capita income, the size of the national economy is an important variable determining the value of the propensity to import.

Large-sized, highly developed economies such as that of the United States have a low trade participation rate because of the wide diversity of domestic resources and extensive *internal* specialization and trade. If the United States were to be divided into two or more separate national states, the trade among the latter that is now internal would become international, with the propensity to import raised far above the level that now exists. The same considerations apply to the Soviet Union, with an added antitrade bias because of ideological and political reasons.

As observed in the introductory chapter of this book, the significance of international trade for a national economy is actually greater than indicated by the propensity to import. For many countries, it is doubtful whether their current populations could be physically sustained in the absence of trade. For others, physical survival would be possible without trade but only at a significantly lower standard of living.

EXPORT DEPENDENCE

In the preceding section the emphasis was on the role of imports in determining the economic welfare of a country, exports being regarded as the social cost of obtaining the benefits of imports. In the long run, however, the volume of a country's imports depends upon the volume of its exports, since the latter are the principal means of

TABLE 6.6

PERCENTAGE OF EXPORTS ACCOUNTED FOR BY
PRINCIPAL EXPORT COMMODITY, SELECTED COUNTRIES*

Country	Export Commodity	Percent of Total Exports
Bolivia	Tin	46
Chile	Copper	73
Colombia	Coffee	41
Ghana	Cacao	62
Iraq	Petroleum	91
Venezuela	Petroleum	93

The data apply to various years from 1970 to 1972.
° Calculated from country data in International Monetary Fund, *International Financial Statistics*, June 1974.

paying for imports. It follows that the long-run economic welfare of a country is indirectly related to its ability to export.

There is a second aspect of a country's export position which has important implications for the short run. Trade, as we know, is based upon specialization. Resources that are allocated to the export sector of an economy depend for their employment upon export markets. If the foreign demand for a country's exports contracts, output and employment in affected industries decline. The more specialized resources used in export industries are, the more difficult it is to absorb them elsewhere and to develop substitute export activities.

From both long- and short-run perspectives, a country is in the most favorable trade position when it has a wide range of export industries. In such cases, the overall export position is less subject to deterioration because of shifts in foreign demand for particular export products. In contrast, to the extent that exports are concentrated in a few industries, the vulnerability of the economy to changing foreign demand is increased.

Again, the more highly developed economies tend in the above respects to be in a more favorable position than less developed economies. For many of the latter, exports are dominated by a very few products, usually of a primary character (raw materials or agricultural commodities). Table 6.6 shows a sample of countries heavily dependent on the export of a single commodity.

THE EMPIRICAL BASES OF TRADE

In this last section it is proposed to examine empirically the bases which theory hypothesizes as the underlying determinants of international trade. Because of the paucity of relevant data, however, the discussion will be very broad and casual, designed to produce general impressions rather than specific and sophisticated results.

It will be recalled from the preceding chapters that there are two general modern theories of trade, corresponding to two different types of market conditions. In the context of *competitive* markets, differences in relative factor endowments are assigned the central explanatory role. In the presence of *imperfectly competitive* markets, economies of scale, product differentiation, and technological gaps constitute the principal elements determining the pattern of trade. Accordingly, the empirical bases of trade consist of differences in relative factor endowments, on the one hand, and the presence of the characteristics of imperfectly competitive markets on the other hand.

Relative Factor Endowments

Unfortunately, conceptual as well as statistical difficulties are encountered in attempting to measure empirical relative factor endowments. In the first place, the classification of factors into the conventional molds of land, labor, and capital is analytically convenient but subject to extensive qualifications as empirical categories because of wide variations in their economic qualities. Thus, land—which includes all nature-given resources—varies with respect to soil, climate, topography, the amount and accessibility of mineral and power resources, etc. In the case of labor and capital the problem is to separate that part of the former which properly belongs to the latter—that is, to include in labor supply only "raw" labor and to include in the supply of capital the human as well as material components. Needless to say, the available data for effecting this separation are very rough and indirect.

Moreover, in contrast to the neat simplicity of a two-factor, two-country theoretical model in which each country's relative factor endowment can be clearly identified as relatively capital- or labor-abundant, the multifactor, multicountry real world obscures the meaning of relative factor endowments.

Notwithstanding these difficulties it is possible to obtain a general picture of the vast differences in relative factor endowments, as we shall now proceed, by stages, to show.

Land-Labor Ratios. Let us begin with the broadest comparison the data will allow us—the distribution of the land area of the world in relationship to population. As the fourth column of Table 6.7 shows, the variation of land area per head of economically active

TABLE 6.7
LAND-LABOR RATIOS IN SELECTED COUNTRIES

Country	Total Area (millions of hectares)*	Agricultural Area† (millions of hectares)*	Economically Active Population, 1970 (millions)	Total Area Per Head of Economically Active Population (hectares)*	Agricultural Area Per Head of Economically Active Population (hectares)*
Australia	768.7	494.7	5.1	150.8	97.0
Canada	997.6	68.7	8.0	124.7	8.6
Argentina.......	277.7	180.0	8.9	31.2	20.2
New Zealand	26.9	13.5	1.1	24.4	12.3
USSR	2240.2	607.3	123.4	18.2	4.9
United States.....	936.3	436.6	81.1	11.4	5.3
France	54.7	33.0	21.8	2.5	1.5
Denmark	4.3	3.0	2.3	1.9	1.3
India	326.8	178.5	216.4	1.5	0.8
Switzerland	4.1	2.2	2.8	1.5	0.8
Italy	30.1	17.6	20.3	1.5	0.9
United Kingdom...	24.4	18.8	25.1	1.0	0.7
West Germany ...	24.7	13.5	26.7	0.9	0.5
Belgium	3.1	1.6	3.7	0.8	0.4
Netherlands	3.7	2.1	4.9	0.8	0.4
Japan	37.2	6.4	52.6	0.7	0.1

° One hectare = 2.47 acres.
† Includes arable land, land under permanent crops, and permanent meadows and pastures.
Source: Food and Agricultural Organization of the United Nations, *Production Yearbook 1972,* vol. 26 (Rome, 1973), table 1, pp. 3–8.

population for different countries is enormous, ranging from over 150 hectares (Australia) to 7/10 hectare (Japan).

In the economic sense, however, land as a factor category encompasses much more than geographic space, so that the amount of area is a poor indicator of land in its economic sense. We cannot possibly here identify and attempt to measure the distribution of the numerous different characteristics of land relevant for the production of different types of output. But we can identify broadly two of the major uses of land as a productive factor and the characteristics associated with each. The uses referred to are (*a*) agricultural production, and (*b*) natural resource production.

In Table 6.7, the second column shows the agricultural area, as contrasted to the total area, with the last column displaying agricultural area per capita of economically active population. It will be noted that the ranking of countries on the latter basis differs in several cases from the original ordering, but the great disparity among countries remains. It is evident that to the extent that comparative advantage in agricultural products is a function of the endowments of agricultural land relatively to population there is a manifest empirical foundation for specialization and trade in such products.

It is also evident, though we shall not attempt to cite supporting data, that the relative supplies of particular types of agricultural land vary widely. For example, the combination of temperature, moisture, and topographic and soil conditions appropriate for growing temperate zone products, such as wheat and beef, is quite different from the combination of characteristics suitable for the growing of tropical products, such as coffee and bananas. That countries such as Argentina and Australia would have a comparative advantage in wheat and beef, while countries such as Costa Rica and Honduras have a comparative advantage in coffee and bananas, is hardly surprising.

Equally obvious is the disparity in the distribution of supplies of natural resources, such as mineral and energy resources. The concentration of the world's known reserves of petroleum in the Middle East and a few other areas is well-known. The distribution of such minerals as bauxite (the ore from which aluminum is made) and tin is likewise extremely uneven.

A unique characteristic of natural resource supplies is that—in contrast to agricultural land, capital, and labor—they are irreplaceable. Consequently, over time a country's relative endowment of a natural resource may drastically change as the result of its exploitation. The relative scarcity of a resource may also increase not simply because of a decrease in its physical availability but because of an expansion in the supplies of labor and capital. Both sets of forces—decreasing physical availability of natural resources and increasing supplies of labor and capital—have served over the past decades to transform the United States from a relatively natural-resource-abundant country to a relatively natural-resource-scarce country. Correspondingly, the United States has shifted from a net-export to a net-import position with respect to natural resource products.

Capital-Labor Ratios. Data on the distribution of the world's stock of capital are extremely limited. There is a paucity of data with respect even to the stock of material capital. For "human capital" there is practically no direct quantitative information, since there are no market measures of this component of capital, so that indirect indicators must be relied upon.

An empirical investigation by G. C. Hufbauer provides us with at least a rough ranking of certain countries in accordance with their capital-labor ratios. A reproduction of Professor Hufbauer's data is given in Table 6.8. It will be noted that the material component of capital stock is given in the first column, and only for manufacturing. The second column shows skilled employees as a percent of total employees in manufacturing employment, and serves for our purposes as a proxy measure of human capital, as explained in an earlier discussion (see Chapter 3).

Unfortunately, there is not available a single measure of capital which combines the material and human components. As can be seen, however, there is a very high correlation between the amount of material capital and of human capital as measured by skills.

We need not regard the estimates given in the table as reliable absolute measures for them to be interesting. It is sufficient for the purpose at hand to observe the great disparity among countries in

TABLE 6.8

RELATIVE CAPITAL SUPPLIES AND
SKILLED EMPLOYEES FOR SELECTED COUNTRIES

	Fixed Capital Per Manufacturing Employee (in U.S. dollars of approximately 1958 Value)	*Skilled Employees as Fraction of Total*
Canada	8,850	.106
United States.	7,950	.108
Austria	4,000	.068
Belgium	4,400	.080
Denmark	2,850	.078
France	4,900	.083
Germany	4,250	.100
Italy	2,600	.046
Netherlands	4,750	.092
Norway	6,100	.080
Sweden	5,400	.129
United Kingdom.	4,000	.095
Australia	5,300	.103
Japan	3,100	.049
Israel	3,900	.114
Portugal	1,500	.027
Spain	1,700	.041
Yugoslavia	2,500	.056
Mexico	2,000	.036
Hong Kong	1,200	.046
India	500	.017
Korea	850	.022
Pakistan	500	.014
Taiwan	1,150	.031

Source: Grateful acknowledgment is made to the National Bureau of Economic Research and Dr. G. C. Hufbauer for permission to reproduce data contained in table 4, p. 157 of G. C. Hufbauer, "The Impact of National Characteristics and Technology on the Commodity Composition of Trade in Manufactured Goods," *The Technology Factor in International Trade*, ed. Raymond Vernon, National Bureau of Economic Research, 1970.

For qualifications and methods of calculation see the above source.

the capital-labor ratio as measured by the technique employed by Dr. Hufbauer.

Land, Labor, Capital, and Types of Economy. We have gained an impression of the vast differences which exist among countries in their supplies of land and of capital, each in relationship to labor. However, with three factor categories there remains another set of comparisons more difficult to make. A country may have a relative abundance of one factor in relationship to one of the other factors but not in relationship to the third factor. For example, from Tables 6.7 and 6.8 above, we can observe that the Netherlands is labor-abundant when compared to land, but relatively labor-scarce when compared to capital.

Of the three factor ratios, that of capital to labor may play a key role. The supply of capital relative to that of labor is especially relevant in determining the degree to which an economy is agricultural or industrial. Agricultural pursuits can be carried on with little capital compared to the capital requirements of industry, other than light, handicraft industries. If a country has a large per capita supply of both capital and land, some portion of its capital is likely to be applied in agriculture in the form of mechanical means of cultivation and harvesting, irrigation works, and so on. But it is also likely to develop industrially, for the scope for the profitable use of capital in industry is ordinarily much greater than in agriculture, at least after a certain amount of capital has been applied to agriculture.

Where both capital and land are scarce relative to labor supply, therefore, a country will tend to be predominantly agricultural. Similarly, where land is abundant compared to labor supply but capital scarce, agriculture will tend to be more important than industry. But where capital is abundant and land scarce, each in relation to labor supply, the economy will tend to be predominantly industrial, with agriculture largely of an intensive-cultivation type.

There are, therefore, three broad types of economies, based on different relative factor endowments, that may be distinguished. The first type we may designate the *balanced economy*. It is characterized by an abundance of both capital and land, relative to labor supply, compared to other types of economy. Or, put in other terms, labor is comparatively scarce, relative to land and capital. Industries requiring a large amount of capital and small amounts of labor, and agricultural production requiring large amounts of land and small amounts of labor, are both encouraged. Since labor is scarce in relation to both land and capital, labor productivity is high and per capita income large.

The second type of economy is *agricultural,* with both land and capital scarce relative to labor supply or with land abundant relative to labor and capital scarce relative to labor. The scarcity of capital precludes any significant industrial development, although the abundance of labor may encourage some light, handicraft industries, particularly if the necessary raw materials are locally available. Per capita productivity and income are low, except where land is relatively abundant.

In between the first two extremes are the *industrial* economies, abundantly supplied with both capital and labor but with relatively small amounts of land. Manufacturing is highly developed; agriculture tends to be of an intensive character. Per capita productivity and income are higher than in the agricultural countries but lower than in the balanced economies.

On the basis of the above criteria, we may classify the principal trading countries of the world as follows:

Balanced Economies	*Agricultural Economies*	*Industrial Economies*
United States	China	Great Britain
Canada	India	Switzerland
Australia	Other Asiatic Countries,	Belgium
Argentina	excluding Japan	Netherlands
New Zealand	Africa	Germany
	South America,	France
	excluding Argentina	Italy
		Japan

It is recognized, of course, that this classification of national economies is, like all broad generalizations, subject to numerous qualifications and specific exceptions.

Imperfectly Competitive Characteristics

Differences in relative factor endowments are relevant in explaining competitive trade but less so as an explanation of imperfectly competitive trade. As an earlier discussion showed (see Chapter 5), the latter is importantly influenced by internal economies of scale, product differentiation, and technological gaps.

Internal Economies of Scale. Two questions arise in attempting to determine the empirical importance of economies of scale as a basis for trade. The first is to what extent such economies are realized in various industries; the second is what determines the location of those industries subject to significant economies of scale.

Concerning the extent to which economies of scale are present, the most important observation is that different industries are apparently subject to widely different experience. One study, based on data for the United States, indicates very significant economies of scale for some industries, such as aircraft manufacture, and *negative* economies for others, such as textiles.[1]

Economies of scale would provide no special basis for trade if all countries were able equally to realize the economies potentially available. As explained in Chapter 5, however, the ability to exploit economies of scale depends upon the presence of a large enough market to absorb the resulting output. If each firm in every country had equal access to world markets no particular advantage would be enjoyed in this respect by the firms in any one country. But in reality market imperfections and artificial barriers (such as tariffs) usually discriminate against foreign suppliers in domestic markets. As a consequence, the size of domestic markets in a country may serve to limit the ability of local firms to capture economies of scale. This implies that countries with large domestic markets will tend to have an advantage over those with small domestic markets in those industries subject to significant economies of scale.

To the extent that the size of domestic markets—as measured in terms of population and per capita income—determine comparative advantage positions in industries subject to significant economies of scale, it is clear that the very large disparities in the size of national markets provide an important empirical basis for trade.

Product Differentiation. As we learned in Chapter 5, the differentiation of products also provides a basis for trade, quite different from that relevant to standardized products. The more extensively products are differentiated, the more important is this characteristic in explaining the pattern of trade.

It is evident that product differentiation varies considerably among different types of goods. In general, primary products, such as unprocessed foodstuffs and raw materials, tend to be standardized, while manufactured goods typically are differentiated in varying

---

[1] See G. C. Hufbauer, "The Impact of National Characteristics and Technology on the Commodity Composition of Trade in Manufactured Goods," *The Technology Factor in International Trade*, Ed. Raymond Vernon (New York: National Bureau of Economic Research, 1970) , table A-2, pp. 212–20.

degrees. More sophisticated types of manufactured goods probably tend to be more highly differentiated than simpler kinds of articles. Thus, according to one calculation, instruments, photographic goods, watches, machinery and appliances, and medicinal and pharmaceutical products are highly differentiated, while textile yarns and threads, cotton fabrics, processed foods, and cosmetics are examples of products with low degrees of differentiation.[2]

The most reasonable hypothesis, supported by empirical studies, is that the extent of product differentiation is related to the level of real per capita income. High per capita income levels are associated with potential market demand for different varieties of goods, as well as with the presence of the technological know-how and the skilled technicians required to produce them. It is not surprising, therefore, to find that the richer, industrialized countries are the principal sources of the more sophisticated differentiated products.

Technological Gaps. Finally, the last element entering into imperfectly competitive trade is the existence of technological gaps, giving innovative firms a monopoly, even though frequently temporary, of newly developed products.

Technological advances are principally a function of research, combined with the availability of the technical personnel and other resources required to apply the fruits of research to production. It is reasonable to suppose, therefore, that international differences in the amount of research and development (R & D) effort and in the availability of scientists, engineers and other technical personnel would lead to technological-gap trade. Empirical studies confirm this hypothesis.[3]

It is to be expected, of course, that the ingredients of technological innovation are not equally distributed among countries. The more highly developed and wealthier countries naturally tend to be in the most favorable position. Thus, in a study made of the importance of eight technologically intensive exports as compared to the exports of sixteen other manufactured products for ten countries in 1964, the United States ranked first, while Brazil was at the bottom; in between, the United Kingdom, West Germany, and France ranked

---

[2] G. C. Hufbauer, "The Impact of National Characteristics and Technology," pp. 212–20.

[3] See William Gruber, Dileep Mehta, and Raymond Vernon, "The R & D Factor in International Trade and Investment of United States Industries," and D. B. Keesing, "The Impact of Research and Development on United States Trade," both in the *Journal of Political Economy*, February 1967.

closer to the top, whereas Japan, Canada, and Mexico were (in that order) closer to the bottom.[4]

Summary It is apparent from the above discussion that certain common threads run through the three characteristics of trade under imperfect competition. Economies of scale, product differentiation, and technological gaps all tend to be related to the degree of economic development and the size and per capita level of real income. The earlier observed concentration of trade in manufactured products among the developed, industrial countries of the world is obviously consistent with this relationship.

RECOMMENDED READINGS

For data on the volume, composition, and geographic pattern of trade, the following are the principal sources:

GENERAL AGREEMENT ON TARIFFS AND TRADE (GATT). *International Trade*. Geneva, Switzerland. Issued annually.

INTERNATIONAL MONETARY FUND, Washington, D.C. *International Financial Statistics*. Issued monthly.

———. *Direction of International Trade*.

ORGANIZATION FOR ECONOMIC COOPERATION AND DEVELOPMENT (OECD). *General Statistics*. Paris. Issued monthly.

———. *Overall Trade by Countries*. Paris. Issued monthly.

UNITED NATIONS, New York. *Commodity Trade Statistics*. Issued quarterly.

———. *Monthly Bulletin of Statistics*.

———. *Statistical Yearbook*.

———. *Yearbook of International Trade Statistics*.

UNITED STATES DEPARTMENT OF COMMERCE. *Statistical Abstract*. Issued annually.

———. *Survey of Current Business*. Issued monthly.

Other appropriate references for this chapter:

GRUBER, WILLIAM ET AL. "The R & D Factor in International Trade and International Investment of United States Industries," *Journal of Political Economy*, February 1967.

KEESING, DONALD B. "Labor Skills and Comparative Advantage," *American Economic Review*, May 1966.

---

[4] See William H. Gruber and Raymond Vernon, "The Technology Factor in a World Trade Matrix," *The Technology Factor in International Trade*, ed. Raymond Vernon (New York: National Bureau of Economic Research, 1970), table 2, p. 238.

————. "The Impact of Research and Development on United States Trade," *Journal of Political Economy*, February 1967.

U.S. TARIFF COMMISSION. *Competitiveness of U.S. Industries.* TC Publication 473. Washington, D.C., April 1972.

VERNON, RAYMOND, ED. *The Technology Factor in International Trade.* New York: National Bureau of Economic Research, 1970. Especially recommended in this volume is the contribution of Hufbauer, G. C., "The Impact of National Characteristics and Technology on the Commodity Composition of Trade in Manufactured Goods."

STUDY QUESTIONS

1. How do you explain the historical increase in the relative importance of trade in manufactured goods compared to that in foodstuffs and raw materials? What evidence is there that a reversal of this trend may be in the offing?

2. Why is international trade highly concentrated among developed market economies? Why is trade generally more important for market economies than for centrally planned economies?

3. Describe and assess the significance of the asymmetrical position in world trade of less developed countries.

4. Define the average propensity to import, and explain why it varies so greatly among countries.

5. In what respects is a wide variety of export products preferable to a more limited number?

6. What is the economic meaning of "land" as a factor of production?

7. Identify the characteristic of mineral and similar natural resource supplies which distinguishes them from other factor supplies.

8. Apply the Heckscher-Ohlin theorem to explain the shift of the United States from being a net exporter to a net importer of natural resource products.

9. Recall the distinction between material and "human" capital.

10. What proxies can reasonably be used to measure human capital?

11. How does the capital-labor ratio of a country help determine whether it is an agricultural or industrial society?

12. Describe the various combinations of land, labor, and capital which underlie the classification of economies as balanced, agricultural, or industrial.

13. Why are relative factor endowments mainly relevant in explaining competitive trade, less so in explaining imperfectly competitive trade?

14. Recall the meaning of internal economies of scale.
15. How does the size of national economies affect their ability to realize economies of scale?
16. Consider which of the imported goods you purchase are significantly differentiated from similar domestic goods.
17. Why is the extent of product differentiation probably greater in the United States than it is in Mexico?
18. What is meant by "technological-gap" trade?
19. What are among the principal determinants of technological innovations?
20. How does the level of real per capita income affect the ingredients of imperfectly competitive trade?

7

The theory of international factor movements

The substantive content of international economic relations consists of (*a*) the exchange of goods and services among countries, and (*b*) the international movement of the factors of production. While (*a*) refers to the movement of the *products* of factors, (*b*) relates to the movement of the factors themselves.

The theory of trade addresses itself to the causes and effects of trade in goods and services and was the subject of Chapters 2 through 5. The theory of trade is built on the assumption that productive factors are perfectly *immobile internationally, though perfectly mobile within each trading country*. The purpose of this assumption is not to describe the real world, where factors have some degree of mobility internationally and some degree of immobility intranationally, but rather to isolate for analytical study the pure theory of trade in a setting free of extraneous influences.

In the present chapter, our primary focus of interest is the causes and effects of international factor movements. As in the pure trade model, certain assumptions will be made for the purpose of distilling from the complicated set of real-world influences on factor movements the essential and central forces of an economic character. Chief among these assumptions are the absence of artificial barriers or restraints on factor movements and the operation of strictly economic motives.

THE MEANING OF FACTOR MOVEMENTS

Before attempting to discover the reasons for and consequences of international factor movements, it is necessary to identify what they are. As far as the movement of labor is concerned, it is self-evident that reference is made to the migration of persons from one country to another as places of more or less permanent residence and of employment. Temporary changes in residence for tourist travel, study, and so on, are therefore not included.

The definition of international capital movements is not so simple. It is important to remember that capital, as a factor of production, refers to the stock of reproducible goods useful in helping to produce other goods and services. In concrete, physical terms, the capital stock of a country consists of its railroads, highways, harbor installations, power plants, dams, buildings, industrial and agricultural machinery and tools, inventory of raw materials, and so on.[1] But an international capital movement does *not* consist of the transfer of specific capital goods from one country to another, though the transfer of capital goods may accompany a capital movement. Rather, an international capital movement means, in the first instance, and as recorded statistically, the movement from one country to another—or, more accurately, from individuals, businesses, or institutions in one country to those in another country—of *money capital* or loan funds. It is bonds, stocks, and other evidences of debt or ownership which are dealt with in domestic and international capital markets. Specific capital goods, like all other goods, are dealt with in the commodity markets, and they are recorded in commodity trade statistics.

Our immediate interest at the moment, however, is the international allocation of *real* capital—that is, of concrete instruments of production. The question, then, is: what is the connection between international monetary capital movements and the distribution of the supply of real capital? The answer is to be found in the nature of the process of real capital accumulation.

---

1 "Human capital" may also be regarded as a component of a country's stock of capital, as we concluded in previous discussions. However, human capital is embodied in persons and obviously cannot be transferred internationally separately from the migration of persons. The significance of this will be discussed below.

In order for any country or region within a country to acquire a larger stock of capital goods, it must have available a current flow of goods and services in excess of its current consumption of goods and services. One method of accumulating capital, therefore, is to *save* (that is, not consume) some portion of the national income or current aggregate net production of goods and services. This is the normal and by far the more important source of real capital formation. But in countries that are meagerly endowed with capital and land per head of population, the ability to save is severely limited by the low level of per capita income and the desire to consume a very high proportion of all that is currently produced.

Fortunately, there is a second method by which a country may increase its domestic stock of real capital. With a given level of national income, the domestic stock of capital goods can be increased without further reducing current consumption, provided that an *import surplus* of goods and services from abroad can be developed. Moreover, the import surplus need not consist of capital goods. Even if only consumer goods are imported, the import surplus permits a diversion of domestic productive agents from consumer goods production to capital goods production.

But how can a country develop an import surplus—especially for a long enough period to allow a significant increase in its stock of real capital? In previous chapters we assumed that the only method of paying for imports was with exports. Now, however, we are dropping this artificial assumption and admitting the existence of international transactions in evidences of debt—that is, of international monetary capital movements. We must now also admit, therefore, that a country may develop an import surplus of goods and services, provided that individuals, businesses, or institutions (including governments) in other countries are willing to lend or give the means of paying for such a surplus. As far as private individuals and businesses are concerned, the willingness to lend abroad depends upon their expectation that the rate of financial return will be greater there than at home. More specifically, is the rate of interest obtainable abroad greater than that offered in the domestic market on securities of similar kinds and degree of risk? If so, there is an incentive to purchase foreign securities or to make what is called a *portfolio* investment. Or is the rate of profits earned by concerns abroad higher than that earned in similar businesses at home? If so, there is an incentive to acquire ownership shares in the foreign concerns or to form a company in that country—that is, to make a *direct invest-*

ment.[2] In either of these two cases—portfolio or direct foreign investments—the receiving country obtains the financial means of paying for an import surplus and increasing its domestic stock of capital.

Apart from private loans and investments from abroad, a country may be enabled to acquire an import surplus by receiving loans or grants from foreign governments or other public institutions. In this case, the *motives* for the capital transfer are likely to be different from those of private lenders and investors, but the result is the same as far as permitting an increase in the domestic stock of capital in the receiving country is concerned. In short, an international monetary capital movement provides the means by which the receiving country can increase its domestic stock of real capital. In effect, a money capital movement constitutes a transfer of purchasing power, which, in turn, permits the receiving country to develop an import surplus. It is the latter which constitutes the *real* capital movement; indeed, as we shall see in a subsequent chapter, the net movement of goods and services is the only way in which a net monetary capital movement can, in fact, occur. The *mechanism* by which a monetary capital flow is transformed into a real capital movement is a difficult subject in itself and will be taken up in a later chapter.

Finally, there is one very important consideration entering into capital movements not found in the case of population movements. A monetary capital inflow into a country, except for grants or gifts, ordinarily carries with it an obligation of repayment at some later date and of interest payment in the interim.[3] Just as a real capital inflow can take place only in the form of a net import surplus of goods and services, so, also, capital *repayment* can be made only in the form of an *export* surplus of goods and services. This raises numerous problems, some of which we shall consider later in other contexts; but at the moment we are interested in its implications from the standpoint of capital supply. How can a capital inflow con-

---

2 Although, in general "portfolio investments" refer to fixed-interest securities or bond capital and "direct investments" to equity or share capital, the technical distinction is somewhat sharper than this. "Direct investments" refer to equity shares in foreign concerns in sufficient amount to give an important voice in their management, and the direct branches of domestic companies. Once a foreign enterprise is defined as a direct-investment company, however, all private investments in the securities of that company by nationals of the investing country are considered to be part of the direct investment. Portfolio investments consist of holdings of foreign stocks, bonds, real estate, etc., which do not constitute an important voice in the management of an enterprise but are held primarily as a source of income.

3 In the case of investments in the form of equity shares, however, there is no problem of fixed principal or interest payments, but foreign holders expect to receive any profits due them.

tribute to a permanent increase in the stock of domestic capital if, later on, an export surplus must be developed to repay the loans received or to liquidate the equity interests of foreigners?

The same question can be raised about the capital expansion of an individual business, financed by floating a loan or stock issue domestically, and essentially the same answer is applicable in both cases. Real capital contributes to the production of goods and services a *net* amount over and above its cost. More specifically, the use of capital involves a more roundabout and efficient method of production that raises output sufficiently not only to repay the cost of the capital but with a surplus left over. Just as an individual business concern may be able, therefore, to increase its *net* assets and income by borrowing, so a country as a whole may add to its net stock of capital and flow of real income by borrowing internationally.

ECONOMIC MOTIVES FOR FACTOR MOVEMENTS

The economic motive for workers to migrate from their homeland to a foreign country is to improve their standard of living. For most workers, the standard of living is primarily a function of real wage rates. Hence, higher real wage rates abroad than at home are a major inducement to migrate. The parallel between this reason for international labor movements and the reason for international trade should be noted: in both cases, it is international price differences which are the immediate motivating force. Just as differences in commodity prices lead to trade, so differences in wage rates—the "price" of labor services—tend to induce labor movements.

Capital movements are also induced by international differences in expected rates of return. Loan capital tends to move to countries where interest rates are higher than domestically, appropriate account being taken of any differential degree of risk. Investment, or equity, capital likewise seeks areas of maximum expected rates of return for a given degree of risk.

FACTOR SUPPLIES AND FACTOR RETURNS IN COMPETITIVE MARKETS

The immediate reasons for factor movements appear to be obvious enough, but of greater interest is what accounts for international differences in wage rates and the return on capital. In seeking an explanation, let us first assume the presence of competitive goods and factor markets. The influence of imperfectly competitive markets will be examined later.

In competitive markets, the price of a factor service tends to be equal to the value of the marginal product of the factor. Wage rates higher in the United States than elsewhere indicate that the marginal productivity of labor is greater in the United States than in other countries. In a similar manner, if the rate of return on capital investment is lower in the United States than in other countries, it can be presumed that the marginal productivity of capital is lower in the United States.

If international differences in factor prices and rates of return are the consequence of differences in the marginal productivity of the factors, the next question is, what is responsible for the latter?

The marginal productivity of factors is influenced by a variety of things. The state of technology and the production function are major influences. So, too, is the pattern of demand. However, if we adopt the assumptions earlier accepted for the Heckscher-Ohlin model of trade, the state of technology, production functions, and the pattern of demand do not significantly differ among countries, hence cannot explain international differences in marginal productivities. This leaves as the major determinant of differences in the marginal productivity of factors *differences in relative factor endowments.*

That relative factor supplies exert a powerful influence on factor productivities is one of the central propositions of economic theory. Other things being equal, the greater the quantity of any factor working with given amounts of other factors, the lower tends to be the marginal productivity of that factor. The principle involved here is that of variable proportions or diminishing returns—one of the oldest "laws" of economics. In a relatively capital-rich, labor-scarce country, the rate of return on capital tends to be lower and the wage rate higher than in labor-abundant, capital-scarce countries.

From these relationships there emerges the following hypothesis: relatively capital-abundant, labor-scarce countries tend to experience a capital outflow and labor immigration; relatively labor-abundant, capital-scarce countries tend to experience labor emigration and to attract an inflow of capital.

The reader will observe at once that, according to the above hypothesis, the underlying cause of factor movements is precisely the same as the underlying basis of international trade as explained by the Heckscher-Ohlin theorem. Given the conditions postulated by the Heckscher-Ohlin theorem—competitive markets, given state of technology, identical production functions internationally, nonreversal of factor intensities, similar patterns of demand—*international trade and international factor movements are each the result of differences in relative factor endowments.*

Moreover, not surprisingly, there is an exact parallelism between the pattern of trade predicted by the Heckscher-Ohlin theorem and the pattern of factor movements. A labor-scarce, capital-abundant country, such as the United States, tends not only to specialize in and export commodities requiring large amounts of capital and small amounts of labor but also to attract immigrants and to export capital. A capital-scarce, labor-abundant country, like India, tends not only to specialize in and export labor-intensive products but also, in the absence of artificial barriers and noneconomic considerations to the contrary, to "lose" labor through emigration and attract capital from abroad.[4] This statement must be qualified, however, to take into account the effects of transfer costs. We noted earlier that the costs of transporting commodities in many cases make trade in them uneconomic. So, too, costs of factor movements may outweigh in particular cases the advantages of movement. Transfer costs are likely to be especially important in the movement of labor. The money required merely for rail and ship fare can alone be a formidable obstacle to the emigration of a poor family to a distant land. Nevertheless, the tens of millions of persons who have emigrated to other lands in the course of history are witness to the fact that the opportunities for *net* gain (after deducting transfer costs) have not been lacking.

A word of caution is now in order. We earlier noted that for the Heckscher-Ohlin theory of trade to hold, the assumptions on which it is built must be valid. Similar caveats must be introduced for the theory of factor movements as stated above. In order for the cause of international factor price differences to be assigned to differences in relative factor endowments, a major assumption is necessary: that supply conditions are of dominating importance. Conceivably, the

---

[4] The conclusion that India would tend in a free market to attract foreign capital must be modified additionally by the fact that relative scarcity is not the only determinant of the marginal productivity of a factor of production. The general social and political atmosphere and the economies of scale are, among others, elements that help determine the marginal productivity of any factor. Hence, the return on capital in India might not be as attractive to foreigners as its relative scarcity alone would indicate. This does not, however, reduce the economic motive for Indians to emigrate.

demand for a factor service in relatively abundant supply may be so great as to cause its price to be relatively high. This is equivalent to the conclusion reached in our discussion of the Heckscher-Ohlin theory of trade that relative factor abundance need not necessarily be associated with a relatively low price of the factor.

A more general theory of factor price differences, therefore, is that they are caused by differences in relative factor supplies in relation to relative factor demands. The assignment of dominating influence to the supply side is a special case of the general theory, with the pattern of demand for goods—and thence the factors producing the goods—being not significantly different internationally.

THE ECONOMIC EFFECTS OF FACTOR MOVEMENTS

In Chapter 4 we investigated the effects of free international trade on the level of the world's and of each participating country's real income. A similar inquiry for factor movements is now in order.

The Level of World Income

Free international trade, we have concluded, increases the efficiency of world production and increases the level of real income. So, too, do free international factor movements induced by economic considerations. If labor and capital move from areas where the net value of their marginal products (and, therefore, their prices) are lower to where they are higher, more is added to world output than is destroyed. For example, suppose that a given type of labor service commands a wage of $15 per day in the United States and the equivalent of only $3 per day in Italy. Then, as one such laborer emigrates to the United States, output rises by $15 per day in the United States and falls by $3 per day in Italy; net gain in world output: $12 per day (ignoring transfer costs). Of course, as Italian labor continues to emigrate to the United States, its marginal productivity would tend to rise in Italy and fall in the United States. But, so long as the marginal productivity of labor remained greater in the United States than in Italy, there would continue to be both an economic motive for continued emigration and a net gain in world output. If the marginal productivity were to become equal in the two countries (a point to be considered shortly), then both the motive for further emigration and the possibility of further gain in world output would be eliminated.

The same analysis applies to capital. World output is increased if capital moves out of the United States, where its marginal productivity is relatively low, to capital-scarce countries, where its marginal productivity is higher.

The Level of National Income

We have shown that there is an unequivocal economic gain to the world as a whole realizable through both free international trade and free international factor movements. From a cosmopolitan point of view, then, the case for free and unimpeded international economic relations is unexceptional.

But all of us, even those sophisticates who regard themselves as "citizens of the world," are identified first as nationals of a particular country. International economic *policies* are formulated by each national state, for the most part with its own *national* interests in mind. In a world organized in this fashion, the effects of trade and factor movements on the national economy of each participating country have more relevance to attitudes and policies than do the effects on the world economy as a whole.

Now we have already shown, in Chapter 4, that free trade leads to a greater real national income for each participating country than it could produce in isolation. Can the same thing be said of international factor movements? Would free movement of labor from labor-abundant to labor-scarce countries and of capital from capital-abundant to capital-scarce countries enlarge the real national incomes of both the sending and the receiving countries?

Let us first consider labor movements and construct a case where the answer has the greatest chance of being affirmative. Suppose that there are two countries, one of which has a population below the optimum and the other with a population far above the optimum. As concrete contemporary examples, we might take Canada as the country with below-optimum population and India as the country with above-optimum population.

Now an increase in the labor supply of Canada—provided that it were not excessive for any given period of time—would in all probability increase the real national income of Canada by an amount *proportionately greater* than the increase in the number of workers. The economic reasons for expecting this result lie in the advantages to be gained from greater specialization and division of labor and perhaps also from the economies of scale permitted by a larger market. In this case, *all* factor owners—labor as well as property holders—would tend to gain from the immigration.

At the same time, average per capita real income in India would tend to be higher after than before the emigration, since the per capita supply of land and capital would be raised. However, whether the remaining (nonemigrating) population would be better off depends upon circumstances. If there were unemployment or under-employed before the migration for lack of land or capital with which to work or if the net marginal productivity of the emigrating workers were zero in India,[5] the population remaining after emigration would undoubtedly be better off on the average. However, emigration might leave the home population worse off than before. This would be the case, for example, if the emigrants were the higher skilled or better educated workers whose productivity was considerably above those remaining behind. Note that in this case it is not "pure" labor alone that migrates but labor together with capital. It will be recalled from an earlier discussion (see pp. 51–52, above) that "human capital," embodied in persons in the form of education and training, properly belongs to capital as a factor category, with labor as a factor category defined in terms simply of labor time. Nearly all persons embody some amount of human capital, so that the migration of persons involves the movement of both labor and capital.

Moreover, there is perhaps a general tendency for permanent migrants (as opposed to temporary or seasonal migrants) to possess an above-average level of education and training. Awareness of opportunities in foreign lands, the degree of adaptability to foreign cultures, and the financial resources needed to move are all likely to be associated with better educated and trained persons. The phenomenon of the so-called "Brain Drain," referring to the migration to the more highly developed countries of scientists, engineers and other educated persons, is a recently well-publicized example. In addition to the loss of human capital in the countries from which such emigration occurs, frequently there is also a loss of material capital in the form of accumulated wealth the emigrants own and transfer to their new place of residence.

From the above discussion we would have to conclude that, although immigrant countries with a suboptimum population tend

---

[5] It has been observed that in some underdeveloped economies, agricultural workers may have a zero marginal product, indicating a redundant supply of labor. In such cases, the wage paid tends to be at or near a subsistence level but above, of course, the marginal product of the labor.

to gain from an inflow of migrants, the effects on the remaining population of emigrant countries may or may not be positive, depending upon particular circumstances. Uncertainty as to the welfare effects of labor movements extends to immigrant as well as emigrant countries when the former already have an optimum or above-optimum population. As an example, consider England, instead of Canada, as an immigrant country. In contrast to Canada, it is fairly clear that England is not underpopulated. Whether or not England is actually overpopulated is a debatable point, but let us assume for the sake of argument that her population is just about at the optimum. Hence, any increase in England's population from the immigration of Indians would result in an above-optimum population. In other words, with the supply of land and capital and the state of technology remaining unchanged, the larger population in England would reduce *per capita* output, even though the aggregate national income would presumably be larger. How, then, can it be said that the movement of labor provides the basis for an improvement in the economic welfare of the immigrant country?

Assuming that competition prevails in the immigrant country, the immigrant workers (as well as native labor) will receive a wage equal to the value of their marginal product. Now it is clear that if the immigrants receive only the value of what they *add* to production (their marginal product), natives will have no less real income available to them than before the immigration took place. Indeed, actually the native population as a whole will have a *larger* per capita real income available, *provided that the immigrant labor is economically discriminated against.*[6] The reason for this result is as follows: as immigration continues to force down the marginal productivity of labor, the total wages received by the immigrants will be less than their total contribution to the national income, with a "surplus" thus being made available for distribution to the native population.

For example, suppose that the value of the marginal product of the first immigrant in his new home is $15 per day. The arrival of a second immigrant reduces the value of labor's marginal product to, say, $14, and the third immigrant reduces it to $13. After three immigrants have arrived, then, each receives a wage of $13 (the value of his marginal product), or a total of $39 in wages. But the

---

[6] See Abba P. Lerner, *The Economics of Control* (New York: Macmillan Co., 1944), pp. 364–65.

national income of the country has increased by $15 plus $14 plus $13, or a total of $42. Hence there is $3 "surplus" available for distribution to the native population. In order, however, for native labor to be at least as well off as before, income received by it would have to be greater than the value of its marginal product—for its marginal product declines at the same time that the immigrants' marginal product declines. This is where discrimination between native and immigrant labor comes into the picture. Now, of course, the immigrants, even though receiving less income per head than the native population, would presumably still have a higher income than in their own country. Hence, *everyone,* native as well as immigrants, could have his economic welfare improved through the population movement. On *social* grounds, however, there might be very strong objections to discriminating in this fashion, and this is perhaps the most important "practical" economic argument against immigration under the circumstances described.

Let us now briefly consider the national economic effects of capital movements. An inflow of capital into capital-poor countries will tend to increase the per capita productivity of the receiving country. It is true, of course, that the national wealth is not increased by the full amount of the capital inflow, for the country has at the same time acquired an external debt. But, as we have argued earlier, capital may produce a surplus over and above its costs, so that, after the loan is repaid, there remains a net gain in the capital wealth of the borrowing country. Presumably, then—barring the dissipation of the loan proceeds in added consumption or uneconomic investments— the capital-receiving country will have its real per capita income increased.

Turning to the lending country, the outflow of capital reduces the domestic supply of capital and therefore tends to reduce the per capita domestic productivity of the population. But note that the capital exported is not lost to the economy. Rather, the locus of its investment has changed—from lower return to higher return uses. Suppose, for example, that capital investments in the United States yield a marginal rate of return of 5 percent, while similar risk investments in Mexico yield a marginal rate of return of 10 percent. The flow of capital from the United States to Mexico, then, will yield a larger return to the American economy (in the form of imports paid for with the interest earnings) than if the capital had been invested within the United States. The per capita output of the American economy—from domestic production and the return on investments abroad combined—will be larger as the result of the capital out-flow.

Factor Price Equalization

It was shown in Chapter 4 that free and competitive trade tends to reduce international differences in factor prices. A still stronger tendency in this direction is exerted by factor movements. Whereas trade affects factor prices indirectly through the repercussions produced by the reallocation of resources, factor movements affect factor prices directly through changing factor supplies. A movement of labor from low-wage areas to high-wage areas increases the supply of labor in the immigrant country and reduces it in the emigrant country; in a like manner, capital movements increase the supply of capital in the receiving countries and reduce it in the sending countries. To the extent that the marginal productivity and price of a factor depends upon its supply in relationship to the supplies of other factors, the result of factor movements is clearly in the direction of eliminating factor price differences. Even so, there are possible exceptions. One exception was cited earlier: an immigrant country with a suboptimum population. A similar exception applies if both labor and capital move jointly in the same direction toward a country abundantly supplied with land, as discussed below. Nevertheless, the presumption remains strong in the general case that factor movements reduce factor price differences.

The impact of factor movements on factor prices is naturally accompanied by redistribution of the national income. The share in the national income of the relatively highest priced factor tends to be reduced, the share of the relatively lowest priced factor increased. This tendency results, of course, from the effects of factor movements on relative factor supplies.

FACTOR MOVEMENTS AND TRADE AS SUBSTITUTES

From our survey of the many respects in which trade and factor movements are parallel in their causes and effects, it is reasonable to suppose that these two components of international economic relations are to some extent substitutes for each other. The greater the volume of trade under the conditions posited by the Heckscher-Ohlin theory, the lesser will be the differences in international factor prices and the motives for factor migration. The greater the movement of factors internationally, the smaller tend to be the differences in comparative costs and the reasons for trade.

Actually, however, neither factor movements nor trade can entirely eliminate the function of the other. To begin with, factors are not, and cannot be, perfectly mobile. The degree of mobility of resources varies tremendously. At one end of the scale, there are those resources which are inherently incapable of movement. Into this category fall land, including climate, mineral deposits, water power, and location. At the opposite extreme is the high sensitivity and mobility of money capital, at least when there is a well-organized international capital market and an appropriate atmosphere prevails. Indeed, capital in general, whether in its monetary form or in real terms, is capable of movement and historically has played a tremendously important role in the creation of a world economy.

The obstacles to the movement of capital are not inherent, therefore, but are rather of an institutional and psychological character. In a world divided into numerous independent national states, each of which has sovereign authority over its own peoples and territory, there is always an additional element of risk and uncertainty in investing capital in a foreign country. In the latter part of the 19th century, these risks and uncertainties were reduced to a minimum because of the institutional framework which then prevailed, and consequently large international movements of capital occurred. In later years and particularly since the early 1930s, however, political uncertainty and divergent and sometimes discriminatory national economic and financial controls have rendered foreign investment a risky business, not to be undertaken without the prospects of a very high return.

In between the complete immobility of land and the potentially great mobility of capital lie human productive agents. Physically, labor is, of course, easily capable of international migration. Even more than in the case of capital, however, the actual international movement of labor is restricted by institutional and psychological barriers. To consider the latter first, there are the ties that bind individuals and families to their homeland: language, customs, habits, friends and relatives, and the whole array of sentiments and emotions subsumed under the name of "nationalism." Nevertheless, the history of international migration demonstrates that while these factors may limit the movement of human beings, they do not prevent them. If the atmosphere is propitious and the motives strong, labor *will* move, although noneconomic motives may in some cases be more important than economic reasons.

Whatever might be the natural tendencies, institutional restrictions, as in recent years, can reduce migration to a mere trickle. Immigration laws, exclusion acts, work permits, and numerous other devices have been invented to reduce, or in some cases eliminate, the possibility of moving to another country.

Since movements of factors do not, in fact, eliminate differences in their relative scarcities in different countries, international trade has a continuing basis as a substitute for factor movements. The steamy jungles required for natural rubber production cannot be transferred to the temperate zones; nor can the soil and climate required for wheat be moved to tropical regions. But natural rubber and wheat can be exchanged for each other in international trade. Similarly, immigration laws may prevent Indian labor from moving into the United States, and the institutions and sociopolitical environment of India discourage American capital from flowing to India, but American tractors can be exchanged for Indian jute.

Just as, in practice, factor movements do not eliminate the function of international trade, neither does trade entirely remove the basis for factor movements. For this to happen, trade would have to result in factor price equalization. But, as we noted much earlier, the conditions necessary for such an effect are so stringent as to be virtually impossible of fulfillment in the real world.[7] Again, then, we reiterate that there is a continuing economic basis for both factor movements and trade.

COMPLEMENTARY ASPECTS OF TRADE AND FACTOR MOVEMENTS

We have concluded that trade and factor movements are substitutes for each other, but only partially so. Rather than regard trade and factor movements as mutually exclusive phenomena, each may be looked upon as performing functions not achievable, or not so easily achievable, by the other. Indeed, we may go further and indicate some important respects in which trade and factor movements are complementary rather than substitutive.

Factor movements, for example, even though they reduce the

---

[7] One of the required conditions, for example, is that transport costs be zero, so that a given good has an identical price in all countries. Needless to say, zero transport costs do not exist.

disparities in relative costs and thereby reduce the opportunities for profitable trade that existed before, themselves create new fields of trade. This is perhaps best seen in the case of long-term capital flows.

Take a capital-poor country that receives long-term loans from abroad which are used, for example, to aid in the industrialization of the country. Some manufactured goods (such as textiles) which were formerly imported may now be produced as cheaply at home as abroad and therefore no longer be imported. But, as per capita real income grows in the country, the volume and composition of consumption changes, creating new demands for a wide variety of goods and services, both domestic and imported. The *composition* of trade is likely to change and the volume of trade to grow. This has been, in fact, the experience of countries that have industrialized.

By an analogous line of reasoning, it is probably true that international trade actually encourages international capital movements, notwithstanding the fact that trade reduces inequalities in the returns received by capital in different countries. In the first place, it must be remembered that capital is capable of movement, in the final analysis, only in the form of goods and services. Trading relations are, then, a necessary accompaniment of international lending and borrowing. Beyond this, however, international trade, by broadening markets and stimulating more efficient use of resources, creates investment opportunities, attractive to foreign as well as domestic investors. Indeed, in the history of long-term capital movements it has most often been the presence, or potential development, of *international* markets that has stimulated foreign investments. Moreover, a high volume of trade is more likely to be accompanied by well-developed financial facilities and institutions and by some degree of stability in political and economic relations, which reduce the risks and uncertainties of foreign loans and investments and encourage a greater flow of capital.

THE COORDINATE MOVEMENT OF CAPITAL AND LABOR

Just as commodity trade and factor movements are, in practice, often complementary, so also may the movements of different factors be complementary under certain circumstances. Suppose, for example, that some countries are well supplied with both labor and capital, compared to others that have a great abundance of land but small amounts of labor and capital. Under such circumstances, there might be a tendency for both labor and capital to move to the relatively land-abundant region. This is well illustrated historically by the mass migrations of peoples from Europe to the Western Hemisphere in the 19th century and the accompanying flow of capital.

In such coordinate movements of capital and labor, each tends to reinforce and encourage the other. Immigration into a lightly populated area enlarges the market, creates additional demand, and opens up new opportunities for capital investment. Likewise, the inflow of capital creates new employment opportunities, raises real wages, and increases the attractiveness of the area to those living in land-scarce countries. Furthermore, capital cannot be separated from the knowledge and skills required to use it. The development of industries in young countries is often dependent, therefore, not only upon the inflow of capital from wealthier and more mature countries but upon the importation of know-how and technology as well. The combined movement of both capital and individuals to the United States in its earlier history and up to, roughly, World War I, for example, gave an incalculable impetus to the rapid growth in the income and wealth of the United States.

FACTOR MOVEMENTS AND WELFARE

In considering the welfare aspects of trade in Chapter 4, we observed that some segments of a population are likely to be harmed while others gain. The same holds for factor movements. As already noted, the income share of high-priced factors tends to shrink as the result of factor movements. The clearest-cut example is the share of labor in a high-wage country which is at or above the optimum level of population prior to immigration, as cited above.

In such cases of conflicts of interest, we may appeal to the welfare principle adduced earlier in connection with the welfare argument for trade. Since everyone *could* be made better off by factor movements, the potential welfare at least is advanced. In this connection two points deserve emphasis. The first is the tremendous magnitude of the potential economic benefits to the world as a whole and to each country realizable from unimpeded trade and factor movements. The second is that the problem of distributing the gains realized should not be exaggerated. As noted earlier, virtually all economic progress is accompanied by distributional effects. From a welfare point of view, it would not make good sense to forgo the advantages of trade and factor movements in order to avoid changes in income distribution, in view of the fact that machinery for controlling distribution exists and can be put into operation. This does not, of course, deny that there may be valid social, political, or other noneconomic values or objectives that, in cases of conflict with economic goals, may take precedence.

THE DYNAMICS OF FACTOR MOVEMENTS: THE MULTINATIONAL CORPORATION

In the preceding discussion, the motives for and effects of international factor movements were analyzed in a static, competitive framework, with assumed conditions equivalent to those postulated in the Heckscher-Ohlin theorem of international trade. This approach is attractive, providing a simple explanation of factor movements that is an extension of the Heckscher-Ohlin theorem of trade. To the extent that relative factor endowments determine the pattern of trade, in accordance with the Heckscher-Ohlin theorem, to the same extent relative factor endowments determine the pattern of international factor movements.

However, it will be remembered that we found it necessary to supplement the Heckscher-Ohlin theorem of trade in order to explain trade occurring under conditions falling outside its framework. In particular, it was noted that a great amount of trade is in response to changes in technology and the development of new products, for the most part in the context of imperfectly competitive market structures. Correspondingly, to explain certain observed factor movements it is necessary to go beyond the simple theory applicable to a static, competitive world and introduce additional explanatory variables related to dynamic changes and usually imperfectly competitive markets. We shall confine the discussion to the outstanding contemporary example of a factor movement best explained in these terms—namely, the foreign operations of multinational corporations.

A multinational corporation (MNC) may be loosely defined for our purposes as an enterprise having a "home" base in one country, together with related facilities in other countries. Typically, an MNC consists of the parent company and wholly or partially owned subsidiaries located abroad. Some specific examples will be cited in the next chapter.

It is to be observed that a firm's acquisition of foreign subsidiaries represents a capital outflow of the type earlier classified as a "direct investment." In contrast to "portfolio investments," in which no control over the operations of foreign firms is involved, direct investments entail the management of foreign operations. In other words, direct investments involve an internationalization of management and entrepreneurship as well as of capital. Indeed, the amount of actual capital movement accompanying a direct foreign investment may be negligible. Such is the case when the acquisition of foreign facilities is financed through borrowing in the local market. (In this example, the capital outflow represented by the direct investment is accompanied by a capital inflow into the investing country, represented by the receipt of foreign loans, leaving only the difference, if any, as the *net* capital movement.)

The distinction between portfolio and direct investments gives an important clue to the special nature of multinational corporations. For one thing, it suggests that MNCs are motivated to extend their operations abroad not simply, or perhaps even significantly, because of a relative scarcity of capital in foreign countries, which, in our earlier competitive model, served as the underlying basis for capital outflows. This contention is supported by the not uncommon practice, alluded to above, of multinational firms of borrowing in local markets a substantial portion of the funds invested abroad. What, then, is the basis for MNCs to set up foreign operations?

The general answer to this question seems obvious: to take advantage of perceived opportunities to make profits—that is, a return on investment over and above the interest cost of the financial resources used. (In this sense, profits may be regarded as the reward for entrepreneurship, including risk-taking.) Moreover, expected profits from foreign direct investments must ordinarily be greater than those expected from an equivalent investment at home, for there are extra risks and costs of foreign investment as compared to home investments. Operating in a foreign culture, with unfamiliar institutions and practices, and subject to the jurisdiction of the foreign as well as home governments, a firm inevitably incurs extra costs and risks.

Given these barriers to foreign direct investments, what induces firms nevertheless to undertake them? Evidently, the multinational corporation must expect to enjoy some special advantage from its overseas activities. Note, however, that there must be an advantage not only as compared to home investment but also as compared to the domestic firms in the same industry located in the foreign country. Other things being equal, a foreign firm is at a disadvantage as compared to domestic firms. The disadvantage arises from the special costs and risks attached to foreign operations, as mentioned above. This suggests that if purely competitive markets exist, a foreign firm would not be able to compete with domestic firms. Hence, the "edge" a multinational corporation has over domestic firms in a foreign country must be attributable to some kind of market imperfection.

Perhaps the most important and common example of a market imperfection giving the multinational firm an advantage over domestic firms is the possession of monopolistic control over products or processes. The source of this control may be varied. An obvious case is the development of a new product or improved variety of an existing product as the result of a technological breakthrough. If the process is patented or if the required technological knowledge is kept secret, the innovating firm clearly has an advantage over others. It will be observed that this is precisely the case earlier described as the basis of "technological-gap" trade. Direct foreign investment to exploit a technological advantage is simply an extension of technological-gap trade. It will be recalled that once a new product is developed for the home market, the innovating firm may seek to expand its market through export sales. However, a growing market for the product in foreign countries tends to induce domestic firms in those countries to undertake production of the good, leading to a "product cycle," in which the innovating country ends up as an importer. To prevent the erosion of its market from such foreign competition, the innovating firm may establish foreign production operations to serve both the local market and outside markets, including the home country. (A very significant fraction of United States imports are provided by foreign subsidiaries of United States multinational firms.)

Besides seeking to forestall foreign competition, a firm may be able to lower its costs of production through the establishment of foreign subsidiaries. For example, once the processes of producing a new commodity have become standardized, less skilled labor can often be substituted for more highly skilled labor, so that the relocation of production in lower-wage countries reduces costs. Again, however, since local firms also have access to the same lower factor prices, if the multinational is to survive in the local market it must have some sort of advantages not available to local firms. Besides patented processes or secret knowledge, these advantages may consist of easier and less costly access to financial resources, specialized management or marketing skills not locally available, economies of large-scale based on "learning-by-doing," etc.

It is evident from the above discussion that direct foreign investments are associated with imperfectly competitive markets. On the other hand, portfolio foreign investments, in which control over foreign firms is not involved, are the typical form of capital movements in competitive markets. This distinction suggests that, in the same manner that we found a parallel between trade and factor movements in the context of a static, competitive model, so, too, is there a parallel between trade and direct foreign investments in the context of dynamic and imperfectly competitive markets.

The Economic Effects of Direct Foreign Investment

There remains for discussion the economic effects of direct foreign investments, especially as these are undertaken by multinational corporations. (In addition to economic effects, there are social and political aspects of multinational firms which have an important bearing on public attitudes and policies and that will be discussed in the next chapter.)

It should be recognized at the outset that we are entering an area of uncertain analysis. Multinational enterprises, for the most part, are oligopolists, the behavior of which is less amenable to the kind of neat and definitive analysis that can be applied to competitive firms. Moreover, even when the behavior can be predicted with a fair degree of confidence, assessment of the welfare effects produced is difficult because of conflicting aspects of the behavior.

Looking first at the positive side and from a cosmopolitan point of view, multinational firms tend to bring about a greater degree of economic integration of national economies. The perspective of the multinational enterprise is global, and it accordingly tends to vault over or bypass national boundaries in its efforts to produce and market its products in the most profitable fashion possible. To the extent that nationalistic barriers and restrictions impede competitive trade and factor movements, thereby preventing the full realization of their potential benefits, MNCs may be regarded as a substitute, albeit perhaps a "second best" one, for the removal of the impediments to freer trade and factor movements. Indeed, some economists contend that direct foreign investments, by penetrating protected national markets, increase world economic efficiency and "offer the possibility . . . of equalizing factor prices, even in the face of the international barriers to the movement of capital and labor."[8]

---

[8] See Charles P. Kindleberger, "The Theory of Direct Investment," *American Business Abroad* (New Haven: Yale University Press, 1969), p. 35.

One of the characteristics of large, oligopolistic industries is the constant drive to achieve technological breakthroughs and to develop new products or variations of existing products. Multinational corporations, in an effort to exploit their advantages, undoubtedly hasten the spread around the world of such product innovations. Perhaps more important, technological knowledge itself, and the specialized skills and organizational abilities required to apply the knowledge to production processes, may be more quickly and widely diffused as the result of the foreign operations of MNCs.

Turning to the negative side of the picture of multinational corporations, most of the objections of an economic character (as opposed to social and political aspects) are simply an extension of the various objections to monopolistic practices. The very fact that multinational firms have some special advantage over local firms implies the possession of monopolistic or oligopolistic market power, with attendant opportunities to pursue antisocial behavior.

As noted earlier, one common motive for direct foreign investment is to prevent the development of competition from foreign producers. To the extent that this purpose is achieved, the multinational firm is in a position to restrict output and raise prices above socially optimum levels and to deny local firms access to the technology and processes under the control of the multinational firm.

More generally, the spread of the multinational corporation, each typically of huge size, clearly tends to increase in the world economy the degree to which economic decisions affecting the lives of hundreds of millions of persons are concentrated in the hands of the relatively very few persons who manage and control the affairs of the giant international enterprises. The contrast is stark, between this method of organizing economic activities and that of the classical competitive model, in which economic power is so diffused as to be negligibly possessed by individual firms, leaving the impersonal forces of the market to direct the economy.

Whether or not on net balance MNCs are economically beneficial or harmful to the world economy in general, and to the home and host countries in particular, is a moot question at the present time. Perhaps it will never be possible to arrive at any sweeping generalization with great confidence. The uncertain net economic effects of MNCs have fostered vigorous controversy over appropriate public policies. The issues involved will be briefly discussed at the end of the next chapter.

RECOMMENDED READINGS

ALIBER, ROBERT Z. "A Theory of Direct Foreign Investment," *The International Corporation: A Symposium*. Edited by C. P. Kindleberger. Cambridge: M.I.T. Press, 1970, pp. 17–34.

BERRY, R. ALBERT, AND SOLIGO, RONALD. "Some Welfare Aspects of International Migration," *Journal of Political Economy* vol. 77, no. 5 (September–October 1969).

JOHNSON, HARRY. "Some Economic Aspects of the Brain Drain," *The Pakistan Development Review*, August 1967, pp. 379–411.

———. "The Efficiency and Welfare Implications of the International Corporation," *The International Corporation*. Edited by C. P. Kindleberger, pp. 35–56.

KINDLEBERGER, CHARLES P. *American Business Abroad*. Chap. 1. New Haven: Yale University Press, 1969.

MACDOUGALL, G. D. A. "The Benefits and Costs of Private Investment from Abroad: A Theoretical Approach," *Economic Record*, March 1960, pp. 13–35.

MEADE, JAMES E. *Trade and Welfare*. Vol. 2, *The Theory of International Economic Policy*, chaps. xix–xxiii, xxvii. London: Oxford University Press, 1955.

RAGAZZI, GIORGIO. "Theories of the Determinants of Direct Foreign Investment," INTERNATIONAL MONETARY FUND. *Staff Papers*, vol. 20, no. 2 (July 1973), pp. 471–98.

STUDY QUESTIONS

1. Describe the two methods that are open to a country through which it may increase its stock of real capital.
2. Distinguish between an international money capital movement and an international real capital movement.
3. Show how an import surplus of consumer goods might permit a country to build up its stock of capital goods.
4. What are the economic motives for international labor and capital movements?
5. State the marginal productivity theory of factor prices.
6. Compare the effects of differences in relative factor endowments on (a) the pattern of trade and (b) the pattern of factor movements.
7. Prove that the world's real output and income would rise if factors of production were to move internationally in accordance with economic motives.

8. Describe the conditions under which a population movement would most favorably affect both the emigrant and immigrant countries. What modifications in the analysis are required under less favorable conditions?

9. What is meant by the "brain drain?"

10. Why do labor movements usually also involve capital movements?

11. Analyze the effects of factor movements on factor prices and the distribution of income.

12. In what sense and under what conditions are trade and factor movements substitutes for each other? Why, in fact, are they never complete substitutes?

13. Show the respects in which trade and factor movements may be complementary.

14. Describe a situation in which you might expect capital and labor to migrate jointly in the same direction.

15. What welfare questions and principles are raised by factor movements? How do these compare to those raised by trade?

16. In what respects are portfolio and direct investments subject to different theoretical analysis?

17. Define "multinational corporation."

18. Describe the conditions which might give foreign firms an advantage over domestic firms.

19. What relationship is there between the theory of trade in imperfectly competitive markets and the theory of foreign direct investment?

20. Argue pro and con that multinational corporations are beneficial to the world economy.

8

A survey of international
factor movements

From the analysis in the preceding chapter we have concluded that the unequal relative endowments of the means of production in different countries create the basis and incentive, in the framework of competitive markets, for both trade and the movement of capital and labor. In addition we noted that, especially with respect to capital, international flows may be in response to different rates of return attributable to market imperfections.

It is the purpose of this chapter to review broadly historical experience with international capital and labor movements.

LONG-TERM INTERNATIONAL CAPITAL MOVEMENTS:
A BRIEF HISTORY OF INTERNATIONAL CAPITAL MOVEMENTS

It will be recalled from the discussion in the preceding chapter that only *real* capital movements are significant from the standpoint of the allocation of resources. While it is often monetary capital movements which allow real capital movements, not all monetary capital movements are significant from this point of view. More specifically, as we shall see later, it is only net *long-term* portfolio investments and direct investments which ordinarily give rise to the real capital movements that are important in the allocation of resources.[1] The data in this chapter on capital movements are confined, therefore, to long-term portfolio and direct investments.

The Pre-1914 Period

The history of long-term international capital movements in the modern era can usefully be divided into four periods: the century or so preceding World War I and ending in 1913; the 1920s; the depression decade of the 1930s; and the period since the end of World War II. Our principal focus will be on the last named period, but it is of interest briefly to recount the previous historical record.

The century ending with the outbreak of World War I was the "golden age" of private international investment activity. It was an especially propitious era for the flow of long-term capital.

In the first place, several countries, with Great Britain in the lead, were rapidly accumulating capital as the result of the Industrial Revolution and the accompanying increase in national income and savings. At the same time, there were vast areas in other parts of the world, including the United States, rich in land and natural resources but short of capital. Moreover, as Britain and certain other European countries—such as France and Germany—became increasingly industrialized their import demand for raw materials and foodstuffs grew. This increased prospective returns from investments in overseas areas whose economies were suited to producing and exporting the primary products demanded by the more highly developed countries.

In the second place, it was a period in which market forces were permitted to operate with a minimum of interference by governments, which generally pursued a policy of laissez-faire. The prevalence of the international gold standard created what amounted to an international currency, minimizing the risks of loss from fluctuating exchange rates, while the absence of major international conflicts after the Napoleonic wars removed this source of economic and political maladjustments and uncertainty.

By far the largest supplier of international capital before World War I was Great Britain, followed, in order, by France, Germany, and the three smaller continental countries of Belgium, the Netherlands, and Switzerland. The principal recipients of foreign capital

---

[1] The dividing line between long- and short-term investments is usually arbitrarily set at one year.

were the other countries of Europe, Latin America, the United States, Canada, Asia, and Africa.

The nature of international investment prior to 1914 may be summed up in one sentence: apart from some loans for political and military purposes by France and Germany, the main stream of investment capital was directed towards undeveloped primary producing countries, and the chief borrowers were those who could offer the highest returns.[2]

On the whole, we should have to agree that the long-term international capital movements which occurred before 1914 probably came as close to conforming to the expectations dictated by economic theory as conditions in the real world allow. The experience of the United States is eloquent evidence of the economic benefits to be derived from the inflow of capital from abroad for there can be no doubt that its development during the 19th century was thereby hastened. Even so, there were unfortunate aspects of the experience during this era which modified the full realization of the economic benefits predicated by theory. We have already noted that in some instances loans were dictated by noneconomic considerations. More serious than this, however, was the tendency for many direct investments in some areas to lead to ruthless exploitation of so-called "backward" peoples and the creation of economic and political rivalries. It may be seriously questioned, for example, whether either the native peoples of Africa or the general citizenry of the imperialist powers which fought over the territorial division of Africa gained any lasting economic benefits. A discussion of colonialism and imperialism falls outside the scope of this book, but it should be pointed out that in their worst manifestations they may destroy the benefits that would otherwise accrue from the international flow of capital.

The 1920s

World War I had a major impact on international capital movements. The immediate impact was to transform the United States from a net international debtor into a significant net creditor and greatly to diminish the foreign investments of most European countries—in the case of Germany to such an extent that she became a debtor country. These changes were the result, of course, of financ-

---

[2] See Royal Institute of International Affairs, *The Problem of International Investment* (London: Oxford University Press, 1937) , p. 129.

ing the war and postwar reconstruction. In the decade following the war, the United States replaced Great Britain as the major source of international capital, accounting for about two thirds of the world's foreign new investment.[3]

More significant, the climate for international capital flows had been radically altered by the political and economic repercussions of the war, with an accompanying change in the character of foreign investment. In contrast to the earlier period, a significant portion of capital flows were for the purpose of relief and rehabilitation of war-ravaged countries, with the capital furnished mainly by the United States government. By 1922, however, the government was out of the foreign loan business, and the capital movements thereafter were on private account.

United States private foreign investments in the middle 20s increasingly consisted of direct investments but were dominated by portfolio loans, many of which were imprudent and used for nonproductive projects. As a consequence, the onset of the world depression in late 1929 led to widespread defaulting on loans.

The Depression Decade

The postwar period of net long-term international capital movements reached its end in 1930. The next few years were marked by a severe drop in output and employment, deflation, a sharp decline in the volume of international trade, the disorganization of the international monetary mechanism, the introduction of trade and exchange controls, the intensification of tariffs and other trade impediments, and political instability. In some measure as a cause, as well as a result, of these developments, new long-term international investments virtually ceased, and outstanding loans were widely defaulted.

Indeed, in the case of the United States, the flow of long-term capital reversed direction after 1930. New dollar issues for foreign account and U.S. direct investments abroad decreased to an insignificant volume during most of the 1930s and were exceeded in amount by the amortization of past loans and net sales of outstanding securities to foreigners.

The decade of the 1930s was also marked by extensive defaults on interest and amortization payments due from foreign borrowers, both private and governmental. Defaults resulted in a general and

---

[3] John H. Dunning, *International Investment* (Suffolk, England: Chaucer Press, 1972) , p. 60.

sharp drop in bond prices, which encouraged large repurchases by foreigners of their own bonds, accounting for the substantial reduction in the foreign portfolio held by American investors which occurred after 1930.

As the result of extensive defaulting and repayments of outstanding foreign loans, the United States ended the decade of the 30s with overseas investments worth about $4,000 million less than at the beginning.[4]

The Period Since World War II

During World War II, a huge amount of capital was made available to the Allied nations by the United States government, mainly through Lend-Lease arrangements. Private international capital flows, on the other hand, practically ceased together.

For the first few years following the end of the war, capital flows were again largely in the form of governmental loans and grants to aid in the relief, rehabilitation, and reconstruction of war-ravaged countries. Subsequent to the economic recovery of western Europe—heavily financed by the United States Marshall Plan—the flow of governmental loan and grant capital continued but was diverted to the less developed countries (LDCs) as part of foreign aid programs. The continuing large participation of governments and various international organizations (such as the World Bank) in the supplying of capital to less developed countries is revealed in the data given in Table 8.1 and represents an unprecedented phenomenon in the history of capital movements.

Private long-term capital flows also resumed after the end of the war, but the real volume did not reach that of the prewar peak year of 1928 until 1956. The latter year marks the turning point of private long-term capital movements, bringing the volume well above the highest level reached at any time in the past. Since then, the flow of private long-term capital has continued to grow, as the data in Table 8.2 for the United States—the predominant, though not only, source—show.

A summary of the net cumulative effects of all past capital flows out of and into a given country is conveniently shown by the balance sheet of the country's international financial position. On the asset side of the balance sheet are listed the claims of the residents (includ-

---

4 Dunning, *International Investment*, p. 61.

TABLE 8.1

OFFICIAL CAPITAL FLOWS TO LESS DEVELOPED COUNTRIES,
1965–1972
(in billions of dollars)

1965	6.20	1969	7.19
1966	6.43	1970	7.98
1967	7.06	1971	8.98
1968	7.05	1972	10.14

The data refer to official loans and grants, extended bilaterally and through multilateral institutions, from countries belonging to the Development Assistance Committee of the Organization for Economic Cooperation and Development (OECD).

Source: World Bank, *Annual Report 1973* (Washington, D.C., 1973), p. 86.

ing the government) against other countries. On the liability side are listed the claims of other countries against the home country. Table 8.3 shows the international long-term investment position of the United States for various years.

Especially impressive has been the huge increase in private long-term claims held by the United States against the rest of the world, accumulated through past capital outflows and reinvested earnings. The data also show that capital flows have not been entirely unidirectional. In recent years foreign long-term capital has been flowing into the United States at an accelerated pace.

One other comment on the international investment position of the United States is in order. The data in Table 8.3 refer only to long-term assets and liabilities. On short-term account, the United States is a large net international debtor. Combining long- and short-term foreign assets and liabilities results in a net creditor position of the United States of about $51 billion in 1972 or about half of the long-term position. However, the net debtor position of the United States on short-term account is the result of the operations of the

TABLE 8.2

LONG-TERM PRIVATE CAPITAL OUTFLOW FROM THE UNITED STATES,
SELECTED YEARS AND TOTAL, 1960–72
(in billions of dollars)

	1960	1962	1964	1966	1968	1970	1971	1972	Total All Years 1960–72
Total	2.5	2.8	6.5	4.3	7.5	8.5	10.9	12.5	78.7
Of which reinvested earnings on direct investments . . .	1.3	1.2	1.4	1.7	2.2	2.9	3.2	4.5	26.7

Sources: U.S. Department of Commerce, *Survey of Current Business*, various issues.

TABLE 8.3

LONG-TERM INTERNATIONAL INVESTMENT POSITION OF THE UNITED STATES
(in billions of dollars)

	1939	1946	1960	1972
U.S. long-term assets abroad				
U.S. government	—	5	17	36
Private	11	12	44	128
Total	11	17	61	164
U.S. long-term liabilities to foreigners	6	7	19	62
U.S. long-term net creditor position.	5	10	42	102

Sources: U.S. Department of Commerce, *Survey of Current Business*, various issues.

international monetary mechanism rather than of the flow of capital in response to differential rates of return of relevance in the present context. (The role of short-term capital movements is explored in Part Three.)

THE NATURE AND SIGNIFICANCE OF RECENT CAPITAL FLOWS

As compared to experience in the preceding half century or so, recent and current experience with long-term capital flows displays marked changes, both quantitatively and qualitatively.

As noted above, the combination of two world wars and a decade of unprecedented depression destroyed the kind of environment favorable to international investment which had prevailed in the period prior to 1914. A resurgence in capital flows began after World War II and rapidly accelerated once postwar reconstruction was completed.

Equally significant as the resumption of large-scale flows of capital has been the transformation in the character of international investment. Before 1914, international investment was largely *private* and of the *portfolio* variety. In the more recent period, a large fraction of capital flows has been of a *public* character (provided by governments and official international agencies), and private flows have become increasingly of the *direct* investment variety. Associated with the latter development has been the prominent role played by multinational corporations.

During the last several years United States direct investments abroad have constituted approximately 80 percent of total United States foreign investments. Foreign investments in the United States, on the other hand, have consisted predominantly of the portfolio variety, direct investments amounting on the average to less than one third the total.

There have also been significant shifts in the distribution of direct investments, both by industry and geographic location. In earlier periods, direct investments were typically of the "colonial" type— that is, for the purpose of developing raw materials for export. While this type of investment continues to be important, especially in the petroleum industry, manufacturing industry now commands the largest share of direct investment funds (see Table 8.4).

Accompanying the shift toward investment in manufacturing industries has been a change in the geographic distribution, away from less developed countries toward developed economies, especially in Western Europe, as shown in Table 8.5.

As noted in the preceding chapter, direct investments, as opposed to portfolio investments, are undertaken largely in the context of imperfectly competitive markets. Indeed, the great bulk of foreign direct investments today is undertaken by a relatively few oligopolistic firms, the multinational corporations (MNCs).

The spread of the activities of MNCs has generated intense controversy, both in their home countries and in the countries where they operate. Criticism of the MNCs is levied on several different counts.

Perhaps the central source of concern is the sheer economic and financial power wielded by multinational corporations. One dramatic indicator of their power position is the comparison between their gross annual sales and the gross national product of countries.

TABLE 8.4

DISTRIBUTION OF U.S. FOREIGN DIRECT INVESTMENTS
BY TYPE OF INDUSTRY, END OF 1972

	Value of Investment (in millions of dollars)	*Percent of Total*
Manufacturing	39,478	42
Petroleum	26,399	28
Mining and smelting	7,131	8
Other industries	21,024	22
Total	94,032	100

Source: U.S. Department of Commerce, *Survey of Current Business*, September 1973, p. 24.

TABLE 8.5

UNITED STATES FOREIGN DIRECT INVESTMENTS
BY GEOGRAPHIC AREA, END 1972

Area	Value of Investments (in millions of dollars)	Percent of Total
Canada	25,784	27
United Kingdom	9,509	10
European Economic Community*	15,745	17
Other Western Europe	5,461	6
Japan	2,222	2
Australia, New Zealand, South Africa	5,393	6
Latin America	16,644	18
Other Areas	13,274	14
Total	94,032	100

* The original six members: France, Germany, Italy, Belgium, Luxembourg, the Netherlands.

Source: U.S. Department of Commerce, *Survey of Current Business*, September 1973, p. 24.

On this basis, General Motors is larger than all but 22 countries![5] Some of the other giant international corporations with annual sales in excess of the gross national products of most countries include Standard Oil of New Jersey, Ford Motor Co., Royal Dutch Shell, General Electric, IBM, Mobil Oil, Chrysler, Unilever, ITT, Texaco, Western Electric, Gulf Oil, U.S. Steel, Volkswagenwerk, Westinghouse Electric, Standard Oil California, and Philips Electric.

Although there are several thousand MNCs, a few hundred dominate foreign direct investment. For the United States, which accounts for about a third of foreign affiliates, 250 to 300 firms control over 70 percent of foreign direct investments.[6] An even greater concentration is found in the United Kingdom and the Federal Republic of Germany, which, together with France, are the principal homes, other than the United States, of the multinational corporation.

The foreign direct investments of MNCs in many cases dominate total investments in the host countries. In Canada, for example, foreign corporations conduct one third of total business activity and account for 60 percent of manufacturing output and 65 percent of mining and smelting.[7] The dominance of foreign companies in the

[5] For this and the immediately following comparisons, see U.S. Senate, Committee on Finance, *The Multinational Corporation and the World Economy* (Washington, D.C.: U.S. Government Printing Office, 1973), p. 8.

[6] United Nations, *Multinational Corporations in World Development* (New York, 1973), p. 7.

[7] United Nations, *Multinational Corporations*, p. 17.

local economy is especially great in high-technology industries. In most of the developed market economies outside the United States, foreign firms own from 50 to 100 percent of such industries.[8]

Moreover, the largest multinational firms tend to play a prominent role in the domestic economy of the home country. Thus, more than one third of the manufacturing output of the United States is represented by the top 187 United States multinational firms, and 264 of such firms are responsible for half of all United States exports of manufactures.[9]

The tremendous power position of the MNCs in most host countries has led to the fear of loss of national independence or of control over the national economy. For less developed countries, the fear frequently is expressed in charges of foreign imperialism, with all the political as well as economic overtones that term connotes. For developed economies which are the principal current host countries of foreign direct investment, it is more a matter of having important sectors of the economy controlled by corporations the management of which is outside the national jurisdiction. Accordingly, there is concern that national control over domestic economic and monetary affairs is weakened and that even the sovereignty of the state itself may be diluted.

Notwithstanding these concerns, the majority of countries have encouraged the inflow of foreign investments. The reason obviously is the economic benefits they perceive to be obtained. Economic theory generally supports the belief that host countries do indeed tend to benefit from foreign direct investments in their industries. In addition to the highly visible extra tax revenue and employment opportunities generated, more important contributions to the local economy may be made by foreign firms in increasing competition in domestic markets—thereby improving allocative efficiency—promoting technical efficiency through demonstration effects as well as through the force of competition and through speeding the transfer of technology and innovation.[10]

In view of the above benefits to be derived from receiving foreign investments, the tendency generally is for governments to negotiate with MNCs rather than to outlaw them. Through negotiation with respect to such matters as taxation and the employment of local personnel in the higher echelons of management, an effort is made to

---

[8] United Nations, *Multinational Corporations,* p. 17.

[9] United Nations, *Multinational Corporations,* p. 15.

[10] See Richard E. Caves, "Multinational Firms, Competition, and Productivity in Host-Country Markets," *Economica* 41 (May 1974) : 176–92.

reduce the objectionable aspects of MNC operations. In some cases, however, especially in less developed countries, the reaction to foreign investments is more severe, with nationalization of properties as an extreme example.

Criticism of MNCs is not entirely confined to host countries. Especially in the United States have the activities of home-based multinational corporations been subject to intense controversy with respect to their effects on the domestic economy. The principal charges against MNCs are that they result in (a) a loss of tax revenue, (b) unemployment, (c) the export of technology, and (d) an aggravation of balance-of-payments problems.

The tax laws provide that foreign subsidiaries of United States corporations may credit the foreign taxes they pay against the income tax liability of the parent corporations on income earned abroad. The rationale of this provision is to avoid double taxation—that is, taxation by the host country and of the home country on the same income. In any event, the result has been a large reduction in the taxes paid to the United States Treasury by American multinational companies. For example, in 1970 the taxable income on foreign earnings of United States corporations was $11 billion, on which a foreign tax credit of $4.6 billion was claimed, leaving net tax collections by the United States Treasury of only $640 million, or 6 percent of the taxable income.[11]

A further tax "break" is given international corporations by the deferral provision, which allows a subsidiary abroad to defer payment of United States taxes until such time as the income is received in the United States.[12]

American labor, as represented by the AFL–CIO, is the chief critic of multinational corporations and has been the leading proponent of legislation to control their activities. The principal complaint of labor is that MNCs "export" both employment and technology to foreign countries at the expense of the American worker.[13] The spokesmen of labor therefore propose that special tax treatment of

11 U.S. Senate, Committee on Finance, *The Multinational Corporation and the World Economy*, p. 17.

12 At the time this is being written (June 1974) proposals in the Congress to amend the tax laws to remove or reduce the special treatment of the MNCs are under consideration. See also the discussion below.

13 See, for example, Nat Goldfinger, "A Labor View of Foreign Investment and Trade Issues," *United States International Economic Policy in an Interdependent World*, Compendium of Papers, Papers Submitted to the Commission on International Trade and Investment Policy, vol. 1 (Washington, D.C., 1971), pp. 913–28.

the MNCs be repealed, the outflow of capital for overseas subsidiaries be curbed, and that regulation of United States-based multinational companies be introduced.[14] It is because the Burke-Hartke bill (discussed in Chapter 11) provides such restraints on MNCs, as well as related restrictive measures on trade, that organized labor has been one of its most enthusiastic supporters.

Whether or not in fact the overseas activities of multinational companies have compromised the competitiveness of United States industry in world trade and have resulted in unemployment at home is a moot question. The "evidence" varies, depending upon assumptions made, from supporting the conclusion that direct investment abroad *adds* to home employment to supporting the conclusion that it is responsible for the loss of thousands of jobs by American workers.[15]

Equally inconclusive is the net effect of MNCs on the foreign trade position and balance of payments of the United States. A careful study by the United States Tariff Commission concludes that on balance the foreign operations of multinational firms have a favorable impact on United States foreign trade competitiveness.[16] As far as international payments are concerned, the objective fact that annual income receipts from direct investments abroad exceed by a considerable margin the annual outflow of capital in additional direct foreign investments seems to support the view that the operations of the MNCs have not been responsible for the deficits in the United States balance of payments. However, the relationship between foreign investment and the balance of payments is far more complex and subtle than indicated by such data, and competent economists arrive at different conclusions as to what the relationship actually is.[17]

In general, it is a fair presumption that, regardless of the validity or invalidity of the criticisms of MNCs, they will increasingly be brought under various national, and perhaps international, regulations.

---

[14] Goldfinger, "A Labor View of Foreign Investment," p. 928.

[15] For a balanced view of the conflicting evidence, see Robert Gilpin, "The Multinational Corporation and the National Interest," Prepared for the Committee on Labor and Public Welfare, U.S. Senate (Washington, D.C.: U.S. Government Printing Office, 1973) , pp. 13–19.

[16] U.S. Tariff Commission, *Competitiveness of U.S. Industries,* TC Publication 473 (Washington, D.C., April 1972) , pp. 163–90.

[17] See U.S. Tariff Commission, *Competitiveness of U.S. Industries,* pp. 21–29.

INTERNATIONAL POPULATION MOVEMENTS

Just as capital tends, under free conditions, to flow from capital-abundant to capital-poor regions, so labor tends to migrate from areas where it is in relative abundance to areas where it is relatively scarce. To a considerably greater degree than in the case of capital movements, however, immigration is significantly affected by other than economic motives. Immigration, after all, involves human beings and is subject, therefore, to cultural and social influences which are largely absent in the impersonal calculation of relative returns available to capital.

Flight from domestic tyranny or, more positively, the search for political and religious freedom; escape from personal maladjustments to family and community life; and broader military and national considerations have all at various times entered into the determination to seek a new life in other lands. Nevertheless, it is a fairly safe generalization that by far the predominant motive behind the vast international migrations of the past was economic—the desire of the immigrant to improve his standard of living.[18]

A cursory glance at the tremendous disparities in the standards of living in different parts of the world today would indicate that a large part of the world's population has strong economic reasons for migrating. Per capita incomes in North America, industrial Europe, Australia and New Zealand, and a few countries of South America are several times higher than in most other countries of the world. Yet immigration into the higher income countries has been in recent years a mere trickle. Why is this? There are many reasons, but one is overwhelmingly the most important: nearly every country today has strict limitations on the number of immigrants it will admit, and some countries are just as strict in controlling emigration from their homelands. The economic motive has, therefore, little opportunity to express itself. It is characteristic of the present era that mass movements of population are largely confined to political and religious refugees from totalitarian countries or to religious and national groups seeking to establish new communities (such as in Israel, India, and Pakistan).

As in the case of international capital movements, the conditions

---

[18] This is the conclusion reached by the noted population authority, Warren S. Thompson. See his *Population Problems,* 4th ed. (New York: McGraw-Hill, 1953), p. 274.

postulated by economic theory as favoring immigration were more nearly fulfilled during the 19th century and up until 1914 than in any other period of history. First, there were numerous regions of the world rich in natural resources and equable in climate but with sparse populations. Second, knowledge of the economic opportunities in the new lands was widespread, and the costs of moving were relatively low. Third, for the most part, individuals were free to move across national boundaries with a minimum of artificial restrictions.

It is not surprising that the United States was by far the most popular area of immigration or that Canada, Argentina, Brazil, Australia, and New Zealand were the other major countries of immigration. Between 1820, when the United States first began to keep accurate records, and 1972 nearly 46 million immigrants entered the country.[19] If immigrants into other parts of America are added, a total of approximately 60 million persons have migrated into the Western Hemisphere since the beginning of the 19th century.

Overwhelmingly the largest number of immigrants arrived before the introduction of strict controls shortly after World War I. Before 1880, immigration into the United States was left to the different states; thereafter, jurisdiction was assumed by the federal government. For the next 30 to 40 years, American controls were selective rather than restrictive—that is, they were concerned chiefly with what sort of immigrants should be admitted rather than with how many. Generally, the requirements for admittance were in terms of such criteria as the state of health, morals, and finances of the immigrants. But, in addition, some racial groups, chiefly Oriental, were excluded, with certain exempt classes. Exclusion of the Chinese began in 1882, of the Japanese in 1907, and of East Indians and other Asiatics in 1917. In 1943 the ban on the Chinese was lifted and in 1946 the ban on East Indians, but the numbers admissible under the quota system (see below) were very limited.

Other immigrant countries followed roughly the same type of selective controls as the United States, though Argentina and Brazil interposed no formal restrictions because of racial origin. In all countries, however, there was increasing insistence upon more severe immigration controls, and, after World War I, national policies generally shifted from a selectivity basis to a restrictive basis. In this movement the United States took the lead.

---

[19] U.S. Bureau of the Census, *Statistical Abstract of the United States: 1973*, p. 94.

After 1922, and until the enactment of new legislation in 1965, the basic method of restriction was the quota system. Under this system, except for immigrants from the Western Hemisphere, there was an absolute limit on the total number of immigrants admitted each year, with an allocation of quotas among different countries according to the proportion of U.S. population already composed of the different national stocks. Since by far the largest part of the population of the United States consists of Caucasians having their national origins in countries of northern and western Europe, the effect of the quota system was to limit severely immigration from other areas.

The national origins quota system was eliminated by a new immigration law signed in 1965. Under the new legislation, immigrants are to be selected on the basis of special labor skills, family relations with U.S. citizens and residents, or need for political asylum. The country of origin is considered only to the extent that no more than 20,000 immigrants are to be admitted per year from any one country.

However, severe limits on the number of immigrants continue in effect. The previous policy of allowing unlimited immigration from the Western Hemisphere (with minor exceptions) is replaced by a maximum annual inflow of 120,000 from that area. For the rest of the world, a maximum of 170,000 is set. Additional immigrants, numbering perhaps 30,000–40,000, may be admitted on the basis of special considerations, mainly family ties with U.S. citizens.[20]

The Brain Drain

While the current policy of most developed economies is to limit the number of immigrants, the restrictions are not uniformly applied but discriminate in favor of professional and technical personnel and skilled labor. As we observed earlier, the migration of such persons involves not only the movement of labor but of capital as well—the "human capital" embodied in labor in the form of education and training.

One of the striking features of immigration in recent years is the marked shift in the composition of immigrants toward the professional and skilled types of labor. Thus, whereas in the period 1907–1923 professional and skilled workers constituted about one quarter

---

[20] Thus, in 1972, 385,000 immigrated into the United States. See U.S. Bureau of the Census, *Statistical Abstract of the United States: 1973*, p. 94.

of the immigrants into the United States, by 1967 the proportion had reached 70 percent.[21] Other developed countries have had similar experiences, with Canada recently having an especially high rate of absorption of human capital.

The elimination by the United States in 1965 of quotas based on national origins led to a large increase in the "brain drain" from less developed countries. In 1956 the proportion of professional and technical immigrants originating in these areas was 25 percent; in 1967 the proportion was 57 percent.[22] The impact of removing the earlier discrimination against non-Western immigrants, together with the emphasis on professional and technical qualifications, is displayed dramatically by data for 1968. In that year, of nearly 13,000 engineers and scientists who immigrated to the United States, Asia was the origin of over 4,000, and of the physicians and surgeons who immigrated to the United States 40 percent were from Asia.[23]

The Economic Effects of Immigration

We concluded in the preceding chapter that, theoretically, population movements in response to economic motives tend to raise the level of the world's real income and to benefit economically both the country of emigration and that of immigration. We found it necessary to modify this conclusion, however, according to specific circumstances. In brief, the benefits of population movements are clearest when they permanently increase the per capita supply of capital and land in the emigrant country and when the receiving country is economically young and undeveloped with sparse population. The benefits are much more doubtful, however, if the country of emigration has both a high birthrate and a high death rate and if the receiving country has already reached its optimum-size population.

It is impossible to reach any firm conclusions on the precise economic effects of historical migrations. It would seem fairly certain that the large population movements of the 19th century took place under conditions which were generally favorable for the realization of economic benefits. There can be little doubt that the United States and the other major countries of immigration benefited from the increased supply of labor. Not only did the increased supply of

---

21 Brinley Thomas, *Migration and Economic Growth*, 2d ed. (Cambridge: University Press, 1973) , p. 309.

22 Thomas, *Migration and Economic Growth*, p. 311.

23 Thomas, *Migration and Economic Growth*, p. 313.

labor in these countries tend to raise per capita productivity by allowing a greater division of labor, but it also greatly encouraged industrial development. We noted before that in economically young countries, with unexploited land and natural resources, both labor and capital are attracted from abroad, each reinforcing the other. Indeed, under such circumstances the addition to the labor supply and the development of new industries may be so closely related that neither would occur without the other.[24] Thus, a study by the United States Immigration Commission indicates that the great industrial expansion in the United States between 1907 and 1911 would have been impossible without the new immigrants.[25]

The welfare effects of more recent migrations, especially of the "brain drain," are a subject of lively controversy. The presumption is that the migrants themselves benefit from voluntary migration. There is also a strong presumption that the receiving countries gain from the addition to their supply of professional and technical manpower. The unsettled question is whether the emigrant countries suffer a net economic loss, and, if so, whether the loss is greater or less than the gain realized by the migrants themselves and the immigrant countries. From a "liberal" and cosmopolitan point of view, a strong case can be made that the world's welfare on net balance is advanced by the movement of human capital, in the same way and for essentially the same reasons as the movement of material capital is beneficial. From the national perspective of particular emigrant countries, on the other hand, the conclusion may be quite different.[26]

RECOMMENDED READINGS

ADAMS, WALTER, ED.   *The Brain Drain.* New York: Macmillan Co., 1968.

DUNNING, JOHN H., ED.   *International Investment.* Suffolk, England: Penguin Books, 1972.

GILPIN, ROBERT.   *The Multinational Corporation and the National Interest.* Washington, D.C.: Committee on Labor and Public Welfare, United States Senate, Committee Print, October 1973.

---

[24] See J. Isaac, *Economics of Migration* (New York: Oxford University Press, 1947), pp. 214–17.

[25] See National Committee on Immigration Policy, *Economic Aspects of Immigration* (New York, 1947), p. 11.

[26] For cogent presentations of the cosmopolitan and national perspectives, respectively, see Harry G. Johnson, "An 'Internationalist' Model," and D. Patinkin, "A 'Nationalist' Model," in Walter Adams (ed.), *The Brain Drain* (New York: Macmillan Co., 1968), chaps. 5 and 6.

GRUBEL, HERBERT B. AND SCOTT, ANTHONY D. "The International Flow of Human Capital," *American Economic Review,* vol. 56, no. 2 (May 1966).

ISAAC, J. *Economics of Migration.* New York: Oxford University Press, 1947.

KINDLEBERGER, CHARLES P. *American Business Abroad.* New Haven: Yale University Press, 1969.

LEWIS, CLEONA. *America's Stake in International Investment.* Washington, D.C.: Brookings Institution, 1938.

NURKSE, RAGNAR. "International Investment Today in the Light of Nineteenth-Century Experience," *Economic Journal* 64:744–58.

SALERA, VIRGIL. *Multinational Business.* Boston: Houghton Mifflin Co., 1969.

THOMAS, BRINLEY. *Migration and Economic Growth.* 2d ed. Cambridge: University Press, 1973.

UNITED NATIONS, NEW YORK. *Multinational Corporations in World Development.* 1973.

U.S. DEPARTMENT OF COMMERCE, Washington, D.C. *Survey of Current Business, various issues.*

United States International Economic Policy in an Interdependent World. Papers Submitted to the Commission on International Trade and Investment. Washington, D.C., 1971.

VERNON, R. *Sovereignty at Bay.* New York: Basic Books, 1971.

STUDY QUESTIONS

1. What were the conditions prevailing during the 19th century which made it the "golden age" of long-term private international capital flows?

2. Why was Great Britain the leading international investor before 1914?

3. Investigate the role which foreign capital played in the economic development of the United States during the 19th century. (Refer to any good text on the history of the United States.)

4. Summarize the effects of World War I on the international capital position of Great Britain, Germany, and the United States.

5. Investigate the type and geographic distribution of post–World War II private foreign investments by the United States. (Regular articles on this subject appear in the U.S. Department of Commerce publication, *Survey of Current Business.*)

6. In what important respects have international capital movements since World War II differed from those that occurred prior to 1914?

7. Define what is meant by an "international debtor country" and by an "international creditor country."

8. Recall the distinction between portfolio and direct investments and the theory applicable to each (see the preceding chapter, if necessary).

9. Define multinational corporation.

10. What are the principal criticisms of multinational corporations from the point of view of host countries? From the point of view of the United States?

11. List the chief motives, economic and other, for international population movements. Which motive do you think is the most important?

12. If all artificial barriers to international migration were lifted, what would you guess would be the effects on the volume and direction of immigration?

13. What fundamental difference is there in the natural opportunities for large-scale international migration now as compared to earlier times?

14. Trace the historic development of American immigration policies.

15. What part did immigration play in the economic development of the United States?

16. Argue for, and against, the lifting or reduction of the immigration barriers currently in effect in the United States.

17. What is meant by the "brain drain"?

18. What benefits does the inflow of highly trained persons into a country provide? What possible adverse effects are there on emigrant countries?

part two

Public barriers to trade

9

The theory of tariffs and other trade restrictions

Up to this point, except for a brief digression on the trade of centrally planned economies, we have pretended that the volume and pattern of international trade are shaped entirely by private market forces, in the absence of public or governmental interferences or restraints on private transactions. In reality, market forces are never entirely free of impediments imposed by governments, even when the basic system of organizing and conducting economic affairs is through market mechanisms. There are numerous devices governments use to change or modify the market volume and pattern of trade. In this chapter we shall examine the reasons for, and economic effects of, the use of such devices.

THE NATURE OF TARIFFS AND OTHER TRADE RESTRICTIONS

In general, governments can affect the volume and pattern of international trade in any one, or combination, of the following ways:

a. By changing market prices or costs
b. By imposing quantitative restrictions on the volume of trade
c. By making it difficult or expensive to engage in trade as the result of technical or administrative rules and procedures

d. By pursuing discriminatory policies with respect to the purchase of goods and services for the account of governments themselves

Let us examine the particular devices used in each of the above cases.

Tariffs

Tariffs are the most widely employed means of changing market prices and costs. A tariff is a discriminatory tax, or "duty," levied on a commodity when it crosses the boundary of a customs area. The tax is discriminatory, in that it is not applied to commodities produced domestically but only to those produced in foreign countries. A "foreign" country for this purpose is any country not belonging to the customs area of the tariff-levying country. Usually a customs area coincides with national boundaries, but often it also includes colonies and territories and, in exceptional cases, embraces two or more national states. A customs area is extended beyond national boundaries when a *customs union* or a *common market* is formed by two or more countries, as will be discussed in Chapter 12.

Tariffs may be levied on goods passing through a customs area en route to a third country—*transit duties;* on commodities leaving a country—*export duties;* or on merchandise entering a country—*import duties.* Generally speaking, the last named type of tariff is the most common and important, and we shall concentrate our attention on it.

Import duties may be *specific, ad valorem,* or, a combination of the two, *compound* duties. Specific duties are levied according to the physical quantity of the import (so much per pound, per yard, etc.) , while ad valorem duties are calculated as a percentage of the value of the import. Hence, the real burden of ad valorem duties remains constant as the prices of imports vary, while the real burden of specific duties varies inversely with changes in the prices of imports.

A list of all the existing import duties levied by a country is called its *tariff schedule.* The schedule may have one or more "columns"; in a single-columned tariff, the rate is the same for a particular good from whatever country it is imported; a double- or multicolumned tariff discriminates according to the country of origin of the import. For example, imports from countries with which there are tariff agreements may be subject to lower duties than are those from other countries.

Tariffs discriminate against foreign producers in favor of domestic producers. The same kind of discriminatory treatment is accorded through *subsidies* to domestic producers (though with quite different other effects, as discussed below). Subsidies may therefore be regarded as a substitute for import tariffs as a means of favoring domestic industries over foreign competitors.

Subsidies may be used not only to reduce imports but also as a method of increasing exports. Export subsidies permit affected commodities to be offered on the world market at a lower price than domestically, thus encouraging a larger volume of exports. A frequent response of other countries is to impose "countervailing" or "antidumping" duties on the import of such commodities, as described below.

Quotas

Whereas tariffs (and subsidies) affect international trade indirectly through distorting relative prices and costs away from free-trade levels, quantitative restrictions directly limit trade to predetermined levels. The primary instrument of quantitative restriction is the *quota*. (Quantitative restrictions may also be imposed through controls on foreign exchange transactions, but these are usually for balance-of-payments reasons and will be discussed in a later chapter in that context.)

Quotas are limits on the amount of a good which may be imported (import quotas) or exported (export quotas) during a given period of time. The limits may be set in physical terms or in value terms. The quota may be on a country basis—that is, varying limits set according to the country of origin—or on a global basis, wherein the total limit is specified without reference to the countries of origin. A "tariff quota" is distinguished from an absolute quota, in that the former does not set a fixed limit on imports but rather the amount beyond which a higher rate of duty is imposed. A tariff quota is often a device for keeping tariffs lower than otherwise would be the case, by allowing at least a specified quantity of imports to enter free of duty or subject to lower rates than ordinarily applicable.

The administration of quotas usually necessitates the use of a licensing system. This in itself raises serious practical problems, especially as to how the limited number of licenses is to be distributed among various applicants. Since the volume of imports is specifically limited, the domestic selling price of the good may be far in excess of its import cost, and the profit realized from obtaining a license may be very high. These windfall profits can, however, be eliminated through a system of auctioning import licenses to the highest bidders.

From the point of view of the country desiring to restrict the volume of imports, quotas are obviously a much more certain and precise instrument than are tariffs. In addition to this, quotas differ fundamentally from tariffs in their effects on international trade. Apart from tariffs so high that they make imports entirely prohibitive, an import duty does not set an arbitrary limit on the volume of the good that can be imported. Anyone may import as much as he wants of the dutiable good, provided that he pays the import tax. Therefore, the price system of the importing country is not divorced from that of other countries, even though its relationship to other price systems is changed by the tariff. In the case of an import quota, however, the price mechanism is allowed to operate only until the quota is filled; beyond that point, price considerations are irrelevant.

Technical and Administrative Protection

Tariffs, subsidies, and quotas are visible interferences with trade that can be readily identified and measured. A miscellany of other devices to restrict trade are less apparent and less measurable in their effects but are no less potentially significant for that reason.

An obstacle to trade that importers and exporters frequently encounter arises out of the absence of a common system for classifying commodities and determining their valuation base for assessing tariffs. Since different rates duty usually are levied on different varieties of a product, the amount of the tariff depends upon how a particular import is classified. Especially for new products or varieties, the uncertainty thus created as to the amounts of the tariff that must be paid naturally has a negative effect on trade.

Once the classification of an import good and the applicable rate of duty are determined, the amount of ad valorem tariff depends upon the value set upon the commodity for the purpose of calculating the duty. The usual practice is to use the wholesale price of the exporting country, less any indirect taxes, as the value base. However, in the case of certain products—benzenoid chemicals being the most important—the United States uses the American selling price as the basis for determining the import duty. Since the domestic prices of products are higher in the United States than in foreign exporting countries, the effect of this valuation system is to raise the amount of the tariff imposed and reduce the volume of imports.

Antidumping levies are another example of the various irritants discouraging foreign trade. "Dumping" is defined as the sale of a product at a lower price abroad than at home. It is an accepted rule among trading countries that if dumping results in injury to an industry in the importing country, the latter has the right to impose antidumping, or countervailing, duties to offset the price differential.

Although the principle of antidumping duties may be justified, in practical application it imposes an appreciable restraint on trade. Whether or not an antidumping duty is warranted in a particular case requires an investigation of the relevant facts, which may take a considerable time to complete. In the meanwhile, traders are faced with the uncertainty of what duties will ultimately be levied. The magnitude of the disruption to trade thereby caused is greatly increased by the tendency for domestic producers to present unjustified claims of dumping by foreign competitors.[1]

Other technical and administrative rules having a restraining influence on trade include safety and health regulations, marks-of-origin and standards and measures requirements, and the formalities of customs clearance. While some of these have a legitimate purpose, all too frequently in fact they serve as an excuse for barring, or of at least increasing the costs, of imports.

Government Procurement Policies

The final category of nontariff, nonquantitative trade restrictions consists of discriminatory purchase policies by governmental agencies. In view of the typically very significant fraction of the total expenditure on goods and services accounted for by governments themselves, the effect of official procurement policies on trade can be substantial.

If governments were to employ the same standard in determining purchases as that used by private firms—that is, choosing the least-cost suppliers—government instead of private procurement would have no effect on trade (except, of course, for differences in the kinds of

---

[1] Between 1958 and 1965, of 194 investigations of dumping charges made in the United States in only eight cases were antidumping duties levied. See William B. Kelly, Jr., "Nontariff Barriers," in Bela Balassa et al., *Studies in Trade Liberalization* (Baltimore: Johns Hopkins Press, 1967), p. 298.

goods acquired) . In fact, however, governments generally have a strong disposition to favor domestic over foreign suppliers. In the case of the United States, the government is mandated to favor domestic suppliers by the "Buy American Act" of 1933 which requires governmental agencies to purchase materials domestically unless, among other things, their cost would be "unreasonable." The interpretation of an unreasonably higher cost has varied from a 6 percent price differential in the earlier years of the Act to the 50 percent differential that has been the common rule for many years. The effect on trade is the same as a 50 percent tariff surcharge.

THE ECONOMIC EFFECTS OF TRADE RESTRICTIONS

The economic effects of trade restrictions are numerous. Although we shall concentrate our analysis on tariffs and quotas, the same general kinds of effects are produced by other forms of trade restriction.

Price-Cost Effects

The immediate impact of tariffs and quotas is on the prices and costs of the commodities affected. There are other, more fundamental consequences, but they are brought about, in a market price system, through the mechanism of changing price and cost relationships, so that it is the latter that we shall consider first.

The most general price effect of tariffs and quotas is to create a *differential* in the international price (and cost) of the affected commodity. Without tariffs or quotas, assuming pure competition and ignoring transportation costs, we know that the price (and cost) of any traded commodity will tend to be the same in all countries. Now introduce a tariff or quota on a particular commodity, and its price will become different in that country from its price in the supplying country or countries. In the case of a tariff, the price differential will be equal to the amount of the tariff (expressed as a specific duty) . In the case of a quota, the price differential may be any amount, depending upon considerations to be examined shortly.

The reason that a tariff creates an international price and cost differential equal in amount to the amount of the tariff can be easily shown. Suppose that the United States imposes a specific duty of 25 cents per pound on Danish blue cheese. Then, under competitive conditions, the equilibrium price of the cheese is 25 cents higher in the United States than in Denmark. For if the price in the United

States, after the tariff is paid, were less than 25 cents higher than in Denmark, importers would lose on cheese imports—the cheese costing the Danish export price *plus* 25 cents per pound. Hence, the import of cheese would be reduced, and its price in the United States would rise. On the other hand, if the cheese commanded a price in the United States higher than in Denmark by more than the 25 cent duty, the profits realized by importers would stimulate greater imports until the price fell.

Now it will be noted that the equilibrium condition just described can be fulfilled in any one of three ways: (*a*) the price of the commodity may *rise in the importing country* by the full amount of the tariff; (*b*) the price of the commodity may *fall in the exporting country* by the full amount of the tariff; or (*c*) the price may rise in the importing country by less than the full amount of the tariff and fall in the exporting country by less than the full amount of the tariff. From the standpoint of fulfilling the equilibrium condition that the price differential equal the amount of the duty, it makes no difference which of these three possible reactions occurs. But, on other grounds, it makes a great deal of difference, as we shall presently see. It is important, therefore, to investigate what determines the kind of price reaction to be expected from a tariff.

The effect of a tariff on the price of a good depends upon the volume and elasticities of demand and supply, in both the importing (tariff-levying) country and the exporting country. A complete analysis of these forces would become too detailed and involved to present here.[2] But the essence of the analysis can be briefly indicated by concentrating on what is probably the most common case in practice—that where, as the result of the tariff, the price falls in the exporting country and rises in the importing country.

Suppose that a country produces at home some part of its domestic consumption of a commodity and imports the remainder from another country. This implies, as we learned early in the book, that the commodity is produced under increasing-cost conditions, with the supply curves in both countries rising from left to right on the conventional diagram. In competitive equilibrium and ignoring transportation costs, the price (and costs) of the commodity are the same in both countries. Now let the importing country impose a tariff on the commodity. Several reactions will follow.

---

2 For a discussion of the relevance of the *volume* of demand and supply to the price effects of tariffs—a point that is largely ignored in what follows—see Gottfried von Haberler, *The Theory of International Trade* (New York: Macmillan Co., 1937), pp. 227 ff.

First, as an immediate reaction, the price of the commodity in the importing country will tend to rise, and the quantity demanded to fall. Second, domestic producers of the good in the importing country will be induced by the higher market price to expand their output. Third, producers in the exporting country will find that the export market has shrunk—both because of the greater domestic output in the importing country and because of the smaller quantity demanded in the importing country. Therefore, the output in the exporting country will tend to fall. Fourth, the costs (average and marginal) of production will rise in the importing country with its increased output and fall in the exporting country with its decreased output. Hence, in the new equilibrium position, the price of the commodity will be higher in the importing country and lower in the exporting country.

The foregoing analysis is shown diagramatically in Figure 9.1. The demand and supply curves of the importing country (M) are on the left, with quantities measured from right to left, while the curves of the exporting country (X) are on the right, with quantities measured, as conventionally, from left to right.

FIGURE 9.1

THE EFFECTS OF A TARIFF

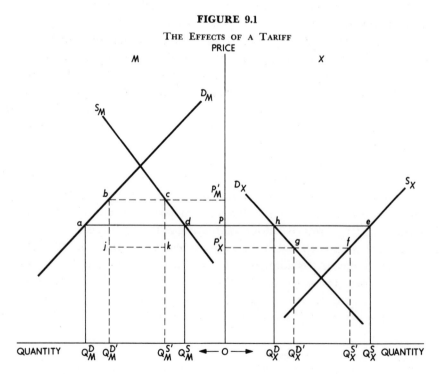

Before the importing country levies a tariff, the equilibrium price of the commodity is OP, the same in both countries. The importing country produces at home OQ_M^s and consumes OQ_M^D, the difference being imported. The exporting country produces OQ_X^s, consumes OQ_X^D, and exports the difference. Equilibrium prevails, for M's import of the commodity just equals X's export, so that the combined quantities demanded and supplied in the two countries are equal.

Now M imposes an import tariff, equal to the distance between OP'_M and OP'_X. As a consequence, the price in M rises from the free-trade level OP to OP'_M, while the price in X falls from OP to OP'_X. These are the new equilibrium prices, for at price OP'_M, M's import demand (equal to the horizontal distance bc) equals X's export supply (gf) at price OP'_X. Hence, the effect of the tariff is to increase the price in M and to reduce the price in X, the arithmetic sum of the two price changes being equal to the tariff.

Accompanying the above price effects of the tariff are an increase in home production of the good in M by $OQ_M^{s'} - OQ_M^s$, a decrease in consumption in M of $OQ_M^D - OQ_M^{D'}$ a decrease in production in X of $OQ_X^s - OQ_X^{s'}$, and an increase in consumption in X of $OQ_X^{D'} - OQ_X^D$.

In the case described above, part of the tariff is "paid by the foreigner," in the sense that the foreign export price is lowered, and part is paid by the consumers of the importing country in the form of a higher price for the commodity. (It should be noted, however, that the government of the importing country collects import duties amounting to the rectangular area $bckj$, possibly relieving thereby the taxpayers of that much other tax burden.)

The extent to which the burden of a tariff can be shifted to foreign exporting countries depends, among other things, upon the importance of the tariff-levying country's demand for the commodity. The greater is the latter country's contribution to total world demand, the larger will be the reduction in the demand for the exporting countries' products as the result of the tariff, hence, the greater tends to be the reduction in export price. On the other hand, a country the import demand of which is an insignificant fraction of total world demand is unable perceptibly to affect the export price by imposing a tariff, so that the domestic price rises by an amount approximately equal to the tariff.

A second factor importantly influencing the effect of a tariff on import and export prices is the elasticities of demand and supply in the importing and exporting countries. Assuming that the tariff-levying country's import demand is a significant portion of world demand, the export price will decrease by a greater amount (and the domestic price in the importing country by a smaller amount) the less elastic domestic demand and supply are in the exporting country. Thus, from the point of view of its ability to make the foreigner bear the burden of a tariff, a country is in the best position when the exporting country's home demand and supply are inelastic. On the other hand, an inelastic demand or supply in the importing country is unfavorable from its point of view, since the domestic price will rise by a greater amount (and the export price will fall by a smaller amount) the greater the inelasticity of the tariff-levying country's home demand and supply are.

The price-cost effect of quotas can be much more drastic than in the case of tariffs. As indicated earlier, a quota may virtually sever international price-cost connecting links, since the market mechanism for relating prices in different countries is artificially stopped from functioning.

One result of quotas is nearly universal: the domestic price in the country imposing the quota is raised above the world price of the commodity. This, of course, is similar to the usual result of a tariff. But there is one important difference: there is no limit on the amount by which the price of the commodity subject to a quota may be raised above the world price. How much the domestic price is raised above the world price as the result of a quota depends, given the elasticities of demand and supply, upon how restrictive the quota is. Other things being equal, the lower the quota is set, the higher will the domestic price be forced upward. As in the case of tariffs, however, quotas may force export prices downward—depending on the elasticities of demand and supply in the exporting country or countries. But if the export price of a commodity is pushed downward because of a quota in the importing country, this does not mean, with a quota of given size, that the price of the commodity in the importing country will be raised by a lesser amount. Rather, it means that the international price and cost differential will be made greater than it otherwise would be.

The above conclusion leads to another important difference between tariffs and quotas. In the case of a tariff, the difference between the export price and the domestic price with the tariff is collected by the government in the form of customs duties. In the case of a straight quota, the difference between the export price and the domestic price goes as a windfall gain to those fortunate enough to be able to import under the quota—meaning, usually, those who have received import licenses. This explains the scramble for import licenses that ordinarily takes place when there is a quota on an import.

The windfall gain to importers could, of course, be taxed by the government. One indirect way of doing this is through the auctioning of licenses to import the quota commodity. Competitive bidding would tend to push the price of licenses up to the point of eliminating expected windfall gains, the government, instead of private importers, receiving the profits.

The Volume and Benefits of Trade

From our preceding analysis it is clear that one of the major effects of tariffs and quotas is to reduce the volume of international trade. In the case of tariffs, this effect follows from the fact that, except in very unusual circumstances, the price of a commodity subject to a tariff is raised in the importing country, thereby reducing the total quantity demanded and, ordinarily, increasing the quantity produced domestically. In the case of quotas, the reduction in the volume of imports is directly brought about by quantitative limits on the volume of imports permitted.

Since international trade yields benefits to the world in the form of higher real income, tariffs and trade restrictions, by reducing the volume of trade, presumably lower the world's real income. The loss involved derives not simply from the quantitative reduction in trade but also from the misallocation of resources. This conclusion may be pointed up by comparing the effect of tariffs and quantitative trade restrictions with that of overall measures, such as exchange depreciation, designed to correct balance-of-payments disequilibrium.

The Allocation of Resources

Effective exchange depreciation also reduces the volume of imports, but it is a reduction that is compelled by the requirements of equilibrium. In contrast to tariffs and trade restrictions, exchange depreciation does not distort cost-price relationships but rather brings them into new alignment. By generally rendering imports more expensive to the depreciating country and by causing the prices of its exports to become cheaper to foreign buyers, exchange depreciation tends to contract the volume of imports and to increase the volume of exports. But internationally traded goods have the same price at the new equilibrium rate of exchange the world over, and resources have been reallocated in accordance with the principle of comparative advantage.

Contrast this situation with the impact of protective tariffs and other trade restrictions. Again resources are redirected, but this time to the production of goods the relative costs of which are *higher* than abroad; otherwise there would be no need to impose a protective tariff. Not only are imports reduced, but exports also tend, in the long run, to be reduced. This is so because of reduced income and import demand in foreign countries, the exports of which are contracted by the tariffs (though this will be negligible if the goods on which the tariffs are imposed constitute only a very small portion of other countries' exports), and because of the tendency for other countries to retaliate by raising their import duties. In other words, resources are reallocated from more efficient export industries to less efficient domestic goods industries.

The distortion of optimum resource use caused by trade restrictions is brought about through the reactions of the latter on international price-cost relationships. As we learned in Chapter 2, the inequality of cost-price ratios in different countries is the condition making international trade mutually beneficial. The *result* of free and unrestricted international trade is to eliminate (except for transport costs) international differences in the price and cost of traded goods and services. But now we have seen that tariffs and quotas *artificially reimpose* international price-cost differences. This creates a situation similar to, though not so extreme as, that which would prevail if countries refused to take advantage of comparative cost differences and insisted upon producing at home all the goods and services consumed at home. In other words, international comparative cost differences create the opportunity for beneficial international trade; tariffs and quotas "freeze" this opportunity, not allowing it fully to be taken advantage of.

The uneconomic effects of tariffs on resource allocation are especially serious when, as is usually the case, the rates vary among different commodities. A still greater distortion of resource allocation results when there are superimposed upon differential rates according to commodities preferential or discriminatory rates on the same commodities according to the country of origin.

Preferential tariff rates are commonly found on trade between the "mother" countries and the colonial possessions or members of an empire. The best known example is the "Ottawa" preference system between the United Kingdom and her dependent colonies and the various members of the British Commonwealth, negotiated at Ottawa in 1932. It has also been common practice for other countries to impose different import duties according to the country of origin, usually on the basis of bilateral agreements. Running counter to this practice is the adoption of the doctrine of "most-favored-nation" treatment, concerning which we shall have something to say in the next chapter.

The uneconomic effects of quantitative limitations on trade are even more severe than in the case of tariffs. When, because of an import quota, the quantity of goods imported is less than the demand for imports at current prices, the link between the price abroad and that at home is entirely severed. The extensive employment of quantitative controls results, then, in a virtual breakdown of the price mechanism as a guide in the international allocation of resources.

Consumption Effects

The effects of trade restrictions are not confined to distorting the allocation of resources and the accompanying loss of some of the specialization benefits of trade. Consumption is also distorted, and the full exchange benefits of trade are prevented from being realized.

Just as the loss from inefficient allocation as the result of trade restrictions is the counterpart of the gain from specialization under free trade, so the loss to consumers as the result of trade restrictions is the counterpart of the exchange benefits of free trade. (On the specialization and exchange benefits of trade, see Chapter 4.) From the point of view of the individual consumer, the loss shows up directly in the form of higher prices and reduced consumption of imported products. More generally regarded, the creation of artificial price differences through tariffs and quotas forces consumption into patterns which yield less total utility than is yielded by given expenditure when prices are equalized internationally. Tariffs and quotas divide consumers in different countries into separate sets, each set subject to different price relationships. Consequently, they are denied the opportunity of maximizing utility through equalizing the marginal utility ratios of each pair of goods.[3]

The Distribution of Income

It will be recalled that one of the effects of international trade, conducted in the context of the Heckscher-Ohlin model, is a redistribution of income in favor of the owners of the relative abundant factor of production and away from the owners of the relative scarce factor of production. (See the discussion p. 61 ff., above.) Import restrictions reverse the direction of this redistribution, favoring the relatively scarce factor at the expense of the relatively abundant factor. In a relatively labor-scarce country, for example, the unimpeded importation of labor-intensive products reduces the demand for labor and the wage rate. Restriction of the import of such products increases the demand for their home production, thus raises the demand for labor and the wage rate. At the same time, of course, the demand for the relatively abundant factor, capital, is reduced and its rate of return decreased.

In addition to the above general effects of trade restrictions on income distribution, particular factors of production that are specialized and not readily transferable among different employments are prone to be harmed, or benefited, by trade restrictions. For example, suppose that a country has a comparative disadvantage in the labor-intensive pottery industry and that pottery workers have specialized skills and training not useful in other industries. The introduction of free trading relations with other countries would tend to cause a contraction in domestic production of pottery and the discharge of pottery workers, who would either remain unemployed or be forced into lower-wage occupations. Restrictions on the import of pottery, on the other hand, would preserve the market for the domestic industry and therewith the jobs and wages of potters.

By the same reasoning, however, specialized workers in *export* industries would tend to be adversely affected by import restrictions.

---

[3] For consumer sets A and B each to realize maximum total utility from the consumption of X and Y, the ratio of the marginal utility of X to the marginal utility of Y must be the *same* for A and B. Otherwise, both could gain utility by trading, each exchanging the good the marginal utility of which is relatively smaller for him for the good the marginal utility of which is relatively greater. When each set of consumers is confronted with a common set of prices, the maximum utility condition is satisfied, since each consumer seeks to equate the ratio of the marginal utilities of X and Y to a common price ratio. Different prices for different consumers interfere with this process.

To the extent that reduced imports lead to reduced exports, import restrictions cause employment opportunities and wage rates in export industries to contract.

Effects on the Balance of Payments

Apart from the effects of tariffs, quotas, and related policies on the allocation of resources and on consumption, they may also be a source of balance-of-payments disequilibrium and an impediment to the adjustment mechanism. Starting from a position of equilibrium, an increase in tariffs by one major country or group of countries reduces the exports of other countries, causing a balance-of-payments deficit and necessitating readjustments of a structural character. Or, to take another example, a major creditor country may, by raising a high tariff wall, make it virtually impossible for its debtors to develop the export surplus which repayment of their debts demands. This is one, though not the only, reason why, for example, there were such widespread defaults in the 1930s on the foreign loans of the United States. At the beginning of that decade, the United States raised its tariffs to the highest level in its history, thereby adding to the effects of the depression in reducing American import demand.

The Effective Rate of Protection

Since tariffs are taxes, like other taxes they are a source of revenue to the government. However, except for some less developed countries, other types of taxes are generally preferred as sources of governmental revenue. The principal purpose of tariffs, as well as of other forms of import restrictions, is to *protect* domestic industries against foreign competition by raising the cost and reducing the volume of imports. The more protective a tariff is, the less revenue it yields to the government.

The degree of protection given to domestic producers by the tariff schedule of a country depends, in the first instance, upon the average height of the tariff wall. It is difficult accurately to measure how high a tariff wall is. A common, but quite misleading, method is to take the ratio which total duty collections bear to the total value of imports. But suppose that on a large list of commodities the tariff is so high that the import of these commodities is very small, while other commodities are on the "free" list (no duties) or are subject to low duties and therefore are imported in relatively large volume.

Since the volume of imports of the highly protected articles is low, obviously the amount of duties collected will also be low; hence the ratio of duties collected to total imports may be small, even though some or most tariff rates are very high.

Perhaps the least unsatisfactory method of measuring the height of tariffs is converting all tariffs to an ad valorem basis and calculating the average. Theoretically, a *weighted* average would be more significant than an unweighted one. But there are serious statistical and conceptual difficulties in choosing the proper weights to be assigned. If duties are weighted by the amount of each commodity imported, we are back to the misleading results described above, with high duties given little weight and low duties high weights. For these reasons, an *unweighted* average, notwithstanding its limitations, may be the most meaningful.

The degree of protection afforded by a given tariff is not always accurately measured by the nominal tariff rate. A far superior measure of the protectiveness of a tariff is given by the so-called "effective rate of protection," which may be either higher or lower than the nominal tariff rate. The distinction between the nominal tariff rate and the effective rate of protection becomes essential whenever the tariff is levied on a finished good which contains imported raw materials or intermediate products subject to tariff rates different from that on the finished good. For example, suppose that woolen fabrics are subject to a 30 percent import duty, while wool is duty-free. The effective rate of protection for the domestic fabric industry is then greater than indicated by the tariff. The difference between the nominal and the effective rates depends upon the proportion of the final value of the fabric contributed by the wool component. For instance, assume that the wool input contributes half the value of the finished fabric. This means that the *value added* by the wool fabric industry is the remaining half the value of the finished product. Hence, the 30 percent tariff on the fabric is in reality a *60 percent* tariff on the value added by the domestic fabric industry!

Should a tariff be imposed on wool greater than that on finished fabric, the effective rate of the fabric tariff would be *less* than the nominal rate. For instance, a 50 percent tariff on wool would place domestic producers of fabrics at a disadvantage compared to foreign producers by 25 percent of the final value of the fabric (continuing to assume that wool contributes half the value of fabric). Subtracting this from the 30 percent duty on fabric leaves a net protection of 5 percent of the value of the fabric, or 10 percent of value added by fabric manufacturers. Thus, the effective rate of protection for the fabric industry would be only 10 percent, compared to the nominal rate of 30 percent. Only when the same rate of duty is levied on a final product and all its imported components are the nominal and effective rates of protection the same.

THE ORIGINS OF TRADE IMPEDIMENTS[4]

In view of the indisputable distortions in the structure of world production and trade and the loss of real income that are caused by tariffs, quotas, and related measures, it may be a source of some wonderment to the student that mankind has devoted so much of its energy to creating such devices. Upon closer examination, however, the apparent paradox disappears. As in other social sciences, so in international economics we must always clearly distinguish between the general and the particular, the impact on society as a whole and that on individuals or groups within the society. With respect to the problem under discussion, it is necessary to examine possible *conflicting interests* on three different levels: (*a*) the national economy versus the world as a whole, (*b*) the national economy versus those productive factors within the economy that are in relatively scarce supply, and (*c*) the national economy versus domestic producers that compete with foreign producers.

THE NATIONAL ECONOMY VERSUS THE WORLD ECONOMY

The arguments in favor of free trade and against all forms of artificial impediments to trade up to this point have had as their base of reference the world as a whole. In the application of theoretical principles to the actual world, we must take account of the fact that an overall, world point of view can seldom be expected to be taken by each of the numerous individual national states which are the component parts of the world economy.

Improve the Terms of Trade

While free trade can be proved on rational grounds to be the best policy for the world as a whole, it is more difficult to reach a similar conclusion from the point of view of the individual national economy. Our earlier analysis proved only that *some* trade is more de-

---

4 The discussion which follows relates to *protectionist* measures. So-called "revenue" tariffs are no longer very important except in underdeveloped areas where the fiscal machinery is inadequate to finance government expenditure from other sources.

sirable, from the national standpoint, than no trade at all; but it has not proved that a *free-trade* policy is always preferable to a policy which includes tariffs, quotas, or other trade restrictions short of complete stoppage of trade.

Indeed, it can be theoretically demonstrated that, *under certain conditions,* an individual country can realize a net gain by imposing tariffs.[5] This can be done, on the analogy of an individual firm, by the country acting monopolistically. A monopolistic firm raises the price at which its product sells (i.e., improves its "terms of trade") by restricting output below the competitive level. A country's terms of trade are improved, and its share of the gain from trade therefore increased, if import prices are lowered relative to its export prices. Now we have already seen in the discussion above of the price effects of tariffs and quotas that the foreign export price of a commodity may be lowered as the result of a tariff or quota in an importing country. Particularly is this the case if (*a*) the country imposing the tariff or quota imports a significant proportion of total world imports of the commodity and (*b*) the supply of the commodity is relatively inelastic in the exporting country or countries. Under such conditions, a country may lower the price it pays for its imports, improving its terms of trade, by, analogously to the monopolistic firm, artificially restricting import demand through tariffs or quotas.[6] *This means, however, that the gain realized by the country imposing the tariff (or quota) is at the expense of other countries;* that is, the distribution of world income is altered in favor of the tariff- or quota-levying country.

The possibility of a country's increasing its gains from trade by raising tariffs is contingent upon the absence of retaliatory action by other countries. In fact, however, other countries would be able to reduce the loss imposed upon them by foreign tariffs through increasing their own tariffs. As Scitovsky has shown, there is, therefore, a strong natural tendency for tariffs to be raised, in a series of retalia-

---

[5] See the analysis, which has been heavily drawn upon in this section, of Tibor Scitovsky, "A Reconsideration of the Theory of Tariffs," *Review of Economic Studies,* vol. 9 (1942); reprinted in American Economic Association, *Readings in the Theory of International Trade,* eds. Howard S. Ellis and Lloyd A. Metzler (Homewood, Ill.: Richard D. Irwin, Inc., 1949), pp. 358 ff.

[6] A distinction must be drawn between the effects of the tariff or quota on the price paid by private importers (and consumers) and the *social cost* of imports to the economy. If the foreign export price falls, the social cost falls to the importing country, even though private importers pay a higher price, with the duty, than before. Similarly in the case of quotas, the domestic consumer ordinarily pays a higher price because of the quota, but the social cost of the good is less if the foreign export price falls.

tions and counterretaliations, until the volume of trade shrinks to a fraction of its former level and any initial gains realized by individual countries are wiped out. Even though, then, there is sometimes the possibility of gain by a national economy through raising its tariffs and improving its terms of trade, such a policy, besides being unneighborly, runs the risk of being self-defeating in the end.

Essentially the same arguments apply to another method of attempting to improve the terms of trade, namely, to levy an *export* tariff. Instead of forcing import prices downward through an import tariff, a country may in certain circumstances be able to force the prices of export commodities upward through an export tariff (or other device to restrict exports). To succeed in this endeavor, the country must furnish a significant portion of the world's output of the good, so that the world's supply of the good is reduced as the result of the tariff. If, in addition, the world's demand for the product is inelastic, the prospect of gaining significantly from the export tariff is improved. As before, however, any gain is at the expense of other importing countries, with retaliatory actions a likely response.

Reduce Unemployment

There are three other arguments for protective tariffs based on the interests of an individual national economy as a whole which, under certain conditions, have a limited validity. The first is that tariffs or other import restrictions may, in times of unemployment, increase employment and national income. As we shall see later, import expenditures, like savings, constitute a leakage in the domestic income stream, while exports add to the domestic income stream. If, therefore, imports can be reduced while exports are maintained, the foreign-trade multiplier will operate to increase national income by a multiple of the reduced import expenditures.

Again, however, the practical consideration arises that this can be an effective means of reducing unemployment only if it is not adopted by all or a large number of countries. Clearly, all countries cannot simultaneously reduce imports and maintain exports. If just one small country is plagued with unemployment, it may be successful in combating it by decreasing its imports. In fact, however, unemployment in a major country tends to spread internationally, and the attempt of such a country to "export" its unemployment through restricting imports results in accelerating the spread.

Apart from its practical limitations, tariffs as a device for mitigating unemployment have the unfortunate effects on the efficiency of resource use described previously. Moreover, alternative policies are possible which would relieve unemployment at home while encouraging greater employment abroad and a larger volume of international trade.

Encourage Industrialization

Another "national" basis for protective tariffs is that a free-trade policy may prevent an argricultural country or an underdeveloped economy from realizing the industrialization upon which, in the modern world, a higher standard of living depends. This is one of the primary arguments for protection and goes back to the early period of economic expansion accompanying the Industrial Revolution.

The Infant-Industry Argument. The "infant-industry" argument is the most famous and widely invoked variation of the general thesis. Alexander Hamilton, in his *Report on Manufactures* (1791), was one of the first to state it clearly. The broader thesis, involving quasi-political and sociological elements as well as economic aspects, was developed on the European continent, especially by Friedrich List in *The National System of Political Economy* (1840). The argument runs that certain individual industries in a country may not have the opportunity to develop because of the competition from already established industries in more highly developed countries, even though, once developed, they would have a comparative advantage. If these industries are protected from foreign competition during their early development, or "infancy," later they will be able to stand on their own feet and survive foreign competition.

Theoretically, the infant-industry argument has a considerable degree of validity. The economic development of countries has not proceeded simultaneously, and historical accident in the location of industries has played a not unimportant role. Even on a theoretical basis, though, the argument can be, and often has been, carried too far. Organizing an industry always requires an interim period before it is firmly established and able to operate efficiently. This has not prevented the rapid development of new industries in competition with older ones *within* countries, and there is no fundamental reason why competition from established industries in other countries should always constitute a much more serious barrier.

Whatever its theoretical merits, the infant-industry argument runs into serious difficulties in practical application. How can it be determined which particular potential industries would, under a protective cover, develop a comparative advantage and be able to withstand foreign competition without continued protection? It is certain that many would clamor for protection, and it is equally certain that the claims of most would not be economically justifiable. Moreover, in the numerous instances where protection turns out to have been a mistake, it becomes extremely difficult to remove the protection and thereby seal the fate of inefficient firms. Lastly, unless the protective tariff is placed on a definite timetable, which is firmly adhered to, the incentive to develop increasing efficiency is weakened, and the basic idea of the program is subverted. Historical experience demonstrates that, in fact, it is much easier for infant industries to obtain protection than it is to remove protection.

General Industrialization.   Broader than the infant-industry argument, but in a similar vein, is the proposition, stated at the beginning of this section, that not only particular industries but general industrialization must be developed if a country is to enjoy a high standard of living. This argument is of especial current interest in connection with the efforts of underdeveloped areas to improve their economic situation.

There are good reasons for believing that a considerable degree of industrialization is indeed necessary for raising the standard of living of many of the underdeveloped areas of the world to a level approaching that of, say, Western Europe. It is also clear, on the other hand, as we shall show later, that the fundamental barrier to industrialization in such areas is not competition from abroad but rather the paucity of capital and technological knowledge and the absence of other conditions favorable to development.

It may be granted that underdeveloped areas have little chance of creating heavy industries, such as steel, for example, in open competition with the highly developed industries of the United States and Western Europe. It may also be true that, in some instances at least, general industrial development carries with it economic by-products which are not realized in the case of the limited and partial industrialization accomplished by the creation of a few infant industries.

The great danger of protective tariffs and quantitative import controls as devices for encouraging overall industrialization, however, is that the wrong kind of industries will be created. There is nothing in the theory of comparative advantage that requires a division of the world into primary producing countries and industrial countries. But it is contrary to economic principles for all countries to attempt to develop the *same* industries. The types of industry which the underdeveloped areas can economically create and maintain are generally those which do not require protection on any large scale, for they are based on natural advantages. Although generalizations are often misleading, we may conclude that, with some possible exceptions, any country that requires general protection in order to industrialize is probably developing an uneconomic structure which is inconsistent with the future realization of its full potentialities.

Military, Political, and Economic Security

Free international trade creates economic interdependencies among participating countries. The more specialized a national economy becomes, the greater is its dependence upon foreign sources of supply for its imports and upon foreign demand for its exports as a means of paying for its imports. Such dependence carries with it vulnerability to economic disturbances over which the national economy has no control. It may also give to foreign countries the power to disrupt the domestic economy as a deliberate policy designed to achieve a military, political, or economic goal.

In wartime, of course, normal trade among belligerents is cut off, and an effort is made to stop the flow of supplies to enemy countries through naval blockades, submarine attacks on shipping lanes, etc. To the extent that a country is dependent upon imports of resources essential for national defense industries, the military security and offensive capability of a country may thus be seriously impaired. Accordingly, one argument for restricting trade is to decrease dependence upon foreign sources of supply of those resources which are strategic for national defense.

A similar basis for justifying trade restrictions is to decrease vulnerability to foreign political pressures. An outstanding example was the long-time policy of the Soviet Union, only recently relaxed, to refrain from extensive foreign trade in order to avoid external pressures from the capitalist world. A more recent example of the political implications of foreign economic dependence is the oil export embargo of Middle Eastern countries, supposedly designed to force a change in the policies of oil importing countries toward Israel.

On the basis of economics, per se, one cannot categorically conclude that trade restrictions for military or political security are, or are not, warranted, for the objectives involved are noneconomic in character. However, there are important economic implications of such policies which must be taken into account in determining whether they are rational policies.

In a certain sense, the security of a country can be increased by restricting trade and thereby reducing economic dependence upon the outside world. It is, however, comparable to the kind of security an individual family can achieve by withdrawing from the market economy and establishing a self-sufficient household economy. In both cases, greater self-sufficiency reduces exposure to external events, *but at the cost of a reduction in the standard of living.* As always, the question, then, is whether the benefits are worth the cost.

For example, as the result of the embargo on oil exports to the United States by the Middle East producing countries, mentioned above, and the resulting energy crisis it produced, President Nixon announced it will be the policy of the United States to seek energy self-sufficiency by 1980. While few observers would disagree with the objective of relieving the United States from the possibility of being blackmailed by the threat of foreign suppliers, the objective must be weighed against the probable tremendous cost to the economy of energy self-sufficiency.

A second observation is that the intended result of greater national security through restrictions on trade may not in fact be achieved. The attempt to promote military security by fostering the exploitation of domestic resources instead of relying upon foreign supplies may backfire by leading to an early exhaustion of domestic resources and a later increased dependence on outside sources.

More generally, the effects of protective tariffs on military security must take into account the close relationship between overall economic strength and military power. Any weakening of the economy is bound to have adverse repercussions on military potential. This holds not only for individual national economies but also for the group of countries which are politically and militarily allied. In other words, economic interdependence among countries which are politically and militarily interdependent is a source of strength rather than weakness. A report by a Senate committee has concluded: "National security depends upon many factors, not the least of which is a community of economically healthy nations devoted to living in harmony and tied together by mutually beneficial trade."[7]

---

[7] *Defense Essentiality and Foreign Economic Policy,* Senate Report No. 2629, 84th Cong., 2d sess. (Washington, D.C.: U.S. Government Printing Office, 1956), p. 28.

THE NATIONAL INTEREST VERSUS THE INTEREST OF OWNERS OF SCARCE FACTORS

As noted previously, one effect of trade is to redistribute income within trading countries, with restrictions on trade tending to cause a reversal in the redistribution back toward the pretrade pattern.

It follows from this that protective tariffs or other import restrictions may be of benefit to one segment of the economy, even though they are deleterious to the economy as a whole. This may help to explain, in fact, many of the bitter historical tariff controversies: between landlords and manufacturers in England over the effects of the Corn Laws on agricultural rents and real wages; between the advocates of protective tariffs in the industrial North and the free-trade agricultural South in the United States; and the arguments for tariffs in Australia on the grounds of protecting the share of workers in the national income.

Whether or not this argument for protective tariffs is acceptable depends upon value judgment comparisons of the welfare of one group within the economy and the welfare of the society as a whole. Such conflicts of interest cannot be solved by objective standards, but one point should be emphasized: free trade, by increasing real national income, makes it *possible* for *everyone's* economic welfare to be advanced; tariffs for the benefit of one particular group of productive agents lower real national income below its free-trade level and therefore reduce the economic well-being of other factor groups. (Exceptions have already been noted in those cases where the national economy as a whole benefits from tariffs.)

Prevent the Pauperization of Labor

One of the most common arguments used in the United States in favor of protective tariffs is that free trade would tend to "pauperize" American labor. The logical basis for this assertion is usually put in something like the following terms: (*a*) wage rates in the United States are far higher than in most other countries of the world; (*b*) therefore, costs of production tend to be lower in other countries; (*c*) hence, under free trade, foreign goods would flood the American markets; and (*d*) American producers would thereby be forced to lower wage rates to a level approximating foreign wage rates.

The critical defect in the above line of reasoning lies at stage (*b*), rendering the remainder of the argument and the conclusion reached invalid. It is not true to say that low money wages necessarily mean low *wage costs per unit of output*. The latter is a function of two elements—money wage rates and the *productivity* of labor. Suppose that the wages of workers in the shoe industry are the equivalent of 25 cents per hour in Italy and $2 per hour in the United States. Suppose, further, that the average output of shoes per man-hour is 1 pair in Italy and 10 pairs in the United States. Then the wage costs per pair of shoes is 25 cents in Italy and 20 cents in the United States.

But, it might be objected, the above example is unfairly "loaded" with the assumption that labor productivity in the United States is so much greater than in Italy. The objection is overcome by the principles of wage determination: real wages are the *fruits* of per capita productivity. Wages in the United States are higher than in Italy because the American worker is more productive than the Italian worker—not, let it be emphasized, because of an inherent superiority, but because of the larger supply of capital, more advanced technology, (possibly) the advantages of large-scale production, and so on. The only way, then, that real wages could be lowered would be through decreases in labor productivity. On the basis of this principle, a grain of truth hidden in the pauper labor argument can be detected. As our earlier theoretical discussion of the effects of trade on income distribution showed, free trade tends to lower the marginal productivity—and therefore market income share—of a country's relatively most scarce factor of production. Labor's income share in the United States might therefore be higher with protective tariffs than under free trade. However, to the extent that free trade results in an aggregate national income greater than would be produced under restricted trade, any adverse effect of free trade on the income share of a particular group could be compensated for and still leave the remainder of the population better off than they would be under restricted trade.

THE NATIONAL INTEREST VERSUS SPECIAL-INTEREST GROUPS

Protective tariffs affect not only the functional distribution of income within a country, but, like most taxes, also affect the *personal* distribution of income.[8] Besides the owners of the relatively scarce factors of production who may benefit from protective tariffs in general, there are numerous individuals and firms who ordinarily stand to gain from nearly every specific tariff. As we have seen, an import duty tends to reduce the volume of import and to raise the domestic price of the commodity on which the tariff is levied. This is bound to be of immediate benefit to domestic producers of the good, or of close substitutes for it, and to those factors of production, if any, which are specific to the protected industry.

On the other hand, as consumers, the public is forced to pay higher prices for the protected commodity. There appears, therefore, to be a conflict of interest between the particular producers who benefit from the tariff and the general public, which suffers higher consumer prices.

The special-interest advocates of tariffs deny that there is such a conflict of interests. In support of this contention, a large battery of arguments has been built up, the chief of which we shall now state and critically evaluate.

Expand Production and Enlarge the Market

The argument that protective tariffs are in the general interest of a country because they expand production and enlarge the market has a beguiling appeal. The interests of various producer groups are closely woven together, so that direct benefits accruing to one group will indirectly redound to the profit of others. Hence, if manufacturing industries are given the benefits of protective tariffs, thereby increasing wages and profits, the market for agricultural and other goods will expand, and the farmers and other producing groups will have reflected upon them the prosperity which only appears to be confined to the protected industries.

Moreover, if it is true, as we have said, that an individual industry may benefit from a protective tariff, is it not true that all producers could be benefited by extending the tariff to protect them?

There are two serious flaws in the above argument. The first is that, with fully employed resources,[9] aggregate domestic production

---

[8] Personal income distribution refers to the distribution of income among families or individuals, rather than according to the productive functions performed by the income receiver (functional distribution of income).

[9] If there is unemployment, the argument reduces to that already described and evaluated above.

cannot be expanded by protective tariffs, for any expansion in one field of economic activity must necessarily be at the expense of reduced output in other fields The main effect of tariffs in this event is to draw resources away from previous employments into the protected industries.

The second flaw in the argument ties in with the statement made in the last preceding sentence. Some of the resources reallocated by the effects of protective tariffs are very likely to be drawn away from the production of export goods. There is, in fact, a probability that export industries would undergo a considerable contraction; for, by leading to a reduction in the volume of imports, protective tariffs tend to reduce the foreign demand for the country's exports. While it may very well be true, therefore, that the *domestic* market would be expanded, any such expansion would tend to be at the expense of the export market. In the final analysis, then, protective tariffs tend to result in a reallocation of resources from the relatively efficient export industries to the relatively inefficient protected industries. This can hardly be said to be of benefit to the economy as a whole.

Equalize the Costs of Production at Home and Abroad

This argument is designed to appeal to the sense of fair play in eliminating "unfair" and "cutthroat" competition from abroad. Some foreign producers, it is said, are able, because of special advantages, to undersell domestic producers. The advantages enjoyed by the foreign producers might be lower wage costs, more favorable climatic conditions, or any of the other numerous factors which help determine costs of production. In order to equalize the position of domestic and foreign producers in these instances, tariffs equivalent to the differences in the costs of production should be levied.

We may agree with everything in this proposition, except the conclusion. There are indeed special advantages enjoyed by the foreign producers of certain products; precisely for this reason international trade is advantageous. Artificially to eliminate the advantages is tantamount to eliminating the gains from trade. As a matter of fact, carried to its logical conclusion, a policy of equalizing foreign and domestic costs through tariffs would totally eliminate trade and would produce the conditions of an isolated and self-sufficient economy with the lower standard of living that inevitably would accompany it.

May there not, however, be a danger that foreigners will be able to produce *everything* cheaper than at home? The answer is emphatically negative. International trade is based on *comparative* advantages, and, as demonstrated in the second and third chapters of this book, it is inherently impossible for a country to have a comparative disadvantage in *all* products.[10] Confusion on this point usually derives from the belief that since wages or some other element of costs are generally lower abroad than domestically, all foreign goods must have lower costs of production. Lower wages do not, however, mean lower *wage costs,* which are a function of labor productivity as well as wages. Low real wages normally are the *result* of low productivity, and high real wages are the result of great productivity. Hence, it is quite possible for high wages to be accompanied by low *wage costs* per unit of output.

Since low wages and a relatively abundant labor supply ordinarily go hand in hand, it is generally true, of course, that low-wage countries do have an advantage in the production of those goods requiring in their production a relatively large quantity of labor. The *proportion* of labor to other factors of production varies, on the other hand, among different goods, so that the advantages thus realized are limited to only certain commodities.

Keep Money at Home

Imports, as we shall see, reduce the domestically held supply of money. Do not imports, therefore, have undesirable repercussions on the economy?

In its crudest form, this argument is based on the most elementary type of fallacious thinking. First, it is based on a mercantilist identity of money and wealth. Even if it were true that tariffs, by reducing imports, keep the domestic supply of money at a higher volume, this would make no direct contribution to the real income and wealth of the country.

Moreover, even though imports, per se, tend to reduce the domestic supply of money, exports tend equally to increase it. If, as we have concluded, a reduction in imports tends to have the ultimate effect of also reducing exports, no net addition to the supply of money is realized. To put it in commonsense terms, any money that is "ex-

---

10 For a comparative disadvantage in one product necessarily implies a comparative advantage in another. Thus, a comparative disadvantage in wheat compared to cloth *means* a comparative advantage in cloth compared to wheat.

ported" to pay for commodity imports will ultimately tend to seek its way back to the country of issue, in the exercise of its only real basis of value—the purchase of goods and services or payment of debts.

It must be granted, however, that in a more sophisticated form the argument is not wholly devoid of meaning. If a country is suffering from unemployment and deflation, an increase in the supply of money may well have beneficial effects, especially through lowered interest rates. Particularly if a country is on the gold standard and has rigid limitations on the ratio between the gold reserve and the supply of money, protective tariffs, if they are successful in promoting an export surplus, may have beneficial repercussions on employment and income, not only directly via the foreign-trade multiplier, but indirectly via easier money conditions. This is a variation of the full-employment argument, considered earlier, and is subject to the limitations noted at that time.

In any event, in most contemporary economies, the supply of money is no longer mainly or even significantly dependent upon the balance of payments. Central bank and fiscal policies are much more potent weapons of monetary control within a country than is manipulation of the trade balance, and they have the additional advantage of not interfering with the most efficient allocation of resources.

Retaliation or Increased Bargaining Power

Retaliation may be appropriately labeled the "small-boy" argument: if you are punched in the nose, hit back, even if you lose your front teeth in the process.

If foreign countries raise their tariffs, a given country will lose some of the benefits of trade formerly received. Retaliation does not, however, recoup the loss but, on the contrary, only aggravates it by still further reducing the volume of trade. As noted earlier, retaliation may yield immediate benefits in the form of improved terms of trade, but the probability is that this will prove ephemeral by leading to counterretaliation.

The bargaining-power argument also involves an increase in tariffs in response to foreign tariff increases. In this case, though, the intent, at least, is honorable, for the avowed purpose is to use offers of rescinding the retaliatory action as a weapon for obtaining reciprocal treatment.

In some instances, there may be validity in this line of reasoning. The danger, however, is that the expected agreement on reciprocal reduction of tariffs will not materialize, in which case it is highly unlikely that the tariffs will be brought back to their original level by unilateral action. Moreover, we may suspect that opposition to lowering tariffs, on the grounds that this would weaken the country's bargaining position, as well as advocacy of higher tariffs to strengthen bargaining power, are both often used as cover for ulterior and less generous motives.

CONCLUSION

With one or two possible exceptions of a very limited kind, none of the arguments for protective tariffs can withstand searching analysis. Some have a degree of theoretical validity under certain assumptions, but in practice they are, more often than not, self-defeating.

The truth is that most specific tariffs are put on the books through the efforts of special-interest groups. We have examined some of the arguments with which these efforts have been rationalized and have found them to be misleading, at least, and often based on crudely fallacious reasoning.

One of the real difficulties in combating tariffs is the failure on the part of the consuming public to realize how its interests are affected. In effect, a tariff amounts to a subsidy to the domestic producers of the dutiable article (paid by the consumers of that article in the form of a higher price), though it is rare for a tariff to be levied for that avowed, specific purpose. Because tariffs (and other trade restrictions) are, in effect, indirect subsidies, the objective being sought could in most cases be achieved through *direct* subsidies without restricting trade. In the event that a subsidy is deemed, on whatever grounds, to be desirable, there are two advantages of providing the subsidy directly rather than through trade restrictions.

The first advantage of a direct subsidy is its greater visibility. The public is more likely to be aware of the cost a subsidy imposes upon it when the subsidy appears in the government budget. The critical scrutiny of taxpayers presumably would provide some safeguard against an unwarranted subsidy.

A more important advantage of direct subsidies over tariffs and other trade restrictions is avoidance of the secondary distorting effects of the latter. To illustrate, suppose that it is desired to expand the domestic production of good X beyond free-trade levels. This could be accomplished by imposing an import tariff, thereby raising the domestic price and inducing an increase in the output of domestic firms. At the same time, however, domestic consumers are also confronted with a higher price of the commodity. Consequently, there is a consumption as well as a production effect of the tariff. The increased production of the good entails a loss of efficiency in resource allocation—that is, the loss of *specialization* gains from trade. The higher price of the commodity to consumers causes an *additional* welfare loss in the form of reduced *exchange* gains from trade. In contrast, a direct subsidy to producers involves only the loss of specialization gains, exchange gains being preserved through the continuation of pretariff prices to consumers. A similar argument applies when it is desired to reduce consumption of a good: a tariff would have the additional effect of increasing domestic production and distorting the allocation of resources, whereas the alternative of a *tax* on consumption, without the tariff, would accomplish the objective while avoiding the loss of specialization gains.

RECOMMENDED READINGS

BALDWIN, ROBERT E. "Nontariff Distortions of International Trade," in Robert E. Baldwin and J. David Richardson, *International Trade and Finance,* chap. 10. Boston: Little, Brown & Co., 1974.

BHAGWATI, JAGDISH AND RAMASWAMI, U. K. "Domestic Distortions, Tariffs, and the Theory of Optimum Subsidy," *Journal of Political Economy,* vol. 71, no. 1 (February 1963) , pp. 44–50.

BLACK, JOHN. "Arguments for Tariffs," *Oxford Economic Papers,* N. S. 11, June 1959, pp. 191–208.

CORDEN, W. M. "The Structure of a Tariff System and the Effective Protective Rate," *Journal of Political Economy,* June 1966.

———. "Tariffs, Subsidies, and the Terms of Trade," *Economica,* N. S. 24, August 1957, pp. 235–42.

GRUBEL, HERBERT G. "Effective Tariff Protection: A Non-Specialist Introduction to the Theory, Policy Implications, and Controversies," *Effective Tariff Protection.* Edited by Herbert Grubel and Harry Johnson. Geneva: General Agreement on Tariffs and Trade and Graduate Institute of International Studies, 1971, pp. 1–15.

JOHNSON, HARRY G. *Aspects of the Theory of Tariffs.* London: George Allen & Unwin, 1971.

YEAGER, LELAND B., AND TUERCK, DAVID G. *Trade Policy and the Price System.* Scranton, Pa.: International Textbook Co., 1966.

STUDY QUESTIONS

1. Define each of the following: import duty, export duty, transit duty, specific rate, ad valorem rate, compound rate, tariff schedule,

single-columned tariff, multicolumned tariff, import quota, and administrative protection.

2. In what sense are subsidies to domestic industry a substitute for tariffs?

3. Compare the restrictive effects on international trade of tariffs and quotas.

4. Define and give examples of technical and administrative protection.

5. What is meant by "dumping"?

6. Ignoring transportation costs and assuming that there are no quantitative restrictions on trade, why will the price of a good on which an import duty is levied tend to be higher in the importing country than it is abroad by the full amount of the duty?

7. In what sense may foreigners be made to "pay" a tariff?

8. Under what conditions is a country unable to influence the world price of a commodity by imposing a tariff?

9. Show the influence of elasticities of demand and supply on the price effect of a tariff.

10. Explain the statement that the effect of free international trade is to eliminate the inequality of price ratios in different countries, whereas the effect of tariffs is artificially to recreate relative price differences. Which of these two effects is the more desirable from the standpoint of the optimum allocation of the world's productive resources?

11. Why would the extensive use of import quotas tend to destroy the function of the price mechanism as a guide in the international allocation of resources?

12. What is meant by the "consumption effects" of trade restrictions?

13. How do tariffs affect the distribution of income?

14. Distinguish between the nominal and the effective rate of protection afforded by tariffs.

15. Under what circumstances may a country obtain a larger share of the gain from international trade by raising its tariffs? Why cannot all countries play this game at the same time? Why is any gain realized by a country through this method likely to prove temporary?

16. An increase in tariffs for the purpose of reducing unemployment is more likely to redistribute the unemployed than to cause a net reduction in the total number unemployed. Explain.

17. State and critically evaluate the "infant-industry" argument for tariffs. In what countries of the world today would you expect to find the infant-industry argument most commonly invoked?

18. Evaluate the argument that tariffs on some commodities are re-

quired for the purpose of increasing the military security of the state.

19. Do high American wages imply high labor costs per unit of output in all American industries? Why not?

20. What is wrong with the proposition that protective tariffs expand production and enlarge the market?

21. Why is it impossible for a given country to be able to sell *all* goods and services at lower prices than other countries?

22. What are the logical implications of the proposal to levy tariffs in an amount that would equalize foreign and domestic costs of production?

23. Granted that imports do tend to reduce the supply of domestically held money, why is this not a valid argument in favor of reducing imports through protective tariffs?

24. Explain in what manner a protective tariff amounts in effect to a subsidy to the domestic producers of the commodity.

25. Show how subsidies to domestic industry in the form of tariffs impose a greater social cost than imposed by direct subsidies.

10

Commercial policies of the United States

The world has never experienced international trade completely free of artificially erected barriers of one kind or another. But the nature and extent of trade barriers have varied greatly in different periods of history, the pendulum swinging from eras marked by exceedingly detailed and stringent controls over trade, to eras during which a free-trade philosophy was more or less closely carried out in practice, and back again to a resurgence of timeworn restrictionism. These vacillating commercial-policy movements have not, of course, taken place in a vacuum: they have been part and parcel of broader historical developments—political, social, and ideological, as well as economic.

It is manifestly impossible within the space of one chapter to give a detailed historical review of the commercial policies of all major countries. In this chapter we shall concentrate, therefore, on the commercial policies of the United States, with special emphasis on the period since 1934. Before embarking upon this, however, it might be useful to have in mind the perspective afforded by a résumé of the main currents of commercial-policy development in the major trading countries in modern times.

A BIRD'S-EYE VIEW OF COMMERCIAL-POLICY HISTORY

Mercantilism

The mercantilist era, which may be roughly dated from about 1500 to 1750, was characterized by a mass of detailed regulations and controls over international trade. England, France, Spain, and Portugal were the chief powers that followed the policies associated with mercantilism. The other great power during this period—Holland—pursued a much less restrictive course with respect to trade, except for that with her colonies.

The main underlying objective of commercial policy was to develop an export *surplus*—a so-called "favorable" balance of trade. In pursuit of this objective, exports were pushed to the utmost—through export subsidies, prohibition of the export of raw materials necessary in the domestic production of more valuable exports, "drawbacks" of excise and import duties, and so on.[1] At the same time, imports were severely restricted, except for raw materials needed for domestic production and except for the precious metals. The devices employed to restrict imports ranged from outright prohibition to high protective tariffs.

The immediate function of an export surplus was to acquire the precious metals. The reasons advanced for considering this to be a prime objective of economic policy varied greatly among mercantilist writers: the crude identification of gold and silver with wealth; the desirability of creating an emergency reserve for the state; as a means of exercising thrift and storing wealth; in order to stimulate domestic economic activity. From the point of view of modern economic theory, many, though not all, of these arguments appear to be based on fallacious reasoning. But such a pervasive doctrine can hardly be explained as simply the consequence of errant logic.

Mercantilism can be explained only in terms of the historical setting out of which it grew: the rise of national states, the almost continuous series of civil wars and international conflicts, the growing power of the commerical class, and the beginnings of scientific thought.

---

[1] "Drawbacks" are rebates to exporters of duties which have been paid on materials used in the manufacture of exported commodities.

The Free-Trade Movement

As the historical circumstances which produced mercantilism gradually changed, the balance-of-trade theory and the restrictionist policies which were appropriate thereto became anachronistic and hostile to the spirit and requirements of the time. Of outstanding importance were the economic and technological developments described as the Industrial Revolution and the accompanying growth of power and influence on the part of the business class. Detailed regulations and controls by the state over both internal and external trade were antagonistic to the developing notions of industrial venture and opportunity for profit after about the middle of the 18th century. At the same time, the intellectual and philosophic basis for rejecting the mercantilist theories was brilliantly provided by a series of writers, culminating in the classic work of Adam Smith. The virtues of free and unhampered private enterprise, both at home and in international trade, and the identification of the public interest with the pursuit of private gain by individuals were rationalized by Smith and classical economic theorists who followed him.

The long and unaccustomed period of peace which followed the Napoleonic Wars provided the atmosphere congenial to the practical implementation of the philosophy of laissez-faire. Gradually the mass of detailed regulations on internal commerce was swept away, and the free-trade movement gained momentum. After a long struggle between the landed aristocracy and the manufacturing interests, the culmination of the free-trade policy in England was reached in 1846 with the repeal of the Corn Laws.

For several decades in the middle part of the 19th century, the free-trade philosophy was in the saddle in the most important trading countries, though at no time were artificial restrictions completely eliminated.

The Revival of Protectionism

The era of laissez-faire and of the companion doctrine of free trade was not destined to continue unchallenged. Toward the last quarter of the 19th century, protectionist sentiment got the upper hand in most of the important trading countries, with the exception of Great Britain and Holland.

The explanation of this trend lies, for the most part, in the efforts of other countries to promote the kind of industrial development which had already come to England; the growing strength of nationalism and imperialism as a political and economic force; and the clamor of powerful special-interest groups for protection against the competition of foreign producers. The "intellectual" basis for protectionism has already been described in the preceding chapter.

The dislocations and maladjustments in the world economy caused by World War I, the rapid growth of competing industries and agriculture which a period of war naturally encourages, and the increasing economic instability which characterizes the highly complex modern industrial economies caused a further weakening of the laissez-faire and free-trade philosophy during the 1920s.

Notwithstanding the rising height of tariff walls, commercial policy in most countries never approached the extremes of mercantilism until the onset of worldwide depression at the beginning of the 1930s. Then, in a desperate attempt to stem the tide of unemployment and deflation, one country after another, with the United States in the vanguard, pushed tariffs to unprecedented heights, subsidized exports, introduced quantitative restrictions, practiced discrimination, and in other ways so emulated mercantilist policies as to evoke the description "neomercantilist." This appellation was especially apposite to Germany after 1933, when her commerical policy became simply a weapon of economic warfare, an integral part of the Nazi ultranationalistic, militaristic program of conquest. But, in a less extreme form, many other countries besides Germany revived mercantilist notions in their attempts to "export" unemployment and to relieve deflationary pressures by developing an export surplus.

Although, as previously indicated, the United States was one of the first major countries to resort to the highly restrictive commercial policies which characterized the depression decade, a few years later American policy underwent an apparently drastic change in outlook. Beginning in 1934 and continuing down to the present, the United States has become the leading official protagonist, as Great Britain was in the 19th century, for freer world trade. The nature and results of this movement can best be understood in the context of American commercial policy under the Reciprocal Trade Agreements program and its successors, so that we shall defer our discussion of it until the later pages of this chapter and the next chapter.

U.S. TARIFFS, 1789–1934

From the very beginnings of the United States as an independent nation and continuously since then, tariffs have been one of the major aspects of her foreign economic policy. Periodic increases and decreases of import duties have characterized the tariff history of the United States, but at no time has the doctrine of free trade been put to practice.

Tariffs for Revenue

Perhaps the primary origin of tariffs in the United States was the convenience which they offered in the early years of the Republic as a source of government revenue. Until the last decade of the 19th century, customs receipts provided half or more of the total ordinary revenue of the federal government. The political proponents of lower tariffs have nearly always, until recent decades, defended a minimum level of tariffs as a source of government revenue. Strange as it may seem to this generation, at times the strongest reason for reducing tariffs was to avoid an embarrassing redundance of revenue! This was the chief reason for reducing rates in 1857 and again in 1872. The basis of the revenue argument has, however, progressively weakened with the growth in government expenditure and the development of alternative sources of revenue, especially the income tax. By 1929 customs receipts constituted less than 15 percent, and by 1938 less than 6 percent, of ordinary government revenue; since then they have yielded a negligible percentage, currently less than 1 percent, of total federal revenue.

Tariffs for Protection

The weakening of the revenue argument for tariffs was accompanied by the growing strength of protectionist arguments. Indeed, there has probably been no tariff in American history which has not had some protectionist elements. According to its preamble, even the first tariff bill (1789), though imposing low rates, had as its purpose not only the provision of revenue but also "the encouragement and protection of manufactures."

The Napoleonic Wars and the War of 1812 greatly reduced the

import of manufactured goods into the United States and stimulated domestic manufactures. Upon the conclusion of peace with England in 1814, a flood of imports from that country flowed into the United States, threatening to ruin the recently established domestic manufacturing concerns. Agreement was general, therefore, even among those who were fundamentally low-tariff in principle, that tariffs should be high enough to protect American industry. The Tariff of 1816 reflected these sentiments; compared to the rates in 1789, which averaged about 8 percent ad valorem, rates on various imports were doubled, trebled, or quadrupled.[2]

While import duties were generally increased still further in the following years, increasing opposition was expressed to high rates, especially in the South. The Tariff Act of 1828 represented the extreme of protective legislation before the Civil War, earning the derisive epithets of the "Black Tariff" and the "Tariff of Abominations."[3] Its extremist character is indicated by the fact that it resulted in average ad valorem rates on dutiable imports of nearly 49 percent and on free and dutiable imports together of over 45 percent.[4] Such violent opposition was provoked in the South by these rates that there were threats of "nullification" and secession. As a consequence, the "compromise" Tariff of 1833 provided for the gradual reduction of all the higher rates and the enlargement of the free list. Although higher rates were restored in 1842, they were again cut in 1846 and 1857, bringing them, in general, to the lowest level since 1816.

Just before the outbreak of the Civil War, the tariff cuts of 1857 were eliminated. As war-financing requirements increased, higher duties were imposed; and in 1864, rates were raised to an average of 47 percent on dutiable goods. This high level of protection con-

---

[2] The percentage figures on the average height of the U.S. tariff, given here and elsewhere in this chapter, are subject to the weaknesses discussed earlier. The reader is warned, therefore, against accepting the figures as accurate measures of the absolute height of tariffs or as indicative of the degree of protection afforded thereby. However, there is evidence that *comparison* of the average rates for different periods of time gives a roughly accurate index of the *changes* in the height of the tariff, and it is only for this purpose that use of the figures is justified.

[3] The bill was apparently never intended to become law but was designed as a political stratagem to weaken the position of protectionist presidential candidates to the advantage of Jackson by including extremely high duties on raw materials. This was supposed to incur the wrath of northern manufacturing interests and result in its defeat; but the plan backfired when the bill was passed.

[4] U.S. Tariff Commission, *The Tariff and Its History* (Washington, D.C.: U.S. Government Printing Office, 1934), p. 73. Most of the factual material in this section is based on this study.

stituted the basis of tariff policy until 1883, when popular demand for reform led to minor downward revisions.

The election of Cleveland in 1884 put the Democratic party in power for the first time since the Civil War. Cleveland put his party on record for tariff reform, but his efforts to reduce rates failed. The Republicans returned to power with Harrison in 1888 on a platform that included as a major plank the protection of American labor against foreign "pauper" labor. The McKinley Tariff of 1890 raised the level of tariffs to close to 50 percent on dutiable articles and embodied the principle of protection as a permanent policy.

Although the Democratic administration which returned to office in 1892 attempted a general revision and reduction of the high duties imposed under the McKinley Tariff, Congress prevented any fundamental changes, except the abolition of the duty on wool. The election of McKinley in 1896 and the ensuing enactment of the Dingley Tariff of 1897 restored the duty on wool and raised the general level of tariffs to a thoroughly protectionist plane. Although some minor downward revision was effected by the Payne-Aldrich Tariff of 1909, no major changes were made until the administration of Woodrow Wilson.

The Underwood Tariff of 1913 threatened the first successful breach of the high protectionist wall which had been built up since the Civil War. Over one hundred items were added to the free list, and hundreds of rates were reduced on other items. The average rate was lowered from over 40 percent to less than 30 percent.

The war prevented the implementation of the Underwood Tariff; and, following the election of a Republican administration in 1920, the previous protectionist trend was firmly reestablished. In response to the postwar plight of the farmer, an emergency act in 1921 added many agricultural products to the protected list. The Fordney-McCumber Tariff of 1922 contained agricultural protection, raised other rates, and gave the President the power to raise or lower rates by as much as 50 percent to "equalize" foreign and domestic costs of production.

The culmination of the protectionist trend in the United States, which, as we have seen, suffered few interruptions from the time of the Civil War, was reached in 1930 with the passage of the notorious Hawley-Smoot Tariff. Probably no other piece of legislation in history has ever aroused as much furor and international ill will as this bill. Notwithstanding the protests of 24 countries, the export markets of which were in many cases seriously threatened, nor the more than 1,000 prominent American economists who petitioned President Hoover to veto the bill, tariffs were raised to the highest level (an average rate of over 52 percent on dutiable imports) in American history.

The unreasonable and frenetic character of the Hawley-Smoot Tariff is demonstrated by the fact that it covered many articles which were in no sense competitive with domestic products. Although many articles were on the free list, a number of them were not produced at all in the United States, while others appear to have been added for purposes of padding.[5]

The foreign retaliation which followed the Hawley-Smoot Tariff is an excellent historical illustration of the probable reaction to the attempt on the part of any major importing country to raise its tariffs, especially during a period of general economic and financial crisis. Partly as an independent policy but also partly in retaliation against the American tariff increases, tariffs in many foreign countries were raised very soon after the enactment of the Hawley-Smoot bill.

Although the decline in income and employment in the United States and other industrial countries was undoubtedly the main factor responsible, the network of tariffs, quotas, and other trade restrictions, which the American tariff of 1930 contributed to and encouraged, constituted an important independent cause of the drastic contraction in world trade which occurred beginning in 1930. The volume of world trade declined by one third between 1929 and the third quarter of 1932, while the gold value of world trade fell by nearly two thirds over the same period.[6] It is also interesting to observe that not only did the volume of U.S. imports fall during the years 1930–33 more than that of any other major industrial country, but the volume of her exports also fell by the greatest amount.[7] It is reasonably safe to conclude that the net effect of tariffs and other trade restrictions during the Great Depression was in the direction of contracting the total market, income, and employment of each country rather than in the direction posited by tariff advocates.

---

[5] Among others on the free list were: broken bells, bread, dried blood, bones, bird eggs, unmanufactured hoofs, ice, ivory tusks, leeches, lava, sheep dip, skeletons, natural teeth, turtles, and worm gut.

[6] League of Nations, *World Economic Survey, 1933–34* (Geneva, 1934), p. 187.

[7] In 1932 the volume of U.S. exports was only 53 percent of 1929, while that of the United Kingdom was 63 percent; France, 59 percent; Germany, 59 percent; Italy, 77 percent; and Japan, 94 percent (ibid., p. 196).

Major Tariff Issues before 1934

The United States won its independence during a period of transition in Europe from mercantilism to laissez-faire and free trade. The prevailing opinion in the United States was also favorable at this time to freedom in trade relations, in part as a reaction against the restrictions and controls to which the colonies had been subjected. Although the theory of protectionism had early been advanced by Hamilton, American tariffs before the Civil War were, generally speaking, based more on the need for revenue than on the desire for protection. Major exceptions to this were the Tariff of 1816—which was designed to protect domestic industries that had developed during the war with Great Britain—and the Act of 1828, which, as we have seen, contained excessively high rates because of a political maneuver that went awry. Concurrently with the free-trade policy of Britain after the removal of the Corn Laws, the United States, in the Acts of 1846 and 1857, also moved toward a low-tariff system.

After the Civil War, although the revenue aspects of tariffs continued to exert an important influence, the principle of protection grew progressively stronger, culminating in the McKinley and Dingley tariffs of 1890 and 1897, respectively. By this time, tariffs had unfortunately become a matter of partisan politics.

The party of Jefferson and Jackson, purporting to represent the interests of the farmer and the "mechanic" against the manufacturing and "monied" interests of the North and East, generally stood for low tariffs for revenue purposes, though certainly not for free trade in any strict sense. The party of Hamilton, the father of the "infant-industry" argument, consistently emphasized the dangers of competition from cheap foreign labor and the virtues of a protected domestic market. The platforms of the two major parties became increasingly bitter and denunciatory with respect to tariffs after the Civil War.

Conflict between Agricultural and Industrial Interests. At the risk of oversimplification, we may say with a good deal of truth that the conflict over protective tariffs in the United States up until roughly World War I was the product of a clash between agricultural interests, mainly in the South, and manufacturing interests, mainly in the North.[8] This was a reflection of the basic position of

---

[8] Some agricultural interests, such as woolgrowers, were protectionist; but the producers of the main staples of American agriculture—especially cotton and tobacco, supplemented by corn and wheat—depended on export markets and were free trade.

the United States in the 19th century as an importer of manufactured goods and an exporter of agricultural products. It was natural for the planters of the South and West to object to the higher prices for manufactured goods which they had to pay because of tariffs and for the manufacturers of the North to desire protection against competition from abroad.

Over the period from the Civil War to World War I, the economy of the United States underwent profound changes in structure, with a tremendous increase in the relative importance of manufacturing industry. Correspondingly, the comparative advantage of the United States shifted from primary products to manufactured goods. Thus, whereas earlier the United States was an importer of manufactured goods and an exporter of raw materials and foodstuffs, it later became an exporter of manufactured goods and an importer of raw materials and foodstuffs. As pointed out in Chapter 6, however, the United States now has a "balanced" economy, under which it continues to have a comparative advantage in certain agricultural goods as well as heavy manufactures.

This change in America's international economic position tended somewhat to blur the division of tariff sentiments. Those manufacturing interests which rely upon raw material imports and finished exports generally became low-tariff protagonists, while producers of foodstuffs and raw materials in competition with the growing volume of primary-products imports joined the ranks of the protectionists. In this connection it should be noted that the Emergency Tariff of 1921 and the Fordney-McCumber Tariff of the following year imposed high import duties on major agricultural products in response to the demands of farmers for protection. These measures were in large part the reaction to the plight of the farmers caused by a war-induced overexpansion of production and a subsequent sharp decline in farm prices. But large segments of American agriculture have since continued to be protectionist.

It would be misleading, however, to believe that the American tariff is the product solely of selfish interests, even though many individual duties have been enacted through the collective influence of small, but mutually supporting, local interests. At one time or another, nearly every one of the theoretical arguments in favor of tariffs examined in the preceding chapter has been invoked. Of these arguments, two of the stronger ones have had considerable influence in the development of the American tariff and thus deserves special mention.

Protection of Infant Industries. The first is the infant-industry argument, which constituted the chief theoretical or intellectual basis for the American tariff during the 19th century and the early part of the 20th. As we observed earlier, this argument is not without merit for a country that is in the early stages of economic development and is faced with the competition of other countries already industrialized. But American history also illustrates its weakness, for high protective tariffs were kept on the books long after industries had lost their "infant" status.

Military Security. The second intellectual basis for American tariffs—to preserve military security—has been applied in more recent decades. This, too, is an argument which may in some circumstances have merit. But we may question its general applicability in a period when American military security is so intimately bound up with the economic and military strength of other free nations, the economies of which are dependent upon the ability to find a market in the United States.

AMERICAN COMMERCIAL POLICY, 1934–62

The highest protective tariff in American history was followed, four years later (1934), by the inauguration of the most ambitious tariff-reducing program in the country's history. Within a quarter of a century, the average level of import duties was reduced from a level of 53 percent in 1930–33 under the Hawley-Smoot Tariff to approximately 12 percent under the Reciprocal Trade Agreements program.

The Reciprocal Trade Agreements Program

The first, and basic, step in the new tariff program was the adoption in June, 1934, of the Reciprocal Trade Agreements Act. By this act, the President was empowered to negotiate treaties with foreign countries for the purpose of reciprocally reducing tariff barriers and without the necessity of ratification by the Senate. The "teeth" in the power to negotiate mutual trade concessions was the authority granted the President to lower or raise duties by as much as 50 percent of the existing level. Later, the base to which the 50 percent limit applied was changed to the duties prevailing on January 1, 1945. The provisions of the act were to extend three years, but extensions were successively made, although with important amendments, which will be discussed later.

Before the conclusion of the General Agreement on Tariffs and Trade in Geneva, Switzerland, in 1947, trade agreements were negotiated by the United States separately with 29 different countries. The general procedure followed in these negotiations may be briefly described.

Negotiating Procedures. Upon a tentative understanding with another country that the basis for reciprocal tariff concessions exists, the Trade Agreements Committee of the U.S. government—consisting of representatives from various departments of the government designated for the purpose of giving information and advice to the President on trade agreements—appoints a "country" committee to make a detailed examination of all factors pertinent to the negotiation. If, on the basis of these investigations, it appears that an agreement is feasible and desirable, the Trade Agreements Committee recommends to the President that formal negotiations be undertaken, and it accompanies the recommendation with tentative lists of items on which tariff concessions might be granted and on which concessions by the other country might be asked.

If the other country involved is willing to negotiate, a tentative list of articles subject to concessions is agreed upon, and formal negotiations are ready to begin. Before actual negotiations are entered into, however, public notice is given of the government's intentions, and a list of the import articles which the United States proposes to consider for concessions is circulated. The public is invited to supply any information which might be useful in the negotiations, including briefs on the part of domestic producers who are fearful that their interests would be jeopardized by tariff concessions.

Most of the agreements concluded before 1947 provide that they shall remain in force for an initial period of three years, after which they are automatically extended for an indefinite period but are subject to termination by one or the other of the contracting parties on giving six months' notice.

Negotiating Principles. Two major principles are embodied in the trade agreements of the United States. The first is the so-called "unconditional most-favored-nation" treatment. Under this principle, adopted by the United States as a general policy in 1923, any benefits or concessions granted to a given country automatically extend, without specific concessions in return, to all other countries. Hence, any trade concession which the United States now extends to any foreign country (except for the Philippines, for which preferences are authorized in all trade agreements) it extends to any country with which it makes an agreement, unconditionally and without restriction.[9] Similarly, any concession granted by the other contracting party to any third country, but often with specified exceptions, must be extended unconditionally to the United States. In effect, therefore, even though trade agreements are bilateral, the concessions are "multilateralized."

The second principle followed in negotiating trade agreements is informal and is designed to avoid the weakening of bargaining power in obtaining concessions from other countries through the operation of most-favored-nation treatment. The principle is that of confining concessions to "chief suppliers." That is, the general policy, in an agreement with any given country, is not to grant a concession unless that country has been, or is likely to become, the principal, or at least a major, source of import of the commodity.

Although the principal objective of trade agreements is to provide for specific tariff concessions on listed articles, they also include certain general provisions concerning trade relations, apart from tariffs, between the signatories. Included in the general provisions are such commitments as the prohibition or limitation on the use of quantitative restrictions (quotas) and trade discriminations. The fullest and most general nontariff provisions, however, are contained in the General Agreement on Trade and Tariffs negotiated in Geneva in 1947.

THE GENERAL AGREEMENT ON TARIFFS AND TRADE (GATT)

During the last war, the U.S. government began to do preliminary work on postwar economic problems and took the initiative, in consultation with her allies, in proposing various forms of international economic cooperation after the war's end. In very general terms, U.S. government policy in the postwar years in the field of commercial relations has been directed toward two main objectives: (a) an international agreement on a code of trading relations and (b) the reduction or elimination of various specific trade barriers through international negotiation.

The most ambitious attempt at developing a code of commercial conduct is the Charter for an International Trade Organization

---

[9] There is an exception, however: the President is authorized to withhold trade concessions from countries which either discriminate against American commerce or pursue policies which tend to defeat the purposes of the Trade Agreements Act.

(ITO). The Charter was the product of nearly five years of preparatory work during the war and over two years of laborious negotiations after the war. Agreement on the Charter was finally reached by the representatives of 54 countries at the end of the Havana Conference in March, 1948. However, there was widespread opposition to the Charter in the United States by business and other groups; as a result the administration was unable to secure congressional approval and the effort to establish the ITO was aborted.

Even while a United Nations committee was at work drafting a charter for the ITO, international negotiations were underway at Geneva, Switzerland, in 1947 for the mutual reduction of tariffs. There emerged from these negotiations the General Agreement on Tariffs and Trade, popularly known as GATT. The United States government was able to participate in the Geneva Agreement without congressional approval under the authority granted by the Reciprocal Trade Agreements Act.

The General Agreement reached at Geneva included not only a schedule of specific tariff concessions, but also general principles of trade conduct similar to those contained in the Havana Charter. Originally, the general principles agreed upon at Geneva were conceived as provisional, pending the adoption of ITO. Upon the demise of the latter, however, GATT became a permanent agreement and was transformed into an international agency responsible for overseeing the implementation of a code of commercial conduct.

General Provisions of GATT

The major general provisions of GATT include unconditional most-favored-nation treatment; elimination of quantitative trade restrictions; the obligation to negotiate for the reduction of tariffs upon the request of another member country; nondiscrimination; freedom of transit; simplification of customs formalities; liberalization of marks-of-origin requirements; and a general "escape" clause allowing deviation from these principles under specified circumstances, such as the right to impose discriminatory, quantitative restrictions for balance-of-payments reasons.

Multilateral Tariff Negotiations. In the Geneva negotiations and subsequent sessions, specific tariff concessions were negotiated. The type of negotiations, though falling within the scope of the Reciprocal Trade Agreements Act of the United States, represented a considerable departure from previous practices. Before Geneva, as we have seen, the United States negotiated its trade agreements separately with each country on a strictly bilateral basis. After Geneva, the negotiations were also conducted bilaterally, on a product-by-product basis, each country usually negotiating as to its treatment of each particular import commodity with its principal past or anticipated supplier of that commodity. However, the understandings reached in the bilateral negotiations were combined to form the schedules of concessions of the several countries set forth in the Agreement and the Protocols. The close contacts among the negotiating teams, the ability of each country to observe how its position was affected not only by its own bilateral negotiations but also by the simultaneous negotiations among other countries, together with most-favored-nation treatment, rendered the proceedings, in effect, *multilateral.*

The two most significant characteristics of GATT, therefore, are, first, its general provisions, which constitute a code of commercial policy, and, second, the essentially multilateral approach to negotiations which it embodies.

The Accomplishments of GATT. No doubt the greatest contribution of GATT consists of the acceptance by the major trading countries of the world of the principle of free international exchange of goods and services, without discrimination or quantitative restrictions, and the commitment to negotiate multilaterally to reduce existing tariffs and other artificial trade barriers. In the hundreds of individual negotiations that have been carried on under GATT, covering tens of thousands of commodities, tariff concessions have been made applying to products constituting more than two thirds of the total import trade of the participating countries and considerably more than half of the total import trade of the world. The most tangible accomplishment of GATT lies in the significant reduction (and "binding") [10] of tariffs that the multilateral negotiations it has sponsored have effected.

Less tangible, but perhaps of equal value in the long run, is GATT's role as an international forum for the discussion of the commercial policies of its members and for the adjustment of disputes arising out of the implementation of the general principles of GATT and the obligations assumed in specific tariff negotiations. The necessity for frequent consultation and discussion is especially great because of the numerous allowable exceptions to the general

---

[10] A tariff rate is "bound" when a country agrees not to raise it.

principles embodied in GATT and the danger that such exceptions, if not controlled, would "take over." For example, one of the basic principles of GATT is that members refrain from quantitative restrictions (quotas) on its imports from other members. An exception is permitted in case a member can demonstrate that import quotas are necessary for balance-of-payments reasons. There are no clear-cut criteria for determining when quotas are necessary to protect the balance of payments. Hence it is provided that members of GATT resorting to quotas for this purpose must consult with other members regarding the nature and extent of the restrictions and their justification. Members resorting to quota restrictions are thus put on the defensive and encouraged to create conditions that will allow the quotas to be removed. Essentially the same procedure helps safeguard against abuses of allowable quotas for promoting the industrialization of underdeveloped members and for the carrying-out of domestic price-support programs.

Weakening of the Trade Agreements Program

The Trade Agreements Act of 1934 was never a permanent part of American law but required a periodic renewal of authority. Until the act finally expired in 1962 and was replaced by new legislation—the Trade Expansion Act—it had been renewed 11 times. As each renewal act expired, further extensions were subject, of course, to congressional amendments. The last several renewal acts, beginning with the one in 1951, included amendments greatly reducing the effectiveness of the program. The chief weakening amendments related to the "escape," "peril-point," and national security clauses, and to the President's authority to negotiate tariff reductions.

The Escape Clause. In the trade agreement concluded with Mexico in December, 1942, an escape clause was included, providing that a concession on any article might be withdrawn, in whole or in part, whenever, as a result of the concession and from "unforeseen" developments, the import of the article increased in such quantity as to cause or threaten "serious injury" to domestic producers of like or similar articles. In 1947 the President issued an executive order requiring the insertion of a similar escape clause in all future trade agreements. The Trade Agreements Extension Act of 1951 made it mandatory for an escape clause to be included not only in all future trade agreements but, as soon as practicable, in all existing trade agreements currently in force.

The procedure and criteria to be followed in escape-clause action were spelled out in the Extension Act of 1951, as modified by amendments in 1953, 1955, and 1958. The Tariff Commission was charged with the responsibility of promptly conducting an escape-clause investigation upon the request of the President, resolution of either house of Congress, resolution of either the Senate Committee on Finance or the House Committee on Ways and Means, upon its own motion, or upon application of any interested party. As part of an investigation, the Tariff Commission held public hearings at which interested parties were afforded an opportunity to testify. Should the Commission find the existence or the threat of serious injury attributable to increased imports of articles on which trade agreement concessions have been made, it recommended to the President withdrawal or modification of the concession or the imposition of an import quota. The President was not obliged to follow the recommendations of the Tariff Commission, but if he failed to do so he had to submit a report to the Congress stating his reasons. Further, an amendment in 1958 provided the President could be overruled by a two-thirds vote of Congress.

The criteria to be employed in defining "serious injury" under the escape clause were successively expanded to enable producers more easily to obtain relief. The 1951 act directed the Tariff Commission to take into consideration, without excluding other factors, "a downward trend of production, employment, prices, profits, or wages in the domestic industry concerned, or a decline in sales, an increase in imports, either actual or relative to domestic production, a higher or growing inventory, or a decline in the proportion of the domestic market supplied by domestic producers." The Trade Agreements Extension Act of 1955 greatly broadened the base for escape-clause action by defining the term "domestic industry" to embrace each single product of multiproduct firms and by allowing a finding of injury even when increased imports were not the primary cause of the injury.

As it turned out in practice, the escape clause was not extensively used to revoke trade agreement concessions. Out of several dozen investigations by the Tariff Commission, injury was found in only about one quarter of the cases, and only about one half of these was accepted for action by the President. Moreover, with the exception of lead and zinc (on which import quotas were levied), the articles affected were of minor importance—such things as clothespins, dried figs, hatters' fur, bicycles, alsike-clover seed, and so on. However, the *indirect* effects of the escape clause as a restrictive device may be considerable, since it subjects foreign exporters to the risk of having their American market suddenly circumscribed.

The Peril Point. Increasing opposition to reduced tariffs by affected American producers led to the "peril-point" provisions in the Trade Agreement Extension Act of 1948. The Extension Act of the next year eliminated the peril-point provision (primarily because of the pressure put on Congress by the administration, who at that time was vigorously opposed to it), but that of 1951 reinstated the provision with some changes. Thereafter, it remained in force in subsequent extension acts.

Under the peril-point provision, the President was required, before entering into any trade agreement negotiation, to transmit to the Tariff Commission a list of the commodities to be considered for concessions in forthcoming negotiations. The Commission was then required to make an investigation and report on (*a*) the maximum decrease in duty, if any, that can be made on each listed commodity without causing or threatening serious injury to domestic industries producing like or directly competitive products or (*b*) the minimum *increase* in duty or additional import restriction that may be necessary to avoid serious injury or threat of injury.

The President could not conclude a trade agreement until the Commission's peril-point report was made or until after the lapse of 120 days from the date the list of articles proposed for negotiation was transmitted to the Tariff Commission. The President was not bound, however, to follow the conclusions of the Tariff Commission; but if he failed to do so, he had to transmit to the Congress a copy of the trade agreement in question, identifying the articles on which concessions had been made inconsistently with the Commission's report and stating his reasons for not carrying out the Commission's recommendations. Thus, in the GATT tariff negotiations in 1956 at Geneva, the United States failed to provide increased import duties on tungsten alloys and violins and violas, as specified in the Commission's peril-point report, and this failure was reported by the President to the Congress as required.

It is quite obvious that the escape-clause and peril-point provisions were closely related. The former was designed primarily to take care of injuries caused by concessions already made in trade agreements, and the latter was designed primarily to prevent concessions from being made in new negotiations that might cause injury in the future.

Before the 1960–62 tariff negotiations between the United States and the European Economic Community (EEC) and other GATT members, the peril-point clause had no great impact on U.S. trade negotiations. But in the last negotiations conducted under the Reciprocal Trade Agreements Act—1960–62—the peril-point restriction proved nearly fatal. While the EEC offered to reduce its common external tariff by 20 percent on about 60 percent of the products requested by the United States, reciprocal concessions offered by the United States included only about one quarter of the products requested by the EEC. This unbalanced offer by the United States was the result of elimination of negotiable items under peril-point determinations. The ensuing deadlock in the negotiations was broken only when the United States offered new concessions at rates below peril-point findings.

The National Security Provision.   In the 1955 renewal of the trade agreements program, a provision was inserted allowing the imposition of trade restrictions on imports that threaten the national security, whether or not the products affected were subject to trade agreement concessions. The determination of whether the import of a product threatened the national security was to be made in the first instance by the Office of Civil and Defense Mobilization, but the final decision rested with the President. The basis for action was greatly extended by an amendment in 1958 providing that restrictions might be applied to nondefense industries if it was determined that imports were weakening the internal economy and thus impairing national security.

Many industries took advantage of the national security provisions as a basis for advancing their claims to protection against imports, including, among others, producers of wool felts, dental burrs, wire cloth, textiles, watches, stencil silk, electrical equipment, and petroleum. Few, however, were successful in convincing the Office of Civilian and Defense Mobilization of the legitimacy of their cases. The most important exception was petroleum. In 1956 the United States imposed import quotas on crude oil and petroleum products under the national security provision, on the grounds that imports were discouraging the domestic exploration necessary to assure an adequate supply of oil in the event of a national emergency.

Authority to Reduce Tariffs.   The last, and perhaps most serious, weakening of the Reciprocal Trade Agreements Act came from limiting the President's authority to reduce tariffs. The original act authorized reductions in tariffs up to 50 percent of the rates in effect in 1934. Later, the base on which 50 percent reductions were permitted was changed to the rates prevailing on January 1, 1945. The President's authority remained thus until the Trade Agreements Extension

Act of 1955. Thereafter, only a small margin of further reductions was permitted, as evidenced by the fact that nearly all the reduction in tariffs accomplished under the program until its expiration in June, 1962, had been achieved by 1953.

The 1955 Extension Act provided for a 15 percent reduction of prevailing rates, spread over three years, and also for a reduction to 50 percent of all rates higher than 50 percent. The last renewal, in 1958, permitted reductions under three alternative methods: by 20 percent, or by 2 percentage points, or to 50 percent, reductions in any event to be effected in no more than four annual stages.

It should be noted that the formal authority to reduce tariffs could never be fully utilized in practice. Apart from the constraint imposed by the necessity to receive reciprocal concession in bargaining negotiations, the President was subject to the pressures exerted by the escape and peril-point clauses and the national security provision described above.

THE TRADE EXPANSION ACT OF 1962

On the expiration in June, 1962, of the 11th renewal of the Reciprocal Trade Agreements Act inaugurated 28 years earlier, the United States was confronted with a critical decision on its future commercial policy. It was hardly conceivable that the reciprocal trade agreements program should be allowed to expire, but a choice had to be made between continuation of the program as it had evolved over the past years or its replacement with a rejuvenated and expanded program. At least two major considerations led to the second alternative.

The first was the exhaustion of the program as an effective instrument of commercial policy. Little scope for further reciprocal trade negotiations remained; indeed, no significant reduction in the level of U.S. tariffs had been made for a decade or more. The President's authority to pursue a positive commercial policy had progressively been so surrounded with restrictions that he barely had left the power merely to "hold the line" on past accomplishments, let alone to advance further.

In itself, this situation was not especially novel and probably would not have led to any large change in program had it not been for a second development—the formation of the European Common Market. The Common Market, to be fully discussed in Chapter 12, presented a sharp challenge to the United States. The reaction to it could consist either of rebuff and defensive withdrawal into possibly bitter and divisive trade bloc discrimination or of efforts to shape it into a unifying and expansionary force in free-world economic relations. The United States chose the latter option, both because she had long supported the movement toward Western European economic and political unification and because her own export position would otherwise have been seriously threatened.

The principal requirement for turning the Common Market into a force for positive benefit to the world economy lay in its establishment of a low-level common tariff wall on the goods and services of nonmember countries. But for this to be possible, the United States, as a main competing country in the world economy, had to be willing reciprocally to reduce its trade barriers. The Trade Expansion Act of 1962 was largely designed with this situation in mind. Indeed, some provisions of the act are specifically directed toward relations with the Common Market.

Let us now see what the major provisions of the Trade Expansion Act were.

Authority to Reduce Tariffs

As we noted earlier, the President's authority to reduce tariffs had been greatly restricted during the last years of the Reciprocal Trade Agreements Act. The Trade Expansion Act reinstituted and expanded this authority.

The general authority extended to the President allowed him to negotiate reductions in U.S. tariffs by as much as 50 percent of the rate existing on July 1, 1962. Provision for even greater reductions under certain conditions was made but did not in fact become significantly operative. The President's authority to negotiate tariff reductions was limited to the five-year period ending July 1, 1967.

A major change in negotiating procedures was provided by the act. Instead of being restricted, as in the past, to negotiating article by article, the President was authorized to negotiate by broad categories of goods.

Escape Clause

The Trade Expansion Act eliminated the former peril-point clause and significantly modified escape-clause procedures. As before, the President was authorized to increase or impose any duty or import restriction necessary to remedy or prevent serious injury to a domestic industry by reason of increased imports due to trade agreement concessions. However, the concept of "serious injury," which in previous legislation had been interpreted very liberally, was considerably narrowed. Moreover, the increase in imports responsible for injury had to be the result in "major part" of trade agreement concessions and such increase in imports must have been the *"major factor"* in causing or threatening injury. The net effect of these changes was greatly to reduce the scope for escape-clause action.

Adjustment Assistance

The tightening of the escape clause was made more palatable by a major innovation which introduced an alternative to increased trade barriers as a remedy for any injuries sustained as the result of tariff concessions. The alternative consists of "adjustment assistance" to firms and workers.

Both business firm and workers may apply for adjustment assistance whenever, upon application of an interested party, it is determined that the applicant is eligible for assistance. The criteria for eligibility are virtually the same as those used in deciding whether escape-clause action is called for. A firm is eligible for assistance whenever, as a result in major part of trade agreement concessions, an article competitive with an article produced by the firm is imported in such increased quantities as to cause or threaten serious injury to the firm. Among other criteria to be applied, idling of productive facilities, inability to operate at a reasonable level of profit, and unemployment are to be taken into account in determining whether injury has been sustained. A group of workers is eligible for assistance if, because of the same circumstances applicable to the firm, unemployment or underemployment of a significant number or proportion of workers occurs. In both cases, increased imports must be the *major* factor causing injury.

Adjustment assistance to firms takes the form of technical assistance, financial assistance, and tax assistance, furnished singly or in combination. Technical assistance is for such purposes as helping an injured firm to become more efficient or to shift into other product lines. Financial assistance may consist of loans or loan guaranties, to enable the firm to modernize, expand, or convert its productive facilities. Tax assistance is given in the form of allowing an injured firm operating loss carrybacks for a longer period than normally permitted, thus reducing the firm's net tax liabilities.

Adjustment assistance to workers include training, unemployment compensation ("readjustment allowances"), and relocation allowances. Primary emphasis is to be placed on retraining displaced workers to prepare them for new jobs. During training periods and thereafter if employment is not secured, unemployment compensation may be paid for up to 52 weeks, or longer if necessary to allow completion of training or if the worker is 60 years or older. Finally, an unemployed worker, head of a family, may obtain an allowance for meeting the expenses of moving to another area where employment or an offer of employment has been received.

TARIFF REDUCTIONS SINCE 1934

The history of negotiated tariff reductions by the United States since the introduction of the Reciprocal Trade Agreements program in 1934 can be divided into three stages. During the first stage, from 1934 to 1947, bilateral agreements were concluded with 29 countries, resulting in a reduction in the average United States tariff by one third the previous level. The second stage, beginning with the establishment of GATT in 1947 and ending with the termination of the Reciprocal Trade Agreements Act in 1962, witnessed a further reduction in tariffs through five rounds of multilateral negotiations, only the first of which was highly productive. The latest stage began with the adoption of the Trade Expansion Act of 1962 and the sixth, or Kennedy Round, of negotiations under the aegis of GATT and concluded in 1967. The Kennedy Round proved to be the most comprehensive and productive tariff negotiating session in history, with 46 countries participating in the agreement to reduce tariffs by approximately one third on trade amounting to $40 billion annually.

Looking at the period as a whole, we can observe a major reduction in the average level of tariffs on the part of the principal trading countries of the world, shown in Table 10.1. As a result of these reductions, the remaining level of tariffs in 1972 for major industrialized countries was only 9 percent on industrial products. For agricultural products, the level of tariffs is higher and varies more widely among countries. Thus, whereas the Canadian agricultural tariff averages 9.6 percent, the Japanese is 40.6 percent, the United States 15.1 percent, the European Economic Community 16.5 percent, and the United Kingdom 10.8 percent.[11]

---

[11] U.S. Tariff Commission, *Trade Barriers,* T. C. Publication 665, vol. 1, chap. 1 (Washington, D.C., April 1974), pp. 4–5.

TABLE 10.1

PERCENTAGE REDUCTION IN AVERAGE TARIFF LEVELS AS
RESULT OF TRADE AGREEMENTS, BASE YEAR TO 1972

	Base Year	Industrial Products	Agricultural Products
United States.	1933	72.1	61.9
Canada	1935	58.2	66.2
Japan	1954	25.0	15.2
European Economic Community	1960	44.3	29.9
United Kingdom	1938	59.6	37.6

Source: U.S. Tariff Commission, *Trade Barriers,* TC Publication 665, vol. 1, chap. 1 (Washington, D.C., April 1974), p. 9.

Lest the impression be given from the above data that tariffs have been practically eliminated, a few sobering qualifications should be noted.

First of all, the measurement of tariff levels is fraught with conceptual difficulties as observed in the preceding chapter. As an indicator of the degree of freedom of trade from tariff restrictions, the data suffer from concealment of very high tariffs on particular products.

It is a general practice of developed countries to levy very low or no tariffs on raw materials not produced domestically, higher duties on semiprocessed manufactures, and the highest rates on finished goods. In the United States, 23 percent of imports are duty free, but on finished products, which account for more than half United States imports, only 3.4 percent are duty free.[12]

The second qualification of average tariff rates as an indicator of the degree of free trade relates to the distinction drawn in the preceding chapter between *nominal* rates and *effective rates* of protection. It will be recalled that whenever there are imported components of domestic products, with different tariff rates applicable to the components and the finished good, the effective rate of protection to domestic industry differs from the nominal tariff. It has been calculated, for example, that the average effective tariff in the United States on a list of 64 product groups is two and a half times the average nominal rate.[13]

Finally, it is important to remember that tariffs are only one form of trade restriction. As tariff rates have been reduced through inter-

[12] U.S. Tariff Commission, *Trade Barriers,* p. 34.

[13] See R. E. Baldwin, *Nontariff Distortions of International Trade* (Washington, D.C.: Brookings Institution, 1970), pp. 163–64.

national negotiation, the relative significance of nontariff barriers to trade has increased.

NONTARIFF BARRIERS TO TRADE

Quantitative Restrictions

The most visible nontariff instrument of trade restriction is the import quota. Practically all countries make use of quotas, with France the leader and the United States near the top of the list of major trading countries employing this device.

Agricultural products are the favorite object of quota restrictions. All major industrial countries heavily subsidize agriculture through price support programs or other measures. To avoid extending the benefits of domestic subsidies to foreign producers quantitative import restrictions or high tariffs are necessary. Thus, the United States has placed quotas, among other products, on certain dairy products, wheat and wheat flour, peanuts, cotton, sugar, and meat, while the European Economic Community imposes a variable levy system for all its major agricultural commodities which effectively eliminates outside competition with domestic producers.

Several major products other than agricultural commodities are widely subject to quota limitations. Coal is the prime example for Europe and Japan, petroleum for the United States. Until the energy crisis led to their relaxation, the United States severely limited imports of crude oil and petroleum products. It will be recalled that the oil import quotas of the United States were first imposed in 1956 on the grounds of national security.

A method of achieving the effect of import quotas without their overt employment has been devised in recent years in the form of "voluntary export restraints." The best known example relates to textiles. Under the threat that import quotas would otherwise be imposed by the United States, Japan agreed, beginning in 1956 to limit her export of various cotton textiles. Controls on trade in cotton textiles were later extended to numerous other countries under an international agreement. In 1970–71 the United States government concluded agreements with major Far Eastern exporters of wool and man-made fiber products to limit their exports to the United States, and at the end of 1973 a general international agreement on the export of textiles of all types was adopted.

In addition to textiles, other products have been subject to voluntary arrangements limiting trade. Rapidly increasing steel imports into the United States led to agreements with Japan, the United Kingdom, and the European Community to restrain their exports. Some 25 other items exported by Japan, accounting for about 9 percent of Japanese shipments to the United States, have been subject to quantitative controls. Mexican exports of strawberries and tomatoes and Formosan exports of canned mushrooms to the United States have also been "voluntarily" restrained.

The overall significance of quantitative import restrictions is indicated by the proportion of imports subject to such restrictions. For industrial products, it has been estimated that over 16 percent of United States imports are subject to quantitative restrictions. The comparable figures for other industrial countries are over 11 percent in Japan, 4.7 percent in the United Kingdom, and 4.3 percent in the European Economic Community.[14] With respect to agricultural imports, quantitative restrictions are greater, but the United States reverses position with the European Economic Community. Thus, the percentage of agricultural imports subject to quantitative restrictions in 1970 was 33.7 for the European Economic Community, 27.9 for Japan, 21.9 for the United Kingdom, and 21.6 for the United States.[15]

Quantitative restrictions on trade may extend to exports as well as imports. The so-called "voluntary" export restraints discussed above are actually disguised import restrictions by consuming countries. Regular export quotas are another matter, for they are undertaken in the supposed interest of the country adopting them.

Export quotas have frequently been applied for political or military reasons. Thus, until the recent détente with the Soviet Union and the Peoples Republic of China, the United States severely restricted its exports to these countries and continues to embargo (that is, impose zero export and import quotas) trade with Cuba and North Korea.

More recently, there appears to be a developing trend on the part of some countries to restrict their exports as a means of raising prices,

---

14 John C. Renner, "National Restrictions on International Trade," *United States International Economic Policy in an Interdependent World.* Papers Submitted to the Commission on International Trade and Investment Policy, vol. 1 (Washington, D.C., July 1971) , p. 667.

15 Renner, "National Restrictions on International Trade," p. 671.

a technique no doubt suggested by the impact of the oil export embargo in 1973 on world petroleum prices.

Other Restrictions

Besides tariffs and quantitative restrictions, there are other trade-inhibiting and trade-distorting policies too numerous to allow more than brief reference.[16] So far as the United States is concerned, the principal other sources of restrictive effects are government procurement policies under the Buy American Act, the difficulties of foreign exporters in complying with United States product standards (with respect to health and safety, labeling, etc.), and the cumbersome and expensive customs procedures and practices. It should be noted, however, that the United States has no monopoly on these trade-inhibiting policies. Nearly all countries have similar policies, in some cases more restrictive, in others less restrictive, than those of the United States.

RECOMMENDED READINGS

BALASSA, BELA ET AL. *The Structure of Protection in Developing Countries.* Baltimore: Johns Hopkins Press, 1971.

BALDWIN, ROBERT E. *Nontariff Distortions of International Trade.* Washington, D.C.: Brookings Institution, 1970.

BROWN, WILLIAM ADAMS, JR. *The United States and the Restoration of World Trade.* Washington, D.C.: Brookings Institution, 1950. A thorough analysis and appraisal of the ITO Charter and GATT.

DIEBOLD, WILLIAM, JR. *The End of the ITO.* Essays in International Finance no. 16. Princeton University, International Finance Section, October 1952.

ELLSWORTH, P. T. *The International Economy,* chaps. ii, iii, xii–xv. 4th ed. New York: Macmillan Co., 1969. An excellent brief survey of trade-policy history, which ties in commercial policies with both broader historical forces and the development of international trade theory.

MEIER, GERALD M. *Problems of Trade Policy.* Oxford University Press, 1973.

PIQUET, HOWARD S. *The Trade Agreements Act and the National Interest.* Washington, D.C.: Brookings Institution, 1958.

---

16 For a fairly comprehensive discussion, see R. E. Baldwin, *Nontariff Distortions of International Trade* (Washington, D.C.: Brookings Institution, 1970), pp. 163–64.

PREEG, ERNEST H. *Traders and Diplomats.* Washington, D.C.: Brookings Institution, 1970.

U.S. TARIFF COMMISSION, WASHINGTON, D.C. *The Tariff and Its History.* 1934.

————. *Trade Barriers: An Overview.* TC Publication 665, April 1974.

STUDY QUESTIONS

1. The term "favorable" balance of trade is still used in its original meaning as developed during the mercantilist era. What is its meaning, and how do you explain its origins?

2. Describe the general economic and political changes, dating from about the middle of the 18th century, which finally led to the abandonment of mercantilism and the victory of a laissez-faire, free-trade philosophy.

3. Why were the policies pursued by many countries during the 1930s often described as "neomercantilist"?

4. From the history of American tariffs, what influence would you say wars ordinarily have on tariff policies? Why?

5. What was the general trend of United States tariff policies from the Civil War to 1934?

6. Which of the protariff arguments described in Chapter 9 would you suppose were the most influential in the passage of the Hawley-Smoot Tariff? Did experience with this tariff strengthen or weaken these arguments?

7. How did the comparative-advantage position of the United States in the 19th century help explain her tariff policies? The free-trade outlook of the South?

8. Describe briefly the procedure through which U.S. tariffs were lowered by agreements made under the Reciprocal Trade Agreements program.

9. What is the significance of the principle of "most-favored-nation" treatment? Why has it not appreciably weakened the bargaining position of the United States in its tariff negotiations with other countries?

10. How have tariff negotiations under GATT differed from those previously conducted?

11. Describe the major general provisions of GATT which constitute a "code of commercial conduct."

12. Explain how the "escape" clause and the "peril-point" provisions in the amended versions of the Trade Agreements Act operated.

13. How do government price-support programs tend to conflict with tariff-reducing programs? Name some specific examples of this conflict in the United States.

14. Describe some of the other artificial obstacles to U.S. imports currently in force.

15. What major considerations led to the adoption of the Trade Expansion Act of 1962?

16. Summarize the chief provisions of the Trade Expansion Act. To what extent does the act represent a continuation of past policies, and to what extent does it break new paths?

11

Current issues in commercial policy

The Kennedy Round of tariff negotiations were completed in 1967, at which time the authority granted by the Congress to reduce United States tariffs expired. For the next several years no further grant of power was given to the Executive to engage in general tariff-reducing negotiations. In 1973, President Nixon proposed a "Trade Reform Act," which would grant the Administration the authority to engage in additional multilateral negotiations. The provisions of the Act will be considered below, following a brief discussion of the major issues that have arisen since the expiration of the Trade Expansion Act of 1962.

THE REVIVAL OF PROTECTIONISM

The "liberal" thrust of United States commercial policy initiated in 1934 carried through the next three decades, culminating in the very significant reduction in tariffs achieved in the Kennedy Round of negotiations. Since then, however, there has been an apparent marked change in the atmosphere, with the emergence of new problems and new attitudes in trade relations. A major element in this change has been the revival of protectionist sentiment in the United States.

Protectionism, overt or latent, has always been strong in the United States (as in most other countries), but it tends to be manifest most intensely during periods of domestic economic disturbance or instability. Whenever any particular industry or sector of the economy encounters difficulties it frequently attributes its problems to "unfair competition" with foreign producers and clamors for higher tariffs, quotas, or other restrictions. There is a bias toward granting such demands, since the claims of complainants are highly visible and forcefully communicated, while the interests of consumers and of the economy in general are so widely diffused as to seem trivial and not worthy of vigorous representation.

The considerable reduction in United States tariffs accomplished by the Kennedy Round of negotiations predictably elicited a spurt of protectionist sentiment. Soon after these negotiations were completed in 1967 several major industries—led by steel, chemicals, textiles, and oil—began a campaign for protective legislation. During the years following several hundred bills were introduced in the Congress calling for import quotas on products ranging from steel, meat, shoes and textiles to strawberries and baseball gloves. The rising threat of the passage of legislation that would destroy the accomplishments of past tariff negotiations and possibly set off a trade war led to the diversionary action of inducing certain foreign countries "voluntarily" to limit their exports to the United States, as described previously.

While the negotiation of agreements limiting the export to the United States of textiles, steel, and other products may have reduced the pressure to enact restrictive domestic legislation, it did not remove the pressure. Rising unemployment, an accelerating inflation, and a steadily deteriorating foreign trade position helped to rejuvenate in the early 70s the protectionist movement. The prime expression of this movement was the Burke-Hartke bill, officially known as the Foreign Trade and Investment Act of 1973 (H.R. 62 in the House of Representatives, S.151 in the Senate).

The basic thrust of the Burke-Hartke bill is comprehensive government control over imports of goods and the export of capital and technology. The bill would impose quotas on all imports not already quantitatively restricted, with some exemptions, such as for goods not produced in the United States (!) and for products in which domestic producers have consistently remained uncompetitive internationally. Quotas would initially be limited to the average level of imports in 1965—69 and set on a country-by-country basis. In the future, quotas would be raised or lowered as necessary to maintain the base-period ratio of imports to domestic production. The authority to set quotas, as well as to invoke escape-clause action and determine "injury" from imports, would be vested in an independent Foreign Trade and Investment Commission consisting of spokesmen for industry, labor, and the public.

The second area addressed in the Burke-Hartke bill relates to foreign investment, especially as undertaken by multinational corporations. We have already examined the nature of the criticisms levied against multinational corporations (see pp. 146–47, above) in particular the charge that they "export" employment and technology. The bill responds to these criticisms by authorizing the President to prohibit any transfer of United States capital abroad, whenever in his judgment the transfer would result in a net decrease in domestic employment, and to prohibit companies from manufacturing abroad or licensing foreign manufacture, whenever in his judgment such prohibition would contribute to increased employment in the United States. In addition, the bill proposes removing the special tax treatment of multinational companies.

Even though the Burke-Hartke bill has received widespread support, including that of organized labor as represented by the AFL–CIO (previously a supporter of liberal commercial policy), it has failed to date to be adopted. Nevertheless, it is significant as a formal expression of powerful protectionist forces, which may be temporarily stemmed—but probably not destroyed—only when some other legislation, such as the proposed Trade Reform Act discussed below, is enacted.

THE COSTS OF PROTECTIONISM

Except for extreme protectionists, most persons would agree that the case for a liberal commercial policy is strong. But for a large middle group in between the extreme protectionists and the doctrinaire free traders, the admitted benefits of liberal commercial policy are not obtainable without paying a price. For many, the alleged price is regarded as too high in comparison to the benefits received in return.

It is indeed true that any reduction in trade barriers is bound to cause some disturbance in certain sectors of the domestic economy. The very essence of the economic case for freer trade lies in the benefits obtainable from the reallocation of resources away from less efficient employments. Previously protected firms and industries can be expected therefore to find the demand for their products reduced (or less rapidly increasing) as competing imports rise in response to lowered barriers.

Moreover, generally speaking, the sectors of the economy likely to be hardest hit by lowered tariffs are among those already suffering from difficulties. It is the relatively *stagnant* industries in the United States in which foreign producers have the greatest comparative advantage—such as pottery, chinaware and glassware, and leather goods. But relatively stagnant industries are precisely the ones least able to adjust to greater import competition. Industries with a rapidly growing demand for their products would generally be able to maintain, or even to continue to increase, their sales, notwithstanding the loss of part of their market to foreign producers. Other industries might find that increased imports would reduce not only the relative market share of domestic producers but their absolute volume of sales as well.

The "classical" answer to this kind of problem—that resources released from industries unable freely to compete with foreign producers should be reallocated to the more efficient export industries—is not always satisfactory to those immediately affected. Resource reallocation is rarely in fact as smooth and easy as theory postulates. What about the workers who have spent a lifetime acquiring special skills not useful in other industries? Investors in the plant and equipment rendered idle by import competition? Those who have built their homes and made their friends in communities where the declining industries are located? Is it fair that these particular groups should bear the brunt of the burden of adjustment to increased imports? Here is where the practical politics of commercial policy liberalization become very important. The list of those who testify in congressional hearings against freer trade reads like the obituaries of declining American industries.

These are, within their own frame of reference, valid complaints deserving consideration. But there are reasonable answers, too, demanding "equal time" before it is concluded that liberal policies should be scuttled to avoid injury to domestic groups.

First, it is worth noting that *not* to lower trade barriers also causes injury. Export industries—domestic and foreign—and consumers generally are injured in just as real, though less obvious and direct, a sense by tariffs and quotas as import-competing industries are injured by the reduction of tariffs and quotas.

The injuries ascribed to reduced trade barriers have been vastly exaggerated in the minds of the American public. From statements commonly made by the more alarmist protectionist groups one gathers the impression that lower tariffs would result in mass unemployment and business failure. Objective analysis fails completely to lend credence to such conclusions.

Although many of the heavily protected, least efficient domestic industries would no doubt be unable to withstand the competition of freer imports, many others could adjust without too much difficulty, through shifts in product lines, improved management, more advanced techniques, and so on. For most U.S. industries, imports are only a small fraction of total domestic sales. As long as there is a generally buoyant economy, increases in imports are easily absorbed by expanding total sales with a margin left for increased sales by domestic producers.

Various studies have been made of the effect of foreign trade on employment in the United States. One, by the U.S. Bureau of Labor Statistics, has estimated that the number of jobs attributable to merchandise exports was about 2.7 million in 1969, while 2.5 million jobs would have been required to produce at home goods comparable to imports in that year.[1]

Perhaps more significant are the marginal employment effects of increases in imports, for it is the latter that most often leads to the demand for import restrictions to preserve domestic jobs. The conclusion of the study by the Bureau of Labor Statistics is that,

Increased imports may be accompanied by increased employment rather than reductions in employment, if total demand is growing.[2]

Even under less favorable conditions in the economy, however, the impact of increased imports on employment is minor. Thus, it is estimated that the job displacement associated with $1 billion of imports is on the order of 77,000, or one tenth of 1 percent of 1969 total civilian employment. As compared to other causes of unemployment, this effect is trivial. For example, it is estimated that 400,000 jobs were lost in 1970–71 because of a cut in military expenditure, while it would have required a 15 percent increase in

---

[1] U.S. Bureau of Labor Statistics, "Foreign Trade and Employment," *United States International Economic Policy in an Interdependent World*, vol. 1 (Washington, D.C., July 1971), p. 498.

[2] U.S. Bureau of Labor Statistics, "Foreign Trade and Employment," p. 498.

competitive imports to have created an equivalent loss of employment.[3]

It is clear that when unemployment generally increases it cannot
be cured by import restrictions. On the contrary, the probability is
strong that greater barriers to imports would aggravate unemployment.[4] A forced reduction in imports can be expected to lead to a
reduction in employment in export industries, both because of the
decrease in foreign incomes as the result of their decreased exports
and because of foreign retaliation against United States goods.

At the same time that increased import restrictions fail to expand
employment opportunities they add measurably to consumer costs. It
is not possible to calculate with complete accuracy the total costs
imposed upon the economy from the lesser efficiency of resource
allocation which the barriers to imports entail. However, reasonable
estimates can be made, and these show the costs to be very significant.
Thus, the total costs to consumers in the United States from existing
tariff and nontariff trade restrictions are estimated at a minimum of
$10 billion annually, and possibly in excess of $15 billion.[5] Import
quotas on sugar alone has raised the costs to consumers nearly $800
million annually.[6]

It should be added that the costs of protectionism extend beyond
those to the American consumer. Trade barriers reduce efficiency not
only in the countries imposing them but on other countries as well,
whose own resources are misallocated because of impaired export
markets. As we shall see in the concluding chapter of this book,
restrictive trade practices by the United States and other developed
economies not only reduce efficiency of resource use but also constitute a serious impediment to the growth of the less developed
countries of the world.

THE CHANGING ENVIRONMENT OF TRADE NEGOTIATION

A resumption of international negotiations further to reduce trade
barriers—and, just as important, to forestall an increase in barriers—

[3] U.S. Bureau of Labor Statistics, "Foreign Trade and Employment," p. 502.

[4] See C. Fred Bergsten, *The Cost of Import Restrictions to American Consumers.*
(New York: American Importers Assn., 1972). Reprinted in Robert E. Baldwin and
J. David Richardson, *International Trade and Finance* (Boston: Little, Brown & Co.,
1974), pp. 129–42.

[5] See Bergsten, *The Cost of Import Restrictions,* pp. 129–42.

[6] See D. Gale Johnson et al., *Foreign Trade and Agricultural Policy,* National Advisory
Commission on Food and Fiber (Washington, D.C., 1967), pp. 40–41.

has been hindered not only by the long hiatus in the granting by Congress of additional negotiating powers to the President but also by changes that have occurred in the meanwhile in the international economic position of the United States and of its major trading partners.

To begin at the national level, the United States has clearly suffered in recent years a loss in its relative position in the world economy. In 1950, the gross national product of the United States was on the order of 40 percent of the world's gross output; by 1973 the share had declined to around 28 percent. From 1960 to 1973, the share of the United States in the total manufactures exports of 14 major industrial countries declined from over 25 percent to around 19 percent.[7] In 1971, for the first time since 1893, the United States balance of trade (exports minus imports) displayed a deficit, amounting to over $2 billion, repeated the next year in tripled amount. In August, 1971, the United States was forced to adopt measures that heralded the collapse of the international monetary system that had been in operation for a quarter of a century (see Chapter 19).

To some extent the above events were in part reflections of perhaps ephemeral internal developments in the American economy, such as accelerated inflation and a decline in productivity. It can hardly be denied, however, that they were also reflections of more fundamental changes occurring in the world economy.

The declining relative position of the United States in the world economy has been accompanied by an upward shift in the positions of the other major industrial countries, in particular, Japan and the European Economic Community (European Common Market). Thus, while the share of the United States in world output was declining over the period 1950–1973, that of Japan more than tripled and that of the original six European Common Market countries increased by 30 percent. In a similar manner, between 1960 and 1973 United States manufactures exports increased in total value by about 240 percent, while Japan increased by over 800 percent, and the Common Market by 375 percent.

The loss of the overwhelmingly dominant position of the United States in the world economy has had very significant implications for commercial policy. In the earlier postwar period the United States

---

[7] U.S. Senate, Committee on Finance, *Staff Data and Materials on U.S. Trade and Balance of Payments* (Washington, D.C., February 20, 1974), table 12, p. 15. The data in the paragraphs following are also from this source.

could take the leadership in the movement toward dismantling trade barriers, secure in the knowledge that its voice would be heeded and assured that its position would not be eroded by trade concessions. The subsequent decline in the dependence of other countries upon the United States as supplier and market would inevitably have changed this picture, even if another development had not come along strongly to reenforce the alteration in the United States position.

The other development referred to was the formation of a large discriminatory trading bloc, the European Common Market. The next chapter will discuss in detail the Common Market and its implications for trade. For our present purpose, it is sufficient to note that it has resulted in dividing the principal industrialized trading countries of the world into three groups: the United States and Canada, the European Common Market, and Japan. (A fourth group, the trade importance of which is not great, but growing, consists of the centrally planned economies.)

The United States gave its official support to the creation of the European Common Market. However, as the Market has grown in economic power and especially since it has been expanded recently to embrace the United Kingdom, Ireland, and Denmark in addition to the original six continental members,[8] the stance of the United States has changed to one of concern. The basis for concern is the discrimination against United States and other third-country exports to the Common Market, within which trade is free among member countries but subject to tariffs and other restrictions with respect to outside countries.[9]

While the actual impact of the Common Market on United States trade has probably been exaggerated, there remains the potential danger of a disintegration of the world's principal trade economy into insulated blocs. Whether or not this potential becomes reality mainly depends upon a renewal of multilateral negotiations to reduce trade barriers and prevent the introduction of new ones. Failing such a renewal of negotiation, an inward-looking regionalism in Europe and protectionist surge in the United States could well destroy much of the progress toward freer trading relations achieved over the past 40 years.

---

[8] France, West Germany, Italy, the Netherlands, Belgium, and Luxembourg.

[9] A recent move, described in the next chapter, further enlarges the area of discrimination through free-trade arrangements between the Common Market and certain other European countries.

Successful further multilateral negotiations will probably require some modifications of past procedures. The relative importance of tariffs as an impediment to trade has receded in comparison to quantitative restrictions and other nontariff barriers to trade. This shift may require changing the rules of conduct embodied in GATT to reflect greater emphasis on the nontariff aspects of commercial policy. As part of this process, the exceptions to the principle of nondiscrimination contained in GATT may have to be reexamined.

THE TRADE REFORM ACT

The prospects for renewal of multilateral negotiations on trade matters are heavily dependent upon the policies adopted by the United States. Unless negotiating authority is extended by the Congress to the Executive branch there is no way for meaningful international action to be taken. In December, 1973, the House of Representatives passed the Trade Reform Act (HR 10710) giving the President new negotiating powers. Although some of the authority requested by the President was reduced and certain amendments of a political nature inserted, the Act broadly retained the provisions sought by the Administration. The principal provisions of the Act may now be briefly summarized.[10]

Rejecting the President's request for unlimited authority to change tariffs, the Act nevertheless empowers the President to:

a. Eliminate existing tariffs of 5 percent or less

b. Reduce tariffs by 60 percent on imports subject to duties between 5 percent and 25 percent as of July 1, 1973

c. Reduce tariffs by 75 percent (but not lower than 10 percent) on products previously subject to duties of more than 25 percent

d. Raise, or impose new tariffs up to levels 20 percent above existing rates or 50 percent above 1934 rates.

These powers would allow tariff reductions to be effected over a period of 15 years.

The Act further empowers the President to negotiate agreements reducing or eliminating nontariff barriers to trade. To eliminate the uncertainty of congressional approval of action on many nontariff restrictions imbedded in domestic law, a new procedure provides

---

[10] For a summary of the Act as passed by the House of Representatives, see the "Weekly Report" of the *Congressional Quarterly* (Washington, D.C., October 20, 1973), pp. 2793–95, and (December 15, 1973), pp. 3256–58.

242 **Introduction to international economics**

that an agreement can be put into effect after giving the Congress 90 days advance notice. However, during this period either the House or Senate can veto the agreement by majority vote.

A third section of the Trade Reform Act empowers the President to join with other countries in granting for ten years preferential trade treatment to developing nations.

The Act also liberalizes the relief and adjustment assistance provisions contained in the Trade Expansion Act of 1962, described earlier. Under the latter, to qualify for relief (in the form of higher tariffs or other restrictions on imports) for injury caused by imports, an industry had to demonstrate that imports were the "major cause" of its distress and, further, that offending increases in imports were directly related to trade concessions granted to other countries. These qualifying criteria are eased in the current Act, by allowing protective measures to be taken if imports are a "substantial cause" of injury to an industry.

A similar liberalization of the adjustment assistance provisions of the earlier legislation increases the benefits and lengthens the period they are available to workers displaced from their jobs by imports. The Act also provides for employment placement services, job training, and allowances for job search and relocation expenses.

Finally, the Act empowers the President to retaliate against other countries engaging in "unfair" or illegal practices with respect to United States exports. However, public hearings are to be required on proposals for retaliatory action, and the Congress has a veto of presidential decisions.

While the above provisions of the Trade Reform Act as approved by the House of Representatives clearly extend a considerable amount of authority to the President to engage in meaningful trade negotiations, amendments of a political nature were included, directed to United States trade relations with the Soviet Union. In 1972, President Nixon entered into a bilateral trade agreement with the Soviet Union that, to be effective, requires the granting of most-favored-nation treatment to the latter—that is, entitlement to the same tariff rates on exports accorded to other countries. Although the most-favored-nation principle has been followed by the United States since 1923 and is embodied in GATT, the United States withdrew such treatment from communist countries (except Poland and Yugoslavia) in 1951. The President's request to reinstate most-favored-nation status to these countries was approved by the House, with, however, a major qualification aimed at the Soviet Union: any extension of trade concessions to that country are contingent upon its relaxation of its policies restricting the emigration of its Jewish citizens. (A further blow to the trade agreement with the Soviet Union was added on to the Act by an amendment in the House forbidding government trade credits to that country unless its emigration policies are relaxed.)

The Nixon Administration was unsuccessful in its attempts to avoid the approval of the above amendments by the House of Representatives, and its hopes for obtaining a reversal in the Senate were dimmed by widespread support in that body for the intent of the amendments adopted by the House. However, after the accession of Ford to the Presidency negotiations between the Administration and Senate leaders regarding the issue of Soviet emigration policies led to a compromise solution. In exchange for assurances (given by the Administration) that the Soviet Union would relax its restrictive emigration policies, the Senate approved the Trade Reform Act, which can be expected to provide the base for further international trade negotiations.[11]

RECOMMENDED READINGS

BALDWIN, ROBERT E. *Nontariff Distortions of International Trade.* Washington, D.C.: Brookings Institution, 1970.

———— AND RICHARDSON, J. DAVID. *International Trade and Finance.* Part 2. Boston: Little, Brown & Co., 1974.

KREININ, MORDECHAI E. *Alternative Commercial Policies—Their Effect on the American Economy.* East Lansing, Mich.: Michigan State University, 1967.

PETERSON, PETER G. *A Foreign Economic Perspective.* Vol. 1, *The United States in the Changing World Economy.* Washington, D.C.: U.S. Government Printing Office, 1971.

United States International Economic Policy in an Interdependent World. Papers Submitted to the Commission on International Trade and Investment Policy. 2 vols. Washington, D.C.: U.S. Government Printing Office, 1971.

STUDY QUESTIONS

1. Define "protectionism" and give some examples of its presence in the United States today.

---

11 In January, 1975, the Soviet Union announced that the conditions imposed with respect to its emigration policies constituted an interference in its internal affairs and were not acceptable. Unless this issue is settled, the provisions of the Act relating to U.S.–Soviet trade will not be operative.

2. Which segments of an economy are most likely to be adversely affected by trade barriers?

3. Why would you expect protectionist forces to be stronger during recession periods than during periods of prosperity?

4. What do the objective data indicate is the effect of foreign trade on United States employment?

5. Through what reactions might increased import barriers lead to decreased exports?

6. How do tariffs and quotas affect the cost of living?

7. What changes in the international economic position of the United States have occurred in recent years?

8. Trace the changes, and reasons therefor, in U.S. official attitudes toward the European Common Market.

9. What significance for trade policies has the development of the European Common Market had?

10. Find out what finally happened to the Trade Reform Act of 1973.

12

Regional economic integration

The classical model of international trade envisages the exchange of goods and services among independent national economies without the interposition of artificial barriers. The model has never been fully implemented in practice. However strong the economic case for unfettered trading relations, opposition to the removal of national barriers has successfully resisted all attempts to make the world conform to the classical prescription.

Nevertheless, the idea of free trade is persistent, displaying a vitality unusual in the realm of economic doctrine. It reaches its full expression *within* each national state as the latter develops into its modern form. But, beyond this, it also finds full expression when two or more national states remove all tariffs and quantitative restrictions on the flow of goods and services between them.

Regional free-trade areas, embracing the national economies of two or more countries, are sometimes feasible, where worldwide free trade has little chance of being adopted in the foreseeable future. Regional groupings for the purpose of freeing trade between them have a considerable historical background,[1] but the greatest interest

---

1 For a brief history of projects of this nature proposed during the interwar years, see United Nations, Department of Economic Affairs, *Customs Unions* (New York: Lake Success, 1947).

in them has developed in recent years, especially in connection with the most ambitious regional project, the European Common Market.

In this chapter we shall explore the economics of what may be broadly called regional *integration.*

THE FORMS AND DEGREE OF ECONOMIC INTEGRATION

There are various forms and degrees of economic integration.[2] The historical prototype is the *customs union,* but both less and more intensive degrees of integration are possible and, in fact, currently in operation or projected.

The Free-Trade Area

The loosest and least intensive form of integration is the *free-trade area.* In a free-trade area, all artificial restrictions on the movement of goods and services among the participating countries are removed, but each country may retain its own tariffs, quotas, or other restrictive devices on its trade with nonparticipating countries.

The best known free-trade area is the European Free Trade Association (EFTA). Originally, EFTA embraced Great Britain, Norway, Sweden, Denmark, Switzerland, Austria, and Portugal (with Finland and Iceland later joining as "associate members"). In 1973, Great Britain and Denmark switched membership from EFTA to the European Economic Community, as described below. When EFTA came into existence in 1960, its seven members (also known as the "outer seven") agreed to eliminate tariffs and quotas among themselves gradually, with each retaining its independence with respect to commercial policies vis-à-vis other countries.

The movement toward free-trade areas extends beyond Europe. For example, a Latin American Free Trade Association was formed in 1960 by Argentina, Brazil, Chile, Paraguay, Peru, Uruguay, and Mexico.

The Customs Union

The customs union is one degree further along the scale of economic integration than a free-trade area. In addition to the complete elimination of tariffs and quotas on intraunion trade, a *common*

---

[2] The following discussion leans heavily on the excellent treatise of Bela Balassa, *The Theory of Economic Integration* (Homewood, Ill.: Richard D. Irwin, Inc., 1961).

external tariff is established on goods entering the union from outside. And, implied by the latter, is the apportionment of customs
revenue between the members of the union according to an agreed
formula.

The best known recent example of a customs union is Benelux—
Belgium, Luxembourg, and the Netherlands. Belgium and Luxembourg had established a customs union as far back as 1921. During
World War II, they agreed to join the Netherlands in an expanded
union. Today, Benelux embraces a single market with a common
external tariff and free internal trade. (Indeed, Benelux is now
closer to being a common market than just a customs union, for
there is virtually free intraunion movement of labor and capital as
well as of goods and services.)

Again, as in the case of free-trade associations, the movement
toward customs union has not been confined to Western Europe. For
example, the formation of a union is in progress in the West Indies,
and it is possible that the Latin American Free Trade Association
will eventually evolve into a union.

The Common Market

A common market represents the next higher degree of economic
integration beyond customs union. Besides (*a*) eliminating trade
barriers among member countries and (*b*) establishing a common
external tariff, a common market involves the important further
integrating step of (*c*) removing national restrictions on the movement of labor and capital among participating countries.

By far the most significant current example of a common market is
the European Economic Community (EEC), established by the
Treaty of Rome of 1957.[3] Popularly known as the European Common Market, the EEC originally included West Germany, France,
Italy, and the three Benelux countries. The membership has since
been expanded to nine countries with the admission in 1973 of Great
Britain, Ireland, and Denmark.

The EEC is more or less an extension of the European Coal and
Steel Community (ECSC), created in 1953 among the same six
countries later forming the EEC. In a real sense, the Coal and Steel
Community was an experiment on a limited scale with the common
market concept, and even with still more highly integrated opera-

---

[3] Several other regional blocs of countries in Latin America and Africa are considering, or are already in process of establishing, customs unions or common markets.

tions. Tariff and quota restrictions on coal and steel were abolished, discriminatory transport rates removed, a common pool of labor and capital funds created, and supervisory institutions with supranational powers formed. The great success of the Coal and Steel Community, together with the invaluable experience gained from it, contributed mightily to the extension of its principles to all goods and services.

The chief provisions of the Treaty of Rome establishing the EEC may be briefly summarized as follows:

1. The gradual elimination of tariffs, quotas, and other barriers to trade among members, to be accomplished within 12 to 15 years starting from 1958. (The target date has been shortened by several years through an accelerated rate of tariff reductions and quota removals.)
2. The creation of a uniform tariff schedule applicable to imports from the rest of the world.
3. The removal of restrictions on the movement among members of labor, capital, and business enterprises.
4. The prohibition of cartels and similar restrictive devices, unless they contribute to improvements in production or to technical and economic progress.
5. The pursuit of common agricultural policies.
6. The creation of two investment funds, one to operate in Europe and the other in associated overseas territories, to channel capital from the more advanced to the less developed regions of the Community.
7. The creation of a Social Fund to help relieve economic injuries to workers resulting from the movement toward integration.

It should be noted that lying behind the European Common Market and inspiring its development is a powerful movement looking toward the eventual political unification of Europe. In addition to creating the economic base for political integration, the Common Market provides a set of administering and implementing institutions—including a Commission, a Council of Ministers, an Assembly, and a Court of Justice—constituting a nucleus from which a European government could someday evolve.

The formation of a common market inevitably increases the interdependence of its members' national economies. In renouncing the use of tariffs, quotas, payments restrictions, immigration and emigration barriers, and control over capital movements as instruments of national policy, the members of a common market remove the chief insulators protecting their national economies from the full impact of external economic developments. The coordination of—or at least the avoidance of inconsistent—national economic and monetary policies is therefore implicit in a common market.

Economic Union

Once a common market has been fully established it arrives at the edge of the last, and highest, stage of economic integration—an *economic union*. The steps required to cross the boundary into economic union are, however, far-reaching.

The single most critical movement from a common market to economic union is monetary and fiscal unification. As long as each country enjoys monetary and fiscal independence, an essential economic ingredient of full-scale integration into a union is missing. On the other hand, the creation of a single monetary and fiscal authority with jurisdiction over two or more countries implies that all other economic relations are brought under the control of a central authority, so that in effect separate national economies are transformed into a single economic entity. Moreover, economic unification carried to this extent strongly implies political unification, for it is hardly conceivable that national political sovereignty could be maintained in the absence of national monetary and fiscal independence.

Needless to say, the barriers to economic union among countries with a long history of nationalism are formidable. It is therefore quite remarkable that the European Common Market countries have declared their intention to move in the direction of monetary unification. In 1970 a committee headed by Pierre Werner, then Finance Minister of Luxembourg, presented a plan for the monetary union of Common Market countries, with a target date of 1980.[4] The plan is to proceed by stages, reaching in the final stage a single common market currency.

The Common Market Commission approved the Werner plan in early 1971, and the Council of Ministers also expressed strong support of economic and monetary union. Whether or not union will in fact be achieved remains to be seen, but the road ahead is rocky, to say the least. From a long-run perspective, the greatest obstacle to

---

4 See "Report to the Council and the Commission of the Realization by Stages of Economic and Monetary Union in the Community," Supplement to EEC *Bulletin* No. 11.

union is the political implications noted above. More immediate difficulties have already been encountered. The integration of Great Britain into the Market will take some time and delay the implementation of the plan for union. The emergence of floating exchange rates after the breakdown of the Bretton Woods system (described in Chapter 19, below) has interfered with realizing the first stage of the Werner plan calling for a reduction in the fluctuation of exchange rates among member countries.

Notwithstanding the above difficulties and others likely yet to appear, the declaration of intention to achieve economic union of the Common Market countries is in itself a remarkable phenomenon.

THE ECONOMIC EFFECTS OF REGIONAL ECONOMIC INTEGRATION

The formation of the European Common Market has aroused intense interest all over the world. Economically, it poses the prospect of creating the largest aggregation of productive power and wealth in the world, next to the United States. Politically and socially it is being advanced as a "third force" in the East-West bipolar power complex.

Our primary interest now is in the economic effects that can be expected to flow from regional economic integration, especially integration of the kind represented by the European Common Market.

To its most enthusiastic protagonists, a common market offers the potentiality of a virtual economic revolution. The free movement of goods, persons, and capital is conceived as the means of releasing vast sources of productive energy hitherto held in check by artificial barriers erected at national boundaries. A favorite appeal to historical support for this sanguine prognostication is to cite the tremendous economic fruits produced by the vast single market of the United States.

The professional economist has been put in the unenviable position of having to throw a little cold water on the burning enthusiasm of the most ardent advocate of regional economic integration. In view of the economist's predilection for condemning artificial hindrances to free trade and factor movements, this may be somewhat surprising. But not really, for it must be remembered that there is another side to the coin of integration when pursued on a regional basis: namely, *regional discrimination. Part and parcel of the process of creating a single regional market is the erection of a wall around the region separating it to a greater or lesser degree from the outside world.* Whether, therefore, regional integration results in a net economic gain depends upon the adverse effects of this substituted barrier to free-world trade as compared to the beneficial effects of tearing down previous barriers. (A second, and related, question is *whose* net economic gain one is referring to—that of the members of the region, or of the outside world, or of the world as a whole?) The only kind of economic integration the unreconstructed "liberal" economist would support without qualification is one that would embrace the world.

This does not mean, however, that there is necessarily an economic case against regional integration; it only means that one should proceed with caution and not overlook the negative as well as the positive effects to be expected. Generalizations are dangerous in this connection, for what might be true in one particular case may not be in another. For instance, conceivably the European Common Market may turn out to be a tremendous success, while the Latin American Common Market may have indifferent or harmful effects. It all depends on circumstances and policies.

We shall now consider more specifically some of the major economic effects of regional integration.

Trade Creation versus Trade Diversion

One of the chief potential economic benefits of economic integration—applicable to free-trade associations, customs unions, and common markets alike—is brought about by the substitution of lower cost foreign supplies of a good for higher cost domestic production. The source of the gain here is precisely the same as that which we earlier concluded follows from the removal of protective tariffs.

Suppose, for example, that prior to the formation of the European Common Market, both Italy and France produced sewing machines, but that Italy had a marked comparative cost advantage, so that France's domestic production was carried on only by reason of a highly protective tariff. On removal of the French tariff, resources in France would be shifted out of the sewing maching industry into more efficient areas, and the French consumer would obtain the benefit of lower priced Italian sewing machines.

Whenever integration has the happy effect of replacing higher cost domestic production with lower cost foreign production, a net economic gain is undeniable, and the gain has aptly been labeled "trade creation."[5]

Unfortunately, however, the removal of tariffs on a regional basis accompanied by the erection of a common external tariff wall may lead to *trade diversion* instead of trade creation. Trade diversion occurs when higher cost sources of supply are substituted for lower cost sources.

For example, suppose that even though Italy has a cost advantage in sewing machines compared to France, the United States has a still greater comparative cost advantage. Assume further that before France and Italy become members of a regional integration arrangement, France has a low tariff, or no tariff, on sewing machines and therefore imports them from the United States, while Italy produces them at home under the cover of a protective tariff. Now France and Italy join in a customs union or common market and impose a common tariff on sewing machines high enough to make American machines more expensive to France, with tariff, than the Italian product without tariff. As a consequence, the source of supply to France is shifted from the lower cost American producers to the higher cost Italian producers. In this case, there is clearly a net economic loss incurred because of the customs union or common market.

There are obviously many other possible combinations of situations in addition to the two preceding illustrations. In some, integration leads to trade creation, in others to trade diversion, and in still others there is no effect (as, for example, when no members of the union or common market produce the commodity under tariff protection either before or after integration). Theoretically, and in general, *a net gain* will be realized if the sum of cost savings through trade creation exceeds the sum of cost increments through trade diversion, and *a net loss* incurred if the reverse balance prevails. But it is more difficult to predict which way the balance will fall in any particular integration scheme.

In the case of the European Common Market, judgments on the relative magnitudes of trade creation and trade diversion vary from the expectation of negligible differences between the two effects to

---

[5] The term was coined, as was also its opposite "trade diversion"—described in the following paragraphs—by Jacob Viner. See his *The Customs Union Issue* (New York: Carnegie Endowment for International Peace, 1950), pp. 41 ff.

the expectation of a significant net balance in favor of trade creation.[6]

One of the important determinants of what the net effect will be is the level of tariffs ultimately established by the Common Market. The lower the common tariff wall is, the less will be the diversion from lower cost outside sources to higher cost inside sources. This, in turn, will probably depend to a large extent upon the commercial policies pursued by other countries, and especially by the United States. If the United States were to react to the Common Market in a protectionist fashion, the danger of the world's being divided into warring and strongly discriminatory economic blocs, leading to a net loss from trade diversion, would be great. But if the United States vigorously pursues a policy of cooperation with the Common Market in reciprocal tariff reductions, the chances of trade creation being predominant are much increased.

The Economic Effects of Free Factor Movements

We recall that a common market not only frees trade among the member countries but also frees the movement of labor, capital, and entrepreneurship. (This does not hold for customs unions and free-trade associations, however, so that the present discussion is not applicable to the latter two types of regional integration.) What benefits, or disadvantages, can be expected to flow from free factor movements?

Recalling our much earlier discussion of factor movements (see Chapter 7), we would presume that their freedom from artificial hindrances would contribute to the welfare of the common market as a whole. The theoretical reason for this conclusion is easily stated: the total output of the community is increased, with the same volume of inputs, when labor and capital move from areas of lower marginal productivity to areas of higher marginal productivity. Likewise, total production is increased if entrepreneurial skills can be freely transferred from areas of relative plentifulness to areas of relative scarcity. The potentiality for further gain from the movement of factors is exhausted only after their marginal productivities have become equalized in different areas.

---

6 For the pessimistic view of the net gain to be realized see Tibor Scitovsky, *Economic Theory and Western European Integration* (Stanford, Calif.: Stanford University Press, 1958), pp. 64–67. For an optimistic view, see Franz Gehrels and B. F. Johnston, "The Economic Gains of European Integration," *Journal of Political Economy*, August 1955.

Moreover, the chances of integration having a negative effect from factor movements, comparable to the possible negative allocation effects described previously, are small. Theoretically, an adverse effect could be produced by diverting factor movements from third countries. But in practice this is not likely to be very significant, especially for labor movements. Because of strict national immigration controls, very little movement of labor occurs across national boundaries to be diverted by regional integration. National restrictions on international capital movements are much less severe, but it is doubtful that any great diversion of the flow from third countries would be caused by the formation of a common market.

In addition to the potentialities for net gains realizable from reducing the national disparities in the marginal productivity of resources, a related and very important, though less measurable, gain may be forthcoming from free factor movements within an integrated region. It is the advantages stemming from the closer communication among the peoples of the region. New ideas, techniques, and skills can be expected to flourish under the impact of closer contact and the removal of national discriminatory policies and attitudes.

While the potentiality for significant gain from free factor movements can hardly be denied, there is one troublesome question to be raised. The gain we have identified is that accruing to the integrated *region as a whole.* Unfortunately, however, there is no assurance that this gain will be equally distributed among the member countries, nor even that some members or sectors may not actually suffer a loss of welfare. This possibility recalls the analogous problem we earlier discussed in connection with the internal distribution within a country of the national gain produced by free trade (see pages 75–76). Not surprisingly, the most reasonable solution may also be similar: a greater emphasis on capital movements, rather than labor movements, and redistributive measures by the regional organization.

Dynamic Effects of Integration

So far we have been considering the economic effects of regional integration on the assumption of given and unchanging factor supplies, state of technology, and economic structure. It is quite probable, however, that potentially the greatest advantages to be gained from integration stem from essentially *dynamic* forces that may be released by integration. Especially important is the extent to which integration will stimulate an accelerated rate of economic growth. Not only is this an extremely relevant consideration from the standpoint of the countries integrating their economies but it is also of prime importance from the standpoint of the outside world, as we shall see later.

We shall now investigate the major forces released or created by integration that may contribute to an accelerated rate of economic growth.

Internal Economies of Scale.   Let us begin with a phenomenon that has been the subject of a considerable amount of controversy among economists: economies of scale.

There are two types of economies of scale: internal and external. Internal economies are those realized by an individual firm as a consequence of expanding its scale of operations. External economies are realized by individual firms, not as the result of their own actions, but as a consequence of expansion in the industry or economy as a whole.

There is doubt in the minds of some economists about the extensiveness and significance of either kind of economies of scale, especially of the external variety. However, several empirical studies in recent years indicate that *in some industries,* though by no means in all, there definitely are marked internal economies realizable as the size of firms expands.[7]

When large internal economies of scale are present in an industry, the ability fully to appropriate them depends upon the size of the market. If the demand for the product is not large enough to absorb the output of firms in the industry operating at optimum scale, economies of large-scale production cannot be fully exploited. In some cases, the market may not be large enough to support even *one* firm operating at optimum scale. For example, it has been estimated that in the manufacturing of rayon yarn, the optimal operation is at an output of approximately 20,000–25,000 tons per year per plant, with costs of production about 8 percent higher for a plant half this size and 25 percent higher for a plant with one quarter the optimum output. Yet a few years ago the entire annual output was only about 10,000 tons in Belgium, 30,000 tons in the Netherlands, 14,000 tons

---

[7] See, for example, Joe S. Bain, *Barriers to New Competition* (Cambridge, Mass.: Harvard University Press, 1956), chap. iii.

in Argentina, 13,000 tons in Mexico, 1,000 tons in Peru and Uruguay, and so on.[8]

In those industries where the appropriation of significant economies of scale requires a total output in excess of the absorptive capacity of the national economy, the integration of several national economies obviously may permit the achievement of lower costs of production.[9] There is evidence that such might be the case in the European Common Market for such industries as atomic energy; steel; the smelting and refining of copper, zinc, tin, and lead; metal engineering; electrical engineering; automobiles; synthetic fibers; paper and allied products; chinaware and glass; furniture; leather; and footwear.[10] There likewise appears to be considerable scope for capturing economies of scale through the integration of Lain American economies.[11]

A related advantage that may be yielded by a larger market is increased competition. Even if a national market is large enough to allow the exploitation of large-scale economies, it may not be large enough to support more than one or a very few optimum-sized firms. Enlargement of the market through regional integration would then permit a larger number of optimum-sized firms to survive and reduce the degree of monopolistic control in the industry. We shall return to this aspect of integration shortly.

External Economies of Scale.   As indicated earlier, the reality of external economies of scale is seriously questioned by some economists (Professor Frank Knight being the leading sceptic) . Others are convinced that external economies are not only genuine but may be of the first order of importance. The weight of the evidence, both theoretical and empirical, seems to be on the side of the latter. Let us briefly explore some of the possible sources of external economies.[12]

In general, the source of external economies lies in the interaction of the various sectors of an economy, with developments in each sector having favorable repercussions on the others. The expansion of one industry may lead to the creation of certain skills of labor

---

[8] See Balassa, *The Theory of Economic Integration*, pp. 135 and 139 and references cited therein.

[9] International trade among nonintegrated countries may also permit the reaping of economies of scale through the presence of large export markets. However, artificial barriers to trade clearly reduce the scope of this possibility.

[10] See Balassa, *The Theory of Economic Integration*, pp. 132–35.

[11] Ibid., 138–42.

[12] A good summary of the evidence is to be found in Balassa, *The Theory of Economic Integration*, pp. 144–62, on which the following discussion draws freely.

techniques of management, or technological developments, which then become part of the economy's "pool" of resources, available to be drawn upon by other industries. A technological improvement in industry *X,* supplying intermediate products to industry *Y,* lowers costs in *Y.* An innovation in industry *A,* supplying industry *B,* may lead to an expansion in the output of *B* that in turn allows the capture of economies of scale by the latter. There may be a circular "feedback" effect—for example, the expansion of coal production may lower the cost of steel, in turn lowering the cost of mining equipment and of coal.

An expansion in the size of markets through regional integration widens the scope for the gains originating in the interplay of sectoral developments. As the situation of underdeveloped economies clearly indicates, the absence of a large enough market frequently stymies the development of particular industries whose absence in turn hinders the development of other industries. Moreover, the larger the market the greater are the opportunities to realize economies through further specialization. For instance, whereas in the United States automobile parts and accessories are produced by a large number of independent firms, in some European countries, because of the limited output of each firm, manufacturers produce component parts themselves.

Increased Competition. One of the less tangible and unmeasurable, but still potentially very significant, benefits of economic integration lies in the more efficient market structures it may encourage. A well-established proposition in economics is that, other things being equal, the more competitive a market is, the more efficient it will be in the sense that the resulting allocation of resources will more nearly approach the social optimum.

It is not inevitable that regional integration will lead to more competitive market structures. Indeed, some observers are of the opinion that integration will result in the formation of cartels and other forms of oligopolistic coordination among the firms of member countries, decreasing economic efficiency.[13]

Others expect a greater degree of competition to evolve because of integration.[14] By a "greater degree" of competition is certainly not meant in this context the theoretical model of *pure* competition. More realistically, it means a decrease in the degree and extent of

---

[13] See, for example, K. Rothschild, "The Small Nation and World Trade," *Economic Journal,* April 1944, pp. 26–40.

[14] See especially Scitovsky, *Economic Theory,* pp. 123–30.

oligopolistic uncertainty and coordination, brought about by a dilution of the influence of each firm. For instance, suppose that within each of several national economies there are only a few firms operating in a given industry, with each national industry protected by tariffs from the effective competition of the firms in other countries. Very likely the firms in the industry in each country will reach an understanding, tacit or overt, not to "rock the boat" by price competition. Inefficient firms are likely to be protected from the competition of efficient firms by agreement to share the market and "live and let live."

Now assume that national barriers to trade and investment are removed through integration of the countries. The vulnerability of each firm in the industry to the actions and reactions of other firms is reduced, for each firm's share of the larger regional market is less than it was of its smaller national market. The oligopolistic interdependence of firms is lessened and the possibility of effective collusion among firms reduced. Inefficient firms lose the protection afforded by the absence in nationally separated markets of competition from foreign producers.

Moreover, the wider markets offered by integration may open the door to the entry into some industries of a larger number of optimum-sized firms. As noted earlier, to the extent that marked internal economies of scale are responsible for oligopolistic concentration of output in the hands of a few firms, integration reduces this barrier to a larger number of firms and more effective competition.

Whether or not the advantages of greater competition are in fact reaped from integration depends in large measure upon the policies adopted by the participating countries. In the case of the European Common Market, it is not yet clear what these policies will be. The treaty establishing EEC forbids, in principle, the formation of cartels and the abuse of dominant market positions. But an exception is allowed for agreements among firms which "contribute to improvements in the production and distribution of goods or to the promotion of technical and economic progress, while reserving a fair part of the resulting profit to the users." Moreover, industrial concentration is not prohibited, and it remains to be seen whether or not various forms of tacit collusion will develop.

Nevertheless, in comparison to the widespread previous practice of many European producers, often with the approval or even outright support of their governments, to engage in restrictive agreements, the Common Market Treaty outlawing cartels and abuses of oligopolistic power represents a significant step in the direction of greater competition. Provided that the spirit of this approach is not too badly violated in practice, the forces operating in the wider market to increase competition will probably predominate over any tendencies toward extending national interfirm coordination to regional industries.

REGIONS VERSUS THE OUTSIDE WORLD

Up to this point we have concentrated our analysis on the effects of regional integration on the participating countries. There remains for discussion the impact of regionalism on the world economy as a whole and on nonparticipating countries in particular.

Generally speaking, we would expect any effects of regional integration beneficial to the participating countries also to be beneficial to the world as a whole, and regionally harmful effects likewise to be detrimental to the whole world. Such, for example, is the case with respect to trade creation and trade diversion. If regional integration leads to trade creation, member countries benefit, while other countries are certainly not harmed. But if it leads to trade diversion, both member countries and other countries whose export markets are diverted suffer economic loss.

Quite conceivably, however, integration could benefit member countries while harming third countries. A distinct possibility of this occurring lies in the *terms-of-trade effect* of integration. If the terms of trade of countries integrating their economies are improved, their share of the gain from trade with the outside world is increased at the expense of the latter.

The terms of trade of a regional group may be more favorable than prior to integration for at least two reasons. First, to the extent that trade diversion occurs, the demand for the export products of third countries is reduced, and this may have the effect of depressing their export prices. Second, the bargaining power of a regional bloc in tariff negotiations with other countries is likely to be much greater than that of each of the participating countries negotiating separately. (This would not apply to integration arrangements not involving a common external tariff, such as free-trade association.)

That some third countries may lose from the trade-diverting and/or terms-of-trade effects of regional integration is a theoretical possibility not to be denied. How significant in actuality such effects are in the case of the European Common Markets is difficult to

260 Introduction to international economics

determine. In any event, the United States has become increasingly concerned over the effects of trade diversion on United States exports, as well as other broader implications of European economic integration. The concern was magnified by two recent events: enlargement of the Common Market to include Great Britain, Ireland, and Denmark; and the agreement, reached in mid-1972, between the EEC and the remaining members of EFTA mutually to abolish tariffs on industrial goods traded between the two groups.

Enlargement of the Common Market from six to nine countries increased the already large aggregation of economic power represented, with the Community having a combined gross national product approximately two thirds that of the United States and a share of world trade of more than 40 percent—nearly double the combined share of the United States, Japan, and the Soviet Union. The fear of large trade diversion as the result of forming an integrated market of this size was compounded when the agreement with EFTA was reached, leaving third-country industrial exports to EFTA members discriminated against.

United States concern over trade diversion has not been generally supported by actual experience. Although the share of the United States imports from the European Economic Community declined from 13 percent in 1960 to 8 percent in 1972, the absolute volume of United States exports to the Community doubled over this period.[15] Moreover, in contrast to the movement in the overall trade balance of the United States, which deteriorated from a sizeable surplus during the 60s to deficits in 1971 and 1972, the surplus balance with the European Community has been maintained, amounting to more than a billion dollars in 1973.

It is not known, of course, what the net impact of the Common Market on the volume of trade has been, for there is no way of determining what would have happened to trade had the market not been formed. It is reasonable to suppose, however, that formation of the market increased the rate of growth in the income of its member countries, which in turn had the effect of expanding the demand for imports, part of which was satisfied by the United States and other outside countries. Any trade diversion, therefore, may have been at least partially offset by the income effect produced by the formation of the Market.

---

[15] U.S. Senate, Committee on Finance, "Staff Data and Materials on U.S. Trade and Balance of Payments" (Washington, D.C.: U.S. Government Printing Office, 1974), p. 16.

Notwithstanding the absence of any clear indication that United States trade in general has suffered from the creation of the EEC, it is evident that the markets for particular products have been adversely affected. The principal products so affected are agricultural. The reason that agricultural exports to the Common Market have suffered is not trade diversion as such, but rather the Community system of variable levies as a means of subsidizing domestic agriculture. The variable levies are set equal to the difference between world prices and domestic support prices. As a consequence, affected products are imported only to the extent that domestic demand exceeds domestic supply at support prices, leaving foreign exporters in the position of residual suppliers. In the event that domestic supply exceeds domestic demand at the support price, the excess is dumped on world markets, thus adversely affecting agricultural exporting countries in the outside world.

Between 1960—before variable import levies were first imposed—and 1970, United States agricultural exports to the EEC increased by about 40 percent, but to other countries the increase was more than 100 percent.[16]

There can be no doubt that the agricultural subsidy program in the European Community restricts trade and is economically inefficient. However, it should be noted that the same general comment applies to similar subsidy programs in the United States and other industrial countries.

Overall, it is doubtful that economic integration in Europe has been responsible for any very significant effects on the United States trade position in the world economy. There is, however, a more general aspect of integration which is potentially of considerable significance—namely, the emergence of economic blocs.

World trade is now dominated by three major blocs of countries: the European Economic Community, the United States and Canada, and Japan. The main thrust of postwar international trade policy, embodied in the General Agreement on Tariffs and Trade, has been eliminating discrimination in trading relations. But the more extensive the regional bloc in Europe becomes, the greater is the volume of trade of the other blocs subject to discriminatory treatment. Moreover, the larger and more powerful a regional bloc is, the less dependent it is on the outside world, fostering an inward-looking

---

16 U.S. Senate, Committee on Finance, *Executive Branch GATT Studies* (Washington, D.C.: U.S. Government Printing Office, 1974) , p. 44.

stance and raising the threat of trade wars with other blocs. A revival of protectionist forces in the other blocs, especially in the United States, would of course increase the probability of the world's degenerating into bitter economic warfare. The main hope of avoiding a development in this direction lies in the vigorous reassertion of the benefits of free trade, and international cooperation under the aegis of GATT.

RECOMMENDED READINGS

BALASSA, BELA. *The Theory of Economic Integration.* Homewood, Ill.: Richard D. Irwin, Inc., 1961.

HUMPHREY, DON. *The United States and the Common Market.* New York: Frederick A. Praeger, Inc., 1962.

KRAUSE, LAWRENCE B. AND SALANT, WALTER S., EDS. *European Monetary Unification and Its Meaning for the United States.* Washington, D.C.: Brookings Institution, 1973.

PATTERSON, GARDNER. *Discrimination in International Trade: The Policy Issues, 1945–1965,* chaps. iv–vi. Princeton, N.J.: Princeton University Press, 1966.

SCITOVSKY, TIBOR. *Economic Theory and Western European Integration.* Stanford, Calif.: Stanford University Press, 1958.

UNITED NATIONS, DEPARTMENT OF ECONOMIC AFFAIRS. *Customs Unions.* 1947.

United States International Economic Policy in an Interdependent World. Papers Submitted to the Commission on International Trade and Investment Policy, vol. 2, chap. 10. Washington, D.C.: July 1971.

VINER, JACOB. *The Customs Union Issues.* New York: Carnegie Endowment for International Peace, 1950.

STUDY QUESTIONS

1. Distinguish between a free-trade area, a customs union, a common market, and economic union.
2. Describe the chief provisions of the Treaty of Rome establishing the European Economic Community.
3. Why does the establishment of a common market strongly imply the close coordination of member countries' national economic, monetary, and social policies?
4. Why does monetary and fiscal unification imply economic union?
5. Regional economic integration necessarily involves trade discrimination. Explain.

6. Show how the formation of a regional economic bloc may lead either to trade creation or trade diversion. Illustrate with examples.

7. Demonstrate the economic advantages likely to accrue to members of the European Common Market as a result of the freeing of factor movements.

8. Define *internal economies of scale*. Why can economic integration be expected to lead to a greater realization of such economies?

9. Define *external economies of scale,* and show how the European Common Market may promote their development.

10. What benefits may economic integration confer with respect to market structures?

11. Under what circumstances are nonmember countries harmed by regional economic integration?

12. How does the "variable levy" system in the EEC work?

13. What are the major trading blocs in the world today? Why is there a potential danger of economic warfare among these blocs?

part three

International monetary relations

13

International payments

Up to this point, very little attention has been paid to the monetary aspects of international relations. In discussing the pure theory of trade, we assumed away the problems connected with monetary relations in order to concentrate on the real (substantive) content and effects of trade and factor movements. In the long run, these real aspects of international economic relations have the greatest significance.

However, the international as well as the domestic exchange of goods and services and movement of capital take place within the context of a monetary framework. How efficiently the system works in real terms heavily depends upon the efficiency of the monetary system. A smoothly functioning and stable monetary system performs a tremendously important facilitative role, creating the framework indispensable for attainment of the optimum volume and pattern of trade and capital movements. A malfunctioning and unstable monetary system inevitably interposes obstacles to realizing the maximum potentials of trade and capital movements. Unstable monetary relations raise problems of their own and, indeed, are the source of most of the short-run concerns of countries in their international economic relations.

267

Preparatory to an exploration of the international monetary system and the problems it raises, this chapter considers the elementary nature of international payments.

THE MEANS OF MAKING PAYMENT: FOREIGN EXCHANGE

The most obvious difference between domestic and international monetary relations is the presence of a single monetary unit in the former and a multiplicity of monetary units in the latter. The world today is divided into over 150 independent national states; there are very nearly as many national monetary systems. Yet, despite this great diversity of systems, superimposed upon them is an international monetary system, consisting of the institutions, arrangements, and practices through which international payments are made. As we shall see later, an international monetary system may take a variety of forms. However, they all have in common the basic purpose of tranferring purchasing power from one currency[1] to another. The problem of tranferring purchasing power internationally arises out of the presence of different national monetary systems. If there were a world-unified monetary system, similar to the system in effect in each national economy, making international payments would not involve problems any different from those relating to making payments from one region to another within the same country.

Since the same currency unit is used in different parts of a given country, domestic payments pose no difficulty. If a New Yorker purchases beef from Texas or an automobile from Detroit he pays in dollars, which is what the seller wants. But if he buys beef from Argentina or an automobile from France, two different currency units enter into the transaction—that of the buyer (dollars) and that of the seller (Argentine pesos or French francs) .

How is payment made when different currencies are involved? The various instruments devised for this purpose are known collectively as "foreign exchange." It is not necessary to describe here the technical aspects of these instruments, such as cable and mail transfers and bills of exchange.[2] Suffice it to say that they constitute means of making payments across national currency boundaries. Thus, for example, if you had to remit 10 pounds sterling to England to pur-

---

[1] "Currency" is used in this discussion as a shorthand expression for "national monetary unit."

[2] The interested reader may consult Morris T. Rosenthal, *Techniques of International Trade* (New York: McGraw-Hill, 1950) .

chase books, you would acquire sterling foreign exchange in this amount, probably in the form of a bank draft which you would mail to the British publisher.

Foreign exchange is bought and sold in organized markets through dealers. Foreign exchange dealers—in the United States, special departments of certain large banks—sell foreign exchange in any currency desired by a customer and purchase any foreign exchange offered to them. Purchases and sales are, of course, at specified prices known as rates of exchange. In the United States, rates of exchange are quoted in terms of cents or dollars per unit of foreign currency. For example, the rate of exchange on the pound at the time you pay for your British books may be $2.395. A £10 draft would therefore cost $23.95 (plus a small commission charge). How exchange rates are determined is considered later.

SOURCES OF FOREIGN EXCHANGE

The presence of a foreign exchange market where means of making payments from one currency into another are available for purchase and sale relieves individuals and business firms of the most immediate problems connected with foreign payments. Except for the special problems arising out of the possibility of variations in foreign exchange rates, making or receiving foreign payments is no more complicated for individual transactions than are domestic monetary settlements.

Even though the question of how foreign payments are made and received has been answered for the individual buyer and seller, it certainly has not been answered yet for the market as a whole. An individual buys foreign exchange from a dealer—but where has the dealer acquired it to sell? Another individual sells foreign exchange to a dealer—but what does the dealer do with it? These questions are clearly interconnected and the answers to them as well.

Let us first consider the sources of the foreign exchange that are dealers' stock-in-trade. Initially we will assume that the international economic relations of each country are confined exclusively to commodity trade, an assumption that later will be relaxed. In this case, there is only one source of foreign exchange: the foreign currency proceeds from commodity exports. Suppose that during some given period U.S. exports consist of the sale to France of machinery for 500,000 French francs. The U.S. exporter wishes to obtain dollars because his costs, taxes, and profits are all expressed in dollars. The exporter therefore sells the franc proceeds[3] of his export to a New York bank foreign exchange dealer. How many dollars are received for the francs depends upon the rate of exchange, which we will assume is $0.20 per franc. Hence, the exporter is paid $100,000 for the 500,000 francs. The exporter is now out of the picture, have finally received payment in his own currency. (The French importer at no time had a foreign exchange problem, since he paid for the machinery in his own currency, francs.) The French franc proceeds of the export are in the possession of the New York bank. What does the bank do with the francs? In the first instance, the bank merely adds the francs to its deposits held in a French correspondent bank. Before explaining this action, let us summarize what has occurred so far by referring to changes in the T accounts of the French importer's bank and the U.S. exporter's bank:

French Bank		U.S. Bank	
Assets	*Liabilities*	*Assets*	*Liabilities*
	Deposit of importer, −500,000 francs Deposit of U.S. bank, +500,000 francs	Deposit in French bank, +500,000 francs ($100,000)	Deposit of U.S. exporter, +$100,000

For simplicity, it is assumed that the French importer's bank is also the correspondent of the U.S. exporter's bank. Observing first the French bank, we see that the importer's account has been drawn down in making payment for the machinery, while the franc deposit account of the American exporter's bank has been increased by the same amount. On the American side, the dollar deposit account of the exporter has been increased from the sale to the bank of French francs, while the franc deposit of the bank with its French correspondent has increased by the same amount.

An important effect of the transactions, the full significance of which is examined in a subsequent discussion, is a change in each country's domestically held stock of money in the form of bank deposits. The total stock of money in France has not changed, but

---

[3] The francs should not be thought of literally as franc currency but rather as some kind of foreign exchange instrument, such as a bank draft. If the latter is used, the French importer purchases a franc draft from his bank, the draft being an order to pay a specified amount of money (in the case at hand, 500,000 francs) to the U.S. exporter or his order.

there has been a switch in ownership from a domestic resident, the importer, to a nonresident, the U.S. bank. In the United States, the export has resulted in an increase in the total stock of domestic money, there having been an exchange between the exporter and his bank of francs for dollars.

Now we return to the question of why the U.S. bank was willing to purchase francs from the exporter. The reason is rather obvious: the bank is in the foreign exchange business, and foreign bank balances are its stock-in-trade. One principal way to acquire the "commodity" in which it deals is through purchasing it from exporters, who in turn have received it in payment from foreign importers. The bank needs foreign exchange balances to have available to sell, for an exchange dealer's profits are derived from the services rendered in providing a market for both buyers and sellers.

We have identified what is nearly always the largest source of foreign exchange to a country, namely, the export of commodities. Falling in the same category is the export of services. The sale to nonresidents of the services of transportation, tourism, insurance, capital funds (the services of which are measured in terms of interest and dividend receipts), and other so-called "invisible" items contributes in the same manner as commodity exports to the foreign exchange receipts of a country.

Besides the export of goods and services, there are other sources of foreign exchange receipts to a country. One of the more important of these is the inflow of foreign capital in the form of loans and investments. For example, when U.S. residents or the government loans or invests money in Canada, the Canadian economy receives U.S. dollars which, from its point of view, constitute foreign exchange.

Closely related to ordinary capital flows between countries is the special form of capital movement known as unilateral transfers. These differ from ordinary capital movements in that no interest payments or recovery of principal are involved. In short, they are in the nature of gifts or grants. Like capital receipts, a unilateal transfer into a country from abroad provides foreign exchange, unless it is directly in the form of commodities.

Finally, a country may be able to mobilize additional amounts of foreign exchange through special transactions undertaken by official agencies for the specific purpose of adding to the private market supply. All such transactions fall into a separate category called the "Official Settlements Account."

There are two principal sources of officially supplied foreign exchange. The first is the liquidation of assets in the possession of the national monetary authority which consist of accumulated foreign currency balances or other assets which can readily be converted into foreign exchange. Among the latter are principally monetary gold and short-term foreign securities that can easily be sold in foreign markets. (Additionally, for members of the International Monetary Fund, the so-called "gold tranche" and Special Drawing Rights are available sources of foreign exchange, as will be explained in a later chapter.) Collectively, all these sources of foreign exchange which a government can draw upon constitute its *international reserves.*

Besides drawing upon its international reserves, a country may be able to mobilize extra foreign exchange through obtaining special credits or loans from foreign countries or international agencies.

Foreign exchange supplied through official settlement transactions has a special significance, distinguishing it from the exchange supplied through other transactions, that will become clear in due course.

USES OF FOREIGN EXCHANGE

We have examined the various sources of foreign exchange that enter into a country's foreign exchange market. It is time now to look at the other side of the picture: the uses to which foreign exchange is put. Not surprisingly, we shall find that these are the exact counterparts of the sources.

Let us begin with the individual foreign exchange dealer, the New York bank in our previous example. The bank acquired 500,000 French franc balances through purchasing them from a U.S. exporter of machinery to France. The bank is interested in foreign exchange balances for only one reason: to have them available to sell. Who, then, are its potential customers?

One clear possibility is importers of French goods. Suppose that an American firm wishes to purchase 500,000 francs worth of French perfume. To pay for the perfume, the firm must acquire this sum of franc foreign exchange, in the form, say, of a franc bank draft ordering a French bank to pay the sum to the French exporter. The draft may be purchased from the U.S. bank which had previously acquired francs from the exporter of machinery. At an exchange rate of $0.20 per franc, the American firm pays the bank $100,000 for 500,000 francs, and the bank's French correspondent pays the francs to the perfume exporter. The monetary results of these transactions are summarized below in terms of the T accounts of the two banks:

French Bank		U.S. Bank	
Assets	Liabilities	Assets	Liabilities
	Deposit of French exporter, +500,000 francs Deposit of U.S. bank −500,000 francs	Deposit in French bank, −500,000 francs ($100,000)	Deposit of U.S. importer, −$100,000

We note that these results are precisely the same as those produced in connection with the export of machinery from the United States, *except for the reversal of entries*. As in the earlier transaction, the export has led to an increase in the domestically held stock of money in the exporting country and a decrease in the stock of money in the importing country. The two transactions together canceled each other in both their foreign exchange and domestic monetary effects. Whereas the export of machinery from the United States increased the foreign exchange balances of the U.S. bank and the U.S. domestic money supply, the import of perfume used up the foreign balances and decreased the domestic supply of money. In France, the import of machinery decreased the domestically held supply of money and increased the foreign liabilities of the French bank, while the export of perfume increased the domestically held supply of money and decreased the foreign liabilities of the bank.

It is clear from the above examples that the foreign exchange dealers—the American and French banks—served only as financial intermediaries, facilitating, but not basically altering, the transactions in goods. Conceivably, the foreign exchange market might have been circumvented entirely. The U.S. exporter of machinery could have been paid $100,000 by the importer of perfume, and the French exporter of perfume could have been paid 500,000 francs by the importer of machinery. Even though such procedures often would not be practical, they illustrate the fundamental nature of the more roundabout, and more efficient, methods of payment through organized foreign exchange markets.

While commodity imports are ordinarily the largest absorber of foreign exchange (just as commodity exports are the largest provider), foreign exchange is needed to make a variety of other foreign payments. The other transactions using foreign exchange are the precise counterparts of those providing it, discussed previously. A country uses foreign exchange to pay for the import of services (foreign travel, foreign transportation, and so on), to finance loans and investments in other lands, to make unilateral transfers to other countries, and to finance official settlement transactions.

RECOMMENDED READING

CRUMP, NORMAN. *The ABC of the Foreign Exchanges.* Rev. ed. London: Macmillan & Co., Ltd., 1957.

HOLMES, ALAN R., AND SCHOTT, FRANCIS H. *The New York Foreign Exchange Market.* New York: Federal Reserve Bank of New York, 1965.

RECOMMENDED READINGS

1. Define the basic purpose of an international monetary system.
2. Compare the problem of making domestic payments with that of making foreign payments.
3. Define "foreign exchange."
4. Check the financial pages of a newspaper for the day's quotation of foreign exchange rates.
5. When the dollar rate of exchange on a foreign currency rises, what happens to the rate of exchange on the dollar in the foreign country?
6. Describe the nature of the business of foreign exchange dealers.
7. Describe several different kinds of transactions that provide foreign exchange in the market.
8. How does an import affect the domestically held supply of money? How does an export affect it?
9. If a U.S. resident were to purchase shares of stock from a resident of Switzerland, what kind of transaction in the foreign exchange market would this give rise to?
10. Show how if a country's imports just equal its exports the domestic monetary and foreign exchange effects of the trade cancel each other out.

14

The balance
of payments

We have learned that in order to make international payments a country needs foreign exchange. Foreign exchange is provided by a variety of transactions, the main categories of which are the export of goods and services, an inflow of capital from abroad, unilateral transfer receipts, and gold exports. Foreign exchange is needed to pay for imported goods and services, to finance capital outflows and unilateral payments, and to pay for any gold imports. International monetary problems arise out of the relationship between these sources and uses of foreign exchange and their interconnection with domestic economic and monetary affairs.

The starting point for an analysis of these problems is the balance of payments. The balance of payments of a country is a summary record of all the international economic and financial transactions of the country during a specified period of time. A partial balance of payments includes the transactions between one country and a given number of other countries (one or more, but not all).

It is important to note that the balance of payments records transactions that take place over a particular period of time. If we want an instantaneous or "still" picture of a country's international economic position, the appropriate measure is not the balance of payments but rather the balance of international indebtedness. The latter is a balance sheet type of statement, showing, as of a given date, claims held by domestic residents against foreigners and vice versa. If claims against foreigners exceed obligations to foreigners, a country is said to be a net international creditor; in the opposite case, it is a net international debtor. In other words, the balance of international indebtedness shows the net results of past transactions on a country's international capital position. We are already familiar with this from our discussion in a previous chapter. By contrast, the balance of payments summarizes international transactions over a given period of time.

A balance of payments can be drawn up for any economic entity if relevant data are known: for an individual, household, community, region, or national economy. The *principles* of a balance of payments are the same in all these cases, although, of course, the content would vary considerably from one to the other. What these principles are we shall examine after having first given a more specific description of the makeup of an international balance of payments.

STRUCTURE OF THE BALANCE OF PAYMENTS

The major purpose of a balance of payments is to provide a summary statistical statement of the sources and uses of foreign exchange. Another way of putting it is to say that a balance of payments summarizes, on the one hand, the transactions of a country which create payment obligations to foreigners (i.e., nonresidents) and, on the other hand, the transactions which provide the means of settling these obligations. Clearly, a distinction between these kinds of transactions is called for.

Debit and Credit Entries

Any transaction of a country that requires a foreign payment or creates an obligation to make such payment is entered in the balance of payments as a *debit* or *payments* item. ("Payments" and "debits" are used interchangeably. A third designation is simply a negative sign.) Any transaction that provides foreign exchange to a country, or that discharges a foreign obligation of the country, is entered as a *credit* or *receipts* item. ("Receipts" and "credits" are used interchangeably. A third designation is a plus sign.) There are some transactions which do not involve an actual international payment or receipt but are included in the balance of payments for the sake of completeness. We shall refer to these at the appropriate time and indicate how they are identified as either debit or credit items.

A few examples will serve to clarify the distinction between debit and credit items in the balance of payments.

The import of goods and services is ordinarily the largest debit items and the export of goods and services the largest credit item in balances of payments. An import is a debit item, for it requires payment to the foreign exporter or creates an obligation to make such payment. An export is a credit item, for it either leads to the receipt of foreign exchange from the importing country or to the creation of a claim for payment against the importing country.

Capital movements are a second source of international payments and receipts. Capital inflows into a country are credit items; capital outflows are debit items. A capital inflow into a country occurs if it receives loans or investments from abroad or if it liquidates foreign assets. Thus, a loan by the U.S. government to the British government constitutes a capital inflow into Britain and is entered in the British balance of payments as a credit item since it provides dollar foreign exchange. From the viewpoint of the United States, the loan represents an outflow of capital and is entered as a debit item. The purchase and sale between residents and nonresidents of evidences of debt or ownership are another form capital movements may take. If U.S. residents purchase securities from Canadian residents, this constitutes a capital movement from the United States to Canada—a debit transaction for the United States and a credit transaction for Canada. Still another form of capital movements occurs when assets held in one country but owned by the residents of another are acquired or liquidated. If General Motors establishes a branch plant in Germany, this is a foreign "direct" investment and appears as a capital outflow from the United States, a debit entry in her balance of payments. On the other hand, if a previously acquired foreign asset is sold to a nonresident, the capital flow is into the seller's country and is a credit entry in her balance of payments.

A final category of capital movements that plays a special role in the international monetary system includes changes in bank balances owned by nonresidents. An increase in foreign balances held by the residents of a country represents a short-term capital outflow and therefore a debit in the country's balances of payments. It is a debit transaction, for in acquiring or adding to bank balances held abroad the country is purchasing an asset which has to be paid for. On the other hand, if a country draws down foreign balances, a capital inflow (credit entry) occurs, for in this case the country is in effect selling an asset which the foreign purchaser must pay for. The same principles apply in identifying increases in domestic balances owned by nonresidents as capital inflows, credit items, and decreases in such balances as capital outflows, debit items.

Other debit and credit entries in the balance of payments are created by unilateral transfers and gold movements. Unilateral transfers into a country are credit items; out of a country, they are debit items. If such transfers are made in kind, such as a gift of wheat by the United States to India, no money payment or claim for payment is involved, but they are still included in the balance of payments to keep the record complete.

Gold is no different from other commodities so far as debit and credit entries are concerned: exports are credits; imports are debits.

Total Debits Equal Total Credits

If balance-of-payments data are accurate and complete, the sum of all debits must equal the sum of all credits. In practice, this is rarely the case, since information on the thousands of individual international transactions of a country's residents is bound to be lacking in completeness and accuracy to the last dollar. Since we know, however, that in fact total debits equal total credits, any discrepancy between the two is attributable to "errors and omissions," which is entered in the balance of payments as a debit or credit, as required to bring the totals to equality.

How do we know that in fact total debits equal total credits? Because balance-of-payments accounting methods have this built-in result. Every international transaction has a dual aspect, each of which is entered separately in the balance of payments, one as a credit item, the other as a debit item. This double-entry bookkeeping assures the equality of debits and credits. One or two examples will illustrate the double-entry nature of balance-of-payments accounting.

Suppose an American firm exports $100,000 worth of equipment to Brazil. This is the first part of the transaction and is entered in the balance of payments of the United States as a credit item. But the export must be settled in some fashion, giving rise to the second aspect of the transaction. In whatever fashion settlement for the export is made, it will be a debit entry in the U.S. balance of payments of $100,000. Consider some of the various possible ways of settlement. A common method would be for the Brazilian importer to purchase dollar exchange from his bank. In this case, the dollar balances of the Brazilian bank held in its correspondent American bank is drawn down by $100,000 upon payment to the exporter. But as we have seen, a decrease in foreign-held balances represents a capital outflow from the country in which the balances are held and a debit entry in that country's balance of payments. If payment for the equipment were made by the importer in his own currency (Brazilian cruzeiros), the debit entry would be the increase in cruzeiro balances held by the exporter or the American bank to whom the foreign exchange was sold. Or perhaps the settlement is in the form of a trade credit extended to the importer. Again, this is a capital outflow from the United States and a debit entry. Another possibility is that the equipment is sent to Brazil as a gift under the foreign aid program, in which case the debit entry is for a unilateral transfer out of the country.

A second example is where the originating transaction is a capital movement. Assume that a California bank makes a loan to a Mexican firm of $1 million. This is a capital outflow from the United States, entered as a debit item in its balance of payments. What is the corresponding credit entry? If the Mexican firm uses the dollars to purchase U.S. exports, these would be the credit entry. If, on the other hand, the Mexican firm sells the dollar proceeds of the loan to its bank for Mexican pesos, and the bank in turn adds the dollars to its balances held in a U.S. bank—a not improbable transaction—a capital outflow from the United States is accompanied by a reverse capital inflow into the United States, no *net* movement of capital having occurred.[1]

Double-entry accounting assures the equality of total debits and credits. There is, however, a more illuminating way of seeing the necessity for overall balance in the balance of payments. A country, like an individual or any economic entity, cannot pay out more than it currently receives except by drawing on its cash reserves, by selling some of its assets, by borrowing, or by receiving gifts—all credit items; nor can it currently receive more than it pays out without accumulating cash reserves or other assets, reducing its liabilities, lending, or making gifts—all debit items.

Balance-of-Payments Accounts

Identifying each balance-of-payments transaction as a debit or credit gives a "vertical" classification, separating entries according to

---

[1] This is an illustration of the principle discussed earlier that net capital movements can only occur in the form of net movements of goods and services.

which side of the balance sheet they fall on. Such classification is essential for making sense out of balance-of-payments data and is based on the obvious need for distinguishing the direction of movement of claims and counterclaims for payment between one country and the rest of the world. A second "horizontal" classification of international transactions is required to make the balance of payments a useful analytical tool. This second classification is based on the proposition that different kinds of transactions, even though they are all debit or credit items, have different significance and implication. We have already implied that such is the case by distinguishing between trade in goods and services, capital movements, unilateral transfers, and official reserve transactions. These we shall now formally designate as the four major accounts in the balance of payments and briefly recall what each encompasses.

The goods and services account—commonly called the Current Account—includes all commodity and service exports and imports. For several reasons the Current Account may be looked upon as the most basic of all payments categories. First, it is always the largest account. Second, the import and export of goods and services constitute the "real" substance of international economic relations, the fundamental economic basis for the existence of a world economy. As we shall see, many transactions in the other payments accounts perform largely auxiliary and supportive functions, facilitating the flow of goods and services but making no independent contribution. Even long-term capital movements, which do have an important autonomous role, can be effectuated only through the movements of goods and services—that is, through Current Account transactions. Third, the Current Account represents the international component of a country's national income. Exports are a component—along with domestic consumption, investment, and government purchases—of the gross national product. Imports represent that part of the national income spent on nondomestically produced goods and services. A full discussion of the relationship between the Current Account and the national income is presented in Chapter 16.

In contrast to the Current Account, the Capital Account embraces transactions consisting not of real commodities and services, but rather of paper claims and debts. The Capital Account has a strategic position in the balance of payments. Long-term capital movements—loans and investments with a maturity exceeding one year—provide the means of financing a new flow of goods and services from the lending or investing country to recipient countries. Short-term capital movements serve mainly as the financial means of temporarily filling in the gaps between international payments and receipts on other transactions. For example, if a country's imports are greater than its exports, the difference may be made up through drawing upon accumulated foreign exchange balances or through an increase in domestic balances held by foreigners or through foreign short-term loans to the country. Each of these is an example of a short-term capital inflow into the country.

The Unilateral Transfer Account includes transactions that are a species of capital movement. They differ from ordinary capital movements in that they do not involve reciprocal obligations or claims. Thus, if the United States makes a foreign aid loan, eventual repayment of which is expected (together with interest) , it is included in the Capital Account. But if a foreign aid *grant* is made, with no obligation on the part of the recipient for principal repayment or interest, it is included in the Unilateral Transfer Account. Other examples are indemnities, reparations, and immigrant remittances.

The Official Reserve Transactions Account contains a record of changes in international reserve assets (gold, foreign currency balances, etc.) and in special credit or loan transactions undertaken to settle any remaining net payments balance in the other accounts combined. Official reserve transactions are not undertaken for independent motives but only in response to the situation with respect to all other balance-of-payments transactions. For example, if total payments on current, capital, and unilateral transfer accounts exceed total receipts in these accounts, it necessarily follows that the difference must be accounted for by an equal amount of net receipts on official reserve transactions account. It must not be concluded from this, however, that official reserve transactions are the reason total debits equal total receipts. In the absence of official reserve transactions, total debits and receipts on all other accounts combined must be equal; the possibility of their being unequal rests upon the presence of a net positive or negative balance on official reserve transactions.

THE UNITED STATES BALANCE OF PAYMENTS, 1972

To illustrate the structure of a balance of payments, let us examine that of the United States for the year 1972, summarized in Table 14.1, below. Several comments on interpreting the data are in order.

First, instead of designating entries as debits or credits, the more

TABLE 14.1

THE U.S. BALANCE OF PAYMENTS, 1972
(in billions of dollars)

I. Current Account		
A. Merchandise trade		
1. Exports	48.8	
2. Imports	−55.7	
B. Military transactions		
1. Foreign sales	1.2	
2. Foreign expenditure	−4.7	
C. Services		
1. Net investment income	7.9	
2. Net travel and transportation	−2.8	
3. Other services, net	0.9	
Balance on current account		−4.6
II. Capital Account		
A. Long-term, net	−1.5	
B. Short-term, net*	−0.5	
Balance on capital account		−2.0
III. Unilateral Transfer Account, net	−3.7	
Balance on unilateral transfers		−3.7
Balance on all above accounts combined		−10.3
IV. Official Reserve Transactions Account, net	10.3	
Balance on official reserve transactions ...		10.3

* Errors and omissions have been included in this account on the presumption that they represent mainly unrecorded short-term capital flows.
Source: *Economic Report of the President, 1974*, pp. 350–51.

usual custom of indicating debits by a negative sign and credits by an implicit plus sign is followed.

Second, for each account a net balance is given, representing the difference between debits and credits in that account. For example, the net negative balance on current account indicates an excess of debits over credits (that is, an import surplus of goods and services) .

Third, total debits equal total credits, as they must. One way of observing this equality is to add algebraically the net balances on all the accounts, which sum to zero.

PLANNED VERSUS REALIZED TRANSACTIONS

The balance of payments is an ex post statement—that is, it is an historical record of the international economic and financial transactions of a country during some *past period*. The record shows the various sources providing means of making foreign payments and the various uses to which the means thus provided were put. And we have learned that the sum total of these means cannot differ from the sum total of their uses.

The information contained in a balance of payments is extremely useful, but only if it is subjected to analysis to draw out significant implications. The fact that the balance of payments must balance is of no analytical interest but is only the consequence of the (very useful) method of accounting employed. The analytically interesting question that follows upon this accounting balance is in what manner and through what processes the balance is brought about. The question arouses curiosity especially in view of the thousands of individual decisions which are ordinarily involved in the international relations of a country, the results of which are summarized in the balance of payments. There is no basis for expecting the independent decisions of so many different individuals, business firms, and government bodies—both at home and abroad—to dovetail into an internally consistent set of relationships.

On the basis of such factors as consumer preferences, the level and distribution of income, the prices of goods and services at home and abroad, interest rates, and foreign exchange rates, a country will wish to import a certain volume of goods and services from the rest of the world, to lend and invest a certain amount of money capital in other countries, and perhaps to make some foreign gifts. In addition, as part of its foreign policy, the government of the country may want to make foreign expenditures and foreign loans and grants for economic and military purposes. All these are payment, or debit, items in the country's balance of payments. On the other side, similar forces operate in each of the other countries of the world to determine the international receipts, or credits, of the country from its exports, capital inflow, and inward unilateral transfers. How, then, could one expect the sum of debits to come out equal to the sum of credits? The answer, of course, is that one would not, except by accident.

Alongside the statement that the balance of payments must balance ex post we have set the improbability that it will balance ex ante. To put it another way, even though *realized* debits and credits must be equal (an ex post statement, referring to the past) , *planned* debits and credits are not likely to be equal (an ex ante statement, referring to a forthcoming period) .

In the likely event that the planned debit transactions of a country are not matched by planned credit transactions, what happens to bring them into actual realized equality? One of two things happens.

The first possibility is that the attempt to carry out plans which are inconsistent with each other may lead to changes in the underlying variables upon which the plans were originally based, thereby causing the plans to be revised. For instance, the attempt of a country to import more goods and services than it can pay for may cause exchange rates on foreign currencies to rise, which in turn would tend to cause a downward revision in import plans and upward revision in export plans. Exchange rates might continue to rise until planned foreign exchange expenditure is brought into equality with planned foreign exchange receipts.

The second possibility is of a quite different nature. Instead of inconsistent plans being forced to undergo revision, they may be allowed consummation through some sort of compensatory action. For example, a country may carry out planned international debit transactions in excess of planned credit transactions by drawing upon accumulated gold or foreign exchange reserves or obtaining a foreign loan for this purpose. Such transactions, undertaken in response to balance-of-payments considerations, are known as *accommodating* transactions. They are to be distinguished from *autonomous* transactions, which are undertaken for reasons independent of the balance of payments. Thus, while a country normally exports monetary gold only when this is necessary to fill a deficiency in foreign exchange earnings from other credit transactions, ordinary commodity exports are autonomous, for they are in response to forces independent of the balance of payments, such as the relationship between demand and supply at home and abroad.

EQUILIBRIUM AND DISEQUILIBRIUM

Equilibrium means a state of balance among opposing forces; disequilibrium means the absence of such a state of balance. Equilibrium is self-sustaining in the sense that, unless and until an external disturbance intrudes, no tendency arises for change in the relationship among the forces internal to the system. Disequilibrium, on the other hand, is inherently incapable of continuing, for imbalance among opposing forces generates change.

Applied to the sphere of economic relationships, equilibrium prevails when the autonomous decisions of various economic entities are consistent with each other. A familiar example is an equilibrium price, which equates the quantity of a good offered for sale with the quantity demanded. If at a given price the quantity supplied differs from the quantity demanded, disequilibrium prevails and the price will tend to change.

The same principles apply to a balance of payments. Equilibrium prevails when planned autonomous debit transactions equal planned autonomous credit transactions in total value. For in this case the intentions of those who wish to engage in transactions requiring foreign payments or creating foreign obligations can be carried out with the means provided by the planned credit transactions of other groups, with no residual payments or receipts balances requiring unplanned settlement. If, however, planned autonomous debits and credits are not equal, the balance of payments is in disequilibrium. An excess of such debits over credits constitutes a *deficit* disequilibrium—or simply a deficit (or adverse) balance of payments. An excess of planned autonomous credits constitutes a *surplus* disequilibrium—or simply a surplus (or so-called "favorable") balance of payments.

It follows from the above that disequilibrium in the balance of payments may manifest itself in either of the ways of reconciling differences between ex ante and ex post relationships previously identified. That is, disequilibrium either shows up in changes in one or more of the variables determining planned decisions or else the differences in planned debits and credits is reconciled through accommodating transactions.

MEASURES OF DISEQUILIBRIUM

From the preceding discussion, we can conclude that an objective indicator of balance-of-payments disequilibrium is the presence of accommodating transactions. Net accommodating credit transactions indicate that autonomous debits exceed autonomous credits—that is, a balance-of-payments deficit exists—while net accommodating debit transactions signify the reverse, a balance-of-payments surplus.

While the distinction between autonomous and accommodating transactions is clear enough theoretically, in practice it is not easy to draw the line clearly, for the distinction rests on motives that cannot be directly observed. The category of transactions that is least doubtful consists of official reserve transactions. Since these transactions are undertaken only by official agencies and for the avowed purpose of adding to the market demand or supply of foreign exchange, they can be presumed to be entirely accommodating. If current, capital, and unilateral transfer transactions are all regarded as autonomous, it follows that the net balance on official reserve transactions is a measure of disequilibrium, a positive (credit) net balance indicating a deficit balance of payments, a negative (debit) net balance indicating a surplus balance of payments. Indeed, such is one of the measures used by the United States government, called simply the "Official Reserve Transactions Balance." Thus, referring to the data presented in Table 14.1, above, we can see that in 1972 the United States balance of payments displayed a deficit of $10.3 billion, as measured by the balance on Official Reserve Transactions.

Interpreting further the United States deficit in 1972 as measured in this fashion, we note that the *combined* balance on the current, capital, and unilateral transfer accounts was *negative* by $10.3 billion. Regarding all these transactions as autonomous leaves the equal, positive, balance in the Official Reserve Transactions account as representing net accommodating transactions, hence a measure of the deficit.

The practical purpose of defining and measuring balance-of-payments disequilibrium is to serve as a guide to policy making. The emergence of a trend toward persistent disequilibrium in one direction, deficit or surplus, is a signal that adjustments of one kind or another are forthcoming, whether automatically produced by market forces or brought about through discretionary policy decisions. The implications of disequilibrium vary in accordance with the type of monetary system in operation and the general condition of the economy, as we shall see in the chapters that follow.

In the case of the United States, a persistent balance-of-payments deficit experienced over many years led to the development of two other, alternative measures of disequilibrium in addition to the balance on Official Reserve Transactions.

The first of these alternative measures is called the "Net Liquidity Balance." The purpose of this measure is to obtain an estimate of *potential* future losses of international reserves in addition to actual current decreases in reserves. The principal potential claim on reserves lies in short-term, liquid claims against the United States held by foreigners. For example, United States bank balances and short-term securities owned by nonresidents are short-term claims that can be quickly withdrawn or liquidated, whereupon they become debit balance of payments transactions (short-term capital outflows), requiring an accompanying additional credit transaction in the Reserve Transactions Account. If, then, during a given year foreigners acquire additional short-term claims against the United States, these represent a short-term capital inflow (credit item) which reduce equivalently the deficit as measured by the Official Reserve Transactions balance but constitute a potential future drain on reserves. On the other hand, if during a given period foreign short-term claims against the United States are *reduced*—constituting a short-term capital outflow, debit entry—to this extent any deficit as measured by the Official Reserve Transactions balance is increased, but the potential future drain on reserves is decreased. The Net Liquidity Balance seeks to adjust the Official Reserve Transaction measure of disequilibrium to take into account the potential future effects on reserves of short-term liquid capital movements.

The Net Liquidity Balance is calculated by removing from the Capital Account liquid short-term private capital flows and adding them (algebraically) to the Official Reserve Transactions balance. Thus, in 1972 there was a net *inflow* of *liquid* private capital of $3.5 billion, even though there was a net outflow of short-term funds of all types. Accordingly, the deficit as measured by the Net Liquidity Balance was this amount greater than that as measured by the Official Reserve Transactions balance—$13.8 billion as compared to $10.3 billion.[2]

The third measure of balance-of-payments disequilibrium is quite different from the two discussed above. It is called the "Basic Balance," which is the algebraic sum of the net balances on current account, unilateral transfer account, and *long-term* capital account. From Table 14.1, it can be calculated that the Basic Balance for the United States in 1972 was --$9.8 billion, showing a deficit of this amount.

The rationale for the Basic Balance measure of disequilibrium is that it reflects most accurately the underlying strength or weakness of the balance of payments, excluding all short-run capital movements, which usually are transitory and subject to frequent reversals of flow. For example, during one period there may be a net short-term capital outflow, followed the next period by a net short-term capital inflow, with a net zero Basic Balance during both periods. As measured by the Official Reserve Transaction Balance or the Net Liquidity Balance, there would be indicated a deficit during the first period and a surplus during the second period. The net zero Basic Balance in this case, indicating balance-of-payments equilibrium, is a more reliable measure of the underlying position. It should be noted,

---

2 All those transactions classified as accommodating, or "means of financing" a net negative or positive balance on autonomous transactions, are sometimes designated as "below the line," with autonomous transactions placed "above the line." Hence, in calculating the Net Liquidity Balance short-term liquid capital flows are transferred from above the line to below the line.

however, that the Basic Balance is most significant as an indicator of the long-run trend in the balance of payments when movements in the balance are observed over several periods.

RECOMMENDED READINGS

The Balance of Payments Statistics of the United States. Report of the Review Committee for Balance of Payments Statistics to the Bureau of the Budget. Washington, D.C.: U.S. Government Printing Office, 1965.

DEVLIN, DAVID T. "The U.S. Balance of Payments: Revised Presentation," *Survey of Current Business,* June 1971, pp. 24–57.

KINDLEBERGER, C. P. "Measuring Equilibrium in the Balance of Payments," *Journal of Political Economy,* November–December 1969.

MEADE, J. E. *The Balance of Payments,* chap. 1. London: Oxford University Press, 1951.

YEAGER, LELAND B. *International Monetary Relations,* chap. 3. New York: Harper & Row, 1966.

STUDY QUESTIONS

1. Define, and contrast, an international balance of payments and an international balance of indebtedness.
2. In what sense do American tourist expenditures abroad constitute an "import" into the United States?
3. Justify the practice of regarding interest and dividend payments as a "service" transaction in the balance of payments.
4. Is the "import" or purchase from abroad of evidences of debt or ownership a capital inflow or outflow? A debit or credit entry in the balance of payments?
5. Suppose you purchase a foreign bond during 1978 and hold it until its maturity in 1984, at which time it is redeemed by the foreign issuer.
    a. During what year or years will this give rise to entries in your country's balance-of-payments capital account?
    b. Assuming that regular annual interest payments are received on the bond, in what years will entries be made in the balance of payments for interest receipts? In what account will the entries be made?
    c. Identify each of the entries made in (a) and (b) above as debit or credit.
6. So far as the balance of payments is concerned, in what respect is an increase in foreign bank balances held by U.S. residents equivalent to a decrease in U.S. bank balances held by foreigners?

7. In what sense is an increase in foreign-held bank balances in the United States equivalent to a short-term loan to the United States? (In answering this, first of all identify on which side of the bank's balance sheet a deposit appears.)

8. If the Ford Motor Company builds a branch factory in England, how is the transaction entered in the balance of payments of the United States? How does this differ from the purchase of bonds issued by a foreign-owned automobile company?

9. Compare a unilateral transfer receipt from abroad with a long-term capital inflow, from the standpoint of (a) debit or credit entry in the balance of payments, (b) subsequent entries in the balance of payments to which they give rise, and (c) effect on the balance of international indebtedness.

10. Suppose a Brazilian exporter ships $100,000 worth of coffee to the United States and receives payment in the form of a dollar deposit account in his name in a New York bank. Describe the entries, appropriately classified, in both the Brazilian and the U.S. balance of payments.

11. If there is a net positive or negative balance in any one of the accounts of the balance of payments, why must there be a net balance, of opposite sign, in one or more of the remaining accounts?

12. Test your understanding of the nature and content of a balance of payments by examining the latest data on the U.S. balance of payments, given in the *Survey of Current Business*.

13. Why are international gold movements recorded in the balance of payments only on a net basis?

14. The "errors and omissions" entry in a balance of payments is an indication that the theoretical principle of equality between total debits and total credits is of doubtful validity. True or false? Why?

15. Name two other ways commonly used to indicate debit and credit entries in the balance of payments.

16. What is meant by the statement that the balance of payments is an ex post record?

17. Why are autonomous debits and credits not likely to be equal?

18. If planned balance-of-payments transactions are not consistent with each other, what kind of reactions may bring them into consistency?

19. Define and illustrate "accommodating" transactions.

20. Define balance-of-payments equilibrium. What are the various signs of disequilibrium?

21. Describe the three measures of balance-of-payments disequilibrium currently in use in the United States, indicating the significance of each.

15

The balance of payments
and the foreign exchange
market

The forces that shape a country's balance of payments are numerous and varied. Over the long run, such basic "real" factors as resource endowment, the state of technology, and consumer preference—in each case, both at home and abroad—exert a decisive influence. Most of the problems associated with balance-of-payments relations, however, arise out of shorter-run influences of a monetary or cyclical character. Among the most important of these are exchange rates, price levels, and income levels. In this chapter we shall concentrate our attention on the key role of exchange rates.

THE MEANING AND IMPORTANCE OF EXCHANGE RATES

If everything influencing the balance of payments, except for exchange rates, were to remain unchanged, a significant variation in exchange rates could be expected to have pronounced balance-of-payments effects. This is simply a way of saying that at least some of the major transactions entering into the balance of payments are a function of exchange rates.

Exchange rates are the links connecting different national currencies and making international cost and price comparisons possible. To a potential U.S. importer, a price quotation of 100 Greek drachmas means nothing until the exchange rate between the dollar and the drachma is known. Suppose that the American firm concludes that at an f.o.b. cost of $10 or less a certain Greek product could profitably be imported, but that at a higher price it would not be profitable to do so. If the Greek export price is 100 drachmas, the good would be imported if the exchange rate is 10 cents or less, for correspondingly the dollar equivalent of 100 drachmas would then be $10 or less. (Reminder: an exchange rate is the price in domestic currency per unit of foreign currency.)

By the same token, whether a given U.S. good is exported to Greece depends in part on the rate of exchange. Suppose that a Greek firm is interested in importing an article from the United States if its f.o.b. cost is 100 drachmas or less, but not if the cost is higher. Assume that the dollar price of the good is $10. Then the good will be exported if the drachma rate of exchange in the United States is 10 cents *or more*. At a 10-cent exchange rate, the equivalent of $10 is 100 drachmas. At a lower exchange rate, the drachma equivalent of $10 is greater. For example, at an exchange rate of 9 cents on the drachma, it costs somewhat more than 110 drachmas to acquire $10 on the foreign exchange market. If the drachma rate of exchange in the United States were, say, 11 cents, then the equivalent of $10 would be approximately 90 drachmas.

This simple example illustrates an important point. Other things being equal, the higher exchange rates are in your country the more costly to you are imported goods and services and the cheaper are your country's export goods and services to foreigners. It is well to keep in mind that exchange rates in different exchange market centers are reciprocals of each other. For instance, a rate of 10 cents per drachma in New York is exactly the same as a rate of 10 drachmas per dollar in Athens. Hence, a higher rate in New York means a lower rate in Athens. As long as exchange transactions are conducted in free and competitive markets, this reciprocal relationship will be assured through arbitrage operations.[1]

---

[1] Arbitrage merely involves buying cheap and selling dear. For example, if the New York rate is 9 cents per drachma, and the Athens rate 10 drachmas per dollar, 90 cents will purchase in New York drachmas worth $1 in Athens. As a result of such purchases and sales, the rate is brought into reciprocal relationship in the two markets.

THE DEMAND FOR FOREIGN EXCHANGE

Implicit in the preceding example is the existence of a functional relationship between the quantity of foreign exchange demanded and the rate of exchange. (We shall also note shortly the functional relationship between the quantity of foreign exchange supplied and the rate of exchange.) Somewhat more loosely, this in turn implies a parallel functional relationship between the debit side of the balance of payments and the rate of exchange. It is true that not all balance-of-payments debit transactions give rise to a demand for foreign exchange—for example, unilateral transfers in kind—but it generally is true that all sources of demand for foreign exchange are debit transactions in the balance of payments.

The functional relationship between the quantity of foreign exchange demanded and the rate of exchange is expressed in the *demand schedule* for foreign exchange. This schedule specifies the various quantities of exchange demanded at various rates of exchange and is constructed on the assumption that all influences on the demand for exchange other than the rate of exchange remain constant. A change in one or more of these other influences on demand results in a shift of the entire schedule.

What are the usual properties of the demand schedule for foreign exchange? An *inverse relationship* between the rate of exchange and the quantity demanded is the most important. We have already noted the chief reason for this inverse relationship: higher rates of exchange make imports more expensive, and lower rates make them cheaper. Hence, ordinarily the volume of imports demanded—and the quantity of foreign exchange necessary to pay for them—move in a direction opposite to the rate of exchange. When the demand schedule for foreign exchange on commodity and service account is expressed in graphical terms, the resulting demand curve falls from left to right in the conventional diagram, with the price (rate of exchange) measured on the vertical axis and the quantity of foreign exchange measured on the horizontal axis (see Figure 15.1).

In technical language, the fall of the demand curve from left to right reflects its having an *elasticity* with respect to the exchange rate that is less than infinite and greater than zero. The elasticity of demand refers to the degree of responsiveness in quantity demanded to a (small) change in price. The coefficient of elasticity is calculated by dividing the percentage change in quantity demanded associated

FIGURE 15.1

THE DEMAND FOR FOREIGN EXCHANGE

with a change in price by the percentage change in price. If the coefficient is one, the demand is unit elastic; if it is greater than one, the demand is relatively elastic; if it is less than one, the demand is relatively inelastic.[2]

The demand for foreign exchange arising out of commodity and service imports has the same elasticity with respect to the exchange rate as the elasticity of demand for the imported goods and services has with respect to their prices in domestic currency. Suppose that the exchange rate falls by 10 percent. Other things being equal, import prices therefore decline by 10 percent. If as a consequence the quantity demanded of imported goods and services rises by, say, 20 percent, the quantity of foreign exchange demanded to pay for imports also rises by 20 percent. Hence, the elasticity of demand for foreign exchange is precisely the same as the elasticity of demand for imported goods and services. Since over usual price ranges the elasticity of demand for goods and services is greater than zero and less than infinity, the same holds for the demand for foreign exchange on goods and services account.

So far we have confined our attention to the demand for foreign exchange arising out of the demand for imported goods and services. Although normally this is by far the greatest component of the aggregate demand for exchange, it is by no means the only one. Foreign loans and investments and outward unilateral transfers are also possible sources of autonomous demand for foreign exchange.

---

[2] Since price and quantity vary in opposite directions, the coefficient of elasticity is negative. However, the sign is conventionally ignored.

However, apart from speculative operations based on anticipated changes in exchange rates, ordinary foreign loans and investments and unilateral transfers are not influenced by the level of exchange rates. Autonomous capital outflows are induced by higher rates of return abroad than at home on comparable loans and investments. While exchange rates affect the foreign currency equivalent of a given loan or investment expressed in home currency, interest and dividend returns are affected in the same manner and to the same extent, leaving the *rate* of return unaffected. This is equivalent to saying that the elasticity of demand for foreign exchange to finance capital outflows is zero. Thus, the effect of capital outflows on the aggregate demand for foreign exchange is to increase it—that is, to move the demand curve to the right—but to leave its shape unaffected.

Unilateral transfers have a similar effect on the demand for foreign exchange—pushing out the curve but not changing its shape. An exception would arise if the transfer is expressed in a fixed amount of the sending country's currency but made in foreign currency. In this case, the demand for foreign exchange to finance the transfer would be unit-elastic.[3]

Adding together the various component autonomous demands for foreign exchange will in all ordinary cases yield an aggregate demand curve of the same general shape as that on goods and services account alone.

THE SUPPLY OF FOREIGN EXCHANGE

The supply schedule or curve of foreign exchange shows the various quantities of foreign exchange that would be supplied at various rates of exchange, all influences other than the rate of exchange being held constant. Autonomous sources of supply are the counterparts of the sources of demand: the export of goods and services, capital inflows, and inward unilateral transfers. To a very large extent these sources of supply of foreign exchange depend upon decisions in other countries. How much a country exports depends chiefly upon how much of its goods and services other countries are willing to import; and how much foreign capital and unilateral

---

[3] A unit-elastic demand curve is a rectangular hyperbola, with constant rectangular areas under each point of the curve. Each such area represents in the case of the demand curve for foreign exchange the product of the exchange rate and the associated quantity of foreign exchange—i.e., the equivalent in domestic currency of that particular quantity of foreign exchange.

transfers flow into the country depend upon how much other countries wish to send to it. These decisions, however, are based on precisely the same kind of considerations underlying home decisions with respect to movements in the opposite direction that we have discussed above. Thus, the export of goods and services from one country, which are the same as other countries' imports from it, is a function of exchange rates, for the latter determine the prices in foreign currencies of the export goods and services.

In constructing a supply curve of foreign exchange, it is essential to keep in mind that a change in the exchange rate in one country is accompanied by an *opposite* change in the rate in other countries. We have seen why the demand curve for foreign exchange has a negative slope: at a higher rate of exchange import foods and services are relatively more expensive, a smaller quantity is therefore demanded, and a smaller quantity of foreign exchange is required to pay for them. But since a higher rate of exchange in our country is equivalent to a lower rate in other countries, at our higher rates our goods and services are cheaper to other countries. More of our goods are therefore demanded by foreigners at our higher exchange rates, but a smaller quantity of foreign currency is received on the average per physical unit of our exports.

Can we say, then, that the supply curve of foreign exchange *rises* from left to right? Not with the same assurance with which we concluded that the demand curve falls from left to right. While the volume of exports certainly tends to increase with an increase in the rate of exchange, the quantity of foreign exchange received for the exports may or may not increase. The outcome depends upon the foreign elasticity of demand for the country's export goods and services and therefore for its currency.

The quantity of foreign exchange supplied in country A at a given rate of exchange is the same as the amount of foreign currency spent for currency A at that rate of exchange. For example, suppose that at a rate of 20 cents per French franc in New York, equivalent to a rate of 5 francs per dollar in Paris, $100 are demanded in exchange for francs. Since each dollar commands 5 francs in exchange, 500 francs are offered for the $100. Hence, the quantity of franc foreign exchange supplied in New York at the rate of 20 cents per franc is 500. In other words, the supply of foreign exchange in a country is directly related to the demand of other countries for its currency.

To continue the illustration, what would be the quantity of franc exchange supplied in New York if the rate of exchange were 25 cents? In Paris the rate on the dollar would then be 4 francs, and U.S. goods and services would be cheaper to the French. The quantity of dollars demanded in France, therefore, will presumably be greater. But, since for each dollar purchased only 4 francs are offered, whether or not the total amount of francs offered increases depends upon the elasticity of the demand for dollars over the range in rates from 5 to 4 francs per dollar. If the elasticity of the demand is greater than unity, the percentage increase in dollars demanded is greater than the percentage decrease in the franc-dollar rate of exchange, and therefore the quantity of francs supplied increases as the rate changes. Thus, let the increase in the dollar rate on the franc of 25 percent, and equivalent decrease in the franc rate on the dollar of 25 percent, which a change in the rate from $0.20 to $0.25 represents, be accompanied by a 30 percent increase in dollars demanded, from $100 to $130.[4] The total number of francs exchanged for dollars is therefore $100 \times 5 = 500$ at a rate of 20 cents per franc and $130 \times 4 = 520$ at a rate of 25 cents per franc.

Now let us assume that the franc demand for dollar exchange over the range from 25 to 30 cents per franc is unit elastic. In this case, the 20 percent change in rate is associated with an equal percentage increase in the quantity of dollars demanded against francs—that is, from $130 to $156. The quantity of francs offered for dollars is then $156 \times 3\frac{1}{3} = 520$, the same as at a rate of 25 cents per franc. General conclusion: when the foreign demand for dollars is unit elastic, the supply of foreign exchange in the United States is zero elastic.[5]

Finally, assume that between a rate of 30 and 35 cents, the franc demand for dollars is inelastic (less than unity). For example, suppose that accompanying the above $16\frac{2}{3}$ percent change in rate, the quantity of dollars demanded increases by only half as much percentagewise—from $156 to $169 ($169 is $8\frac{1}{3}$ percent greater than $156). The quantity of francs supplied at a rate of 35 cents is then $169 \times 100/35 = 483$, approximately. When the foreign demand for your currency is inelastic, an increase in the rate of exchange causes a decrease in the quantity of foreign exchange supplied.

The preceding conclusions are summarized graphically in Figure 15.2. The supply curve of francs in New York (SS) rises from left to right between a rate of exchange from 20 to 25 cents per franc, for

---

[4] Percentage changes in arriving at elasticity coefficients are calculated on the lower of the figures as the base.

[5] The elasticity of supply is measured by the percentage change in quantity divided by the percentage in price, exactly as for the elasticity of demand.

FIGURE 15.2

FRANC SUPPLY IN NEW YORK BASED ON DOLLAR DEMAND IN PARIS

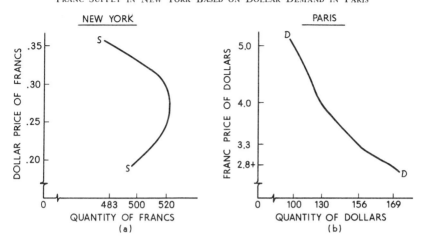

over the corresponding franc-dollar rate of between 5 and 4 francs the foreign demand for dollars (DD) is elastic. The supply curve of francs is vertical over the range in rate between 25 and 30 cents, because the foreign demand for dollars over the equivalent range in rates of from 4 to $3\frac{1}{3}$ francs per dollar is unit elastic. The supply curve of francs bends backward between rates of from 30 to 35 cents, because over the equivalent rates of from 100/30 to 100/35 francs per dollar the foreign demand is inelastic.

DEMAND, SUPPLY, AND EQUILIBRIUM

We may now place the demand and supply curves of foreign exchange on the same set of axes, as in Figure 15.3. The supply curve has been drawn to rise continuously from left to right, based on the assumption of an elastic foreign demand for the country's currency over all the exchange rate ranges included. In a later discussion, we shall assume that the supply curve bends backward above a certain exchange rate and then explore the consequences.

The first observation to make about the demand and supply curves of foreign exchange in Figure 15.3 is that they are the foreign exchange counterparts respectively of cash autonomous, ex ante debit and credit balance-of-payments transactions during the same period. As noted earlier, not all balance-of-payments transactions are conducted through the foreign exchange market, but those that are show up on the demand side if they are debits and on the supply side if they are credits. However, the demand and supply curves do not reveal what quantities of exchange actually are demanded and supplied until the rate of exchange is specified. Even at a specified rate of exchange, we do not know what the realized quantity of exchange bought and sold will be without further information, for the curves reveal only *desired* actions, which may or may not be realized. Indeed, it is this characteristic of the curves that directly relates to exchange equilibrium or disequilibrum.

The exchange market is in equilibrium only at one particular rate of exchange—the rate at which the quantity demanded equals the quantity supplied. This is called the *equilibrium rate of exchange.* In Figure 15.3 the equilibrium rate is shown as R_e.

If the exchange market is in equilibrium at the prevailing rate of exchange, there is no reason for the rate to change, unless and until one or more outside influences—assumed to remain constant in constructing the demand and supply curves—changes. At the equilibrium rate of exchange all the foreign exchange demanded for various autonomous debit transactions in the balance of payments is furnished by various autonomous credit transactions, obviating the need for any accommodating transactions.

But now suppose that an initial equilibrium in the exchange market is disturbed by a change in one of the outside forces mentioned previously. For example, suppose that the national income of the country rises, causing the demand for imports to increase, and

FIGURE 15.3

THE EQUILIBRIUM RATE OF EXCHANGE

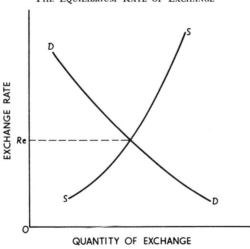

QUANTITY OF EXCHANGE

thereby the demand for exchange to increase. This shows up in the movement of the whole demand curve upward and to the right, such as to $D'D'$ in Figure 15.4. The initial equilibrium rate R_e is clearly now a disequilibrium rate, for the quantity of foreign exchange demanded at R_e exceeds the quantity supplied at that rate. As a consequence, something has to "give," but exactly what gives depends upon the kind of system prevailing.

The typical free-market response to an excess demand situation is a rise in price. In the case at hand, this would mean an increase in the rate of exchange. If the rate of exchange is free to move in accordance with market forces, it would tend to rise until rate R'_e in Figure 15.4 is reached, for this is the new equilibrium rate, at which equality is restored between the quantity demanded and that supplied.

A rise in the free-market rate of exchange is thus one of the manifestations of disequilibrium. At the same time, it is a major method of restoring equilibrium in the face of disequilibrium.

Most exchange rate systems, however, prevent the exchange rate from freely responding to market forces. As we shall see, this is the case most notably under the gold standard system, but it is also the practice under other systems as well. What, then, happens when disequilibrium develops at the prevailing rate?

One possibility is the introduction of controls to suppress the market demand or to push the supply outward. One type of such

FIGURE 15.4

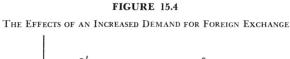

THE EFFECTS OF AN INCREASED DEMAND FOR FOREIGN EXCHANGE

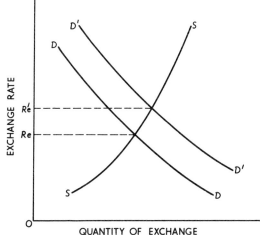

controls involves the requirement of licences to import goods and services and to make foreign loans and investments. Other control devices include import tariffs and quotas and export subsidies.

If market forces are to be allowed free expression without inhibiting controls, the maintenance of stable exchange rates in the face of an excess demand for foreign exchange requires the provision of additional amounts of foreign exchange on the market. The extra supply may be furnished through private channels in response to the excess demand situation, or it may be furnished through the sale of foreign exchange by the central bank or other government agency out of official reserves. In either case, the additional foreign exchange is provided by *accommodating* transactions, which serve to fill in the gap between the quantities of exchange autonomously demanded and supplied and to keep the exchange rate stable.

In summary, we have found three signs of a deficit balance-of-payments disequilibrium. The first is a market-induced rise in exchange rates; the second is the imposition of controls over international transactions; the third is the presence of accommodating transactions. In the next chapter we shall pursue the implications of each of these.

RECOMMENDED READINGS

ALIBER, ROBERT Z., ED. *The International Market for Foreign Exchange.* New York: Frederick A. Praeger, Inc., 1969.

MEADE, JAMES E. *The Balance of Payments,* chap. 1. London: Oxford University Press, 1951.

YEAGER, LELAND B. *International Monetary Relations,* chap. 2. New York: Harper & Row, 1966.

STUDY QUESTIONS

1. Satisfy yourself that higher rates of exchange are associated with more expensive imports and cheaper exports.
2. Why, in a free market, is a New York rate of exchange of $0.02 on the Belgian franc equivalent to a rate in Brussels of 50 francs per dollar?
3. What do you understand by the statement that the quantity of foreign exchange demanded is a function of the rate of exchange?
4. In constructing a demand or supply schedule of foreign exchange, which variables are admitted and which are excluded?

5. Why is the rate of exchange and the quantity of foreign exchange demanded inversely related?

6. What determines the elasticity of demand for foreign exchange on goods and services account?

7. Why is the elasticity of demand for foreign exchange on ordinary capital account zero?

8. What would cause the supply curve of foreign exchange to bend backwards?

9. If a country wished to increase the amount of foreign exchange supplied in its market through raising the rate of exchange, what foreign demand conditions for its exports would be most favorable?

10. Define the equilibrium rate of exchange.

11. Why are accommodating transactions not included in the sources of demand and supply of foreign exchange in determining the equilibrium rate of exchange?

12. Identify three different manifestations of exchange market disequilibrium.

16

Disequilibrium and adjustment of the balance of payments

We have defined balance-of-payments disequilibrium as existing when, over any given period, aggregate autonomous international payments (debits) and receipts (credits) are not equal. This is an inherently unstable situation, containing forces leading to change in the direction of bringing autonomous payments and receipts into balance. The process through which equilibrium is restored is called the adjustment process.

THE GENERAL NATURE OF PAYMENTS ADJUSTMENT

Balance-of-payments disequilibrium creates the most serious adjustment problem for the country experiencing it when it is of a deficit nature and persists over a prolonged period.

A *deficit* disequilibrium exists when autonomous payments exceed autonomous receipts. If the inequality between autonomous payments and receipts is in the opposite direction, there is a *surplus* disequilibrium. As a rule, a deficit in the balance of payments is more bothersome to a country than a surplus because the burden of adjustment tends most often to lie more heavily on deficit than on surplus countries. However, since one country's deficit is necessarily accompanied by one or more other countries' surplus, they are equally incapable of being sustained indefinitely.

As observed in an earlier discussion, because of the multifarious decision-making entities engaged in international transactions and the diversity of their motivations, the matching of autonomous decisions in an equilibrium pattern is not to be expected as the norm. But more or less continuous disequilibrium does not necessarily imply a constant state of balance-of-payments difficulties. Real problems arise mainly from any tendency of a country's international payments to suffer disequilibrium in just one direction—especially in the direction of a deficit—over a long period. Periodic deficits followed by surpluses, leading to an approximate balance over a period of from, say, two or three years, are not likely to create too many serious problems. In practice, therefore, balance-of-payments equilibrium does not require the continuous balancing of autonomous decisions, which would be an impossible goal, but only their approximate balancing over a reasonable period of time. We shall later indicate the pragmatic basis for determining in any particular case how long a "reasonable" period is.

Since balance-of-payments disequilibrium is a state of imbalance between autonomous international payments and receipts, adjustment implies a change in the relationship between these two sides of the ledger. To remove a deficit, autonomous receipts must expand relatively to payments; to remove a surplus, payments must expand relatively to receipts. For such adjustments to occur, there must be changes in the underlying variables to which autonomous payments and receipts are functionally related. A complete list of these variables would embrace the economic universe, for all parts of an economy are interrelated. However, for theoretical analysis to be illuminating and practically useful, attention must be concentrated on the dominating and key variables. In the case of the balance of payments, these key variables are exchange rates, prices, income, and controls, a change in any one of which will tend significantly to affect the balance of payments because of their strong functional relationship to autonomous balance-of-payments decisions. The following discussion shows how adjustment in the balance of payments may be effected by changes in these variables. For the greater part, we shall assume that disequilibrium is of a deficit variety. Generally, the same principles would apply, operating in reverse, to a surplus disequilibrium.

ADJUSTMENT THROUGH EXCHANGE RATES

Under ordinary circumstances, there is some exchange rate at which, given the other key variables influencing the balance of payments, the balance of payments of a country will tend toward equilibrium. Hence, it follows that if the balance of payments is in disequilibrium at one level of exchange rates, equilibrium adjustment can be accomplished by an appropriate change in that level.

We are familiar with the reason for the power of exchange rates to shape the balance of payments. Other things being equal, the higher exchange rates are in a country, the lower are the prices of its export goods and services to the rest of the world and the more expensive to it are import goods and services. Even though some autonomous transactions, such as capital movements and unilateral transfers, may not be directly influenced by exchange rates, we can be quite certain that in the aggregate autonomous payment and receipts are directly affected.

How responsive the balance of payments is to a change in the exchange rate depends upon the elasticities of the home demand for import goods and services and of the foreign demand for the country's export goods and services. The more elastic these demands are, the greater is the effect of a given exchange rate movement on the balance of payments. The less elastic the demands are, the greater is the degree of rate movement necessary to eliminate a given disequilibrium.

Ordinarily, the effect of a rise in exchange rates is to reduce autonomous international payments and increase autonomous receipts, and vice versa, for a fall in rates. A rise in exchange rates is known as *exchange depreciation,* because the international value of the currency in terms of other national currencies falls as rates on the latter increase.[1] A fall in exchange rates is called exchange *appreciation,* and it involves an increase in the international value of the currency.

For exchange depreciation and appreciation to reduce a balance-of-payments deficit and surplus, respectively, however, certain minimum elasticity conditions are required. This can best be seen in terms of the demand and supply curves of foreign exchange, as described in the preceding chapter. As long as the demand curve for

---

[1] The term *devaluation* also means a decrease in the international value of a currency, but it is properly used only when the currency is valued in terms of gold and the gold content is reduced.

foreign exchange has a negative slope (falls from left to right) and the supply curve has a positive slope (rises from left to right), a rise in the exchange rate reduces the quantity of exchange demanded and increases the quantity supplied, and a fall in the rate has the opposite effects. As we know from an earlier discussion, the demand curve will almost surely have a negative slope and thereby contribute to balance-of-payments adjustment through rate changes. But the supply curve of exchange over some range in rates may have a negative slope—that is, bend backward as in Figure 15.2. In this event, a rise in rate *reduces* the quantity of exchange supplied, so that from the supply side, exchange depreciation would increase rather than reduce a deficit.

We recall that the reason for a backward-bending supply curve of foreign exchange is an inelastic foreign demand for the country's exports. If such is the case, in order for exchange depreciation to reduce a deficit and appreciation to reduce a surplus the elasticity of demand for foreign exchange must be great enough to offset the negative effects produced on the supply side. Expressed in terms of the slopes, rather than the elasticities, of the curves, the required condition is that the supply curve approach the demand curve above the point of intersection from the right and below the point of intersection from the left. Figure 16.1 shows a case where this is not true. A rise in the rate of exchange above *R* would cause the quantity of exchange supplied to decrease more than the decrease in quantity demanded, and a fall in rate would cause the quantity supplied to

FIGURE 16.1

UNSTABLE RATE SITUATION

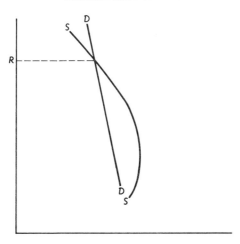

increase more than the quantity demanded. This is the opposite set of reactions to that usually expected from price changes, with the consequence that usual exchange rate variations to adjust the balance of payments are not appropriate under such circumstances. (Another consequence is the instability of the rate, a matter that is discussed in a later context.)

Apart from the probably rather special case considered above, exchange depreciation must be regarded as one of the prime methods of correcting a balance-of-payments deficit. Indeed, of all the methods of adjustment it is the most natural in a free-market system. In the absence of any kind of government control or intervention in the market, balance-of-payments disequilibrium would automatically be corrected through exchange rate movements produced by market forces. Earlier we noted that variations in the exchange rate are a sign of disequilibrium; now we may add that they are also a method of balance-of-payments adjustment.

To illustrate how in a completely free market balance-of-payments adjustment would be effected through exchange rate movements, let us assume that a country's initial balance-of-payments equilibrium is disturbed by an autonomous capital outflow. The situation is depicted in Figure 16.2. Before the movement of capital occurs, the rate of exchange is in equilibrium at R, based on the then-prevailing autonomous demand (D) and supply (S) curves of foreign exchange. The outflow of capital causes the demand for foreign ex-

FIGURE 16.2

ADJUSTMENT OF CURRENT ACCOUNT BALANCE TO CAPITAL
OUTFLOW VIA EXCHANGE RATE CHANGE

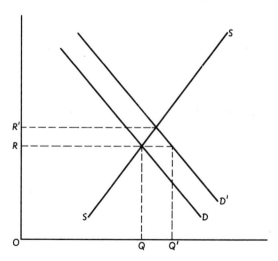

change to increase to D'. The immediate impact of the capital move-ment is a deficit disequilibrium, for at rate R the quantity of foreign exchange demanded exceeds the quantity supplied. In terms of the balance of payments, the disequilibrium is manifested in an excess of autonomous debits over autonomous credits. For equilibrium to be restored, an excess of credits over debits—equal in amount to the capital outflow—must be generated on the combined other auton-omous accounts. For example, if prior to the capital outflow all transactions were in goods and services in the current account, equilibrium would require that the current account develop a net credit balance (equal to the surplus of exports over imports) to match the capital outflow. The adjustment mechanism in the present case that brings about the surplus of credits on other accounts is the rise in the exchange rate. At rate R' (Figure 16.2), adjustment is complete and equilibrium is reestablished. It will be observed that the rise in the rate of exchange produces the surplus of credits on other accounts, equal to QQ' and the outflow of capital, in part through contracting debit transactions which use foreign exchange and in part through expanding credit transactions which provide foreign exchange.

Adjustment of the balance of payments through the exchange rate is automatically generated by market forces in a pure market system with respect to international monetary relations. In the next chapter, this will be called a "floating" exchange rate system. In most his-torical systems, however, exchange rates are not free to move in response to free-market demand and supply, but are limited in their movement in various ways and to varying extents. But this does not preclude the exchange rate as an instrument of adjustment to be employed at the discretion of the monetary authority. Whether an automatic market response or the decision of the monetary authority, exchange variation has the same kind of influence on the balance of payments. The major difference between automatic and discretion-ary variations in rate is that the latter is subject to nonmarket desiderata and judgments with respect to the degree and timing of rate changes. The implications of this difference will be discussed in the next chapter.

ADJUSTMENT THROUGH PRICE CHANGES

The exchange rate is a price, but a very special one, for changes in it alter the relationship between the prices of all domestic goods and services and the prices of all foreign goods and services. Exchange depreciation lowers the domestic price level relative to foreign price levels, and exchange appreciation raises the domestic price level relative to foreign price levels. It is evident that the same kind of changes in relative national price levels could be effected with exchange rates held stable through differential rates of absolute price changes at home and abroad. A uniform decrease in domestic prices, foreign prices remaining stable, would have equivalent effects to exchange depreciation so far as relative national price levels are concerned. As we shall see later, however, price deflation and exchange depreciation have quite different effects in other respects.

As in the case of exchange rate variations, the power of price level changes to adjust the balance of payments depends upon the elasticities of demand for imports at home and abroad. If the foreign demand for a country's export goods and services is elastic, a drop in their prices results in an increase in the quantity of foreign exchange proceeds. If the foreign demand is inelastic, the quantity of foreign exchange earned at lower export prices is smaller than at higher prices. On the demand side, lower home prices will nearly always cause a smaller quantity of foreign exchange to be demanded, the decrease being greater the higher the cross-elasticity of demand between imported goods and domestic goods.[2]

Again, as in the case of exchange rate variations, price changes may either be automatically produced through market forces or deliberately brought about through discretionary policy measures. Inflation and deflation of prices are not, however, symmetrical with respect to the ease with which they may be effected, whether through automatic forces or discretionary policies. More will be said on this point in the next chapter.

ADJUSTMENT THROUGH INCOME CHANGES

Autonomous balance-of-payments transactions are a function not only of exchange rates and prices but also of income. At given and unchanged exchange rates and prices, higher levels of income at home tend to cause a greater volume of imports, and higher levels of income abroad tend to cause a greater volume of exports. (Income levels at home and abroad also probably affect autonomous capital movements, but the relationship here is generally less reliably pre-

---

[2] The cross-elasticity of demand between imported and home goods is defined as the percentage change in the quantity of import goods demanded, divided by the percentage change in the price of home goods.

dictable.) Hence, a balance-of-payments deficit may be corrected through either a decrease in the level of home income or an increase in foreign income.

The responsiveness of imports and exports to income changes at home and abroad is measured by the *marginal propensity to import* or by the *income-elasticity of demand for imports.* The *average* propensity to import is defined as the ratio of imports to the national income, symbolically expressed as M/Y, where M represents imports and Y represents national income. If we wish to investigate effects of a change in income on imports, the appropriate measure is the *marginal* propensity to import, defined as $\triangle M/\triangle Y$, where $\triangle$ signifies change. To measure the ratio of *relative* changes in imports to changes in income, the income-elasticity of demand for imports is the most appropriate concept. It is defined as the percentage change in imports divided by the percentage change in income—that is, $(\triangle M/M) \div (\triangle Y/Y)$.

The balance of payments of a country and its national income are intimately interrelated, changes in one causing changes in the other. National income is defined, in real terms, as the aggregate domestic production of goods and services and, in money terms, as aggregate expenditure on domestically produced goods and services. Goods and services exported out of current home production are part of the national income. Imports, on the other hand, even though they are available for domestic use, are not part of the national income, for they are produced elsewhere (and are therefore part of the national incomes of the producing countries). Hence, viewing the national income as aggregate expenditure on home-produced goods and services, foreign expenditure on a country's exports is included, while domestic expenditure on imported goods and services is excluded. This yields the following identity:

$$Y \equiv C + I + X - M$$

where Y represents the national income, C is consumption expenditure, I is investment expenditure, X is exports, and M is imports. (For simplicity, government purchases of goods and services are not separately identified.)

It will be noted that the foreign component of income, $X - M$, consists of the current account of the balance of payments. If the net balance on current account is zero (that is, $X = M$), expenditure on imports, which does not enter the national income flow, is exactly offset by foreign expenditure on the country's exports, which does enter its income flow. In this case, the effect of foreign trade on the country's money national income is neutral. If exports exceed imports (a net credit balance on current account), foreign trade exerts an expansionary influence on the money national income, while a net debit balance on current accounts has a deflationary effect.

The same conclusions can be reached by a slightly different route. Exports stand on the same footing as domestic investment expenditure in their effects on money national income: each is an "injection" into the income-expenditure flow, swelling the stream of income receipts generated by the purchase of goods and services. They are also alike in that, contrasted to consumption expenditure, they are to a large extent determined independently of the current level of domestic income. In other words, whereas the volume of consumption is mainly determined by the level of domestic income and does not significantly change except in response to a prior change in income, both investment and exports are importantly influenced by other factors. In the case of exports, the chief determining force is the national incomes of *other* countries which provide the markets for the home country's export goods and services.

Imports, on the other hand, have a national income role similar to that of saving. Both are "leakages" in the income-expenditure flow, in the sense that they represent dispositions of income receipts which do not reenter the domestic income stream (although import expenditure does enter the income flow of the exporting countries). They are also similar in both being primarily functions of the national income, their volume and changes in volume being largely determined by domestic income and changes in income.

On the basis of the above relationships it is perceived that if exports change, national income will change in the same direction, and that if income changes—because of variation in exports or for other reasons—imports will change in the same direction. In short, income is an increasing function of exports and imports are an increasing function of income. Hence, starting out in both balance-of-payments and income equilibrium, if the balance of payments is disturbed by an autonomous change in exports, balance-of-payments adjustment will tend to occur through a change in imports induced by the income effects of the change in exports. On the other hand, if the national income changes with exports remaining constant, the consequent induced change in imports will cause balance-of-payments disequilibrium, assuming that equilibrium existed before the change in income occurred.

To give precision to these relationships between the balance of payments and the national income, the conditions of income equilibrium for an open economy need to be stated. First, let us recall the income identity

$$Y \equiv C + I + X - M$$

By deducting the import component of consumption and investment expenditure and of exports separately, the identity may be rewritten as

$$Y \equiv C_d + I_d + X_d \qquad (a)$$

where the subscript indicates production out of domestic resources. We know that the national income is also necessarily equal to the sum of the various possible uses to which income receipts are devoted—namely, expenditure on domestically produced consumer goods and services and on imported goods and services, plus the unspent residual, saving—yielding the identity

$$Y \equiv C_d + M + S \qquad (b)$$

Combining the two identities (a) and (b) and reducing gives

$$I_d + X_d \equiv M + S \qquad (c)$$

This last identity states that the sum of expenditure on domestically produced goods, added to the home stock of goods, plus those exported, necessarily equals the sum of expenditure on imports, plus saving.

The terms in (c) may be rearranged as follows:

$$S \equiv I_d + X_d - M \qquad (d)$$

This is an extremely useful and revealing relationship. If a country's exports and imports are equal $(X_d - M = 0)$, then domestic investment is limited to home saving. But if imports exceed exports, the identity tells us that domestic investment is greater than home saving by the amount of the import surplus. One very significant aspect of this is the potential role of foreign trade in providing extra resources for economic development when domestic saving is insufficient to finance adequate capital formation. The third possibility is for exports to exceed imports, in which case domestic investment is necessarily less than saving, with the difference equal to foreign investment.

All the above relationships are ex post, referring to realized events of a past period, and necessarily hold by definition of the terms. But they are not necessarily equilibrium relationships. Equilibrium prevails, as we have seen in the concept's application to the balance of payments, when ex ante, or planned, decisions of various groups are consistent with each other, so that the decisions can be carried out harmoniously and with no built-in tendency for change to occur. Applied to national income, equilibrium exists when planned "injections" into the income-expenditure flow equal planned "leakages" from the flow. Since expenditure on domestically produced goods added to capital stock (or investment) and exports are injections, and imports and saving are leakages, when these are all on a planned or ex ante basis the income equilibrium equation becomes

$$I_d + X_d = M + S \qquad (e)$$

The terms are the same as in identity (c) above, except for the important difference that the equality *must* hold for the identity, but holds only in equilibrium for equation (e). Hence, when we use the identity sign $(\equiv)$, reference is made to ex post relationships, while the equality sign $(=)$ indicates an equilibrium relationship.

The condition for income equilibrium may be restated as corresponding to identity (d) above.

$$S = I_d + X_d - M \qquad (f)$$

Now we are ready to examine the interrelationship between the current account of the balance of payments and the national income. To simplify the analysis, let us first assume that the net balance on all autonomous balance-of-payments transactions, other than those in the current account, is zero. Therefore, current account balance $(X_d = M)$ is the condition for balance-of-payments equilibrium.

It is at once evident from the income equilibrium equation—either (e) or (f) above—that income equilibrium and balance-of-payments equilibrium need not necessarily coexist. But let us assume that during an initial period income equilibrium and balance-of-payments equilibrium both prevail. Hence, equation (f) above is satisfied under the special assumption that $X_d = M$.

Suppose now that exports decrease. This might occur for any of numerous reasons—a contraction in foreign income, the imposition of tariffs or quotas by other countries, a shift in foreign preferences, and so on. The decrease in exports immediately causes a deficit disequilibrium in the balance of payments. It also immediately causes a decrease in the national income, since exports are a component of income. The question we wish to investigate is what effects the decline in income will in turn have on the balance of payments.

We observed earlier that imports are a function of the national income and defined the relationship between changes in them as the marginal propensity to import, $\triangle M / \triangle Y$. By what amount imports will change as a result of a change in income is discovered by multiplying the change in income by the marginal propensity to import. For instance, assume that $\triangle M / \triangle Y = 2/10$. Then a change in income of, say, $100 causes imports to change, in the same direction, by $20.

Knowing the value of the marginal propensity to import, we need know only the change in national income to calculate the induced change in imports. The first question, then, is how much income changes as a result of an autonomous decrease in exports. Let the decrease in exports be $100. The *immediate* effect on income is to reduce it by the same amoumt. But this is not the end of the story, for the reduction in income in turn will induce changes in all the variables functionally related to income, with "feedback" effects on income. The result is a series of repercussions manifesting themselves in successive income-expenditure rounds, but in dwindling force, until a new equilibrium level of income is reached. This phenomenon is known as the foreign trade *multiplier* effect.

To illustrate how the multiplier works, let us assume the following values for the variables functionally related to income:

Marginal propensity to save: $\dfrac{\triangle S}{\triangle Y} = 2/10$

Marginal propensity to import: $\dfrac{\triangle M}{\triangle Y} = 3/10$

Marginal propensity to consume: $\dfrac{\triangle C_d}{\triangle Y} = 5/10$

Marginal propensity to invest: $\dfrac{\triangle I}{\triangle Y} = 0$

The accompanying table shows the series of changes that occur in successive income-expenditure periods, beginning with a decrease in exports of $100 in the first period.

The decrease in exports occurs in period 1, causing income for that period to decline by an equal amount. The decline in income in

Period	ΔS	ΔM	ΔC_d	ΔI_d	ΔX_d	ΔY
1					−100	−100
2	−20	−30	−50	0	0	−50
3	−10	−15	−25	0	0	−25
4	−5	−7.5	−12.5	0	0	−12.5
Equilibrium Values:	−40	−60	−100	0	−100	−200

period 1 induces in the next income-expenditure period a decrease in saving, imports, and consumption, in each case by an amount determined by their respective marginal propensities times the decrease in income of the preceding period. Since we have assumed a marginal propensity to invest of zero, no induced changes in investment expenditure occur. It is also assumed that no further changes in exports occur after the initial decrease. The decrease in income during each period after the first equals the decrease in consumption expenditure for that period, for under our assumptions, consumption is the only component of income that is induced to changes by prior changes in income.

It will be observed that saving, imports, and consumption expenditure fall by smaller amounts in each successive period, steadily approaching equilibrium values when further change ceases. These equilibrium values are listed in the bottom row of the table. As indicated, the new equilibrium level of income is $200 less than originally, the decline being accounted for by the autonomous decrease in exports of $100 plus the induced decrease in consumption of $100. The new equilibrium level of saving is $40 less than originally, and imports are $60 less than originally. The income equilibrium equation, $I_d + X_d = M + S$, is satisfied, since, starting from the base of the original equilibrium, $\Delta I_d + \Delta X_d = \Delta M + \Delta S$.

Since the decline in income is twice the amount of the decrease in exports, the foreign trade multiplier in this case is 2. More generally, the value of the multiplier is equal to the reciprocal of the sum of the marginal propensity to save and the marginal propensity to import. That is, letting K stand for the multiplier,

$$K = \frac{1}{\Delta S/\Delta Y + \Delta M/\Delta Y}$$

The chief effect of the decline in income set off by the autonomous fall in exports which we are interested in at the moment is the induced decrease in imports. We see that imports are $60 less than originally, the decrease being brought about by the contraction in income of $200, in conjunction with an assumed marginal propensity to import of 3/10. Hence, a considerable adjustment in the balance of payments has occurred, the deficit of $100 in period 1 being reduced to $40 at the new equilibrium level of income. The adjustment has been effected entirely through the income effects of the decline in exports, working through the multiplier.

However, balance-of-payments adjustment is not complete, a deficit of $40 remaining. What accounts for the incomplete adjustment? Evidently, the failure of national income to decrease by an amount large enough to induce a decrease in imports of $100 instead of only $60. With a marginal propensity to import of 3/10, income would have to fall by $333.33 to induce a contraction in imports of $100 (since $333.33 $\times$ 3/10 = $100).

The next question, then, is why income did not fall by a greater amount. The answer is because its fall was "braked" by induced decreases in saving and imports. Referring to the table, we notice that in each period the decline in income is less than the decline in the preceding period by exactly the sum of the decreases in saving and imports. Had the induced changes in saving and imports been smaller, income would have contracted by a greater amount. In other words, the multiplier is greater if the denominator in the formula

$$K = \frac{1}{\triangle S/\triangle Y + \triangle M/\triangle Y}$$

is smaller.

However, the real culprit is saving, for whatever decreases in imports occur directly contribute to balance-of-payments adjustment. For example, suppose that $\triangle S/\triangle Y = 0$ and $\triangle M/\triangle Y = 5/10$. The multiplier retains a value of 2, and the new equilibrium level of income is $200 less than originally, as under the previous assumptions. But in this case imports fall by $100 and adjustment is complete.

The presence of a marginal propensity to save greater than zero prevents complete balance-of-payments adjustment through income effects, unless the income braking caused by saving is offset by the presence of a marginal propensity to invest $(\triangle I/\triangle Y)$ greater than zero. Saving is a leakage in the income-expenditure flow, but investment is an injection. Hence, even if saving decreases as income falls, if investment expenditure also decreases by the same amount income will not be restrained in its descent as under our previous assumptions. To put it another way, the multiplier will be greater when the marginal propensity to invest is greater than zero, the formula becoming

$$K = \frac{1}{\triangle S/\triangle Y + \triangle M/\triangle Y - \triangle I/\triangle Y}$$

If

$$\triangle S/\triangle Y = \triangle I/\triangle Y, K = \frac{1}{\triangle M/\triangle Y}$$

Inserting a value of 3/10 for the marginal propensity to import yields a multiplier of $3\frac{1}{3}$, so that the decrease in income set off by a decline in exports of $100 would be $333.33, with an induced decrease in imports of $100. Adjustment is therefore complete.

Unfortunately for a nice, clean adjustment theory, however, there is no reason for expecting the marginal propensities to save and to invest to be equal, since the decisions are made for different motives and largely by different groups. It is just as possible for $\triangle I/\triangle Y$ to be *greater* than $\triangle S/\triangle Y$ as for it to be equal or unequal in the opposite direction. If $\triangle I/\triangle Y > \triangle S/\triangle Y$, *over*adjustment of the balance of payments will occur, for in this case income changes more than enough to restore equilibrium.

Finally, one other element in the adjustment process through income effects needs brief mention. It is called the "foreign repercussion." To illustrate what is meant by this, consider the effects of the autonomous decrease in our country's exports on the incomes of other countries whose imports from our country decrease. If the contraction in the imports of these other countries is autonomous (that is, not induced by a prior reduction in their incomes), it will have the effect of increasing their incomes. As their national incomes rise, there will tend to be an induced expansion in their import demand, depending upon their marginal propensities to import. And part of their greater import demand can be expected to be directed toward the exports of our home country, thus contributing to the adjustment of its balance of payments.

The foreign repercussion can be significant or it can be negligible in the adjustment process, depending upon circumstances in the particular case. One relevant factor is how important a country's trade and national income are in relation to world trade and income.

For a country like the United States, with the largest volume of trade and income of all countries, the feedback effect of changes in her income on trade may be considerable. On the other hand, for smaller countries, the foreign repercussion is likely to be much weaker, for the impact of changes in their income or trade on other countries' incomes is negligible.

The general conclusion emerging from the above discussion is that balance-of-payments adjustment through income effects is potentially powerful but with no assurance that it will not be either insufficient to effect complete adjustment or so strong as to cause overadjustment and, hence, disequilibrium in the opposite direction.

The adjustment process we have illustrated is automatic and operates on the assumption that the income changes initiated by balance-of-payments disturbances have free rein to work themselves out, uninhibited by countervailing government policies. However, this does not preclude the government's reinforcing, or substituting for, automatic market forces through appropriate measures. If, for example, automatic income effects are too weak to bring about balance-of-payments equilibrium, further income changes can be fostered through monetary and fiscal policies. In general terms, deflationary monetary and fiscal policies tend to reduce balance-of-payments deficits (or increase surpluses), while expansionary monetary and fiscal policies tend to reduce balance-of-payments surpluses (or increase deficits).

Obviously, government also may interfere with automatic adjustment, restraining the income changes which balance-of-payments disturbances produce. The reasons for doing so may be very strong, as is shown in the next chapter.

The Cash-Balance Effect

The conclusion that income effects do not assure that adjustment in the balance of payments may not be under- or overachieved is actually too pessimistic. The model that leads to the conclusion stated is a partial equilibrium model, in the sense that all the variables affecting imports, except for income, are assumed to remain constant. In fact, however, other variables influencing the trade balance cannot remain constant while direct income effects are working themselves out. For one thing, prices are very likely to be affected, as described in the next section. Even more important is the so-called "cash-balance effect," which we shall examine now.

We have seen that with fixed exchange rates a deficit in the trade balance reduces the domestically held supply of money. Unless the monetary authority of the country takes action to offset the impact of a trade deficit on the domestic supply of money, the supply continues to contract as long as the trade deficit continues. But clearly, money supply cannot contract indefinitely, nor will it do so. As the public's holdings of money decline, a liquidity squeeze develops which leads the public to attempt to restore their desired cash balances. Assuming that the monetary authority refrains from satisfying the public's desire to hold more cash through an expansion in money supply, there are in general only two means available to individuals and business firms of acquiring additional cash: (*a*) buying less (or selling more) goods and services, and (*b*) liquidating securities (stocks, bonds, mortgages, and so on). The first method reduces import demand and/or increases exports, thereby directly contributing to the elimination of the trade deficit and drain of the money supply. The second line of action causes a decline in the prices of securities, which is equivalent to an increase in interest rates. Higher interest rates in turn tend to reduce expenditure on goods and services, especially investment expenditure but perhaps consumption expenditure as well, in either case including expenditure on imports. To the extent that the decrease in demand falls on domestic or export goods, the money national income falls (and by a multiple, depending upon the size of the multiplier), inducing a decrease in imports.

Recognition of the cash-balance effects of a trade deficit is important for two reasons. In the first place, it reinforces the "pure" income effects previously identified and insures that any failure of the latter completely to adjust the balance of payments will be offset by cash-balance effects. Second, the analysis points to the fundamental conclusion that the balance of payments is essentially a monetary phenomenon, with the implication that a deficit disequilibrium cannot continue in the absence of monetary policies working counter to the automatic adjustment mechanism. A balance-of-payments deficit cannot continue persistently unless the monetary authority of a country "feeds" it by replacing the money drained out by the deficit.

Combined Price and Income Effects

As the discussion of the cash-balance effect has shown, the direct income effects of changes in the balance of payments do not work in a vacuum. Separation of price and income effects is convenient for expository purposes, but in reality both are normally present, exerting their influence jointly, sometimes in a complementary fashion, at other times in opposition to each other. However, it remains true that the mechanism of adjustment relies upon *either* price *or* income effects—depending upon the exchange rate system in operation—as the trigger mechanism initiating the adjustment process and as the primary adjustment variable.

An excellent example of the interaction between price and income effects is provided by the adjustment mechanism through exchange depreciation. The initial impact on the balance of payments of exchange depreciation stems from the increase in exports and decrease in imports resulting from the effects of depreciation in lowering export prices (in foreign currencies) and raising import prices (in domestic currency). However, an increase in exports and decrease in imports causes national income to increase, producing secondary income effects on the balance of payments in the direction of inducing a greater volume of imports. The final improvement in the balance of payments is therefore likely to be less than that initially provided by the price effects of the depreciation.

Regardless of the type of exchange rate system in operation and the trigger mechanism setting off the adjustment process, an improvement in the balance of payments on current account requires a change in the relationship between a country's production of goods and services and its expenditure on goods and services. A convenient framework for analyzing the required change and the role of income and price effects is the so-called "absorption" approach.

The Absorption Approach

As noted previously, the national income equation is

$$Y = C + I + X - M$$

The elements of national income may now be separated into two groups. The first group represents expenditure on goods and services by domestic residents, or the economy's "absorption" of goods and services. It consists of consumption expenditure (C) plus domestic investment expenditure (I), including import components. The second group consists of the trade balance, exports minus imports $(X - M)$. Hence, letting A represent absorption and B the trade balance, the income equation is rewritten

$$Y = A + B$$

If the trade balance B is to increase (through either an increase in exports or decrease in imports), clearly either Y must rise, or absorption A must fall, since

$$B = Y - A$$

(This is equivalent to the proposition implied in our earlier income analysis that for the balance of payments to improve, saving must increase relatively to domestic investment.)

If there are idle resources available to be drawn upon, or already employed resources can be more efficiently used, an increase in the real national income (output of goods and services) is an avenue for improving the balance of payments, provided that the increase in income is not wholly absorbed domestically. How much extra absorption is induced by an increase in income depends upon the economy's marginal propensity to spend income. If, as normally is assumed to be the case, an increase in income does not induce an equal increase in expenditure or absorption, the balance of payments is improved.

Applying the absorption analysis to exchange depreciation, we observe that the initial impact of depreciation, assuming favorable elasticity conditions and the presence of unemployed resources, is to increase the real national income through expanding the output of export goods and of import-competing goods. The balance of payments improves to the same extent.[3] As a secondary repercussion, the increase in real income induces an increase in absorption and to this extent reduces the initial improvement in the balance of payments. The final net effect of depreciation on the balance of payments thus depends upon the relative magnitudes of the increase in income and the induced increase in absorption. As indicated before, the normal presumption is a favorable outcome, on the grounds that induced absorption tends to be smaller than the increase in real income.

The situation is quite different if balance-of-payments adjustment is to take place in the context of a fully employed economy operating at the outset at capacity. In this case, real income cannot increase, except to the extent that the efficiency of resource use is improved. Apart from the possibility of the latter, the burden of adjustment must therefore fall on reduced absorption.

But how is absorption to be reduced? Exchange depreciation offers

---

[3] The balance of payments improves by a larger amount if the increase in expenditure on import-competing goods is less than the decrease in expenditure on imports —that is, if absorption decreases.

slim possibilities. To the extent that reduced import expenditure is accompanied by increased expenditure on home-produced goods, absorption is not contracted. Other possible effects of depreciation in reducing absorption exist, but they are extremely tenuous and of limited magnitude.[4]

The moral of the story is that exchange depreciation may not be an effective instrument of balance-of-payments adjustment when the economy is fully employed (though some economists believe that it can be effective through the diversion of resources to the more efficient export sector which depreciation encourages). Instead of, or in addition to, depreciation a policy of expenditure reduction through monetary and fiscal restraints may be necessary to correct a balance-of-payments deficit in a period of full employment. An alternative is the imposition of controls, discussed next.

ADJUSTMENT THROUGH CONTROLS

The last general method of balance-of-payments adjustment is through direct controls over international transactions. This method differs radically from the others in that it seeks directly to suppress market forces rather than working through them. It therefore may be argued that direct controls cannot establish a genuine equilibrium, on the grounds that the latter is a free-market concept which is inherently inconsistent with direct controls. However, this is a semantic issue in which we need not become involved. In an era when government controls over various aspects of the economy are pervasive, controls over international transactions cannot be precluded as a possible method of balance-of-payments adjustment, whether or not one wishes to label the result a "true" equilibrium.

Much more important than the semantic question is whether controls can be *effective* in terms of measured results. Suppose that in an effort to eliminate a balance-of-payments deficit a country introduces exchange controls limiting the freedom to import goods and services and to export capital. Since the controls do not lessen the *desires* of residents to import and send capital abroad (and, indeed, may even stimulate their desires), there is the strong tendency for the controls to be circumvented through extralegal channels. "Black markets"

---

[4] Among these efforts are the so-called "money illusion," the Pigou effect, and a redistribution of income. For discussion of these, see S. S. Alexander, "Effect of a Devaluation on a Trade Balance," International Monetary Fund, *Staff Papers*, April 1952.

frequently evolve in countries with exchange controls, wherein foreign exchange is illegally bought and sold for purposes not officially sanctioned.

Even if controls are strictly adhered to, they may not be successful in achieving intended results. For example, if demand for imported goods is not allowed free expression, it may simply be shifted to domestic goods and services, causing a rise in prices and diversion of resources out of export industries. In this case exports fall and the balance-of-payments deficit remains uncorrected.

Notwithstanding such difficulties in successfully adjusting the balance of payments through controls, they msut be admitted as a potentially effective method of adjustment when employed in conjunction with other measures. For instance, if the effectiveness of controls is threatened by the diversion of demand to home goods, contractionary monetary and fiscal policies might be employed to avoid adverse repercussions on exports. Of course, in this event one might say that the adjustment is being accomplished through the income effects of these measures rather than through direct controls. However, the controls may well serve to hasten the process.

Most important, in some cases there may be no acceptable alternative to direct controls as a means of handling a balance-of-payments deficit. Market methods may not work because of destabilizing speculative transactions or because of noneconomic forces at work. Thus, as is shown in the next chapter, exchange depreciation may set off an outward movement of capital based on the expectation of further depreciation, rendering this method of adjustment ineffective.

RECOMMENDED READINGS

ALEXANDER, S. S. "Effect of a Devaluation on a Trade Balance." International Monetary Fund, *Staff Papers*, April 1952.

HINSHAW, RANDALL, ED. *The Economics of International Adjustment.* Baltimore: Johns Hopkins Press, 1971.

The International Adjustment Mechanism. Proceedings of a Monetary Conference. Boston: Federal Reserve Bank of Boston, 1970.

JOHNSON, HARRY G. "Towards a General Theory of the Balance of Payments," in his *International Trade and Economic Growth.* Cambridge: Harvard University Press, 1961, pp. 153–68. Reprinted in American Economic Association, *Readings in International Economics*, chap. 23. Homewood, Ill.: Richard D. Irwin, Inc., 1968.

MACHLUP, FRITZ. *International Trade and the National Income Multiplier.* New York: Blakiston Division, McGraw-Hill, 1943.

MEADE, J F. *The Balance of Payments.* Parts 4 and 5. New York: Oxford University Press, Inc., 1951.

MUNDELL, ROBERT N. *The Monetary Mechanism of International Adjustment.* London: University of Surrey, 1967.

OECD. *The Balance of Payments Adjustment Process.* A Report by Working Party no. 3 of the Economic Policy Committee. Paris, 1966.

YEAGER, LELAND. *International Monetary Relations,* chaps. 4–7. New York: Harper & Row, 1966.

STUDY QUESTIONS

1. Review the concept of balance-of-payments disequilibrium. Distinguish between deficit and surplus disequilibrium.
2. What are the dominating and key variables with which the balance of payments is functionally related?
3. Define exchange depreciation and appreciation.
4. State the conditions required for exchange depreciation to eliminate a balance-of-payments deficit.
5. Illustrate adjustment of the balance of payments to a capital outflow through exchange rate movement.
6. What makes the exchange rate as the price of foreign currency different from the other prices?
7. Explain why and in what sense price deflation and inflation are comparable in their balance-of-payments effects to exchange depreciation and appreciation, respectively.
8. Define: average propensity to import, marginal propensity to import, income-elasticity of demand for imports.
9. State the national income identity for an open economy.
10. In what respect are investment expenditure and exports similar in their income roles?
11. What is meant by the statement that imports are a "leakage" in the income-expenditure flow?
12. Explain why, ex post, $I_d + X_d$ must equal $M + S$.
13. If a country has an import surplus, what must be true of the relationships between domestic saving and domestic investment?
14. What change in the income identity is required to convert it into an equilibrium equation?
15. Define and explain the determinants of the size of the foreign trade multiplier.

16. Under what conditions will balance-of-payments adjustment through income effects alone be complete?

17. What is meant by the "foreign repercussion," and what role does it have in balance-of-payments adjustment?

18. If the government wishes to reinforce the market process of adjustment through income effects, what monetary and fiscal policies would be appropriate in the face of a balance-of-payment deficit? In the face of a balance-of-payments surplus?

19. Explain the cash-balance effect and how it reenforces the income effect with stable exchange rates.

20. In what sense is the balance of payments essentially a monetary phenomenon?

21. Why is the final effect on the balance of payments of exchange depreciation less than the initial effect?

22. Explain the "absorption" approach in balance of payments analysis.

23. Why is it more difficult to correct a balance-of-payments deficit when there is full employment than when there are idle resources?

24. On what grounds may it be argued that balance-of-payments equilibrium and direct trade and exchange controls are inconsistent?

25. What difficulties may be encountered in successfully adjusting the balance of payments through direct controls?

17

Alternative international monetary systems

In the preceding chapter four different general processes of balance-of-payments adjustment were identified: variations in exchange rates, price changes, income changes, and direct controls. One or more of these methods of adjustment must be activated if a country's balance of payments suffers disequilibrium in a given direction for a prolonged period. But which method, or combination, is used depends upon the kind of international monetary system in operation. This chapter examines the major historical systems and discusses their respective advantages and disadvantages. The contemporary system will be reserved for discussion later.

CLASSIFICATION OF SYSTEMS

Alternative monetary systems may be classified according to various criteria, the principal ones being (a) the degree of stability of exchange rates and (b) the extent to which market forces are allowed freely to operate. Depending upon the combination of (a) and (b), the third criterion is (c) the balance-of-payments adjustment mechanism associated with the system.

Based on these criteria, there are four "pure" types of system:

325

1. Stable exchange rates, with market operations free of direct controls, and primary adjustment through automatic price and income changes. We shall call this the pure gold standard system.
2. Floating rates, determined by free-market forces, with primary adjustment through exchange rate variations. We shall call this a floating rate system.
3. Exchange rate stability, though frequently with exceptions, and direct controls over trade and payments. Primary adjustment through direct controls. We shall call this an exchange control system.
4. Short-term exchange rate stability, but with occasional changes in rate and with government intervention limited to operations in the market with no direct controls. The primary adjustment mechanism consists of discretionary exchange rate changes. We shall call this "managed flexibility."

Most actual operating systems contain some mixture of elements from two or more of the above pure types. However, usually there are certain dominating characteristics of an operating system which permit its identification primarily with one of the pure types.

THE GOLD STANDARD SYSTEM

We shall begin the discussion with the gold standard system, for it was the first historical system in modern times and continues heavily to influence the contemporary system.

The dominating characteristic of the gold standard is the stability of exchange rates, within very narrow margins, produced by free-market forces.

The Mechanism of Rate Stability

Exchange rates under the gold standard have fixed par values determined by the gold content of the standard national monetary units. Each country legally defines its standard monetary unit as consisting of a specified quantity of gold. To keep the national currency equivalent in value to its declared gold content, the government stands ready to buy and sell gold in unlimited quantities at the price implied by its relationship to the standard monetary unit. Thus, for example, in 1930, when both the United States and England were on the gold standard, the dollar was defined as containing 23.22 grains of fine gold, and the pound was defined as containing approximately 113 grains of fine gold. The U.S. government freely bought and sold gold at the implied price of $20.67 per fine troy ounce.[1] The British government freely bought and sold gold at the implied price of £3/17s./10 1/2d. per troy ounce, 11/12 fine. The par rate of exchange between the pound and the dollar was equal to the ratio of their gold contents or—the same thing—to the ratio of the prices of gold in each country. Hence, in 1930 the par rate between the pound and the dollar was 113 ÷ 23.22, or £1 = $4.86+.

From the above relationships it follows that the actual rate of exchange between two gold standard currencies cannot vary above or below the par rate of exchange by more than the cost of shipping gold (including insurance) from one country to the other. If the rate should rise or fall by more than this margin, dealers can earn profits by exporting or importing gold and selling or buying exchange with the proceeds, until the prevailing exchange rate is brought nearer to the par rate.

Suppose, for example, as was approximately the case at one time, that the cost of shipping 113 grains of gold from the United States to England is 2 cents. In this event, with a par rate of £1 = $4.86+, the market rate could not continue to fall below about $4.84 or to rise higher than about $4.89. If the market rate fell to $4.84, dealers would buy sterling bills, acquire 113 grains of gold in England for each pound, and sell the gold in the United States at $4.86+, making a slight profit on the transaction, equal, for each pound bought, to the difference between the $4.84 paid for the sterling bill plus $0.02 shipping and insurance charges on the gold, and the $4.86+ for which the gold was sold. The rate at which it pays to import gold ($4.84 in this example) is the "gold import point," and at this rate the demand for exchange is infinitely elastic. On the other hand, if the market rate were to rise to $4.89, it would pay dealers to buy gold in the United States, ship it to England, and sell the sterling proceeds for dollars, since it costs only $4.86+, plus $0.02 shipping charges, to get 113 grains of gold to England, where it commands £1. The rate at which it is profitable to export gold is the "gold export point," and at this rate the supply of exchange on the market is infinitely elastic.

In terms of demand and supply analysis, it is precisely because of the infinite elasticity of demand at the gold import point and infinite elasticity of supply at the gold export point that the market rate of

---

[1] There are 480 grains in a troy ounce, and 480 ÷ 23.22 = 20.67.

exchange is prevented from fluctuating outside this range. This is shown graphically in Figure 17.1.

DZD′ is the original demand and *SVS′* the original supply of exchange. The rate of exchange is originally at *r*. Now let the demand for exchange increase to *DZ′D′*. The rate rises to the gold export point, at which rate the quantity of exchange supplied from the export of goods and services is OQ_s. But at this rate the quantity of exchange demanded to pay for imports is OQ_d. The excess demand, $OQ_d - OQ_s$, is satisfied from the exchange proceeds of the export of gold which private dealers find it profitable to sell abroad. In terms of the balance of payments, the current account net debit balance is matched by the gold account net credit balance.

It should be noted that the movement of gold through the above mechanism represents an *accommodating* balance-of-payments transaction. That is, gold movements occur only because there is an imbalance between autonomous demand and supply of exchange over the range in rate between the gold points. As we know, this is a sign of balance-of-payments disequilibrium.

However, gold movements are not the only indication of disequilibrium, for they may be partially or wholly dispensed with through the effects of substitute short-term capital movements. Suppose the market rate of exchange begins to rise toward the gold export point. Exchange dealers are confident that the rate will never

FIGURE 17.1

THE EXCHANGE RATE UNDER THE GOLD STANDARD

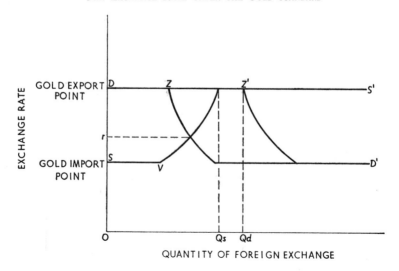

QUANTITY OF FOREIGN EXCHANGE

exceed that point and will probably sometime fall back toward par. The rise in rate may therefore induce dealers to acquire the currency in exchange for foreign currencies while it is temporarily cheap. (Reminder: a rise in exchange rates means a decrease in the international price of the currency.) The inflow of short-term funds from abroad is an accommodating capital movement which restrains the increase in the exchange rate, perhaps preventing it from reaching the gold export point. In the reverse case of a decline in exchange rate, accommodating short-term capital outflows may absorb the extra supply of foreign exchange and prevent the rate from reaching the gold import point.

We shall see later that a current account balance-of-payments deficit or surplus tends to produce certain monetary effects under the gold standard which also encourage stabilizing short-term capital inflows or outflows. We may summarize, then, by saying that, under the international gold standard, rates of exchange are stable, not only because of automatic gold flows at maximum and minimum rates, but also because of the tendency for short-term capital movements to provide additional exchange when the rate rises and to absorb excess exchange when the rate falls.

Adjustment Process

Accommodating gold and/or short-term capital movements signal disequilibrium in the balance of payments, occurring because autonomous payments and receipts are unequal at the fixed rate of exchange. Such disequilibrium cannot continue indefinitely, for neither gold nor capital movements are inexhaustible means of financing differences between autonomous payments and receipts. This is clearest in the case of a deficit disequilibrium. During a deficit period, a country loses gold from its reserve stock, or experiences either a reduction in its foreign short-term assets or an increase in its foreign short-term liabilities, or a combination of these. Obviously, the amount of gold that can be lost is ultimately limited by the stock on hand. The same is true for the amount of foreign short-term assets that can be drawn upon. While there are no formal limits of a similar nature on the volume of short-term foreign liabilities that can be created, there are effective limits set by the willingness of foreigners to accept further claims against the deficit country. The more serious and prolonged the deficit is, the less willing foreigners are likely to be to accumulate further claims against the deficit country, for the greater becomes the risk that its currency will be forced into devaluation.[2]

If disequilibrium cannot persist, how is balance-of-payments adjustment to be effected? A change in the exchange rate is inconsistent with the gold standard idea of a fixed gold value of the currency and is resorted to only if it is unavoidable. Direct controls over trade and payments are likewise anathema to the gold standard principle of market freedom. There is left, then, the remaining adjustment mechanism of price and/or income changes.

The classical theory of gold standard adjustment places primary emphasis on price changes which are brought about by what David Hume (1711–76) called the "gold-specie-flow mechanism." A country with a deficit balance of payments loses gold, while a country with a surplus balance of payments gains gold. Under the traditional gold standard, the domestic supply of money is based on gold holdings. Hence, a deficit balance of payments causes a decrease in the domestic supply of money, while a surplus increases it.

According to the quantity theory of money, the price level is a function of the quantity of money in circulation. A balance-of-payments deficit therefore leads to a decrease in the price level, and a surplus leads to an increase in the price level. This in turn causes deficit countries' exports to rise and imports to fall and surplus countries' imports to rise and exports to fall, thereby eliminating the disequilibrium.

The classical theory of the adjustment mechanism is therefore composed of three connecting main stages: the first is the connection between the balance of payments and the supply of money; the second is the connection between the supply of money and the price level; the last is the connection between the price level and the balance of payments.

From the standpoint of present-day theory, classical theory retains much of its validity, but in the light of changed institutional conditions and later theoretical developments, it requires modification. The weakest link in the classical formulation of the adjustment mechanism is stage two above—the relation between money supply and the price level. The relation between money supply and the price level posited by the classical theory is based on the quantity theory of money, which states that changes in the supply of money

---

2 Devaluation of a currency means a lowering of its gold content and a decrease in its international value. Hence, assets denominated in that currency become worth less in terms of other currencies.

cause changes in the same direction in the price level. It is outside the scope of this book to evaluate the quantity theory, but two of its underlying assumptions should be noted.

The first is the assumption that there is full employment. In the presence of a considerable amount of unemployment, the chances that an increased supply of money will cause prices generally to rise are much less than if there is full employment, for the physical volume of output may keep pace with increased money expenditure. The classical theory of the adjustment mechanism is less applicable, therefore, when there is unemployment.

The second assumption is that costs and prices are flexible, that is, responsive to a decrease in aggregate money expenditure. If costs and prices are "sticky," a decrease in aggregate money expenditure causes a contraction in the volume of output and employment rather than a decline in costs and prices. Several elements contribute to cost and price inflexibility. Labor is ordinarily resistant to wage cuts, and, if labor is organized in strong unions, the power to resist is strengthened. Some costs (including wages, under collective bargaining agreements) are contractually fixed for given periods. More generally, any type of monopolistic element tends to reduce cost and price flexibility. It is common practice, for example, for firms in an oligopolistic market (a few large firms in the industry) to follow a concerted policy of price maintenance even in the face of declining demand for their output.

To question the universal validity of the quantity theory of money is not equivalent to questioning the very important role of monetary changes in the adjustment mechanism. The decrease in the domestically held supply of money a balance-of-payments deficit automatically causes, and the increase in money supply a surplus causes, are nearly certain to contribute to adjustment, provided that offsetting actions by the monetary authority are not taken. As money supply continues to contract in a deficit balance-of-payments situation and the liquidity of the economy correspondingly is reduced, at some point expenditure decisions will be affected. Consumption and investment, as well as import, expenditure may be reduced as a direct consequence of reduced liquidity. In any event, a lowered money supply is likely to cause interest rates to rise, which in turn has a dampening effect on expenditure.

If costs and prices are flexible and responsive to changes in aggregate expenditure, adjustment would follow along the lines indicated by classical theory. But even if prices do not respond to changes in expenditure, *income* does. And, as we know, income changes also provide a means of balance-of-payments adjustment.

At this point, however, we have left the classical world and entered the world of modern theory with its emphasis on adjustment through income, rather than price, changes. But there is no conflict between classical price and modern income effects. On the contrary, they complement and reinforce each other. As we concluded in the preceding chapter, adjustment through automatic income effects alone will be complete only under special conditions. The monetary effects of disequilibrium tend to strengthen the adjustment process by leading either to price changes or additional income changes or both.

Evaluation of the System

As far as the *effectiveness* of the automatic adjustment mechanism under the gold standard is concerned, combined price and income changes can generally be relied upon to perform an adequate job. Together with the encouragement to international trade and growth given by stable exchange rates, this constitutes a powerful argument in favor of the gold standard system. During its heyday in the latter part of the 19th century and until World War I, the gold standard provided a monetary framework which encouraged and facilitated the vast expansion in output and trade occurring during that era.

However, several conditions favorable to the operations of the gold standard were present before 1914 but have disappeared since. Among these, perhaps the most important was the willingness of countries to accept the basic premise underlying the system—namely, the subordination of the national economy to the dictates of external economic and monetary relations. Simultaneously to maintain stable exchange rates and freedom of trade and payments requires adjustment of the balance of payments to serious disturbances through the price and income effects previously described. If this adjustment mechanism is resisted or counteracted by monetary and fiscal policies, trouble is bound to develop sooner or later, with the consequence that either fixed gold values of currencies, or freedom of trade and payments—or both—will be abandoned. This is precisely what happened during the 1930s, when one country after another, beginning with Great Britain in 1931, abandoned the gold standard. Why?

The immediate reason was the world economic crisis and the

breakdown of confidence that followed it, but more fundamentally the reason lay in the rejection of the internal consequences of the gold standard adjustment mechanism. Price and income deflation is an effective method of eliminating a deficit disequilibrium in the balance of payments, but, in conjunction with downward price and cost inflexibility, unemployment is a frequent accompaniment. On the other hand, unless there is slack in the economy, the gold standard mechanism tends to cause inflation in countries with a surplus balance of payments. But today most countries are committed to full employment and price stability as major national goals. Few are willing to pay the price of internal economic and monetary instability for the sake of external equilibrium.

Conflict between domestic equilibrium at full employment and reasonably stable prices and balance-of-payments equilibrium is most prone to occur in a system of stable exchange rates and freedom of trade and payments. Under such a system the internal and external economy are closely bound together, developments in one directly affecting the other. The effects of autonomous changes in the trade balance on the national income were earlier explored in our discussion of the foreign-trade multiplier and adjustment through income effects. It is appropriate now to consider briefly the reverse relationship—the effects on the balance of payments of independent changes in the national income.

Suppose that a country is suffering from a recession and unemployment but is in balance-of-payments equilibrium. To rid itself of unemployment and restore prosperity, expansionary monetary and fiscal policies are called for. But as income and employment respond to these policies, the demand for imports will tend to increase, leading to a balance-of-payments deficit. Some partial compensation may be forthcoming through the foreign repercussion, but rarely could it be counted upon to prevent a deficit from arising. Thus, to achieve equilibrium at full employment the country is exposed to balance-of-payments disequilibrium. If the country has large gold and foreign exchange reserves it may be able and willing to allow the deficit to continue for a considerable period. But if its international reserves are inadequate to finance a deficit for long, an expansionary domestic policy is inconsistent with its commitment to the rules of the gold standard.

In short, the gold standard imposes constraints upon domestic policies which can be expected at least on occasion to clash head-on with important goals.

FLOATING EXCHANGE RATES

The dilemma created by the gold standard would seem to have an obvious and easy solution: let the burden of balance-of-payments adjustment be borne by exchange rates rather than by domestic income and prices. To ease further the problem of maintaining external equilibrium without burdensome constraints on domestic policies, let exchange rates respond freely to market forces of demand and supply. Such a system is, of course, that of freely floating exchange rates.

The above paragraph summarizes in capsule form the outstanding advantage of a freely floating exchange rate system. Some further discussion of it is warranted, both for its own sake and for the light it may throw on alternative systems.

As compared to the gold standard, the chief distinguishing characteristic of floating rates is national monetary independence. In a gold standard system, national currencies are linked together through their common tie to gold and are in effect parts of a unified international monetary system. This is the underlying reason countries are not free in such a system to pursue independent domestic policies without regard to the policies of other countries and the state of the balance of payments. In contrast, with freely floating exchange rates, each country's monetary system stands in an independent position, permitting the pursuit of domestic policies without the constraints imposed by balance-of-payments considerations.

This monetary independence is provided by the absorption of external shocks through exchange rate changes rather than through changes in the domestic supply of money and income. Consider, for example, the effects of an autonomous decrease in exports. Under the gold standard, as we have seen, a deficit in the balance of payments is thereby immediately created, with gold exports and/or accommodating short-term capital inflows providing the means of financing it. Accompanying these is a decrease in the domestically held supply of money. But with floating rates the fall in exports causes an immediate rise in exchange rates which moderate the decrease in exports and causes imports to contract. No accommodating finance is necessary[3] and, correspondingly, the domestic supply of money remains unaffected.

---

[3] However, accommodating transactions may occur if instantaneous adjustment in the balance of payments through the rise in exchange rate is not effected. For example, a private short-term capital inflow may be induced by the rise in rate, as discussed later, in which case the domestic supply of money is reduced.

Nor does the country have to undergo price and income deflation as a result of the decline in exports. Imports are reduced through the rise in exchange rate automatically caused by the fall in exports rather than through a contraction in income or deflation of prices as under the gold standard.

Notwithstanding these undoubted advantages of floating exchange rates, the system is not free of objections. The central objection to floating rates is that the insulation they give the domestic economy against external disturbances is at the cost of a loss of efficiency in the international economy. Exchange rates are key variables in the international economy. When they are stable, they provide the channels through which the price mechanism can transmit allocative signals internationally as accurately as domestically. When exchange rates are severely unstable, transmission channels waver, making international price and cost comparisons difficult and introducing an extra element of risk and uncertainty which interfere with the optimum allocation of resources internationally.

How seriously floating rates would interfere with the international allocative mechanism depends first of all upon the frequency and amplitude of fluctuations in rates. Relatively small fluctuations would have negligible effects, while frequent, severe gyrations could be extremely disrupting to normal trade and investment. The degree of rate instability in a floating rate system is therefore a major consideration deserving discussion.

The immediate determinant of the degree of rate instability experienced under floating rates is a country's balance of payments. Sharp shifts in the trade balance or in capital movements naturally would tend to cause correspondingly large movements in exchange rates. However, it must be noted that under similar circumstances with stable exchange rates the impact would not be escaped but would rather appear as a deficit or surplus in the balance of payments. While exchange rate fluctuations are indeed disruptive, balance-of-payments disequilibrium is also disruptive. There is no a priori basis for expecting in general the consequences of exchange rate fluctuations in response to changing balances of payments to be more disturbing than those produced by balance-of-payments disequilibria. In the latter case, repercussions on income and employment and on the money supply and the rate of interest automatically occur, which in turn may lead to policy changes, including various controls with disruptive and distorting effects.

Opponents of floating exchange rates, however, believe that there is an extra element of instability present with floating rates that is absent under fixed rates—namely, speculative capital movements. Suppose that the exchange rate begins to rise. If speculators expect it to continue to rise, they may purchase foreign currencies, hold them until the exchange rate reaches a peak, then sell them. As a consequence, the exchange rate rises more than it otherwise would because of the extra demand for foreign exchange in the first stage and falls more because of the extra supply in the last stage. With a fixed exchange rate, there is no opportunity for profit from such destabilizing capital movements.

Although destabilizing speculation is a possibility with floating rates, several qualifications should be noted. In the first place, speculation may have stabilizing instead of destabilizing effects. A movement in the exchange rate that is expected to be temporary and later reversed in direction tends to induce stabilizing short-term capital flows. An increase in rate leads to the sale of foreign currency balances (short-term capital inflow) to take advantage of a temporarily high price of the home currency, while a decrease in rate leads to the purchase of foreign currencies while their prices in the home currency are temporarily low. Hence, rate increases are restrained by the extra supply of foreign exchange furnished by speculative capital inflows and rate decreases restrained by the extra demand for foreign exchange to finance speculative capital outflows.

Pressure on the exchange rate may not, of course, be only temporary. The equilibrium rate may move to a higher level, for example, because of a nonreversible balance-of-payments deficit at a lower exchange rate. In this case speculative capital outflows may hasten the process of arriving at a new equilibrium rate, but the exchange depreciation is attributable fundamentally to forces that are present regardless of speculation.

It is also to be noted that the possibility of destabilizing speculation is not the sole property of a floating rate system. Only if exchange rates are rigidly fixed and confidently accepted as such can the possibility of destabilizing speculation be eliminated. In the much more usual case of stable rates subject to periodic adjustment to new levels through discretionary decisions by a monetary authority, the inducement to speculation is at its height. For example, if a country is faced with a serious balance-of-payments deficit, any exchange rate adjustment can confidently be predicted to be in an upward direction (devaluation), so that speculative purchases of foreign currencies offer the prospect of profits with practically no risk of loss. This is known as a "one-way option" and will be discussed further in connection with the Bretton Woods system (Chapter 19).

Apart from the influence of speculative commodity and capital movements, a more basic influence on exchange rate flunctuations is the elasticities of the demand and supply of foreign exchange. These, in turn, we found earlier to be mainly a reflection of the elasticity of demand for imported goods and services and of foreign demand for the country's export goods and services. The less elastic the demand and supply functions are, the greater the fluctuation in rate caused by any given shift in demand or supply.

The most unfavorable circumstances for the operation of a freely fluctuating rate system exist when both the demand and supply of foreign exchange are highly inelastic. Indeed, in an extreme case, the exchange rate may be in an unstable equilibrium position. This would be the result if the supply curve is backward-bending and intersects the demand curve from above to the left, as illustrated in Figure 16.1. Any movement in the rate above or below the point of intersection would set off a cumulative reaction, forcing the rate further in the same direction. Even though eventually the rate would settle in stable equilibrium (because the elasticity of demand is bound to increase as the rate rises), the rate is subject to great fluctuations.

In the last analysis, whether floating rates are the most appropriate system depends upon the relative importance attached to the ease of balance-of-payments adjustment as compared to the gains from specialization and economic integration. For a small country an intensely specialized part of the world economy and therefore heavily dependent upon international trade, fixed exchange rates vis-à-vis its principal trading partners provide an appropriate monetary framework, comparable to that provided by a single currency to regions within a national economy. On the other hand, a large country with extensive internal trade and less dependence upon international specialization may find that the specialization advantages of fixed exchange rates are outweighed by the balance-of-payments adjustment advantages of floating rates. Hence, the so-called "optimum currency area," in which exchange rates are fixed, varies according to the importance of foreign trade.[4]

Historical experience with floating exchange rates has been limited. Experience in the early 1920s and again for a short time in the early 1930s generally showed more of the weaknesses than the

---

[4] Another criterion of the optimum currency area is the mobility of factors of production. Regions or countries among which there is a high degree of factor mobility, which facilitates adjustment, constitute according to this criterion an optimum currency area. See Robert Mundell, "A Theory of Optimum Currency Areas," *The American Economic Review*, September 1961, pp. 657–64.

strengths of the system.[5] But these were not fair tests, since free rates were adopted only as interim measures during transitional and troubled periods. The Canadian experiment with a floating rate from 1950 to 1962 demonstrated that it can be surprisingly stable. However, again the test was not a fair one, because of the close ties between the Canadian and U.S. dollars.

Most recently, floating rates have been undergoing new and extensive trials. As we shall see later (Chapter 19), beginning in early 1973 all major currencies began to float. As usual, though, the float was regarded as provisional, pending the reestablishment of "orderly" exchange rate relationships.

EXCHANGE CONTROLS

Although they are widely different methods of organizing the international monetary system, the gold standard and freely fluctuating exchange rate systems have in common the reliance upon automatic market mechanisms. In sharp contrast, an exchange control system is designed to suppress or circumvent market forces.

In a thoroughgoing exchange control system, all international economic and financial transactions of the country are legally subject to the prior approval of the control authority. All current foreign exchange receipts are required to be sold to the control authority, and all foreign exchange is purchased from it. Sometimes "free" markets for certain kinds of transactions are permitted, but these are limited in scope and are actually a part of the control system.

Typically, exchange rates are fixed at official levels, except for transactions in the free-market sector, if such exists. Typically, also, the official exchange rate overvalues the home currency—that is, the rate is held below the equilibrium level. Were not this the case, the necessity for exchange controls for balance-of-payments purposes would usually disappear.

Various devices may be employed to keep the balance of payments under control. The heart of the system, of course, is the direct control over international transactions. But other, ancillary methods are also frequently used, such as "multiple" exchange rates. This means the setting of different exchange rates for different kinds of transactions. For example, to discourage luxury imports a high rate of exchange can be set on foreign exchange purchased for this purpose,

---

[5] See League of Nations, *International Currency Experience,* chaps. v and vi, (Geneva, 1944).

while a lower rate is applicable to imports of raw materials and foodstuffs. As indicated above, there may even be some transactions for which exchange can be bought or sold at free rates.

Exchange controls have been instituted for a variety of historical reasons. One obvious basis is the presence of a centrally controlled economy, with exchange controls being simply a logical extension to the international sector. Apart from this, exchange controls have originated in most cases in one or more of the following circumstances: economic or monetary crisis, associated with the threat or outbreak of war or severe political disturbances; internal economic or monetary instability, in the form either of deep recession or serious inflation; the presence of a persistent and intractable deficit balance of payments; as part of a national program for economic development, with the objective of direct "rationing" of scarce foreign exchange.

Exchange controls in the 20th century first began to flourish during the economic, monetary, and political crises of the late 1930s. They were continued and extended during World War II and, with few exceptions, maintained in the early postwar years. It was not until late 1958 that Western European countries felt stable and strong enough to dismantle most controls and reestablish a large measure of freedom in international payments. Even so, selected controls, especially over capital movements, have been retained by most European countries down to the present day. More extensive controls are commonly found today in the underdeveloped countries of Latin America, Africa, and the Near and Far East.

Exchange (and quantitative trade) controls, with some exceptions, are now outlawed, in principle, among the major trading countries of the Western world. This is in recognition of their generally uneconomic effects. Freedom of trade and payments ordinarily offers the best assurance that resources will be efficiently allocated domestically and internationally. Direct controls tend to distort or destroy the price mechanism guiding resources into their most productive uses.

Nevertheless, exchange controls cannot reasonably be entirely excluded from the arsenal of weapons at the disposal of governments in their search for economic stability. Free-market forces do not always produce optimum results, and in some cases they lead to quite intolerable results. To cite some examples, consider first a country suffering from severe inflation. Until the inflation is brought under control, a freely fluctuating exchange rate system—the "most free" of all free-market systems—tends to lead to a self-feeding upward spiral of exchange rates and prices. If exchange rates are held stable without exchange controls, the balance of payments may develop a deficit too large to handle with available gold reserves or other accommodating finance. Exchange controls may then be the least undesirable alternative feasible.

A second case for controls arises when a country experiences an outflow of "hot" capital or other large-scale destabilizing capital outflows because of internal political instability, the threat of war, and so on. Exchange depreciation is likely only to aggravate such movements of capital, while the attempt to maintain stable rates could lead to an early exhaustion of the country's international reserves.

More generally, exchange controls can be defended not so easily on their own merit as on the grounds that under some circumstances no more satisfactory alternative is available. A serious balance-of-payments deficit disequilibrium requires *some* method of adjustment. Exchange depreciation or income and price deflation may not always do the job, or may do it with unacceptable consequences. It is then a matter of judgment whether direct controls are preferable.

FLEXIBLE EXCHANGE RATES

The last monetary system to be discussed is a hybrid one, sharing characteristics of the gold standard, freely floating rates, and exchange controls. It may be called a system of "managed flexibility" of which there are two varieties: a flexible rate system and an "adjustable-peg" system. The latter will be considered in the next chapter.

By a flexible rate system we mean one in which exchange rates are neither kept at fixed, predetermined levels, nor allowed freely to fluctuate in response to private market forces and yet in which there is freedom of market transactions. This combination is brought about through the operations of an agency of the government—usually called the Stabilization Fund—which indirectly controls movements in exchange rates through sales and purchases of foreign exchange. The Fund is furnished by the Treasury or Central Bank, under whose aegis it operates, with both gold and foreign exchange balances and domestic currency. Domestic currency is used to buy foreign exchange on the market when it is desired to prevent or retard a fall in exchange rates; foreign exchange is used to buy domestic currency when the objective is to prevent or retard a rise in rates or to force rates downward.

The adjustment mechanism depends upon the policies adopted by the monetary authority managing the system. To the extent that the rate is kept stable, even in the face of persistent or basic changes in autonomous demand or supply of foreign exchange, the mechanism is essentially the same as under the gold standard. On the other hand, if the authority were to remain neutral and allow the market to be shaped entirely by private demand and supply, it would become a virtual floating rate system.

However, neither of the above policies is normally to be expected, for the presumptive purpose of the system is to avoid the disadvantages of both fixed and freely floating exchange rates. The chief disadvantage of the latter can be avoided by *offsetting temporary fluctuations* in rates through appropriate market operations; the principal disadvantage of fixed rates can be avoided by *allowing the rate to change as a means of* correcting a persistent disequilibrium.

Flexible rates, however, are not panaceas for balance-of-payments problems. Like any system of discretionary management, it is necessarily liable to mismanagement. A major source of mistaken judgment is in determining the "correct" rate of exchange in the face of dynamic changes in underlying conditions behind autonomous transactions. A rate that is set too low overvalues the home currency and leads to balance-of-payments deficits; a too-high rate undervalues the currency and leads to balance-of-payments surpluses.

In attempting to predetermine the equilibrium rate of exchange, the concept of "purchasing power parity" may be applied. This holds that the equilibrium rate is one that establishes equality in the purchasing power of the home and foreign currencies. It is calculated by multiplying a past period's demonstrated equilibrium rate by the ratio of price changes at home and abroad that have occurred since the past equilibrium period. For instance, if home prices have quadrupled on the average while foreign prices have doubled, the equilibrium rate of exchange is now twice as high as formerly.

There are several weaknesses in the purchasing-power-parity doctrine, both theoretically and in practice. A major theoretical defect is its assumption that only relative price changes affect the balance of payments, ignoring possibly equally or more significant changes of a structural or cyclical nature.

However helpful purchasing-power-parity calculations may be in forecasting equilibrium exchange rates, only experience can reveal whether in fact they were. Of course, mistakes can be corrected, but the danger is always present that others will be made in the opposite direction. Too frequent rate changes detract from the potential advantage of rate stability and, moreover, encourage destabilizing speculative activity. Reluctance to allow rates to change, on the other hand, reduces the attractiveness of the system in providing a means of adjustment other than through income and price deflation or direct controls.

Finally, a major weakness of flexible rates, revealed during their period of germination during the 1930s, is their tendency to result in conflicting national policies. Country *A's* decision to allow or force the exchange rate on *B's* currency to rise is inconsistent with *B's* decision to prevent the rate on *A's* currency from falling. Such conflicts were not uncommon during the 1930s, until cooperation among national monetary authorities was instituted under the Tripartite Agreement (among the United States, the United Kingdom, and France, later adhered to by others) in 1936. This experience played a large role in shaping the postwar monetary system discussed next.

RECOMMENDED READINGS

BROWN, WILLIAM ADAMS, JR. *The Gold Standard Reinterpreted, 1914–1934.* 2 vols. New York: National Bureau of Economic Research, 1940.

FRIEDMAN, MILTON. "The Case for Flexible Exchange Rates," *Essays in Positive Economics.* Chicago: University of Chicago Press, 1953.

JOHNSON, HARRY G. "Theoretical Problems of the International Monetary System." *Pakistan Development Review,* 7:1–28. Reprinted in *International Finance.* Edited by R. N. Cooper. Baltimore: Penguin Books, 1969, pp. 304–34.

———. "The Case for Flexible Exchange Rates." Reprint Series no. 41. Federal Reserve Bank of St. Louis, June 1964.

MACHLUP, FRITZ AND MALKIEL, BURTON G. EDS. *International Monetary Arrangements: The Problem of Choice.* Princeton, N.J.: Princeton University Press, 1964.

MCKINNON, R. I. "Optimum Currency Areas." *American Economic Review* 53:717–24. Reprinted in *International Finance.* Edited by R. N. Cooper. Baltimore: Penguin Books, 1969, pp. 223–34.

MUNDELL, ROBERT. "A Theory of Optimum Currency Areas." *American Economic Review,* September 1961.

TRIFFIN, ROBERT. *The Evolution of the International Monetary System: Historical Reappraisal and Future Perspectives.* Princeton Studies in International Finance, no. 12. Princeton, N.J., 1964.

YEAGER, LELAND. *International Monetary Relations,* chap. 4 and Part 2. New York: Harper & Row, 1966.

STUDY QUESTIONS

1. What determines par rates of exchange under the gold standard?
2. How does a government maintain a fixed gold value of its currency?
3. Explain in what sense accommodating short-term capital movements are a substitute for gold movements.
4. What limits the ability of a country to remain on the gold standard if it has a persistent balance-of-payments deficit?
5. Explain the gold-specie-flow mechanism.
6. How is the classical theory of the gold standard adjustment mechanism dependent upon the quantity theory of money?
7. How do inflexible costs and prices affect the assumptions of the classical theory of adjustment?
8. What premise underlies the gold standard system with respect to national economic and monetary policies?
9. What is the nature of the objection to the gold standard adjustment mechanism in today's world?
10. Give an example of a situation in which domestic economic goals and balance-of-payments equilibrium are inconsistent.
11. Contrast and explain the difference in the degree of independence of national monetary systems under the gold standard and under freely floating exchange rates.
12. State the objections to freely floating rates from the point of view of international trade and investment.
13. Distinguish between stabilizing and destabilizing speculation, and explain what determines which kind will develop under freely floating rates.
14. Why are inelastic demand and supply curves of foreign exchange unfavorable to the operation of freely floating rates?
15. Define "undervalued" and "overvalued" currencies.
16. What is meant by multiple exchange rates?
17. List some of the conditions under which exchange controls may be justified.
18. Discuss the major objection to exchange controls.
19. How are exchange rate movements controlled in a flexible rate system?
20. Explain the purchasing-power-parity theory and its weaknesses.
21. What are the main weaknesses of a flexible rate system?
22. What is meant by an "optimum currency area," and how does it relate to the issue of floating versus fixed exchange rates?

18

The Bretton Woods system

After World War II, an international monetary system was created that belongs to the category of "managed flexibility" described in the preceding chapter. It was therefore closely related to the flexible rate system, but it had its own unique characteristics not found in any prior historical experience.

For reasons that will soon become evident, the postwar monetary arrangements go under the name of an "adjustable-peg" system. It is also known as the Bretton Woods system, for its basic framework was laid in a conference in 1944 at that New Hampshire site.

As we shall see in the next chapter, the original Bretton Woods system collapsed in 1971, though the institutions for international monetary cooperation created at the time the system was established have continued. It is planned to reform the original system, reinstituting it with modifications. The types of modification envisaged and various specific proposals of reform are discussed in Chapter 20.

Even though the original Bretton Woods system lasted only a quarter of a century, it is worthwhile our examination for two reasons. First, it represented an historic break with previous systems and is significant in its own right. Second, its principal institution—

the International Monetary Fund (the IMF) —continues to flourish, and many of the central precepts underlying the system will undoubtedly reappear in somewhat modified form in an emerging new system.

The creators of the Bretton Woods system[1] were intensely aware of the unsatisfactory monetary experience of the prewar decade. The gold standard, which had been the bulwark of the world economy before World War I, became less and less appropriate in the years following and finally collapsed early in the 1930s under the impact of the economic and monetary crises set off by the Great Depression. The demise of the gold standard left a vacuum, which was filled by a succession of experiments with freely floating rates, flexible rates, and exchange controls. None of these produced satisfactory results. The hope and objective at Bretton Woods was to create a new system that would avoid the undesirable aspects of its predecessors while capturing their best features. The main things to be avoided were the rigid exchange rates and associated deflationary adjustment mechanism of the gold standard; the instability of freely floating rates; the conflicts of national policies and competitive exchange depreciation of the flexible rate system; and the repressive and distorting techniques of exchange controls. The features to be captured were the stability of the gold standard, the easy adjustment mechanism and market freedom of floating rates, the discretionary control over market forces of the flexible rate system, and the selective use of controls when necessary, borrowed from the exchange control system. Finally, entirely new institutions and practices had to be devised to provide the appropriate means of accomplishing these objectives.

Irreducible conflicts are evident from inspection of the above lists of things to be avoided and to be sought. For example, exchange rates cannot be both fixed and flexible, and adjustment cannot be both automatic and controlled. Compromise was therefore unavoidable, and some of the problems of the system as it operated in practice can be attributed to this. Nevertheless, it is a bold experiment which deserves careful criticism.

---

1 Many experts from different countries contributed to the development of the system over a discussion period of several years. The principals, however, were Lord Keynes of the British Treasury and Dr. Harry White of the U.S. Treasury, each of whom advanced a plan bearing his name. In the end, the White Plan, as it emerged from the process of intense discussion and compromise, won the day and became the basis of the system adopted. However, Keynes' ideas were not buried and have enjoyed a revival in recent proposals for reforming the Bretton Woods system, as shown in the next chapter.

THE ESSENTIALS OF THE ADJUSTABLE PEG

The basic notion underlying the Bretton Woods system is that of the adjustable peg. Essentially, this means that exchange rates are kept stable (that is, "pegged") around declared par values but with the rates subject to repegging at different levels when balance-of-payments considerations justify such actions. In other words, rates are stable but not unalterably fixed. The obvious intent of such a system is to gain the advantages of gold standard stability without having to suffer the rigors of its adjustment mechanism.

Pegging the rate of exchange at a specified level involves two operations. The first is deciding at what rate to peg the currency. Having made this decision, it is implemented by declaring a par value of the currency in terms of some standard. In the Bretton Woods system, the standard was gold. The second operation consists of the methods used to maintain the rate stable at or near the declared par. One method of doing this is for each national monetary authority freely to buy and sell gold at the officially set price. Apart from the United States, which followed this practice in modified form,[2] a different method is generally used. It is the flexible rate technique of operations in the market by stabilization funds.

In contrast to a flexible rate system, however, under an adjustable-peg system, countries are committed in principle not merely to eliminate day-to-day fluctuations in exchange rates (beyond small margins around par), but to keep them stable as long as possible, consistent with the achievement of other objectives.

Among these objectives the most important are (*a*) freedom of trade and payment on current account transactions from quantitative restrictions and (*b*) domestic economic stability, including full employment and a reasonably stable price level. If either of these goals is threatened by balance-of-payments pressures, relief through repegging exchange rates at a different level is admitted as a legitimate action.

However, again in contrast to other systems, changing the par value of a currency is not regarded as a prerogative which may be exercised unilaterally and without the prior approval of other countries. In the absence of such an agreement, the commitment to rate

---

[2] Monetary gold operations of the United States were confined to purchases and sales from and to foreign official institutions. Domestic residents are not permitted to hold monetary gold (except for numismatic purposes), but this prohibition is scheduled to be relaxed at the end of 1974.

stability would be in danger of violation through frequent and unwarranted rate changes.

ROLE OF THE INTERNATIONAL MONETARY FUND

It should be clear from the above discussion of the basic principles of an adjustable-peg system that it cannot operate as intended without international agreement to adhere to its principles and an appropriate institutional framework for their implementation. The International Monetary Fund (IMF) was created to serve these purposes.

The IMF and its sister institution, the International Bank for Reconstruction and Development, were formed in 1944 at the Bretton Woods Conference. The Fund began operations in 1946 and stands today at the center of the current international monetary system, with a membership of over 120 countries, including all the important trading countries of the world outside the Soviet Union and mainland China blocs.

The basic approach of the IMF is to provide machinery for consultation and collaboration among member countries, as well as direct assistance in carrying out obligations imposed by the Articles of Agreement, or constitution. A permanent international organization, the IMF is guided by a policy-making board of governors on which all member countries are represented; the executive directors, who are responsible for day-to-day operations; and a technical staff of international civil servants.

Principles of the Fund

As we have noted, the Bretton Woods system was based on an adjustable-peg system. Hence, the obligations of members and assistance provided to them were designed to implement the principles of this system.

The first of these principles listed earlier is the stability of exchange rates. This principle was embodied in the obligation of each member of the IMF to declare a par value of its currency in terms of gold and to refrain from changing the par value, except to correct a "fundamental disequilibrium." Market rates of exchange were to be kept within 1 percent of par values. This was accomplished in most cases through the operations in the market of national stabilization funds.

A second principle of the adjustable-peg system is freedom of current account transactions from quantitative controls. The Articles of Agreement of the IMF prohibit such controls, unless special circumstances warrant exception. Controls over capital movements, however, are permissible. The acceptability of capital controls was based on prewar experience with the disrupting influence that erratic and destabilizing capital flows can have.

The obligation both to keep exchange rates stable and to refrain from imposing quantitative controls over current payments cannot be discharged if the means of financing temporary balance-of-payments deficits are not available. Suppose that a member country enters a period of several months, or even a year or two, of payments deficit. The quantity of foreign exchange autonomously demanded exceeds the quantity autonomously supplied. Hence, the rate of exchange rises, and unless private accommodating capital inflows occur, the monetary authority is obliged to provide additional foreign exchange on the market to keep the exchange rate from exceeding the allowable upper limit over the par rate. If the country possesses sufficient official reserves of gold and foreign exchange to finance the deficit, this may create no special problem. But if official reserves are inadequate, and arrangements cannot be made to obtain international credit, either the exchange rate will break through the official upper limit or controls on payments must be imposed, or both.

The authors of the IMF were well aware that if its principles were to be operationally meaningful, member countries would have to have access to extra foreign exchange reserves when needed to tide them over temporary periods of balance-of-payments deficits. One of the greatest innovations introduced by the IMF was its creation of a "revolving pool" of credit, available to members for this purpose. In the technical language of the Fund, such credit is known as "drawing rights."

The IMF acquires the resources for lending mainly through member subscriptions. Upon joining the Fund, a member is assigned a *quota,* the size of which determines the amount of subscription it must pay into the Fund, as well as its drawing rights and voting power. Quotas are based on such factors as national income and volume of trade.

Quota subscriptions are payable 25 percent in gold and the remainder in the member's national currency, though the gold portion may be less for countries with small gold and foreign exchange reserves. Additional resources can be mobilized, if needed, through arrangements to borrow from several of the larger members.

When a member "draws" upon the Fund, it receives foreign exchange out of the Fund's holdings in return for an equivalent amount of its own currency paid to the Fund. While this appears to be simply a purchase operation, in reality it is a loan operation. The member is required to repurchase within five years any of its currency held by the Fund in excess of the member's quota, and in the meanwhile interest is charged on drawings outstanding. The repurchase is made with gold or acceptable foreign exchange. The Fund's holdings of a member's currency may be reduced in another way: through its purchase by *other* members. This would normally happen if the member develops a balance-of-payments surplus vis-à-vis other members who then draw upon the Fund to help finance their deficits. Indeed, the Fund's resources are designed to be used in precisely this way—that is, as a "revolving pool" of credit, drawn upon by a given member only occasionally and for short periods of deficit and replenished as deficits give way to surpluses. In short, the Fund extends credit to meet *temporary* balance-of-payments deficits.

Restriction of the resources of the Fund to financing short-term, temporary deficits is further assured by limitations, both quantitative and qualitative, on members' drawing rights. The general rule, violated only exceptionally, is that a member may not purchase foreign exchange from the IMF if the purchase would cause the Fund's holdings of that member's currency to increase by more than 25 percent in any 12-month period or to exceed 200 percent of its quota. Moreover, a member has more or less automatic drawing rights only up to one quarter of its quota—the so-called "gold tranche." Beyond that, drawings are subject to determination by the Fund on the basis of the applicant's balance-of-payments situation and its program for restoring equilibrium.

In the direction of more liberal access to the Fund's credit, "standby arrangements" may be made with individual members, assuring that drawings may be made up to specified amounts and within a specified period, provided that agreed-upon policies are pursued by the member.

Finally, there remains the crucially important question of adjustment to balance-of-payments disequilibrium. As noted previously, the IMF is able to help members ride out short-term disturbances. But persistent disequilibrium is another matter. Any stable-rate, free-market system requires for its successful operation a reasonable degree of balance-of-payments stability on the part of the major trading countries. Periods of short-run disequilibrium are to be expected—indeed, are inevitable. As we have seen, the IMF is prepared to help take care of these. Persistent disequilibrium, however, is neither inevitable nor sustainable. The IMF is unable—and in any event would be unwilling—to finance a member's continuing deficit.

Responsibility for maintaining long-run equilibrium rests primarily with each individual country. A member of the IMF is expected to pursue monetary and fiscal policies consistent with this responsibility. However, occasions may arise when, either because of inappropriate policies or because of forces over which a country has no effective control, persistent balance-of-payments disequilibrium develops. Domestic inflation is a common example of the former; shifts in demand and technological changes are examples of the latter. Moreover, a country may find itself caught in the dilemma of a conflict between domestic stability and balance-of-payments equilibrium. This possibility arises out of the relationship between the balance of payments and the national income, as we found in an earlier discussion. To bring its balance of payments into equilibrium a country may have to accept an underemployment equilibrium level of income.

The authors of the IMF recognized that these kinds of problems would arise. To meet them is the chief purpose of the right given to member countries to change the par value of their currencies—that is, to "repeg" their currencies. This is allowable under the Articles of Agreement to correct a "fundamental disequilibrium." But to safeguard the principle of exchange stability, changes in par must receive the prior approval of the Fund, unless the change is less than 10 percent of the initially declared par.

The Articles of Agreement do not define the "fundamental disequilibrium" which justifies the repegging of currencies at different levels. However, from the context of the nature of the system and from operating interpretations over the years, the meaning is fairly clear. Fundamental disequilibrium can be said to exist when a persistent balance-of-payments disequilibrium is not amenable to correction at prevailing exchange rates except through controls over current transactions or at the cost of serious unemployment or inflation. This is a pragmatic rather than theoretical definition but appropriately so as a guide to policy decisions. The objective is to avoid both unnecessary exchange rate variations and the worst consequences of rigid rates, the latter consisting mainly of current-account controls and/or domestic instability.

EVOLUTION OF THE BRETTON WOODS SYSTEM

From the date of the beginning operations of the Bretton Woods system in 1946 to its breakdown in 1971 it underwent several important modifications. One of the most significant of these was the transformation in the direction of an earlier version of the gold standard, in operation during the latter part of the 1920s, known as the "gold exchange standard." The latter is a system in which one or more national currencies are fixed in terms of gold and become "key" currencies to which other currencies are tied and in terms of which international reserves are in part kept.

The United States dollar early became a key currency in the Bretton Woods system. Of the members of the IMF, the United States alone carried out its obligations to maintain the par value of its currency through maintaing a fixed relationship of the dollar with gold. Other countries discharged their corresponding obligation by maintaining a fixed relationship of their currencies to the dollar, thus only indirectly to gold.

Two important consequences followed from the dollar's acquired special status in the system. The first was the increasing use of the dollar by other countries as an international reserve asset, sharing this role with gold. As we shall see in the next chapter, while the use of dollars as reserves contributed to maintaining liquidity in the system, it increased the system's vulnerability to crisis situations.

The second consequence of the dollar's special role was the asymmetrical position into which the United States was placed, as compared with other countries, with respect to exchange rate adjustment. While other countries could change the par values of their currencies by establishing a different relationship to the dollar, the United States was effectively denied an equal freedom of action, for changing the gold value of the dollar would, in itself, leave unaffected dollar rates of exchange on other currencies.

While the evolution of the system into a gold exchange standard with the dollar as a key currency turned out to be a structural weakness which helped bring about its downfall, another modification was deliberately introduced in 1969 to strengthen the system. In response to the liquidity problems arising out of the growing use of the dollar as a reserve asset and an accompanying decline in the relative importance of gold as a reserve medium, an entirely new form of reserve, called "Special Drawing Rights" was invented. Special Drawing Rights (SDRs) were an extremely important innovation which, however, were introduced too late to have a great impact on the Bretton Woods system. The greatest significance of SDRs is for the future. Their contribution to the Bretton Woods system and their potential role in a future system will be discussed in the next two chapters.

RECOMMENDED READINGS

ALIBER, ROBERT Z. *The Management of the Dollar in International Finance.* Princeton Studies in International Finance, no. 13. Princeton, N.J., 1964.

BERNSTEIN, EDWARD M. "The Evolution of the International Monetary Fund." In A. L. K. ACHESON ET AL. *Bretton Woods Revisited.* Toronto: University of Toronto Press, 1972, pp. 51–65.

FLEMING, J. MARCUS. *The International Monetary Fund, Its Form and Functions.* Washington, D.C.: International Monetary Fund, 1964.

GOLDENWEISER, E. A., and BOURNEUF, ALICE. "The Bretton Woods Agreements," *Federal Reserve Bulletin,* September, 1944.

INTERNATIONAL MONETARY FUND. *Annual Reports.* Washington, D.C.

SCAMMELL, W. M. *International Monetary Policy,* chaps. v–vii, 2d ed. New York: Macmillan Co., 1964.

TEW, BRIAN. *The International Monetary Fund: Its Present Role and Future Prospects.* Princeton University, Essays in International Finance, no. 6. Princeton, N.J., March, 1961.

STUDY QUESTIONS

1. Justify the inclusion of both flexible rate and adjustable-peg systems in the category of "managed flexibility."
2. List the characteristics of previous historical systems that the Bretton Woods system seeks to avoid and those it seeks to capture.
3. In what important respects does the adjustable-peg system differ from the gold standard? From freely floating rates? From flexible rates?
4. How do most countries maintain the market values of their currencies at or near par? How does the United States?
5. What rule does the IMF impose concerning quantitative payments controls?

6. What is meant by the IMF's "revolving pool of credit"? In what sense does it "revolve"?

7. Why are drawings upon the IMF in reality the extensions of credit by the Fund?

8. State the limits on the amounts and conditions of drawing rights on the IMF.

9. Why can the IMF not help finance a member's persistent balance-of-payments deficit?

10. Why are adequate international reserves indispensable for the operation of an adjustable peg system?

11. Under what circumstances may a country justify repegging its currency?

12. Describe a gold exchange standard.

13. What is meant by the status of the dollar as a "key" currency?

19

Breakdown of the Bretton
Woods monetary system
and its aftermath

After more than a quarter century of operations, the Bretton Woods system was suddenly and radically disrupted by the announcement of President Nixon in August, 1971, that henceforward the United States would no longer convert dollars into gold. In a series of subsequent events, the basis of the system, as originally envisaged, was effectively destroyed, and the search for a new system inaugurated.

As a prelude to a discussion of the momentous changes following the action of the United States in 1971, a brief look at the system's accomplishments and its increasingly manifest weaknesses is in order.

EARLY ACCOMPLISHMENTS OF THE BRETTON WOODS MONETARY SYSTEM

The Bretton Woods system is notable as representing the first effort in modern times to establish an international monetary order through an explicit agreement of the major trading countries of the world. The basic principle embodied in the agreement and implemented through the creation of the International Monetary Fund is acceptance of international cooperation in formulating policies of an inherently supranational concern. This principle, which has remained intact even in the face of a breakdown in the original operating rules according to which the monetary order was to function, is perhaps the most fundamental and lasting contribution of Bretton Woods.

The viability of a structured order of international monetary cooperation was severely tested from the outset of the Bretton Woods system.

The International Monetary Fund, which was to be at the center of the postwar monetary system, began its operations at a very inauspicious time. The extensive physical destruction and economic and monetary disorder that were the legacy of World War II precluded immediate return to any kind of normal international monetary relations. The demands of the time were for massive reconstruction and rehabilitation of war-torn economies—demands which the IMF was not constructed to meet. The United States stepped into the breach with massive economic aid under the Marshall Plan. In the meanwhile, the IMF attempted, with only limited success, to persuade member countries to reduce the maze of controls and restrictions on payments which were in widespread use in the early postwar years and which were contrary to the principles of the system, except as temporary measures during the transition to more normal relations.

In a remarkably short time, the economies of Western Europe and Great Britain, which were an essential part of the world economy and were the most severely disrupted by the war, were restored and a degree of monetary stability was established. By the latter part of 1949, it was decided that it was time to lay the foundations for the creation of an equilibrium pattern of trade and payments without the prop of extensive economic aid from the United States. In September of that year, the principle of currency repegging was applied on a large scale upon the devaluation, with the consent of the Fund, of most European currencies.

During the next several years, progress toward establishing the conditions envisaged at Bretton Woods was steadily achieved. Although Marshall Plan aid was largely terminated by 1950, the United States continued to support Europe financially, with the aim of restoring the international reserves that had been depleted by war and reconstruction. At the end of 1958, the United Kingdom and several other major European countries virtually removed restrictions on current account transactions, thus conforming to one of the basic principles of the IMF.

As the conditions appropriate to the functioning of the IMF were gradually established, it became correspondingly more active. The usefulness of the Fund was dramatically demonstrated during the Suez crisis in 1956. The closure of the Suez Canal and disruption of oil pipelines in the Middle East fields created a sharp, but temporary, balance-of-payments crisis for certain European countries, especially the United Kingdom and France. To help bolster their payments position and to check speculation against their currencies, the Fund made available large credits to these countries. Several similar operations were carried on in subsequent crisis situations, in each case with support from the Fund serving to help prevent an international monetary crisis. In the meanwhile, the Fund made available credit to many of its members under more normal circumstances.

Paradoxically, as the Fund's participation and influence in the international monetary system grew, a new set of problems arose with which the Fund's ability to cope was questionable. These may be called the problems of confidence, liquidity, and adjustment.[1]

THE LIQUIDITY PROBLEM

Once the IMF had settled down into a more or less "normal" pattern of operations, an unanticipated problem began to emerge— the provision of an appropriate amount of internationally liquid assets.

Liquidity refers to the readiness and ease with which assets can be converted into forms acceptable in making payments. The internationally liquid assets in the possession of a national monetary authority constitute the international *reserves* of the country.

As observed in the preceding chapter, sufficient international reserves are indispensable in the operations of a system with fixed or stable exchange rates and a commitment to international payments free of controls. In the absence of an adequate quantity of international reserves to finance temporary balance-of-payments deficits, there is a general tendency for deficit countries to impose trade and payments restrictions. Alternatively, to reduce the magnitude of deficits, countries may be forced to restrict aggregate demand and employment. In either case, the shortage of liquidity restrains international trade and investment and may result in a general deflationary bias in the world economy.

---

[1] See Fritz Machlup and Burton G. Malkiel, Ed., *International Monetary Arrangements: The Problem of Choice* (Princeton, N.J.: Princeton University Press, 1964).

Gold Reserves

In the Bretton Woods system, gold was originally assigned the role of being the primary international reserve medium, as well as the international unit of account in terms of which each member's currency was defined. Growth in the world's stock of monetary gold depends upon the annual quantity of gold newly mined, less that part going into industrial and artistic uses and private hoards. There is obviously little, if any, connection between the system's need for additional monetary gold—based on growth in the volume of trade and investment—and the amount of it forthcoming. In fact, as the volume of trade and investment expanded rapidly during the 1950s and 1960s, the world output of gold grew at an increasingly slow pace. Moreover, as monetary uncertainty increased, the private demand for gold as an investment and speculative asset increased, leaving a smaller portion of new output for official reserve use.

Key Currency Reserves

As the Bretton Woods system evolved, the stock of international reserves changed composition, with reserve assets other than gold assuming an increasingly larger role. By far the most important of these other reserve assets consisted of the "key" currencies, especially the United States dollar and, to a lesser extent, the British pound sterling.

It was noted in the previous chapter that the Bretton Woods system rapidly became a form of a gold exchange standard, in which the dollar was tied to gold and other national currencies were tied to the dollar. Hence, other countries regarded the dollar as a reserve medium, "good as gold," since it was convertible into gold at a fixed price.

But how can countries acquire dollar reserves? The answer is, through developing a balance-of-payments surplus settled in dollars. For the rest of the world to acquire dollars, the United States must incur a balance-of-payments deficit. For a prolonged period, beginning roughly in 1950, the United States obliged by persistently running a deficit in its balance of payments. The deficit was financed chiefly in two ways: through the export of gold, and through the acquisition by foreign countries of dollar claims and balances. By the beginning of 1974, foreign holdings of dollar balances and other liquid claims against the United States had accumulated to a grand total in excess of $90 billion, of which more than two thirds were in the hands of foreign official institutions.[2] Foreign gold reserves as of the same date amounted to only slightly more than one third as much as dollar reserves.

While the balance-of-payments deficits of the United States fed the rest of the world with international reserves, at the same time the reserve position of the United States deteriorated. As long as other countries were willing to accept dollars in lieu of gold in settlement of the United States deficit, no immediate reserve problem for the United States arose. However, the equality of the dollar with gold as a reserve asset depended upon confidence in the continued convertibility of dollars into gold upon the demand of foreign official holders of dollars. As the total quantity of dollars held by foreigners increased, the ability of the United States to maintain convertibility into gold became increasingly doubtful. The gold stock of the United States was close to $25 billion in 1949, with foreign dollar holdings approximately $6.0 billion. By a quarter of a century later, the United States gold stock had decreased by more than 50 percent to approximately $12 billion—and foreign short-term dollar claims had jumped by about 1,400 percent—to $90 billion.

As the accumulation of dollars in the possession of foreigners continued to grow, it became evident that the process would sooner or later have to come to an end. The longer the United States balance-of-payments deficits continued, the more doubts were raised about the future value of the dollar and its acceptability as a reserve asset. On the other hand, the United States could not continue indefinitely to incur balance-of-payments deficits. Hence, the following dilemma arose: to preserve the status of the dollar as a reserve medium, the payments deficit of the United States had to be eliminated; but elimination of the deficit would mean a drying up of the source of additional dollar reserves for the system.

IMF Credit and Special Arrangements

The need for a source of reserves other than gold and dollars became increasingly evident. Drawing rights on the International Monetary Fund were, of course, a continuing means of acquiring extra foreign exchange available to member countries to finance

---

2 See *Federal Reserve Bulletin*, March 1974, p. A76.

temporary balance-of-payments deficits. Periodically, quota subscriptions of member countries, and therewith drawing rights, were increased. In addition, special devices were invented to provide extra reserves to countries in a crisis situation. One such device is the IMF's so-called "General Arrangements to Borrow," under which extraordinary credit can be mobilized. Another device consists of bilateral "swap agreements" between central banks, under which reciprocal lines of credit are made available.

None of the devices above was a solution, however, to the long-run liquidity problem. IMF credit was never intended to be more than a temporary source of extra reserves, and swap arrangements are designed chiefly as a means of bailing countries out of a crisis situation. A solution to the problem of furnishing appropriate amounts of international reserves required a new approach. Such an approach, representing perhaps the most significant innovation in the Bretton Woods system, was the introduction of an entirely new reserve medium, Special Drawing Rights.

Special Drawing Rights

After several years of growing concern over the liquidity problem, an agreement was reached at the IMF annual meeting in Rio de Janeiro in 1967 to issue Special Drawing Rights—SDRs. In 1969, the agreement was ratified, and the first allocation of SDRs was made in 1970, followed by additional allocations in each of the two succeeding years. By the beginning of 1974, over $9 billion of SDRs had been created. Presumably, future issues will be forthcoming as the IMF determines it to be appropriate. SDRs are allocated to members of the IMF in proportion to their quotas in the Fund.

What are SDRs? Physically, they are merely bookkeeping entries in a special account with the International Monetary Fund. Although SDRs were originally defined in terms of gold, in mid-1974 it was agreed as part of a package of reform measures (discussed in the next chapter) to value the SDR in terms of a "basket" of national currencies. However, the SDR continues to be a fiat or "paper" money that can literally be created with a stroke of the pen. It is for this reason that it is popularly known as "paper gold."

Unlike dollars and other reserve currencies, SDRs are not ordinary money usable in private international transactions. Rather, they are accounting units the use of which is confined to intergovernmental transactions. A member country having a balance in its SDR account with the IMF may acquire foreign currencies from other members in exchange for a transfer of SDRs. Thus, the United States may acquire German marks from Germany's central bank, paying for the marks with SDRs, resulting in a decrease in the SDR account of the United States and corresponding increase in Germany's SRD account. Countries are willing to accept SDRs as payment for their currencies because of the general agreement to do so, and the knowledge that SDRs can always be used for acquiring the currencies of other members.[3]

The purpose of SDRs, of course, is to provide additional international reserves to member countries. Such reserves may be needed to supplement other reserves (gold, dollars, ordinary drawing rights on the IMF) during periods of balance-of-payments deficits. If it is determined that additional reserves are needed to provide an optimal volume of reserves, the IMF (with the approval of its members) can create additional SDRs.

The most important innovation the SDR system represents is the deliberate creation of a fiat reserve asset to be added to gold, key currencies, and ordinary drawing rights as reserve media. This permits an expansion of international reserves in response to a policymaking decision in lieu of letting the volume of reserves be determined by the vagaries of gold mining in relation to the private demand for gold and by the balance of payments of reserve countries. From a longer-run point of view, the greater significance of SDRs may lie in their gradual displacement of both gold and dollars (and other key currencies) as reserve media.

THE ADJUSTMENT PROBLEM

From a long-run point of view, the crucial weakness of the Bretton Woods system was the absence of an efficient balance-of-payments adjustment mechanism. Because of continual changes in the underlying variables determining balance-of-payments relations—relative national income and price levels, tastes, technology, interest rates, etc.—disequilibrium in the balance of payments is a normal phenomenon. But for any one country, disequilibrium, especially of the

---

[3] Originally, there were limits on the obligations to accept SDRs, primarily for the purpose of calming any fear of a country that it might be loaded up with SDRs during the initial trial period before the system had been proven out. However, in the reform of the system discussed in the next chapter, these limitations are to be relaxed.

deficit variety, cannot persist indefinitely. The ability to sustain a deficit is based on the amount of international reserves possessed. The function of reserves, however, is to permit the financing of *temporary* deficits. No country possesses an inexhaustible stock of reserves that would permit it to finance deficits indefinitely.

It follows that any tendency for the balance of payments to display a persistent deficit must sooner or later be overcome. The process through which a deficit (or surplus) is eliminated is the adjustment mechanism.

We are familiar from an earlier discussion (in Chapter 16) with the principle types of adjustment mechanism: through changes in relative national income or price levels, through movements in exchange rates, or through the imposition of direct controls over foreign transactions. The Bretton Woods system, it will be recalled, generally outlaws (with certain exceptions) the employment of direct controls. This leaves changes in income or prices or in exchange rates as possible methods of adjustment. However, a basic principle of the Bretton Woods system is that exchange rates are to be held stable, unless a "fundamental disequilibrium" warrants exchange rate adjustment.

On the presumption that by "fundamental disequilibrium" is meant a tendency toward a continuing disequilibrium—in contrast to temporary, reversible payments imbalances—the Bretton Woods system thus implicitly recognizes the repegging of exchange rates as a principal means of adjustment. At the same time, the obligation to maintain stable rates of exchange in the face of temporary disequilibrium makes the distinction between fundamental and temporary disequilibrium of crucial importance. The operational difficulty encountered has been the timely recognition of the presence of fundamental disequilibrium.

Although several exchange rate adjustments were in fact adopted by various members of the IMF prior to the breakdown of the system in August, 1971,[4] the general tendency was for countries to resist

---

[4] The principal exchange rate revisions were made by major European currencies in 1949, by France in 1957 and 1958, by Germany and the Netherlands in 1961, by the United Kingdom and a number of other countries tied to sterling in 1967, by France and Germany again in 1969. In all the above, except for Germany and the Netherlands—the currencies of which were revalued upward—devaluations occurred. Besides the above repegging of rates, the Canadian dollar, as a special case, was allowed to float without official peg from 1950 to 1962. In the latter year, the Canadian dollar was once again assigned an official par value, which was maintained until the reinstitution of a floating rate in 1970. Also, the German mark was allowed to float in May, 1971.

adjusting rates until forced to by the pressure of their balance-of-payments position. Resistance to changing the official par value of a currency stems from several different sources. Devaluation is frequently opposed as an indication of the failure of the government's policies and as a loss of national prestige. Upward revaluation of a currency is also commonly resisted, with opposition especially strong on the part of the economy's export industries (the markets of which tend to be contracted as the result of the revaluation).

In the face of a persistent tendency toward balance-of-payments disequilibrium, the failure appropriately to change the international value of a currency implies either the operation of other adjustment mechanisms or the cumulative worsening of the disequilibrium. Frequently, alternative adjustment mechanisms are not acceptable. Adjustment through price and income changes may conflict with domestic goals of full employment and price stability. Adjustment through quantitative controls distorts the allocation of resources and reduces economic efficiency. Consequently, the tendency is to adopt a "wait-and-see" attitude, hoping that somehow the disequilibrium will correct itself in time.

The use of exchange rate adjustment only as a last resort has several unfortunate aspects. Maladjustments will have accumulated and the disequilibrium deepened, requiring a larger rate adjustment than would have been necessary earlier. Moreover, undue delay in correcting disequilibrium can easily cause an aggravation of the problem from speculative flows of capital. Thus, the longer a deficit balance of payments continues the more probable becomes an eventual depreciation of the currency, and the longer a surplus balance of payments continues the more probable becomes an appreciation of the currency. Hence, the risk of capital loss from transferring funds from deficit to surplus countries is virtually nil, while the prospect for capital gain is great. With the cards stacked in favor of such speculative capital movements, there is a built-in tendency toward worsening the disequilibrium.

The additional pressure on the exchange market from speculative capital flows compounds the problem of choosing the equilibrium exchange rate at which the currency should be repegged. There is no reliable method of predetermining equilibrium rates, and the deeper the disequilibrium is, the more difficult the problem becomes. As we observed earlier, the purchasing-power-parity theory—which states that equilibrium rates are determined by relative national price level changes since some prior equilibrium period—cannot be relied upon, especially when structural changes have occurred. In the final analysis, only experience with an exchange rate will reveal whether or not it is an equilibrium rate.

Because of the difficulty in predetermining equilibrium rates of exchange, the risk is great that in repegging a currency the level chosen will either overvalue or undervalue it. An overvalued currency is one with too low exchange rates for equilibrium, leading to a continuing deficit in the balance of payments. An undervalued currency has too high exchange rates on other currencies, causing a balance-of-payments surplus to develop. In most instances, a deficit country unsure of the correct equilibrium rate prefers to err in the direction of undervaluation in setting a new rate to avoid the risk of having soon to repeat the operation. But, of course, this tends to result in a surplus disequilibrium for the depreciating country and a deficit for others. For example, it is probable that the European devaluations in 1949 were excessive and bear some responsibility for the deficit balance of payments of the United States in the years following.

THE CONFIDENCE PROBLEM

The confidence problem manifests itself in large-scale speculative capital movements, usually induced by the expectation of an imminent sharp exchange rate movement. As noted above, such an expectation is commonly based on the failure of balance-of-payments adjustment in the face of persisting disequilibrium. Thus, the confidence problem is largely a by-product of the adjustment problem.

Speculative capital movements can occur in nearly any kind of international monetary system. As will be recalled from a previous discussion (see pp. 335–36 above), speculative capital movements are normal in both a floating exchange rate system and a fixed-rate system. It is also to be noted that such capital movements can be stabilizing as well as destabilizing.

However, the Bretton Woods adjustable-peg system was peculiarly vulnerable to sudden, massive destablizing speculative capital flows, followed by relatively large exchange rate adjustments. The reasons for this vulnerability have already been given in the previous section: delay in adjustment, requiring finally a sharp change in exchange rates, and the absence of any significant risk from transferring short-term funds out of countries with continuing deficits into surplus countries.

Several crises of confidence in particular currencies were experienced during the 1960s. For example, a continuing deficit in the balance of payments of the United Kingdom, accompanied by dwindling official reserves, suggested in 1967 that the pound would soon be devalued. The withdrawal of foreign-owned capital from England put additional pressure on the pound and the expected devaluation was realized in November, 1967, with the value of the pound reduced from approximately $2.80 to $2.40.

Another episode of international monetary crisis occurred during 1968–69. The stage was set by the persistent balance-of-payments *surplus* of West Germany, leading to widespread anticipation of an *upward* revaluation of the mark. As a consequence, huge amounts of foreign short-term capital flowed into Germany, creating an embarrassing accumulation of reserves in the hands of the monetary authority. (The monetary authority was obliged to purchase excess supplies of foreign currencies in order to keep the mark near its official par value.) The counterpart of the inflow of capital into Germany was, of course, an *outflow* of capital from other countries. Especially hard hit was France, whose economy and balance of payments were suffering from the dislocations caused by riots and strikes in the spring of 1968. The already existing prospect of devaluation of the franc, combined with the anticipation of a higher valued mark, set off an extensive flow of funds out of France, mainly into Germany. To stem the tide and protect French reserves, the government imposed stringent exchange controls. The crisis cooled, but the final settlement came only after both the mark and the franc were revalued—the former upward, the latter downward.

The system was able to weather—albeit somewhat shakily—the above and other similar crises, until 1971, when the United States dollar came under speculative attack. The events that followed marked the collapse of the Bretton Woods system as it had operated until that time. It is therefore worth examining in some detail this culminating crisis of confidence.

THE DOLLAR CRISIS, 1971

As background, it is important to recall the key role of the United States dollar in the Bretton Woods system. Although gold was intended to be the standard in terms of which members of the International Monetary Fund were to fix the par values of their currencies, in practice the dollar evolved as the operating standard for most countries. However, the dollar, in turn, was tied to gold in a specified relationship and was freely convertible, for official foreign holders, into gold at the specified par value ($35 per ounce), so that other currencies were, at one remove, also tied to gold.

Maintaining their exchange rates stable in terms of the dollar, countries typically kept a large fraction of their international reserves in the form of dollar balances and short-term dollar securities. As noted in an earlier discussion, the proportion of total international reserves consisting of dollars steadily increased with the continuing deficit in the United States balance of payments and the dwindling flow of new gold into monetary reserves. The dollar thus also became the principal "intervention currency"—that is, the currency which monetary authorities sold or bought in foreign exchange markets to keep exchange rates within the 1 percent margin around par values prescribed by the Bretton Woods agreement.

The status of the dollar as an international reserve asset rested fundamentally on the strength of the United States economy and its leading position in the world economy. The symbol of the dollar's status was its convertibility, at a fixed ratio, into gold upon the demand of official foreign holders of dollars. However, the ability of the United States to maintain convertibility into gold declined because of a continuing balance-of-payments deficit, accompanied by an ever-increasing accumulation of dollars in the possession of foreign official agencies.

Uneasiness about the future of the dollar grew as the balance-of-payments position of the United States deteriorated after the mid-1960s. The deterioration was manifested in a reversal of the long-time trade surplus into a trade deficit, while the volume of foreign payments to finance the Viet-Nam conflict and an increasing amount of private overseas investments was expanding. It became increasingly evident that the dollar was overvalued—that is, that the exchange rate of the dollar on other currencies was generally too low—and that a devaluation of the dollar was going to be necessary to correct the United States balance-of-payments deficit.

Expectations that the dollar would soon be devalued reached a climax in early 1971. A massive outflow of short-term capital from the United States ensued. During the first three quarters of 1971 the United States balance-of-payments deficit jumped to an annual rate of some $23 billion, as measured by the so-called "Net Liquidity" basis, or $31 billion as measured by the "Official Reserve Transactions" basis.[5] In the previous year, the Net Liquidity deficit had been less than $4 billion and the Official Reserve Transactions deficit less than $10 billion. Clearly, a realignment of the international value of the dollar could no longer be postponed.

But a problem presented itself: How could the United States effectively raise exchange rates on other currencies? The dollar could be devalued in terms of gold simply by raising the official dollar price of gold. However, devaluation would not change exchange rates as long as other currencies remained tied to the dollar. The position of the dollar as the effective international standard seemed to foreclose the option of exchange rate realignment between the dollar and other currencies through unilateral action by the United States. Effective devaluation of the dollar in terms of other currencies required the cooperation of other countries in agreeing to increase the dollar value of their currencies. However, by mid-August, 1971, the dollar crisis had reached a stage that demanded immediate action, whereas extended negotiations would be required to obtain an internationally agreed new set of exchange rates.

It was in this setting that the United States acted unilaterally to meet the mounting pressure on the dollar. On August 15, 1971, President Nixon announced the suspension of the convertibility of the dollar into gold, accompanied by certain other measures, in particular a temporary 10 percent surtax on imports.

Closing of the "gold window" represented a sharp break with a long historical tradition of maintaining convertibility of the dollar into gold. More than that, it meant removal of the anchor holding exchange rates in a predetermined pattern, as provided in the Bretton Woods system. The exchange rate of the dollar on other currencies was no longer narrowly fixed, but depended upon what action other countries would take with respect to the dollar value of their currencies. Only in the event that foreign official agencies were willing to purchase enough dollars to prevent appreciation of their cur-

---

[5] *Economic Report of the President, 1972* (Washington, D.C.: U.S. Government Printing Office, 1972), p. 150. The Net Liquidity measure of the deficit is the sum of the net balances on the current account, long-term capital account, nonliquid short-term private capital account, and the errors-and-omissions account (presumed to be largely unrecorded private capital flows). The Official Reserve Transactions measure consists of net changes in the government's liabilities to foreign official agencies, plus net changes in official reserve assets.

rencies vis-à-vis the dollar would exchange rates remain unaffected by the closing of the United States gold window. Not surprisingly, in view of the nearly certain near-term decline in the value of the dollar below its previous level, few countries were willing to add to their already large holdings. Thus, the international value of the dollar began to float, depreciating against most other major currencies. Obviously, the Bretton Woods system of stable exchange rates had collapsed. But had it collapsed permanently or only temporarily?

The monetary authorities of the leading trading countries certainly were not prepared to replace stable exchanges with floating rates on a permanent basis. On the other hand, it was recognized that a greater degree of rate flexibility than previously was necessary. There were, therefore, two tasks to be undertaken: in the short run, the establishment of a new pattern of stable exchange rates that would correct the current balance-of-payments disequilibria; in the longer run, a reform of the system to remove the weaknesses that led to its breakdown.

The first of the above tasks centered on determining the appropriate realignment of exchange rates and the method of accomplishing the realignment. It was clear that the international value of the dollar had to be lowered relatively to most major currencies. By how much it should be lowered with respect to each other currency was a difficult question to resolve. One solution (proposed by the United States) was to let the market determine the level of equilibrium exchange rates through a transitional period of the free floating of rates. This approach was rejected, however. The alternative approach—to negotiate a new pattern of rates—was agreed upon, and the negotiations were completed at the Smithsonian Institution in Washington in December, 1971. At the same time, the United States surcharge on imports was removed.

As the result of the Smithsonian Agreement, exchange rates among major currencies were significantly altered as compared to the rates in effect prior to August 15. The currencies of the two countries with the largest balance-of-payments surplus—Japan and Germany—had their dollar values increased by nearly 17 percent (Japan) and 14 percent (Germany). The dollar value of most other major currencies also increased, though by lesser amounts. Equivalently, of course, the dollar was depreciated.

In the process of establishing the new set of exchange rates, the United States agreed to devalue the dollar—that is, to lower its official gold content—by slightly less than 8 percent. (The devaluation became effective in May, 1972.) Many other countries did not declare a par value in terms of gold, but instead established a "central rate" in terms of the dollar. It was agreed that actual rates of exchange would be maintained within a margin of $2\frac{1}{4}$ percent on either side of par values or central rates. It will be noted that this represented an increase in the allowable margin of 1 percent provided for originally in the Bretton Woods system.

EMERGENCE OF FLOATING RATES

It was the expectation that the realignment of exchange rates accomplished by the Smithsonian Agreement would remove the underlying cause of the disequilibrium which had culminated in the crisis of August, 1971. Accordingly, it was thought that the new pattern of exchange rates would be sustainable until a basic reform of the system was agreed upon.

As it turned out, these expectations were realized for only a short period. The first break in the pattern of exchange rates established by the Smithsonian Agreement occurred when the British pound came under heavy pressure in the middle of 1972, leading to the decision by Great Britain to cease support of the exchange rate and to allow the rate to respond to market forces. Over the next six months the value of the pound dropped 10 percent below the level set the previous December.

Great Britain was not the only country experiencing balance-of-payments difficulties. At the same time that the pound was under downward pressure, the Japanese yen was subject to upward pressure, reflecting a large surplus in her balance of payments. Throughout the latter half of 1972, the Japanese monetary authority had to purchase large amounts of dollars in the foreign exchange market to keep the value of the yen within the limits prescribed by the Smithsonian Agreement.

During the course of 1972 it also became evident that the deficit in the United States balance of payments was not being corrected by the December devaluation of the dollar. Even though pressure on the balance of payments from speculative capital outflows had been removed, the "basic balance"—on the current plus the long-term capital accounts—continued to show the same large deficit incurred in

1971. The failure of the basic balance to respond quickly to the devaluation was hardly surprising, in view of the considerable length of time it takes for the effects of currency realignment fully to manifest themselves. Nevertheless, the continuing deficit of the United States, together with continuing disequilibria in the balances of payments of Japan and other major trading countries, led to increasing nervousness in exchange markets. By early 1973, barely more than a year after the Smithsonian Agreement, another international monetary crisis was brewing.

As usual, the principal manifestation of a crisis was a large movement of short-term capital, mainly out of the United States into Germany. During the first seven trading days of February, the German central bank purchased some $6 billion in order to prevent the mark from appreciating against the dollar. Such pressure on exchange markets made a second realignment of exchange rates unavoidable. Action was taken on February 12, 1973: the United States announced a further devaluation of the dollar, by 10 percent, to be accompanied by a corresponding appreciation in terms of the dollar of the six nonfloating currencies of the European Common Market (France, Germany, Belgium, the Netherlands, Luxembourg, and Denmark). At the same time, Japan and Italy rescinded their previous policies of maintaining stable exchange rates and joined Great Britain in allowing their currencies to float.

Market pressures quickly demonstrated that the new rate structure was not viable. The six nonfloating European Common Market currencies faced renewed market pressure in late February, followed by a closing of international exchange markets. This time it was decided to give up the apparently fatuous attempts to maintain stable exchange rates. At a conference in Paris, it was agreed that the remaining nonfloating Common Market currencies were henceforth to be allowed to float jointly vis-à-vis the outside world.[6] Thus, when exchange markets reopened on March 19, 1973, all of the world's major currencies were floating. The Bretton Woods system of stable rates, which had actually deceased in August, 1971, was finally buried. The transformation of the system from one in which exchange rates were pegged—with occasional repegging at different levels—into one in which rates fluctuated widely is pictorially illustrated in Figure 19.1.

---

[6] A "joint float" meant that the six currencies would float as a unit against the dollar, while maintaining stable rates—within a margin of 2.25 percent—among themselves. As for other Common Market countries, Britain and Ireland floated together and Italy floated alone.

FIGURE 19.1

COMPARATIVE EXCHANGE RATES
Major U.S. Trading Partners: Exchange Rates Relative to the U.S. Dollar*

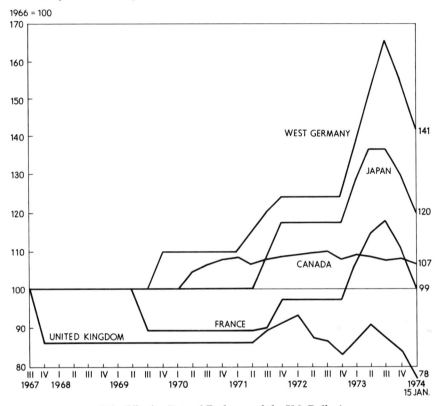

U.S.: Effective Rate of Exchange of the U.S. Dollar†

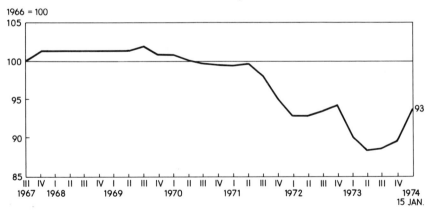

* The indexes are based on the central rates except in periods of currency float where the values shown are market rates.

† Derived from weights based on overall U.S. trade during 1972.

Source: *International Economic Report of the President,* 1974, p. 12.

RECOMMENDED READINGS

DUNN, ROBERT M., JR. "Exchange-Rate Rigidity, Investment Distortions, and the Failure of Bretton Woods." *Essays in International Finance,* no. 97. Princeton, N.J.: Princeton University, February 1973.

GILBERT, MILTON. "Problems of the International Monetary System." *Essays in International Finance,* no. 53, April 1966.

The International Monetary System in Transition, a Symposium. Chicago: Federal Reserve Bank of Chicago, 1972.

KAFKA, ALEXANDRE. "The IMF: the Second Coming?" *Essays in International Finance,* no. 94, July 1972.

MACHLUP, FRITZ AND MALKIEL, BURTON G. EDS. *International Monetary Arrangements: The Problem of Choice.* Princeton, N.J.: Princeton University Press, 1964.

MEIER, GERALD M. *Problems of a World Monetary Order.* New York: Oxford University Press, 1974.

MIKESELL, RAYMOND F. *Financing World Trade,* chap. 3. New York: Thomas Y. Crowell Co., 1969.

OFFICER, LAWRENCE H. AND WILLETT, THOMAS D., EDS. *The International Monetary System.* Englewood Cliffs, N.J.: Prentice-Hall, Inc., 1969.

STUDY QUESTIONS

1. Why was the International Monetary Fund slow in operating as intended in the early postwar years?
2. What is meant by the "liquidity problem"?
3. Why does insufficient international liquidity impose a deflationary bias on the world economy?
4. What determines the volume of international reserves in the form of gold?
5. How do other countries acquire reserves in the form of dollars?
6. What dilemma arose in connection with the use of dollars as a reserve currency?
7. Describe what SDRs are, how they are created, what purpose they serve.
8. What is the basic function of international reserves?
9. Explain the history of exchange rate adjustments in the Bretton Woods system.
10. What consequences followed from the resistance in the Bretton Woods system to timely exchange rate adjustments?

11. Why was the Bretton Woods system especially vulnerable to de-stabilizing capital movements?

12. What is meant by a "crisis of confidence" in a currency?

13. Describe the events leading to the dollar crisis in August, 1971.

14. What was the significance of the cessation of the dollar's convertibility into gold?

15. Why was it difficult for the United States unilaterally to devalue the dollar?

16. Describe the actions adopted in the Smithsonian Agreement in December, 1971.

17. Why did the realignment of exchange rates in late 1971 and again in February, 1973, not succeed in restoring stable exchange rates?

18. Investigate exchange rate movements of the dollar in recent months.

20

Reform of the international
monetary system

Shortly after the dollar crisis in August, 1971, the
Board of Governors of the International Monetary Fund adopted a
resolution at its annual meeting calling for a thorough study of the
"measures that are necessary or desirable for the improvement or
reform of the international monetary system." Less than a year later
a report was submitted by the Executive Directors of the Fund out-
lining various issues of reform.[1] In the meanwhile the Board of
Governors created a Committee on Reform of the International
Monetary System and Related Issues—popularly known as the "Committee of 20"—to work on specific proposals for reform.

It was originally planned that, based on recommendations of the
Committee of 20, a fully reformed monetary system would be
adopted within two years—that is, by the fall of 1974. It soon became
evident, however, that this timetable was too optimistic. Apart from
the inherent complexity of the issues, the difficulty of negotiating a
new system was compounded by the continuing uncertainty in exchange markets, aggravated by the international oil crisis and the
outbreak of worldwide serious inflation. Nevertheless, in June, 1974,

---

[1] *Reform of the International Monetary System*, A Report by the Executive Directors to the Board of Governors (Washington, D.C., 1972).

at the sixth and last meeting of the Committee of 20 an *Outline of Reform* was agreed upon.[2]

The Committee's Outline of Reform was presented in two parts. The first part is intended as a guide to future action, it being recognized that final reform of the system will have to wait until conditions in the world become more settled. The second part consists of interim measures intended to be implemented immediately. The principal provisions of each of these parts will now be examined in turn.

THE OUTLINE OF REFORM

The three major weaknesses of the Bretton Woods system identified in the preceding chapter—relating to liquidity, confidence, and adjustment—are all addressed in the *Outline*. Clearly, however, the seminal defect of the earlier system, and the one concerning which the most significant issues arise, was the excessive rigidity of exchange rates and the consequent absence of a satisfactory mechanism of balance-of-payments adjustment. We shall therefore begin with this aspect of the reformed system.

Adjustment Mechanisms

The central principle of the Bretton Woods system was the maintenance of stable exchange rates within narrow limits around declared par values, with changes in par values admitted only in the face of a "fundamental disequilibrium." This basic principle is retained as a guide to the future system but significantly modified in the direction of greater flexibility.

In the language of the *Outline,* "The exchange rate mechanism will remain based on stable but adjustable par values, and countries should not make inappropriate par value changes" (Paragraph 11). Moreover, changes in par values are to continue to be subject to the approval of the International Monetary Fund, with the intent of avoiding competitive depreciation or undervaluation of currencies. Considering how similar these provisions are to the Bretton Woods system, it may be asked in what manner greater flexibility has been introduced.

The most far-reaching modification—and, in the light of earlier

---

2 The text of the *Outline of Reform,* with accompanying annexes, is given in a supplement to the *IMF Survey,* June 17, 1974, pp. 193–208.

attitudes on the part of monetary officials, astounding innovation—is the admission of floating exchange rates as one possible response to balance-of-payments disequilibrium. To be sure, the *Outline* makes it clear that the floating of rates is not to be regarded as the norm but adopted only in "particular situations." Moreover, floating rates are to be subject to authorization, surveillance, and review by the International Monetary Fund, in accordance with agreed guidelines (discussed later). If a country fails to conform with these guidelines, or if the Fund decides that continued floating is "inconsistent with the international interest," authorization to float may be withdrawn.

Notwithstanding the restrictions imposed on rate floating, its admission into the system represents a major modification of earlier practice. Undoubtedly, the change in attitude toward floating rates was the consequence of the manifest inability to restore stable rates in the period following the breakdown of Bretton Woods, together with the absence of any disastrous experience with floating rates during that period. The pragmatic necessity of admitting the legitimacy of floating rates in particular circumstances is further recognized in the *Outline* by its acceptance as the general system to be in operation during the interim period, prior to the full establishment of the permanent system sometime in the future, as discussed below.

If exchange rate floating is to be resorted to only in unusual circumstances, what is to be the "normal" means of correcting balance-of-payments disequilibrium? As in the Bretton Woods system, if acceptable domestic measures are inadequate, a change in par values is retained as the principal method of adjustment. However, in an obvious effort to overcome the excessive resistance to rate adjustments experienced earlier, the *Outline* places much greater emphasis on this means of correcting disequilibrium.

To begin with, countries are exhorted to make "appropriate" par value changes *promptly,* and it is suggested that the International Monetary Fund may establish simplified procedures for approving small changes in par values.

Secondly, exchange rate adjustment is to be undertaken when needed to avoid protracted payments imbalances by surplus as well as deficit countries. (The intent here is to remove the asymmetrical pressure on deficit countries, as in the past.)

Thirdly, the IMF is to have an enlarged role as overseer of the adjustment process. The world payments situation in general and the balance-of-payments position of particular countries are to be kept under continuing surveillance. The surveillance function is to be assigned to a new organ, the "Council," that will have the "necessary decision-making powers to supervise the management and adaptation of the monetary system, to oversee the continuing operation of the adjustment process and to deal with sudden disturbances which might threaten the system" (Paragraph 31). The Executive Board is to serve as an arm of the Council in the discharge of its functions.

If it is determined that a member country is in payments imbalance, the country is expected to consult with the Fund concerning its situation and the measures proposed to be taken. An assessment by the Executive Board "will establish whether there is a need for adjustment." Once it is decided that adjustment is needed, the country is expected to take appropriate action to correct its payments imbalance. If it does not do so, the "Fund will have available graduated pressures to be applied" to the country. What precisely such pressures would be has not been agreed upon, though various possibilities are suggested in Annex 2 of the *Outline*.

Whether or not the Fund will be in a position to impose effective sanctions against countries failing to adhere to suggested adjustment policies is a moot question that only future events can clarify. However, it is significant that agreement has been reached to extend the authority of the Fund beyond the limits previously enjoyed. As the chairman of the Committee of 20 stated, "The reformed system aims to take a step forward to greater international authority in all the main areas, but not a frighteningly large step."[3]

The SDR and Reserve Assets

The second major area of reform contained in the *Outline* relates to the international standard unit of account and the reserve-creating process.

As we observed in earlier discussions, in the Bretton Woods system gold was the ultimate standard in terms of which the par values of currencies were expressed. As the system evolved, only the United States dollar was directly tied to gold, with most other currencies defined in terms of the dollar. An accompanying characteristic of the system was the role of the dollar as well as of gold as international reserve assets. Both the liquidity and the confidence problems described in the preceding chapter were to a large extent the consequence of these arrangements.

The anachronism of gold serving as the international standard of value—or *numeraire*—has long been pointed out by academic econ-

---

[3] *IMF Survey,* June 17, 1974, p. 189.

omists. A long step toward reducing the role of gold was taken in 1969 with the introduction of Special Drawing Rights (SDRs) as a kind of substitute for gold (see pp. 359–60, above). A major second step, approaching the final demonetization of gold, has now been taken in the reformed system by assigning to the SDR the status of *numeraire* in terms of which the par values of currencies are to be expressed. Presumably this action spells the end of the long history of insistence upon the need for the international monetary standard to consist of gold, silver, or other commodity.

Consistent with raising the status of the SDR to that of international standard is the *Outline*'s declaration of the SDR as the "principal" international reserve asset. While gold and certain national currencies may continue to serve as means of payments settlements, it is intended that their previous importance as international reserves be reduced as the SDR becomes the primary reserve medium. To make this decision effective, the *Outline* proposes several measures.

The first relates to satisfying the liquidity needs of the system. "As part of the better international management of global liquidity, the Fund will allocate and cancel SDRs so as to ensure that the volume of global reserves is adequate and is consistent with the proper functioning of the adjustment and settlement systems" (Paragraph 25). This wording strongly suggests that the volume of international reserves is to be subject to the discretionary management of the IMF to a much greater extent than previously.

The other measures are designed to make SDRs more attractive as reserve assets—by setting an appropriate interest rate (initially at 5 percent) on SDR balances, relaxing the original restrictions placed on their use and protecting their capital value. The manner of accomplishing the last named objective is left for future determination, but as an immediate step in that direction the Fund has announced that the SDR will be set equal to a "basket" of 16 currencies.[4]

---

[4] The currencies included in the basket are those of the 16 countries with a share in world exports in excess of 1 percent of the average over the period 1968–72. The relative amounts of the currencies in the basket were set broadly proportionate to the share of the countries in world trade, with the dollar, however, assigned a larger weight than its share of world trade. Thus, the basket consists of 33 percent dollars, 12.5 percent West German marks, 9 percent British pounds, etc. (See *IMF Survey,* June 17, 1974, p. 185.) As the value of any currency in the basket changes vis-à-vis other currencies in the basket, the value of the SDR in terms of that currency moves in the opposite direction. For example, if the dollar were to depreciate, the dollar value of an SDR would appreciate, while the value of the SDR in terms of the mark, pound, etc. would fall.

Special Provisions Relating to Developing Countries

The reforms described above relate to the most significant aspects of the international monetary system. Additional changes in the system for the most part concern technical matters of secondary importance, such as the management of reserve currency holdings and control over disequilibrating capital flows, which need not detain us here. One point of more substantive interest, however, relates to the special provisions for developing countries.

One of the "main features" of monetary reform listed in the *Outline* is "the promotion of the net flow of real resources to developing countries." The measures directed toward this goal are more in the nature of declarations of intent than specific programs. Countries with a deficit balance of payments are enjoined in their adjustment policies not to reduce the access of developing countries to their financial markets or development assistance; countries with surplus payments position are to seek to increase their aid to developing countries. Further, developing countries are to be given special consideration in the application of the general rules of conduct relative to adjustment processes and the employment of controls on trade and capital flows.

The issue concerning development finance that gave rise to the greatest controversy in the deliberations of the Committee of 20 relates to the so-called "link." The basic idea of the link, strongly advocated by spokesmen for developing countries, is to provide financial assistance to the latter through the allocation of Special Drawing Rights, thereby linking increases in the system's liquidity with aid to developing countries. To the extent that new issues of SDRs are allocated disproportionately to developing countries—rather than, as originally, in proportion to quotas in the IMF—command over the world's resources is transferred to such countries. At the same time, the SDRs would soon appear in the reserve holdings of other countries as developing areas used the SDRs to finance import surpluses.

Some countries, the United States among others, have opposed the link on the grounds that the creation of liquidity for monetary purposes and economic aid to developing countries should not be mixed. The *Outline* reflects the inability of the Committee of 20 to arrive at an agreement with respect to the link proposal, but it is described as a possible future arrangement. As perhaps a consolation to developing countries for the *Outline's* lack of firm commitment to the link, it is proposed that a new facility in the Fund be created to extend "longer-term balance-of-payments finance" to developing countries.

Immediate Steps

The reforms contained in the *Outline* as discussed above are for the most part intended as guidelines for future action, the Committee of 20 having concluded that, in view of unsettled conditions in the world economy, the process of reform must be "evolutionary." At the same time, it was felt to be necessary that immediate steps be taken to help resolve monetary problems caused by the energy crisis and widespread inflation.

The main thrust of the immediate measures proposed in the *Outline* is to minimize the instability in international monetary relations during the interim period of floating exchange rates. To this end two major steps were proposed.

The first, immediately adopted by the IMF, was to create a special "oil facility" under which resources will be made available to member countries to assist in meeting the balance-of-payments problems resulting from increased costs of petroleum. It is of interest to note that at the time the creation of the oil facility was announced (June 13, 1974), it was indicated that certain oil producing countries (in the Middle East and Venezuela) had provisionally agreed initially to provide to the Fund the equivalent of about three billion units of SDRs to finance the extension of credits under the oil facility.

The second "immediate step" contained in the *Outline* is to establish a set of "guidelines" for the management of floating exchange rates in the interim period pending the return to a system of par currency values. The guidelines are principally directed toward minimizing exchange rate fluctuations and avoiding competitive rate alterations. To this end, countries are enjoined to intervene in foreign exchange markets as necessary to prevent or moderate short-run "sharp and disruptive fluctuations" in rates and to resist longer-term rate movements if these are in response to "temporary" factors. However, members should not "act aggressively with respect to the exchange value of its currency"—that is, deliberately reinforce a movement in market rates—unless in pursuit of a "target" zone. In the latter case, the member is to consult with the Fund as to the reasonableness of the target rate zone. Further caveats on exchange intervention, designed to avoid adverse repercussions on other member countries, are included, all within the general prescription of close consultation with the Fund.[5]

UNRESOLVED ISSUES

If the *Outline of Reform* adopted in mid-1974 and described above is fully implemented, the international monetary system will be considerably different from that created at Bretton Woods, but it will retain one of the principal features of the latter—stable, though adjustable, exchange rates. As a consequence, the central problem of the Bretton Woods system—the timing and appropriate amount of exchange rate adjustment—will continue to be the major challenge confronting monetary authorities.

As we have seen, the proposed reforms address this problem and seek to correct the defects of the earlier system by introducing greater flexibility of exchange rates and increasing the sensitivity of the adjustment process. Nevertheless, by retaining a system of par rates of exchange with a limited range of permitted variation as the norm, the issue of rate adjustment is not resolved but simply placed in a different context.

Automatic versus Discretionary Decisions

As the Chairman of the Committee of 20 has stated, "The reformed system is an *internationally managed* system."[6] Management requires, however, that there be some set of operating rules to guide policy decisions. These rules can be largely automatic or discretionary. A prime example of an automatic system is the so-called "crawling peg," which deserves a brief description.

Crawling Pegs. In a crawling peg system ("sliding" or "gliding" parities are other names used) daily fluctuations in exchange rates would be confined within relatively narrow limits around par rates, but the latter would not be fixed. Par exchange rates would be determined by a moving average of actual market rates over some predetermined period of the immediate past. Thus, if actual market rates have been rising toward the upper limit of the previous par, the latter would be adjusted upward. The amount of rate adjustment,

---

[5] For a detailed statement of the guidelines see the IMF Press Release No. 74/30, reproduced in *IMF Survey,* June 17, 1974, pp. 181–83.

[6] Address by Jeremy Morse, reported in *IMF Survey,* June 17, 1974, p. 188. Italics supplied.

however, would be very small over short periods, being limited to, say, no more than 1/26 percent each week and 2 percent each year.

A major advantage of crawling pegs is that it permits continual adjustment to payments imbalance through the exchange rate. In addition, because of the narrow limits of rate movements over short periods, destabilizing capital movements would be discouraged.

Objective Indicators. Somewhat less automatic than crawling pegs but serving the same purpose is the adoption of a set of "objective indicators" of the appropriateness of rate adjustments to serve as a guide to policy decisions. This approach was submitted early by the United States as its principal proposal for reforming the system.[7]

With exchange rates maintained within relatively narrow margins around par values, payments imbalance manifests itself in changes in international reserves, a deficit country losing reserves, a surplus country gaining reserves. Hence, the United States Secretary of the Treasury in presenting his proposal for reform suggested that "Disproportionate gains or losses in reserves may be the most equitable and effective single indicator we have to guide the adjustment process."[8]

The advantages of such a system are thought to be twofold: it would place pressure on countries to take timely action to correct serious disequilibrium, and it would remove the usual asymmetry between the positions of deficit and surplus countries.

The principle of objective indicators found expression in the *Outline of Reform* but in a qualified way that removes them far from being an automatic guide to exchange rate decisions. Thus, in its consulting and surveillance functions with respect to the need for balance-of-payments adjustment, the IMF "will attach major importance to disproportionate movements of reserves" (Paragraph 7 of the *Outline*) but as only one of several other criteria.

The *Outline of Reform* makes it clear that, in the last analysis, the system proposed will depend upon its proper discretionary management in the context of consultation and cooperation through the International Monetary Fund. How well the system will function once it is fully operative only experience will tell, but many economists are strongly skeptical of the prospects for success of any system dependent upon discretionary management and regard freely floating exchange rates as the optimal system. However, since a floating rate system is apparently not acceptable to policy makers (except as a

---

[7] See *IMF Survey*, August 9, 1972, pp. 70–72.

[8] Ibid., p. 71.

temporary deviation from the norm), it is of interest to examine in this concluding section the theoretical advantages which a flexible rate system, properly managed, might have.

THE MANAGEMENT OF EXCHANGE RATES TO ACHIEVE INTERNAL-EXTERNAL BALANCE

At a purely theoretical level, a system of managed exchange rates has certain potential advantages over both freely floating and fixed-rate systems. The advantages arise out of the option to employ the exchange rate as a policy variable subject to discretionary management—an option not available under either of the other two systems. The exchange rate is a very important element in economic relations. If the rate is rigidly fixed, then other variables must adjust to the fixed rate. If the exchange rate floats freely in response to market demand and supply, then monetary and fiscal authorities are denied its power as an instrument for achieving both internal and external goals.

The generally accepted internal national goals, relevant in the present context, are full employment and the maximum degree of price stability consistent with full employment. The term "internal balance" is used to describe this goal. The external goal, identified as "external balance," is balance-of-payments equilibrium without the use of distorting restrictions on trade and long-term capital movements.

Internal and external balance are interdependent. The link directly connecting them is the balance of trade, which appears as a component both in the income equilibrium equation and in the balance-of-payments equilibrium equation, as follows:

$$(1)\ Y = C + I + (X - M)$$
$$(2)\ B = (X - M) - K = 0$$

The first equation states that income is in equilibrium when aggregate output or supply, Y, is matched by aggregate demand, consisting of consumption (C) and investment (I) expenditure, plus the difference between exports (X) and imports (M). (Government expenditure as a component of aggregate demand is not separately identified for simplicity but may be regarded as included in C and I.) The second equation states that the balance of payments, B, is equal to the trade balance—exports minus imports—minus any net long-term capital outflow, K. The condition for balance-of-payments equilibrium is that B equal zero—that is, a positive trade balance equal to a net long-term capital outflow, or a negative trade balance equal to a net long-term capital inflow (with K being negative in the latter case).[9]

It is clear, as was earlier learned (see p. 312 ff., above) that income equilibrium and balance-of-payments equilibrium may not coexist. However, since imports vary directly with changes in income, there is always some level of income which will produce balance-of-payments equilibrium. Unfortunately, that level of income may be too low (or too high) for internal balance, causing either domestic unemployment or inflation. In other words, internal balance requires that income be in equilibrium at the full-employment level and with a minimum degree of inflation, whereas payments equilibrium may require a lower or higher level of income, accompanied, respectively, by unemployment or inflation.

The problem of reconciling internal and external balance when the rate of exchange is fixed arises because there are more policy targets than policy instruments available. The instrument for achieving internal balance is monetary-fiscal policy, regarded as a single policy variable capable of changing the national income to any desired level. With the exchange rate fixed, monetary-fiscal policy is also the instrument for achieving external balance, capable of changing the balance of payments in any desired direction. Both targets cannot be reached simultaneously with the one policy instrument, except fortuitously.[10] Suppose, for example, that a country is suffering from unemployment, accompanied by a payments deficit. To reach internal balance, an expansionary monetary-fiscal policy is required, but this would enlarge the external deficit. A similar "dilemma" situation is the coexistence of internal inflation and an

---

[9] The concept of balance-of-payments equilibrium employed here is equivalent to the so-called "basic balance" measure of equilibrium. A more general definition of equilibrium would include all *autonomous* capital flows, whether or not long-term. The rationale for using the present concept is briefly explained in footnote 10, below.

[10] In some models, monetary and fiscal policies are treated as separate instruments, thus meeting the requirement of an equal number of instruments and targets even when the exchange rate is fixed. However, this approach is based on a concept of external balance which admits interest-induced short-term capital movements into the equilibrium equation. Consequently, monetary policy, through its effects on interest rates, can produce external balance, while fiscal policy is assigned the target of internal balance. (For the original formulation of the model, see Robert Mundell, "The Appropriate Use of Monetary and Fiscal Policy under Fixed Exchange Rates," *IMF Staff Papers* [Washington, D.C.: International Monetary Fund, March 1972], pp. 70–77). However, net short-term capital movements are not consistent with long-term balance-of-payments equilibrium and have therefore been excluded from the external balance equation in the present discussion.

external surplus, since an opposite monetary-fiscal policy is called for in the two cases.

The admission of the exchange rate as an added policy variable can resolve the dilemmas and permit the simultaneous attainment of internal and external balance. In the first case, unemployment is taken care of by an expansionary monetary-fiscal policy, while the balance-of-payments deficit is cured by exchange depreciation. In the second case, inflation is removed by a contractionary monetary-fiscal policy, while the external surplus is eliminated by exchange appreciation.

The above may suggest that the simplest way of avoiding dilemma cases is to allow exchange rates freely to float. It is true that dilemmas would thereby be avoided, since external balance would automatically be produced by market forces, hence a single monetary-fiscal instrument would be sufficient to achieve the single policy target of internal balance. However, at a purely theoretical level, it can be shown that in some cases maintaining exchange rates stable would be preferable to allowing the rates to respond to the market.

Consider the situation of a country simultaneously experiencing inflation and a balance-of-payments deficit. If a contractionary monetary-fiscal policy is applied while the exchange rate is held stable, inflation is reduced and, *as a consequence of reduced inflation,* the external deficit is reduced. On the other hand, if the exchange were permitted to rise in response to the external imbalance, the problem of eliminating inflation would be aggravated because of the higher prices of imported goods and the reduction in imports and increase in exports the depreciation brings about.

A second case also favors maintaining stable exchange rates. Suppose that a country suffers from unemployment and a balance-of-payments surplus. An expansionary monetary-fiscal policy would work in the direction of restoring both internal and external balance without any change in the exchange rate. If the rate were to float downward in response to the external surplus, on the other hand, the problem of eliminating unemployment would be aggravated by the reduced exports and increased imports induced by the exchange appreciation.

The preceding discussion shows the theoretical rationale for a flexible exchange rate system. Optimum policies for internal-external balance in some circumstances include exchange rate adjustment, in other circumstances exchange rate stability. To be able to adopt optimum policy combinations obviously requires that the exchange rate be a policy variable, neither rigidly fixed nor automatically responsive to market pressures.

Unfortunately, the theoretical merits of flexible rates are not easily realized in practice. In the first place, there is the problem of properly managing the system in accordance with the set of appropriate guidelines. The difficulties of managing monetary-fiscal policies are well-known; adding the exchange rate as another policy instrument compounds the problem. Secondly, since exchange rates are inherently multilateral, in order to avoid inconsistencies or conflicts, their management must either be under a single authority or through the coordination of policies by separate authorities. Since a single international monetary authority is not feasible in the foreseeable future, separate national monetary agencies must coordinate their policies. The *Outline of Reform* clearly seeks to provide the framework for this coordination under the supervision of the International Monetary Fund.

RECOMMENDED READINGS

COOPER, RICHARD N. "Flexing the International Monetary System: The Case for Gliding Parities," in *The International Adjustment Mechanism*. Boston, Mass.: Federal Reserve Bank of Boston, 1970, pp. 141–56.

GRUBEL, HERBERT G. ED. *World Monetary Reform*. Stanford, Calif.: Stanford University Press, 1963.

HALM, GEORGE N. "Toward Limited Exchange-Rate Flexibility, *Essays in International Finance,* no. 73. Princeton, N.J.: International Finance Section, Princeton University, March 1969.

HIRSH, FRED. *An SDR Standard: Impetus, Elements and Impediments.* Princeton University, Essays in International Finance, no. 99, June 1973.

INTERNATIONAL MONETARY FUND, Washington, D.C. *Reform of the International Monetary System.* 1972.

――――. *IMF Survey* and *Supplement,* June 17, 1974.

KAFKA, ALEXANDRE. *The IMF: The Second Coming?* Princeton University, Essays in International Finance, no. 94, July 1972.

MACHLUP, FRITZ. *Plans for Reform of the International Monetary System.* Princeton University, Special Papers in International Economics, no. 3, 1962.

―――― AND MALKIEL, BURTON G. EDS. *International Monetary Arrangements: The Problem of Choice.* Princeton, N.J.: Princeton University Press, 1964.

MUNDELL, ROBERT. "The Appropriate Use of Monetary and Fiscal Policy under Fixed Exchange Rates," IMF *Staff Papers*. Washington, D.C.: International Monetary Fund, March 1972, pp. 70–77.

PARK, Y. S. *The Link Between Special Drawing Rights and Development Finance*. Princeton University, Essays in International Finance, no. 100, September 1973.

SWAN, T. W. "Longer-Run Problems of the Balance of Payments," in American Economic Association, *Readings in International Economics*, chap. 27. Homewood, Ill.: Richard D. Irwin, 1968.

TRIFFIN, ROBERT. *Gold and the Dollar Crisis*. New Haven, Conn.: Yale University Press, 1960.

WILLIAMSON, JOHN H. *The Crawling Peg*. Princeton University, Essays in International Finance, no. 50. Princeton, N.J., December 1965.

STUDY QUESTIONS

1. What was responsible for the failure to reform the international monetary system by the original target date?

2. According to the proposal in the *Outline of Reform*, how would you describe the exchange rate system to be established in the future?

3. What role is given to floating exchange rates in the *Outline of Reform?*

4. In what ways is exchange rate adjustment treated differently in the proposed reformed system as compared to the Bretton Woods system?

5. What is meant by the *numeraire* of a monetary system? What change in the *numeraire* of the international system has been made?

6. In what ways have SDRs been made more attractive as reserves?

7. Describe what is meant by the "link" and what purpose it would serve.

8. Why has the IMF created a special "oil facility"? How will it operate?

9. List some of the guidelines for the management of floating exchange rates proposed in the *Outline of Reform*.

10. In what sense is the proposed reformed system an "internationally managed system"?

11. Describe a "crawling peg" system.

12. What "objective indicator" was proposed by the United States?

13. Define internal and external "balance." How are they interdependent?

14. Describe two situations in which it would be desirable to maintain exchange rates stable, even in the face of external imbalance, and

two situations in which allowing exchange rates to respond to external imbalance would be preferable.

15. Why is the exchange rate a "policy variable" only in a system of managed flexibility?

16. What major difficulties do you perceive in the successful implementation of the reformed system proposed in the *Outline?*

21

The balance-of-payments problem of the United States

        The balance-of-payments evolution of the United States since the end of World War II illustrates the problems arising out of international monetary relations and offers us the opportunity to submit the principles we have been discussing to the laboratory of experience.

    The U.S. balance of payments had displayed four stages of development since 1945. The first stage, embracing the years 1946–49, was characterized by a huge balance-of-payments surplus and is often referred to as a period of "dollar shortage." The second stage, 1950–57, was a transition period, characterized by a "planned" deficit. The third stage, beginning in 1958 and lasting through 1970, was marked by a persistent unplanned deficit and is sometimes called the period of "dollar glut." The latest stage, which we may label the period of "dollar crisis and devaluation," began in 1971 and continues to the present time. Early in this period the international monetary crisis and the collapse of the Bretton Woods system occurred, followed by the widespread floating of exchange rates as described in Chapter 19. Because of these structural changes in the international monetary system we shall postpone discussion of the crisis stage until the next chapter.

DOLLAR SHORTAGE, 1946–49

The immediate postwar years were a period of reconstruction and rehabilitation of war-torn and disrupted economies. Western Europe, including Great Britain, had suffered the most damage, and the economic and political future of the Western world depended upon its speedy rehabilitation.

Europe emerged from the conflict with demands on her resources far in excess of her domestic capacity to meet them. A backlog of consumer wants, plus the requirements for restoring and expanding productive capacity through large investment expenditure, created a heavy demand for imports, while reducing the capacity to export. The ability to pay for imports with large international service income, as in prewar years, was seriously impaired by the war liquidation of overseas investments, the loss of shipping, and the temporary reduction in tourist travel in Europe.

In addition, structural changes in world trade had been produced by the war to the detriment of Europe's international trading position. In the prewar years, Western Europe had a substantial dollar balance-of-payments deficit settled with net earnings in other areas as an integral part of a system of worldwide multilateral settlements. But during and after the war, the position of the United States as a supplier so expanded that nearly all areas of the world became short of dollars, and the basis for the prewar multilateral settlement system was greatly weakened.

Finally, Western Europe was beset in the early postwar years with inflation and, until her currencies were devalued in September, 1949, with overvalued currencies. These monetary sources of disequilibrium served to aggravate the more fundamental real sources of difficulty and to obstruct the processes of adjustment.

Given these conditions, the prospects for Europe without extraordinary financial aid from the United States were portentous. Without a prolonged and agonizing period of adjustment, the possibility of restoring the prewar standard of living and of reentering a free and multilateral world trading system unencumbered by quantitative trade and payments controls was slim indeed. Politically, there was a great danger that democratic political and social institutions would collapse under the heavy strain of economic hardship and disorder.

In response to these threats, the United States adopted a variety of financial aid programs, the most important of which was the European Recovery Program—more popularly known as the Marshall Plan. Billions of dollars in grants and loans were made available to European countries. This aid undoubtedly provided the extra margin of resources making it possible for Europe to get back on her feet economically within a remarkably short space of time, and gradually to dismantle the direct controls over external trade and payments. Indeed, after a few years' transition, as we shall soon see, the Europe of 1946–49—confronted with economic and political collapse and a massive dollar shortage—was transformed into a dynamic economy of unprecedented prosperity and growth with a large dollar surplus in her balance of payments.

The phrase "dollar shortage" refers to the fact that Europe did not have enough current dollar earnings and dollar assets to draw upon to finance the import surplus required for her rehabilitation. Hence, the role of the extraordinary financial assistance extended by the United States was to fill the gap between Europe's needs and resources.

The counterpart of the rest of the world's (especially Europe's) dollar shortage was the surplus in the balance of payments of the United States. This is shown by the data in Table 21.1, which have been rearranged from the way they are ordinarily presented. Against the current account balance are set the means of financing it. It may reasonably be assumed that the $5.4 billion of private capital outflow and remittances represented autonomous and normal means of financing. This left approximately $26 billion of financing by other

TABLE 21.1

U.S. BALANCE OF TRADE AND MEANS OF FINANCING IT, 1946–49
(in billions of dollars)

Export of goods and services (excluding military transfers)	$67.0
Import of goods and services	35.1
Excess of exports	$31.9
Means of financing excess exports:	
U.S. private capital (long and short term)	2.9
U.S. private remittances	2.5
U.S. government financing:	
Loans	11.7
Grants (excluding military transfers)	13.1
Liquidation of gold and dollar assets	4.8
Errors and omissions	−3.1
Total Net Financing	$31.9

Sources: U.S. Department of Commerce, *Survey of Current Business,* various issues.

means, nearly all of which consisted of U.S. government grants and loans.[1]

Clearly, the export surplus of the United States could not have been nearly so large as it was had the U.S. government not extended grants and loans to foreign countries. Indeed, if the U.S. government had refused to extend foreign grants and loans, the rest of the world would have been *incapable* of running such a large current account dollar deficit. What, then, are we to say: that the dollar shortage of the world was *caused* by U.S. government grants and loans? Or that the grants and loans were made as a *result* of a shortage?

The question is largely one of semantics, for either point of view can be defended, depending upon one's perspective. It is quite clear that the financial assistance making possible Europe's import surplus and U.S. export surplus was in response to a huge excess demand for imports by Europe over the means of financing them without foreign aid. In this sense, at least, U.S. assistance represented accommodating finance, and the dollar shortage may be regarded as having been an independent phenomenon.

TRANSITION: 1950–57

By the end of 1949, the period of rehabilitation of Europe's economy was essentially over and extraordinary American economic assistance under the Marshall Plan terminated. U.S. government foreign grants and loans—apart from military programs—dropped sharply.

The improved dollar-payments position of the world showed up clearly in the increase of dollar and gold reserves of foreign countries. Whereas during the years 1946–49 the world drew down its gold and dollar reserves by nearly $5 billion (see Table 21.1), 1950 marked the beginning of a period of their replenishment. In the eight-year period 1950–57, the net recorded accumulation of dollar reserves and gold from the United States by other countries amounted to over $10 billion, as shown by the balance of payments of the United States given in Table 21.2.

From these developments it might be argued that not only was the dollar shortage ended, but that its opposite—a dollar "glut"—had already begun to develop. By a dollar glut is meant the presence of a

---

[1] The $4.8 billion liquidation of gold and dollar assets was offset to the extent of $3.1 billion by "errors and omissions," probably largely representing unrecorded (and for the most part clandestine) capital movements to the United States.

TABLE 21.2

U.S. BALANCE OF PAYMENTS, 1950–57
(in billions of dollars)

Export of goods and services (excluding military transfers)	$156.3
Import of goods and services	134.4
Excess of exports	$ 21.9
Means of financing excess exports:	
Private capital (net)*	10.8
Remittances	4.7
U.S. government grants and loans (net)	20.0
Total financing	$ 35.5
Excess of financing over export balance	$ 13.6
Increase in foreign U.S. balances and short-term dollar claims (net)	8.6
Purchases of gold from U.S. (net)	1.7
Errors and omissions (net)	3.3
Total	$ 13.6

* U.S. capital outflow, less long-term foreign investments in the United States.
Source: U.S. Department of Commerce.

balance-of-payments surplus of other countries vis-à-vis the United States—that is, a U.S. balance-of-payments deficit. As measured by the increase in foreign held dollar balances and gold outflow, the United States indeed did incur a balance-of-payments deficit.

Nevertheless, there are good reasons for not regarding the surplus dollar receipts of other countries during this period as evidence of a genuine dollar glut. It will be observed from Table 21.2 that the current account surplus of the United States continued, as in the preceding period, to exceed the net private capital outflow and remittances. Government loans and grants were therefore necessary to finance the excess. But the volume of assistance rendered was considerably greater than the amount needed to cover the dollar deficit of other countries. This was apparently the result of a conscious decision on the part of the U.S. government for the purpose of allowing other countries to reconstitute their international reserves, which had been seriously depleted during the war and early postwar period. Moreover, there remained during the period various quantitative restrictions by most other countries on their dollar payments. Had the market demand for dollar exchange not been held in check by artificial controls, no doubt the surplus dollar receipts would have been significantly reduced, perhaps eliminated.

In any event, it is clear that the world dollar-payments situation was significantly different from that of both the preceding years of dollar shortage and the following years of dollar glut.

DOLLAR GLUT: 1958–70

The objective data on the balance of payments for the period of dollar glut now under examination do not reveal any sharp changes in the structure of the international payments position of the United States compared to the preceding transitional period. As Table 21.3 shows, a large current account surplus continued to be realized, accompanied by a still larger deficit balance on capital and unilateral transfer accounts. What, then, distinguishes this period from the earlier one?

The principal difference is that whereas previously the United States regarded the deficit in its payments as a desirable and planned contribution to the restoration of liquidity in the international monetary system, the deficit after 1957 was neither planned nor accepted as desirable. Indeed, for the first time in memory the balance of payments became a cause for concern and anxiety both to the United States and to foreign countries.

It is true, as we noted in earlier discussions, that the continuing deficit in the United States balance of payments provided additional international reserves for other countries, thereby supplementing the inadequate growth in gold reserves and helping to overcome an increasing liquidity shortage. However, as other countries' holdings of dollars increased, the net reserve position of the United States deteriorated. At the end of 1957, the total liquid liabilities of the United States to foreigners was less than $16 billion; at the end of

TABLE 21.3

U.S. BALANCE OF PAYMENTS, 1958–70
(in billions of dollars)

Export of goods and services*	442	
Import of goods and services	387	
Balance on current account		+55
Remittances and pensions	−10	
Private capital (net)	−34	
U.S. government grants and loans	−42	
Errors and omissions	−11	
Balance on capital and unilateral transfer accounts		−97
Deficit on combined current, capital, and unilateral transfer accounts		−42
Means of financing deficit:		
Increase in liabilities to foreigners, plus decrease in reserve assets		+42

* Excluding transfers under military grants.
Sources: *Survey of Current Business*, various issues.

1970, the total was over $43 billion.[2] Moreover, United States reserve assets (of gold, drawing rights on the IMF, and foreign exchange balances) suffered a net decline from $23 billion to $14 billion over the same period. As a consequence of both these developments, the United States found itself in the uncomfortable position of having a ratio of foreign short-term liabilities to short-term assets far in excess of unity, in contrast to a ratio far below unity at the beginning of the period.

CAUSES OF THE U.S. DEFICIT

In seeking an explanation for the remarkable transformation in the U.S. balance of payments from a position of huge surplus in the early postwar period to chronic deficit after 1957, the data in Table 21.3 yield an important general clue. We observe that, in contrast to more usual deficit situations, the current account displayed a large net credit balance. Obviously, the deficit was the result of net debit balances on the capital and unilateral transfer accounts exceeding in total sum the current account credit balance. Given the very large outward movement of private capital, combined with the continuation of government foreign loan and grant programs, equilibrium required that the current account develop a larger surplus than was realized in fact. One way of stating the cause for the deficit, then, is in terms of the failure of the current account fully to adjust to changes in the capital and unilateral transfer accounts. This relates to what is known as the "transfer" mechanism, which is the adjustment process by which *monetary* transfers—capital movements and unilateral payments—are converted into *real* transfers in the form of the net movement of goods and services.

As a first approach to the reasons for the failure of the U.S. balance of payments to reach an equilibrium adjustment, let it be noted that the strains placed upon it were of an extraordinary nature. The strains were of two kinds. First is the sheer magnitude of the capital movements and unilateral transfers to which the current account must respond for equilibrium to prevail. A net outflow of capital plus U.S. government foreign grants and loans totaling over $75 billion for the 13-year period 1958–70 must be regarded as an unusually heavy burden for the balance of payments to bear.

Second, a high proportion of total U.S. foreign payments was motivated by political and military considerations having little or no

[2] *International Economic Report of the President,* February 1974, table 40, p. 104.

connection with market forces. In addition to government foreign loans and grants, included in this category are military expenditures abroad which averaged $3 billion per year during 1960–64 and $3.7 billion during 1965–67, reached $4.5 billion in 1968 and $4.9 billion in 1970. Since equilibrium adjustment in the balance of payments is largely dependent upon market decisions with respect to the import and export of goods and services, the presence of such large non-market transactions can be presumed to complicate the problem of adjustment.

In view of the huge size of the U.S. economy, there was no question of its physical *capacity* to produce an export surplus sufficient to match outward movements of capital and unilateral transfers. The problem, rather, was that market forces were not strong enough in the right direction to generate a matching surplus. Indeed, the trend at the end of the 1960s was toward a large reduction in the current account surplus of the United States, from an annual average of $5 billion during 1960–67 to only $1.6 billion during 1968–70.

The market forces determining the amount of an export surplus include as major elements aggregate demand and supply at home and abroad, price competitiveness, and the commodity pattern of trade. The influence exerted by each of these elements has varied during different periods.

An important structural factor was the changed supply situation in Western Europe as compared to the early postwar years. For the first few years following the war, Europe's productive capacity remained far below the demands upon her economy, while the U.S. economy, physically intact, easily was able both to meet pent-up domestic demand and to furnish extensive aid to other countries. The remarkable recovery and expansion of European productive capacity not only relieved the United States of the burden of continued massive assistance but transformed Europe from the status of a deficit supply area to that of a dynamic competitor of the United States in world markets.

This switch in the relative positions of Europe and the United States was fostered by several other developments. Accompanying Europe's economic expansion—and partly responsible for it—was rapid technological advances, while many American industries were operating with outmoded equipment and techniques. As a result of the improved efficiency of its industries and the lag in U.S. industries, productivity per man-hour in Europe increased during the 1950s at a more rapid rate than in the United States. A similar favorable differential was enjoyed by Japan which, like Europe, was undergoing an extraordinary economic expansion.

The competitiveness of other countries in world markets was strengthened by price factors. All countries suffered inflation during and after the war, but the inflation in Europe was more severe than in the United States. This was an important contributing reason for the dollar shortage. The situation was radically changed in 1949 by a wave of exchange depreciation. The pound sterling was devalued by 30.5 percent. Others followed suit, though devaluing by a smaller percentage, until countries accounting for four fifths of world trade (excluding that of the United States) had realigned the dollar value of their currencies. Whereas previously European currencies generally had been clearly overvalued in relation to the dollar, this was no longer true. Indeed, for some countries the devaluation may have been excessive, leaving their currencies *undervalued*.

In any event, the major countries sharing world markets with the United States became increasingly capable after 1949 of competing with the United States in terms of price. American industry was no longer in a world "sellers' market," limited in its export sales only by the availability to other countries of dollar exchange. The competitiveness of other countries was sharpened by the vigorous efforts of their industries to expand export sales. Depending as a rule on exports to a much greater degree than their American counterparts, European and Japanese manufacturing firms display a responsiveness and adaptability to foreign demand for their products that is outside the tradition of most U.S. firms. Among other ways, this manifests itself in export pricing policies. Even though in their domestic operations foreign firms are generally no more competitive than U.S. firms, in the export field they are.

By the beginning of the period of the dollar glut in 1958, however, and for the next several years, the combination of a high degree of price stability in the United States and the resumption of inflationary trends in Europe still permitted the United States to realize a large export surplus, notwithstanding the adverse factors described above. This situation abruptly came to an end in 1964. Starting in that year and progressing through 1970, inflationary forces in the United States gathered momentum under the impact of a declining rate of unemployment and rapidly expanding aggregate demand. A not surprising accompaniment was a shrinkage of the export surplus, as noted previously.

Observing the trade position of the United States over the entire postwar period, it becomes clear that a deterioration had occurred. The long-term tendency has been for the volume of world trade to expand at a faster rate than world production. While U.S. imports have followed this pattern, its exports have not. This contrasts sharply with the experience of major United States competitors in world trade—especially West Germany and Japan—whose exports have expanded much more rapidly than world output. Thus, the United States share of total "free world" exports contracted from 21 percent in 1960 to 18 percent in 1970.[3]

Aside from the factors already mentioned as contributing to this result, certain structural changes were at work reinforcing the trend. One of these was the declining U.S. share of agricultural products in world trade. Since agricultural products account for roughly 15 percent of U.S. exports—a much higher proportion than for most other industrial countries—the effect was to brake the expansion of total U.S. exports.

A similar adverse effect was produced by the fact that while world trade in agricultural products had been relatively declining, trade in manufactured consumer goods had undergone the greatest expansion. The United States, however, is not a major exporter of such goods, nor did the proportion which they bore to U.S. total exports (about 12 percent of nonagricultural exports) change over the period. On the other hand, the U.S. import demand for consumer goods rose—to over 25 percent of total imports as compared to 17 percent in 1960.

In summary, the deficit in the U.S. balance of payments was the consequence of the failure of the current account to develop a credit balance sufficiently large to cover the net debit balance on autonomous capital and unilateral transfer accounts. This failure in turn was the result of changes in supply conditions, a declining price competitiveness of the United States in world markets, and structural changes in the pattern of trade unfavorable to the U.S. position.

RECOMMENDED READINGS

Hansen, Alvin H. *The Dollar and the International Monetary System.* New York: McGraw-Hill, 1965.

Harris, Seymour E. *The Dollar in Crisis.* New York: Harcourt, Brace & World, Inc., 1961. A collection of papers on various aspects of the balance-of-payments problem of the United States.

---

[3] United States Senate, Committee on Finance, *U.S. Trade and Balance of Payments* (Washington, D.C.: U.S. Government Printing Office, 1974), table 11, p. 14.

KINDLEBERGER, C. P. *The Dollar Shortage*. New York: John Wiley & Sons, Inc., 1950.

LARY, HAL B. *Problems of the United States as World Trader and Banker*. New York: National Bureau of Economics Research, 1963.

MACDOUGALL, DONALD. "The Dollar Problem: A Reappraisal," *Essays in International Finance,* no. 35. Princeton, N.J.: International Finance Section, Princeton University, November 1960.

SALANT, WALTER J., ET AL. *The United States Balance of Payments in 1968*. Washington, D.C.: Brookings Institution, 1963.

STUDY QUESTIONS

1. What is meant by dollar "shortage" and dollar "glut"?
2. Argue pro and con that the dollar shortage was not an independent phenomenon but was the result of U.S. foreign aid to Europe.
3. What circumstances during the period 1950–57 support the conclusion that the U.S. balance-of-payments deficit during that period was not an indication of balance-of-payments disequilibrium?
4. Review the implications of the U.S. balance-of-payments deficit for its international liquidity position.
5. Explain the meaning of the "transfer" problem.
6. State the requirements for balance-of-payments equilibrium when a country has net autonomous outward capital movements and unilateral transfers.
7. In what way did the economic recovery and expansion of Europe and Japan contribute to the shift from dollar shortage to dollar glut?
8. How did the widespread currency devaluations in 1949 affect the U.S. balance of payments?
9. What is meant by the statement that the devaluation in 1949 may have left European currencies "undervalued"?
10. What is the nature of the special strains placed on the U.S. balance of payments over the past several years?

22

Dollar crisis and devaluation

The year 1971 marks the beginning of a new era in the history of the United States balance of payments. The events during that year which set it apart from the preceding periods were twofold: (*a*) the pressures on the balance of payments which had been accumulating since 1958 finally exploded, and (*b*) as a consequence, the dollar was devalued, bringing down the keystone of the postwar international monetary system, as described in Chapter 19, and creating an entirely new balance-of-payments setting for the United States as well as for other countries. In this chapter, both these developments and their aftermath will be explored. As a prelude, it will be instructive to investigate why the balance of payments of the United States was allowed to deteriorate into a crisis situation.

THE FAILURE TO ADJUST

We concluded in an earlier discussion that the fundamental weakness of the Bretton Woods monetary system was the absence of an efficient adjustment mechanism. This weakness extended to the United States in magnified form. Because of the central status of the dollar as a reserve currency and operating international standard, the United States did not have the option enjoyed by other countries of exchange rate adjustment. Consequently, the United States was confronted with the choice of either pursuing a policy of "benign neglect" or of attempting to correct its payments deficit by other means.

Benign Neglect

A policy of "benign neglect" means in effect ignoring the balance of payments. The rationale for such a policy can be found on either of two grounds.

One basis is, being denied adjustment through the exchange rate, no other acceptable effective means of adjustment are available, leaving inaction the least undesirable course to follow. Such an option would not be available to most countries, but the powerful position of the United States in the world economy made it a possible policy for her.

A more positive rationale for benign neglect was constructed on the grounds that the United States did not really have a balance-of-payments problem, notwithstanding conventional indications to the contrary. According to this view, the payments deficit of the United States was simply a reflection of the dollar's status as an international financial asset. Foreigners *wish* to acquire and hold dollars, not only as working balances in the conduct of international commercial relations but also as liquid assets that are at once safe and yield a return. In this latter respect the United States is like a bank, with international depositors holding short-term claims against it. While a bank needs reserves to meet net cashings of claims against it, the reserves necessary are only a fraction of its deposit liabilities, since only in crisis situations will the exercise of claims be more than a fraction of outstanding deposits. So, too, it was argued, the United States need not have international reserves greater in amount than a fraction of its foreign short-term liabilities.

The status of the dollar, which is demanded as a world money, has been dramatically displayed in the creation and development of the so-called Eurodollar market. Eurodollars are deposits in banks located outside the United States denominated in dollars. Tens of billions of such dollar deposits, held by foreigners as well as United States citizens and firms, are used to make short-term loans to a variety of borrowers, including governments. Borrowers in the market are frequently interested in acquiring dollars as a means of purchasing other currencies. Lenders are attracted to the Eurodollar market instead of domestic United States financial markets because of the higher rate of return that can be earned there.

The view that the United States balance-of-payments deficit was no cause for concern, being simply a reflection of the demand for dollars as an international liquid financial medium, may have been consoling to policy makers, but it was not completely convincing. Any implication that the United States could continue indefinitely to incur a payments deficit was certainly misleading. Even "sound" banks can overextend themselves and run into a liquidity crisis.

Skepticism as to the viability of a policy of benign neglect was warranted because of its implicit assumption that other countries were willing indefinitely to accept an international dollar standard. In this system, the responsibility for balance-of-payments policies would rest with other countries. If the United States were to continue to incur deficits in its balance of payments, those countries with surplus dollar receipts would have the choice of either further accumulating dollar balances or letting the values of their currencies in terms of the dollar appreciate. The United States could accordingly assume a passive role with respect to exchange rates and the balance of payments. The subservience of other countries to the dominating position of the United States implicit in such a system is hardly likely to make it acceptable.

Attempted Corrective Measures

In any event, benign neglect never became an established official policy of the United States. By around 1960, the government evidenced sufficient worry about the balance of payments to take measures for its relief.

Operation Twist

One of the most interesting early policies adopted went by the name of "operation twist." The basic idea here was to allow short-term interest rates to rise while holding long-term rates steady. The hope was that higher short-term rates would make dollar holdings more attractive to foreigners, while keeping long-term rates low would favor domestic economic growth. The policy was successful in keeping the intended differential in rates over the first half of the 1960s, but thereafter inflationary pressures pushed both short- and long-term rates upward, with the spread between them disappearing except for a brief period. In any case, the policy could not be expected fundamentally to change the balance of payments; its primary purpose was to reduce the conversion of dollars into gold—that is, to change the form in which the deficit in the balance of payments was expressed.

Capital Controls

A second major policy decision was reached in 1963. This was to restrict the outflow of capital from the United States. The first implementation of the decision was the imposition of a so-called "interest equalization tax," under which U.S. residents who purchased foreign securities have to pay a tax of up to 15 percent of the purchase price.[1] By thus making the net return on foreign securities less attractive, the outflow of capital in this form was discouraged.

Capital controls were extended in 1965 through a program of voluntary restraint on the part of American firms and banks and business firms with overseas investment and loan operations. Three years later, the voluntary program was transformed into a mandatory program accompanied by a considerable tightening of restrictions on capital outflows in the form of direct investments abroad. At the same time, new and more restrictive guidelines on the extension of foreign credits by banks and other financial institutions were instituted by the Board of Governors of the Federal Reserve System.

That the capital-control program of the United States had some success in reducing the payments deficit below the level it would have otherwise reached is fairly clear. However, the program has always been regarded as only a temporary device, and in his economic message to the Congress in 1969, the President affirmed the Administration's intention to relax and ultimately remove restrictions on capital movements (which in fact was done in 1974).

The rationale of capital controls as a method of reducing the U.S. balance-of-payments deficit is straightforward. As indicated in the preceding chapter, the outflow of private capital from the United States spurted around the middle of the 1950s to a new high level and became the largest monetary transfer debit item in the balance of payments.

---

[1] The tax was 15 percent for equity shares and for bonds maturing in 15 or more years, with lower rates applicable on bonds of shorter maturity. Securities of underdeveloped countries and of Canada were exempted.

It is incorrect to assume that a dollar's payment on capital account contributes a dollar to the balance-of-payments deficit. Some capital movements, in fact, involve no foreign exchange expenditure at all and are self-transferred in real terms. The chief example are direct investments in which plant and equipment are sent from the United States for installation in foreign branch plants. In such cases, the balance-of-payments deficit is unaffected. Foreign investments are also frequently accompanied by other kinds of transactions which provide additional foreign exchange receipts. Foreign firms with connections with U.S. firms may, because of the connections, purchase equipment from the United States, thereby expanding her exports. Another example are license agreements under which foreign firms are permitted to use patented processes in return for royalty or copyright payments to the American firm holding the patent or copyright.

Even when a particular capital outflow is unaccompanied by any direct return flow of receipts as in the preceding examples, there is an indirect feedback effect tending partially to compensate for the foreign expenditure. Over the long run, the most important feedback is the payoff from the loan or investment in the form of interest and dividends. The significance of this for the U.S. balance of payments is indicated by the magnitude of interest and dividend receipts from past foreign loans and investments. Since 1971 these receipts have exceeded $10 billion per year.

Interest and dividend receipts are not the only feedback from foreign loans and investments; the transfer adjustment mechanism works in the direction of expanding a country's export of goods and services in response to capital outflows. The mechanism consists mainly of increasing the income—and perhaps price level—of the countries receiving the capital, leading in turn to increases in their demand for imports. To the extent that the capital-sending country participates in satisfying this increased demand, its balance of payments adjusts to the capital movement.

Notwithstanding the above favorable feedback effects of capital outflows on the balance of payments, it is highly probable that such outflows have a net adverse effect on the balance of payments over the short and medium term. The payoff in interest and dividends takes several years to equal the initial principal amount of capital outflow. The transfer mechanism, as we explained in an earlier discussion, operates imperfectly and, in any event, slowly. The conclusion is that, while a dollar's capital outflow certainly does not add a dollar to the balance-of-payments deficit, it almost surely adds some significant part of a dollar. It follows that a reduction in capital outflow from the United States reduces the country's balance-of-payments deficit during the period in which the reduction occurs.

Nevertheless, there are strong objections to controls over capital movements, as there are to trade controls. First, they interfere with the most efficient use of resources, leading to allocative distortions which sap international trade and investment of their full potential benefits. Second, the United States, together with the other major trading countries, is committed to the principle of freedom of trade and payments, unless exceptional circumstances warrant a temporary deviation. The leadership of the United States in establishing this principle makes its own adherence to it all the more important. Third, as indicated above, capital controls are more in the nature of a temporary palliative than a method of fundamental correction of payments imbalance, since over the long run, interest and dividend receipts decline as a result of restricting capital outflows.

Redistribution of the Burden of Defense and Economic Aid

Comparable to the reduction of private capital movements as a means of relieving the balance of payments is the reduction of public capital and unilateral transfer outflows for overseas economic and military aid. This could be accomplished by unilateral action, but since foreign aid is an instrument of foreign policy, it is not easily amenable to significant change on balance-of-payments grounds. Alternatively, an effort could be made to maintain the total of foreign aid while reducing the share borne by the United States, requiring, of course, an increase in the share of aid contributed by other countries.

The United States in recent years has relied principally upon the second approach. Even though it has unilaterally reduced the amount of foreign economic aid, its foreign military aid has increased. On the other hand, a concerted effort has been made through diplomatic channels to obtain the acquiescence of allied countries to assume a larger share of foreign aid. How successful the campaign has been is difficult to determine. However, according to the published data, the aggregate volume of government loans and grants, excluding military grants, has remained relatively stable over the last several years at an annual volume close to $4 billion.

Ad Hoc **Measures**

The measures described are the most general that the United States has adopted to date to relieve its balance of payments. Other actions have been confined to a hodgepodge of piecemeal *ad hoc* measures of doubtful effectiveness and questionable justification. Among these are the following: a reduction in the duty-free goods American tourists are allowed to bring into the country; a program to encourage foreign tourists to visit the United States and Americans to see America first; the "tying" of foreign aid to U.S. goods— that is, requiring recipients of aid money to spend it in the United States; a tightening of "buy American" provisions in government procurement, discriminating further against foreign supplies; and an export promotion campaign directed toward business firms. It is doubtful that these measures yield any significant benefit to the balance of payments. At the same time, some of them (such as "buy American" practices and tied loans) constitute a disguised depreciation of the dollar and violate principles of trade and payments freedom to which the United States is committed.

DOLLAR CRISIS

The efforts of the United States to rid itself of payments imbalance through the measures described above were unsuccessful. The deficit in the balance of payments continued unabated through the decade of the 1960s. This was hardly surprising, since the measures adopted to eliminate the deficit were more in the nature of palliatives than cures, while the market forces producing the deficit underwent no fundamental change of direction.

Given the assumed inability of the United States to depreciate the dollar against other currencies, there was, in reality, no effective method of balance-of-payments adjustment available save one, and this was unacceptable from a domestic point of view. That potentially effective method was internal deflation through monetary and fiscal contraction.

The deficit in the balance of payments automatically worked to reduce money supply, but this effect was counteracted by domestic monetary policies, so that the money supply of the United States continued to rise over the years of payments deficits. In a similar manner, fiscal policy was generally directed toward domestic goals rather than to the balance of payments.

The reason for the failure to apply monetary and fiscal brakes on the economy is not difficult to apprehend. While undoubtedly effective as a means of improving the balance of payments, unfortunately such policies tend also to cause a slowdown in economic growth and unemployment. If restriction of money supply and aggregate demand had the effect only of reducing the price level while maintaining full-employment production, it would be a much more acceptable method of correcting the balance of payments. In fact, however, the downward inflexibility of wages and prices causes a contraction of aggregate demand to have its primary impact on output and employment rather than on prices. Full employment has such a high priority among national economic goals that its sacrifice for the sake of the balance of payments is not often acceptable. This is all the more so in view of the relatively large reduction in national income required to reduce imports. With a marginal propensity to import on the order of 5 percent, it would require a contraction in income of $20 to reduce imports by $1.

Twelve years of uninterrupted deficits and the apparent absence of any prospect for improvement in the United States balance of payments led, by 1970, to a spreading belief that some sort of drastic measure was in the offing. The nervousness thus engendered resulted, as usual under such circumstances, to a sharp reversal in short-term capital flows. Whereas in 1969 there had been a net inflow of foreign private liquid funds into the United States of nearly $9 billion, during 1970 there was a net outflow of over $7.5 billion. As a consequence, the Official Reserve Transactions balance displayed a large increase, financed by a big jump in short-term liabilities to foreign official agencies and a decrease in United States reserve assets.

The developments in 1970 confirmed the opinion of observers that a crisis was fast approaching. Accordingly, the outflow of dollars accelerated at the beginning of 1971, reaching massive proportions in the succeeding months. The deficit in the balance of payments during the first three quarters of 1971 rose to an annual rate of over $31 billion as measured by the Official Reserve Transactions balance and over $23 billion as measured by the Net Liquidity balance.[2]

The subsequent events were described in Chapter 19 and need be only briefly recalled now. The United States suspended the convertibility of the dollar into gold on August 15, 1971. In December, the Smithsonian Agreement provided for a widespread realignment of exchange rates, resulting in the depreciation of the dollar of be-

---

[2] *Economic Report of the President,* 1972, table 33, p. 150.

tween 8 and 9 percent.[3] During the course of the following year it became evident that the realignment of exchanges effected under the Smithsonian Agreement was not sufficient to produce balance-of-payments equilibrium. In the early part of 1973, a resurgence of capital outflows from the United States occurred, requiring foreign central banks to purchase $10 billion in order to support the value of the dollar in terms of their own currencies. This led to a second realignment of exchange rates, with a further devaluation of the dollar in February, 1973, by 10 percent, accompanied by the announcement that the Japanese yen was to be allowed to float. Again, the realignment of currencies did not succeed in restoring confidence. Speculative outflows of dollars continued, until in March, 1973, efforts to maintain stable exchange rates were abandoned. Thereafter, exchange rates of the major currencies were allowed to float.

THE EFFECTS OF DOLLAR DEPRECIATION

In the months immediately following the introduction of floating exchange rates in March, 1973, the dollar depreciated further below its last formal devaluation the preceding February. By the third quarter of 1973, however, the exchange value of the dollar had begun to recover, and by year's end was restored to approximately the level established after the devaluation in February. Thereafter, during the first half of 1974, the weighted exchange value of the dollar underwent only relatively minor fluctuations. It appeared that some reasonably stable exchange value of the dollar had been reached.

That exchange rate adjustments contributed to a major improvement in the United States balance of payments would seem to be evident. The current account of the balance of payments (goods and services, excluding unilateral transfers) underwent a turnaround of over $10 billion between 1972 and 1973—from a deficit of $6 billion to a surplus of over $4.5 billion—and this favorable trend continued into the first part of 1974.

Equally significant, the outflow of speculative capital from the

---

[3] To measure the effective change in the international value of the dollar when dollar rates of exchange on other currencies vary in different degrees, it is necessary to weight the different changes in rates according to their relative importance in influencing the international position of the economy. For a discussion of different weighting techniques, and measures of changes in the value of the dollar, see *Economic Report of the President*, 1974, pp. 220–26.

United States was staunched by the increased strength of the current account position and the apparent end to further large-scale decreases in the international value of the dollar. A return flow of short-term private liquid capital to the United States began after the attempt to maintain stable exchange rates was abandoned, so that by the fourth quarter of 1973 the net balance on this account displayed a positive entry of $3.6 billion, in contrast to the large net negative balance during the first quarter of that year.

Notwithstanding the correlation between improvement in the balance-of-payments position of the United States and the depreciation of the dollar, it would be a mistake to assume an exclusive causal relationship between the two. Other factors affecting balance-of-payments relationships have not remained constant while exchange rate realignments were occurring. For example, the dramatic improvement in the United States merchandise trade balance during 1973 was in some significant measure due to a world food shortage and the consequent rapid increase in United States agricultural exports. At the same time, an also rapid expansion in manufactures exports from the United States was in part attributable to a cyclical splurge in economic activity in the countries furnishing the major markets for these exports.

Although it is not possible to assign specific weights to the various factors responsible for improving the United States balance of payments, there is no doubt that (*a*) the dollar had become overvalued during the 1960s, and (*b*) removal of the overvaluation was a prerequisite for correcting the persistent balance-of-payments deficit.

Unfortunately, the progress made over the period 1971–73 toward establishing equilibrium exchange rates suffered a serious blow as the consequence of a huge increase in the price of petroleum and an acceleration in the rate of worldwide inflation.

The quadrupling of the price of oil following upon the restrictive policies adopted in 1973 and continued in 1974 by oil exporting countries created massive balance-of-payments deficits for oil importing countries, totaling to tens of billions of dollars in 1974. Even the United States, one of the countries least dependent upon imported oil, found the payments surplus which exchange rate adjustments and other factors had begun to generate during 1973 give way during 1974 to the reemergence of a sizable deficit. Other countries faced a much more serious payments situation.

In the absence of any relaxation of the restrictive policy of oil exporting countries, the longer-run outlook for balance-of-payments relations was rather bleak. In order for the trade in petroleum to be maintained, some means of financing the deficits of importing countries must, of course, be found. Oil exporting countries, especially Middle Eastern, cannot possibly use more than a small fraction of their enlarged revenue to increase their imports of other goods and services. Hence, these countries will accumulate huge amounts of foreign exchange—perhaps as much as $200 billion by the end of 1976. In order to avert an international financial crunch, at least a large part of these funds must somehow be "recycled" back into the hands of oil importing countries. The recycling could be in the form of foreign investments by oil exporting countries, long-term loans, and grants to developing countries, bilaterally or through multilateral agencies. In the absence of a sufficient return flow of financial resources to the oil importing countries, the latter could be forced to adopt deflationary policies, with serious implications for the stability and prosperity of the world economy.

Concurrent with and aggravated by the oil problem has been an acceleration of worldwide inflation. Nearly all countries are experiencing serious inflation, though to differing degrees. The inevitable consequence is continual disturbance to balance-of-payments relations and constantly shifting equilibrium rates of exchange (which is one of the principal reasons for not attempting in the near future to reestablish stable par rates of exchange).

The combination of the oil (and other raw material and food) shortages and inflation had created by the latter part of 1974 an atmosphere of impending crisis in the world economy, unmatched since the period of the Great Depression in the 1930s. Indeed, there was the growing fear that the United States and other major industrial countries were on the brink of once again falling into deep depression. That such a possibility was even contemplated was evidence that the world economy was confronted with problems extending far beyond merely balance-of-payments disequilibrium.

RECOMMENDED READINGS

ALIBER, ROBERT Z. *Choices for the Dollar.* National Planning Association, Pamphlet no. 127. Washington, D.C., May 1969.

BERGSTEN, C. FRED. *Global Role of the Dollar: Recommendations for the U.S. International Monetary Policy.* New York: Praeger Publishers, 1973.

DESPRES, EMILE, ET AL. "The Dollar and World Liquidity," *The Economist,* February 5, 1966, pp. 526–29.

HABERLER, GOTTFRIED AND WILLETT, THOMAS D. *A Strategy for U.S. Balance of Payments Policy.* Washington, D.C.: American Enterprise Institute of Public Policy Research, 1971.

McKINNON, RONALD I. "Private and Official International Money: The Case for the Dollar," *Essays in International Finance,* no. 74. Princeton, N.J.: International Finance Section, Princeton University, April 1969.

MEIER, GERALD M. *Problems of a World Monetary Order.* New York: Oxford University Press, 1974.

SWOBODA, A. K. "The Euro-Dollar Market: An Interpretation," *Essays in International Finance,* no. 64. Princeton, N.J.: International Finance Section, Princeton University, February 1968.

STUDY QUESTIONS

1.   What is meant by a policy of "benign neglect"?
2.   State the basis for the proposition that deficits in the United States balance of payments do not need to be eliminated but are simply reflections of its international financial position.
3.   What is meant by an international "dollar standard"? Why is it not likely to be welcomed by other countries?
4.   Describe "operation twist" and indicate what consequences it was intended to have.
5.   What feedback effects on the balance of payments can be expected from capital exports?
6.   Why would a dollar's decrease in capital outflow probably reduce the balance-of-payments deficit but by less than a dollar?
7.   What are the main objections to controls over capital movements?
8.   How could the United States have eliminated its payments deficits through monetary and fiscal policies? Why were these policies rejected?
9.   Briefly review the events leading to the dollar crisis in 1971.
10.   Why did the attempts in 1971 and again in early 1973 to establish stable exchange rates fail?
11.   Review the major changes in the U.S. balance of payments following the introduction of floating exchange rates in 1973.
12.   Even if the depreciation of the dollar was not alone responsible for reducing the U.S. payments deficit, why was it a necessary step?
13.   How did the oil crisis and inflation affect the international economy?
14.   What is meant by the "recycling" of oil dollars?

part four

The international economics of development

23

The challenge of economic development

The vast majority of the world's population is living close to the perilous border of bare subsistence. This no doubt has been the case for a long, long time, but only recently has it commanded the interest and attention it deserves. Today, the poverty in which the great mass of peoples live stands high, perhaps at the very top, of world economic problems demanding solution. The impoverished countries themselves place economic development first on the priority list of goals. Equally significant, developed countries, individually, and collectively through various international organizations, have joined the battle and declared their intention to help raise the standard of living of the poorer countries.

The reasons for the tremendous interest in economic development are several and varied. On the part of the less developed countries, there are the natural desire to participate in the fruits of economic progress so manifest elsewhere and an emerging consciousness that poverty is not an immutable state but a condition amenable to change through deliberate measures. For many countries with a newly acquired political independence and escape from colonial status, accompanied by the emergence of nationalist pride, economic growth is both a sign and prerequisite of independence.

413

Developed countries, for their part, have been motivated to accept the growth of less developed countries as an important goal and to help in its realization for humanitarian, political, and economic reasons. Of these, the political motivation has probably been dominant. On a general level, it has come to be widely believed that world peace and stability cannot be firmly established with the bulk of the world's population suffering from deprivation and seething with discontent, while the remainder of the world lives in relative affluence. On more particular levels, the economic development of certain countries is regarded as an important instrument of the foreign policy of the major powers. The interest of the United States in Latin America, of France in parts of Africa, and of the Soviet Union in Cuba are examples.

Whatever the motives are, the important fact remains that economic development has become a major concern of the contemporary world.

THE MEANING AND EXTENT OF UNDERDEVELOPMENT

It has become common practice to refer to certain countries of the world for whom economic growth is of paramount importance as "less developed countries," or LDCs, while others are labeled "developed countries." As the term implies, less developed is a relative condition. All countries, including the most advanced, are less developed than they are capable of becoming. There is, therefore, a considerable amount of arbitrariness in classifying countries as either "developed" or "less developed."

However, there is no useful purpose served in attempting to draw fine distinctions. The pragmatic basis for identifying the LDCs is per capita real national income. If the mean of the world's per capita income is taken as the line dividing the less developed from the developed countries, approximately two thirds of the world's population belong to the LDCs. The range of variation in income is huge: the per capita income of the richest country in the world is more than 60 times that of the poorest! Though there are enormous statistical difficulties in measuring and comparing real incomes of different countries, the margin for error without essentially changing the picture this figure evokes is wide.

Whatever income level is reasonably adopted as the criterion, it is clear from the data presented in Table 23.1 that the great majority of countries in Asia, the Middle East, Africa, and Latin America falls into the category of LDC.

TABLE 23.1
ESTIMATED PER CAPITA NATIONAL INCOME FOR
SELECTED REGIONS AND COUNTRIES, 1970
(U.S. dollar equivalents)

Regions and Countries	Per Capita Income (for the year 1970 unless otherwise indicated in parenthesis)
Developed Market Economies*	2,690
United States	4,294
Europe	2,070
Africa	180
Cameroon	166
Egypt	200
Ethiopia	71
Malawi	70
Kenya	131
Morocco	212
Uganda	127
Tanzania	94
Caribbean and Latin America	510
Argentina	1,000
Brazil	368
Chile	614
Bolivia	202
Colombia	366
Ecuador	250
Guatemala	337
Haiti	80
Mexico	353
Paraguay	230
Peru	293
Middle East (1969)	400
Asia (excluding Japan, 1969)	110
Afghanistan	83
Indonesia	93
Thailand	169
Malaysia	329
Philippines	228
Japan	1,658

° Europe, North America, Australia, New Zealand, Israel, Japan, South Africa.
Source: United Nations, *Yearbook of National Accounts Statistics,* vol. 2 (1974), table 1B, pp. 8–12.

THE MEANING AND PURPOSES OF DEVELOPMENT

If per capita real income is taken as the criterion of the state of economic development, the corollary is that *growth* in per capita real income is the measure of success in attaining the goal of development.

The emphasis on per capita real income derives from its being the single best, though by no means the only, measure of the economic welfare of a country. Real income consists of the flow of produced goods and services. The quantity of goods and services available for current consumption, investment, and government use is limited to the quantity domestically produced (plus any net inflow from other countries). Other things being equal, the standard of living or level of consumption in a country therefore depends upon the real income it produces. The standard of living of LDCs is low mainly because their real income, in relation to their population, is low.[1]

It is observed that it is not the toal national income, but income per head of population, which we have adopted as the chief indicator of the state of economic development. If the population of a country grows at the same rate as its national income, the base determining the standard of living remains unchanged. The presumed goal of economic growth, therefore, is an increase in real national income proportionately greater than any accompanying increase in population.

Because the rate of population growth in most less developed countries is high—and tends to increase as the death rate is lowered through improved medical conditions and nutrition—the difficulty of realizing growth is compounded. In recent years the gross output of developing countries as a group has increased at an impressive annual rate of about 6 percent, but the increase in population has exceeded $2\frac{1}{2}$ percent, leaving the per capita growth rate at only about 3 percent. Moreover, for the least developed countries, population increases have tended to match increases in output, leaving a zero rate of growth in per capita output.[2]

THE PROCESS OF ECONOMIC GROWTH

Economic growth is a complicated and many-sided process which defies simple analysis. We cannot pretend, within the space of a few pages, to do more than indicate briefly some of the major elements of economic growth, for the purpose of providing background for the understanding of the problem of developing economically backward areas.

---

[1] Per capita income, of course, is an average figure which conceals the extent of variations above and below. If income within a country is very unequally distributed, the mass of people have a very low standard of living even though average income is at a respectable level.

It should also be noted that income levels may be a poor indicator of living standards because of claims on output other than the current consumption. For example, to the extent that a country diverts its income to maintaining a military establishment, the availability of consumer goods and services is correspondingly reduced.

[2] See World Bank/IDA, *Annual Report 1973*, p. 7.

Sociopolitical Elements

Experience in recent years with attempts at economic development in various parts of the world is leading to wider acknowledgment than formerly that the process of economic growth is not only—and perhaps not even mainly—an economic problem. It can more properly be described as a social phenomenon, with cultural, political, and economic aspects.

A propitious social environment is indispensable for economic growth. A strong desire for an improvement in material living conditions and a reasonable prospect that energy devoted to this end will yield rewards are prerequisite conditions. To material-conscious Americans this may appear to be a far-fetched obstacle. But in many parts of the world, cultural values traditionally de-emphasize economic welfare. In part, the lack of drive for material betterment may be the product of a historic poverty, from which escape has only rarely been found on the part of individuals and which has come to be accepted as an immutable part of the natural order of things. Contacts with other cultures with a higher standard of living— whether through movies, tourists, radio, or GI's—tend, however, to weaken the hold of parochial cultural values and fatalistic acceptance of the status quo. But there probably has never been such a widespread urge to acquire higher living standards as there is today.

Still, economic development implies a plasticity of attitudes and institutions which cannot be created overnight. The illiterate peasant is not easily persuaded to change his timeworn methods of cultivation; the practice of having large families—as a means of providing old-age security or larger household earning power or, in some cases, as the result of religious or moral tenets opposing birth control—is not subject to sudden reversal; the social and sometimes legal barriers to occupational mobility may be formidable.

On a broader scale, governmental organization and administration in less developed countries are frequently outmoded and inefficient. Resistance to political changes is notoriously strong, especially when, as frequently is the case, nepotism and corruption have become standard practices. Reform of monetary, banking, and fiscal systems is particularly important in creating the basis for economic development. And in those not uncommon cases where landownership is concentrated in the hands of a few wealthy, absentee landlords, a reform program for the redistribution of land tenure may be required to give the incentive to greater productive effort.

Other examples could be cited of the social changes, often of a revolutionary character, in the habits, institutions, and general outlook of the people which economic development involves. Such considerations could easily lead to an extremely pessimistic outlook on the prospects of development in most of the presently less developed countries. There are several reasons, however—while fully admitting the difficulties and complexities of the sociocultural adaptations required for economic growth—for not adopting a defeatist attitude as to possibilities.

One reason is historical experience. After all, every developed country today was at one time itself underdeveloped. And in each case the beginning and progress of economic growth involved deep social and cultural changes. We need only remind ourselves of the static tradition-bound, nonmaterialistic-oriented societies of Western Europe in the precommercial and preindustrial era or of the feudalistic social organization in Japan just prior to the beginning of its rapid economic development to realize that social and cultural matrixes extremely uncongenial to the changes implicit in economic growth need not constitute an insuperable barrier.

Second, there is no clearly defined causal sequence in which cultural change precedes and economic growth follows. Though in the present state of our knowledge of the process of economic growth, ignorance far outbalances firmly established principles, one point seems incontrovertible: the process is a *total* one, involving interaction among a multitude of economic, social, political, and cultural forces. Economic growth is itself a powerful source of change in the noneconomic aspects of society. Two of the most nearly universal characteristics of economically developing societies are industrialization and urbanization, and perhaps no two more potent forces affecting the ideology and social structure of a society can be found.

Finally, it may well be that apparent resistance to social change is a function of lack of opportunity to gain from change. Social psychology teaches that man's wants and desires are to some extent shaped by the means available for satisfying them. If, then, there is opened up the prospect of economic growth and higher standards of living, resistance to the necessary sociocultural adaptations may be greatly reduced. This is one of the chief underlying justifications for a committed program of external assistance to less developed countries by developed countries—a point to be discussed more fully later.

Limitations of space forbid any more extended consideration here of the crucially important sociocultural aspects of economic growth. In what follows we shall concern ourselves primarily with the economic aspects of growth.

ECONOMIC OBSTACLES TO GROWTH

The LDCs have low per capita income because their output of goods and services—the source of income—is low in relation to their population. It follows that in order to realize economic growth productivity per capita must somehow be increased. Quite apart from the sociopolitical resistances mentioned above, the economic obstacles to raising per capita productivity can be formidable.

Limited Resources

The potentiality for growth is constrained in the first place by the quantity and quality of existing productive resources. If a country is fortunate enough to be well endowed with an abundant supply of natural resources and of land area possessing favorable attributes of soil, climate, and topography, the base for economic growth is laid in advance by nature. The economic history of the United States offers an outstanding illustration of these advantages.

Many less developed countries of the world are handicapped at the outset by the small amount or poor quality of natural resources available per head of population. Agricultural development may be limited by such factors as poor soil, adverse climatic conditions, lack of sufficient rainfall, or rugged topography. The development of particular industries may be precluded, on an economic basis, by the paucity or inaccessibility of domestic raw materials, especially if the raw materials are weight-losing and costly to transport.

We must be cautious, however, not to exaggerate the limitations on growth potentiality set by the quantities or qualities of natural domestic resources. There are outstanding examples of countries with relatively high standards of living, yet poor in natural resources, either quantitatively or qualitatively. Switzerland and the Netherlands, for example, fall into the upper range of per capital incomes; yet they are both among the countries of the world with the least amount of arable land per capita and without any important domestic sources of industrial raw materials.

Moreover, natural resources of economic value are not absolutely fixed. On the contrary, they are in good part a function of technology. The Netherlands has expanded its supply of arable land through walling off areas from the sea. What is today regarded as worthless rock may tomorrow become a valuable source of minerals or energy, as the history of uranium has dramatically shown. It will probably be only a matter of time before salt water can be cheaply converted into fresh water, at which stage enormous areas of land now too arid to be useful will become potentially rich and valuable for agriculture.

Nor must it be forgotten that various inputs are generally substitutable over a considerable range in producing a given output. Both capital and labor may often be substituted for land or other natural resources. Even food can be grown chemically, and an acre of land can be made to yield several times greater output through the use of fertilizers, hybrid seeds, and so on.

The second resource-constraint on development is the economic quality and quantity of labor. One of the most important reflections of a stagnant economy with low per capita income is a working population plagued with malnutrition and ill-health, illiteracy, lack of initiative, inadaptability to new ideas and new processes, indifference to self-betterment, and similar inabilities and attitudes, constituting a hard core of resistance to economic growth. This is indeed one of the main reasons for the "self-breeding" character of deep poverty. For most LDCs, it is hardly an exaggeration to say that the first step toward a higher standard of living is improvement in the health, physical stamina, and level of education and skilled training of the mass of people. The dilemma, as always, is how to get started—with lack of facilities and, especially, lack of teachers.

Apart from the qualities of the population and working force, most LDGs simply have too many people in relation to their endowments of natural resources and supply of capital. This, in fact, is one of the chief explanations for a state of underdevelopment. As we have stated many times before, per capita productivity and real income are in part a function of the ratio of land and capital to population. Other things being equal, the lower this ratio is, the lower will be the standard of living. To put it another way, with given supplies of land and capital and a given state of technology, there is some population number that is "optimum." The concept of an optimum population is tricky to handle, but, however refined the definition, hardly anyone would deny that the typical less developed country today has a population in excess of the optimum.

From a static point of view, the "solution" to an above-optimum population is to increase the supply of capital. But, unfortunately, this may not be enough, for populations are not static, especially in the face of increased production. The third problem with respect to labor supply and population, then, relates to their future growth.

If, in a particular area of the world, the population is relatively sparse, an increase in population may have a favorable impact on economic development by providing a widening market and opportunities for a greater degree of specialization within the economy. The United States in the 19th century and Canada and Australia still today offer excellent examples of the favorable effects of growing populations.

In countries already highly overpopulated, the situation is different. Overpopulated areas generally have both high birthrates and high death rates. An improvement in hygienic conditions and nutrition—perhaps essential for increasing labor productivity, as suggested earlier—has the immediate effect of reducing the death rate without, however, correspondingly lowering the birthrate. Indeed, the birthrate may even rise, because of better health and care of expectant mothers, a decrease in the practice of abortion, and so on. The consequence is a tendency for the population to increase in response to economic progress, thereby threatening to make the progress only temporary. In many countries this may prove to be one of the greatest stumbling blocks on the road to a higher standard of living. Because of the admixture of economic, social, political—and often religious—aspects entering into the determination of the birthrate, only carefully worked-out policies, appropriate to the particular cultural complex of each country, can hope to succeed in solving the problem.

The third resource-constraint on growth is the limited supply of capital and saving to form new capital. For the total output of an economy to grow by 1 percent per year, net new capital formation of around three to four times this amount may be necessary. Suppose that the population is growing at an annual rate of 2.5 percent. In this case, it takes net new capital formation of from 7.5 to 10.0 percent of the national income to keep the standard of living from falling. However, in the typical stagnant LDC, the volume of domestic saving is hardly sufficient to support such a rate of investment, let alone to support the higher investment required for growth. It has been suggested that at least 15 percent of the gross national product must be devoted to capital investment for an economy to "break out of the vicious circle of poverty and underemployment."[2]

The paucity of saving in LDCs is usually accompanied by limited incentives to invest available saving in growth-oriented investments. The profitability of private investment in an industry depends upon the existence of an adequate market for its product. But in low-income countries the domestic market for anything but the most elemental types of commodities is, simply because of the low level of per capita income, exceedingly narrow. Even though the creation of additional industries would generate additional income and purchasing power, no *single* industry is ordinarily able in itself to create an adequate demand for its own product. On the other hand, the simultaneous development of many industries tends to raise the level of income and demand enough to provide an adequate market for each. In effect, the workers and other factor owners in each industry constitute a market for the products of all other industries.

The balanced expansion of the economy in many sectors at the same time would be the most direct way of breaking the stalemate just described. But how to accomplish such a multisector expansion is one of the challenges facing LCDs.

Static Technology

How much output a given set of employed resources produces depends upon the state of technology. Output can be markedly increased without any change in the quantity or quality of the factors of production by applying a more advanced technology. In the case of developed countries, improved technology has been a major element in economic growth.

The level of technology in use in a country is a function not only of the state of knowledge, but also of the availability of the professional, technical, and skilled personnel required to apply the knowledge, and of the opportunities and incentives to do so.

Even though technical knowledge itself tends in the long run to be a "free good" that can be imported from developed countries, it may be slow in some cases to reach the LCDs, especially when it becomes the protected monopoly of private firms. The research and

---

2 See *The Role of Foreign Aid in the Development of Other Countries,* A Study Prepared at the Request of the Special Committee to Study the Foreign Aid Program, U.S. Senate, by The Research Center in Economic Development and Cultural Change of the University of Chicago, Committee print (Washington, D.C.: U.S. Government Printing Office, 1957) , p. 4.

development expenditure underlying the advancement of technical knowledge, on the other hand, is typically extremely limited in the LCDs themselves.

Perhaps the other two variables determining the level of technology are more responsible than the lack of knowledge for the slow pace of technological advance usually found in less developed countries. As indicated earlier, the shortage of technical and skilled personnel and the absence of a large and expanding market are characteristic of LDCs, both of which favor the continuation of traditional technology. To the extent that technological changes involve capital investment, the shortage of capital additionally restrains innovation.

Inefficient Organization

We have identified the principal objective constraints on development imposed by limited resources and markets and the state of technology. There remains an important final constraint on growth that is of a different character, relating to social and economic organization.

With given resources employed with a given technology, output is a function of the efficiency of resource use. Efficiency is of two varieties: technical and economic.

Technical efficiency requires that no more resources be used than necessary to obtain any level of output and depends, therefore, on proper management at the operating level of the individual firm or producing unit.

Economic efficiency is much broader than technical efficiency, embracing the latter as only one of its elements. The criterion of economic efficiency is costs of production, optimal efficiency being associated with minimum costs.

It is a fair presumption that LDCs on the average are less efficient in the use of their resources than are developed countries. Lesser technical efficiency is attributable in part to the lack of skilled entrepreneurial and managerial personnel but perhaps more especially to the absence of a strong motivation to squeeze the maximum output out of resources. Production in LCDs is predominantly agricultural, commonly carried on largely by self-sufficient peasant family units. Frequently there is not enough land available to provide full-time employment to all working members of the family, leading to underemployment or "disguised unemployment." Under such circumstances, the absence of the drive to be technically efficient is quite understandable.

Economic inefficiency is undoubtedly a far more pervasive and serious hindrance to development than is technical inefficiency. Economic efficiency requires the operation of a system of social accounting which properly measures opportunity costs and marginal contributions to output and allocates resources accordingly. In developed economies, the allocative system is based on the market pricing mechanism. In the LCDs, the market mechanism functions at a very low level, with the allocative system tending to be dominated by traditional modes of resource use. It is hardly an exaggeration to say that development is not possible on any significant scale without breaking out of tradition-bound methods of resource allocation. This is, of course, simply an aspect of the sociopolitical framework of development discussed earlier.

THE RELEASE OF DEVELOPMENTAL FORCES

Notwithstanding the obstacles and constraints on the growth of LCDs we have examined, the potentiality for development is always present, though in varying degrees for different countries. Indeed, development *is* occurring in a vast number of LCDs. The central question is the process through which development takes place, and what methods are most fruitful in initiating or accelerating the process.

A definitive answer to this question has so far not been found. What we do know, as indicated earlier, is that development is an extremely complex phenomenon. Fortunately, we need not attempt here to sort out the multifarious elements of the development process. We can, however, undertake the more modest task of examining the possible role in development of international economic relations.

We shall devote the next chapter to this assignment. To set the stage for the forthcoming discussion, let us see if international economic relations could conceivably help overcome the obstacles to growth discussed above.

At a superficial level at least, the potentiality of developmental support from the international sector is apparent. The scarcity of resources can be relieved through trade and capital movements; the restraint of limited markets can be removed by access to world markets; the more advanced technology of developed countries and the technical know-how to apply it might be borrowed or transmitted through economic contacts; inefficiency of resource use can be reduced by the opportunities for economic advancement afforded through trade and the example and competitive pressures of more efficient foreign producers.

In the next chapter we shall see how international economic relations may indeed contribute to development in all the above connections. But we shall also see that it is not simply a matter of LCDs suddenly being integrated into the world economy and experiencing growth promptly therewith.

RECOMMENDED READINGS

DENISON, EDWARD F. *Why Growth Rates Differ.* Washington, D.C. Brookings Institution, 1967.

HAGEN, E. E. *On the Theory of Social Change.* Homewood, Ill.: Richard D. Irwin Co., 1962.

HOSELITZ, BERT F., ED. *The Progress of Underdeveloped Areas.* Chicago: University of Chicago Press, 1952. Especially useful in giving historical and cultural aspects of economic development.

McCLELLAND, D. C. *The Achieving Society.* Princeton, N.J.: Princeton University Press, 1961.

MEIER, GERALD M. *Leading Issues in Economic Development.* 2d ed. Parts 1 and 2. New York: Oxford University Press, 1970.

SPIEGELGLAS, STEPHEN AND WELSH, CHARLES J., EDS. *Economic Development: Challenge and Promise.* Englewood Cliffs, N.J.: Prentice-Hall, 1970.

STUDY QUESTIONS

1. What is meant by the term "less developed area"? Canada has vast unrealized economic possibilities. Do you include her among the less developed countries?

2. Explain the statement that "the process of economic development is not only—and perhaps not even mainly—an economic problem."

3. Indicate some of the major cultural and political changes implicit in economic development.

4. Why is the gross national product an unsatisfactory measure of the state of development?

5. See if you can calculate how long it would take for a growth rate in output of 6 percent per year, accompanied by a population growth rate of 3 percent, to double per capita output.

6. Why is the capacity of LDCs to save more limited than that of developed countries? What significance does this have for growth?
7. How do limited markets serve to restrain capital formation?
8. Distinguish between technical and economic efficiency.
9. What are the reasons for economic inefficiency in LCDs?
10. In what sense is technology a "free good"?
11. Show how each of the economic obstacles to growth discussed in the text might be relieved through international economic relations.

24

The role of international trade and capital movements in development

With the possible exception of certain centrally planned economies such as mainland China, none of the less developed countries (LDCs) of the world expect to achieve their goals of development in isolation from the world economy. The live issues are not whether international economic relations are important in the development process but rather *how* important they are, and more especially, under what conditions their contribution to development would be greatest.

THE IMPORTANCE OF TRADE IN DEVELOPMENT

In classical thought, trade was regarded as an "engine of growth"— that is, as providing the opportunity and the stimulus for a country to become economically developed. This view has been strongly challenged, as we shall see later. However, the dominant current economic theory concurs in the general conclusion of the classical economists, though on the basis of an elaborated analysis. Let us examine the ways in which trade can foster development according to contemporary thinking.

427

Trade and Efficiency

We begin with the proposition made familiar in the early chapters of this book: trade in accordance with the principle of comparative advantage increases the efficiency, and therewith the real national income, of participating countries. It will be recalled that the sources of the gain from trade in competitive markets are twofold: from specialization in production (the specialization gain) and from exposing consumers to a common world set of products and prices (the exchange gain). A third source of increased efficiency, applicable when domestic markets tend to be imperfectly competitive, is the pressure that free trade exerts upon domestic producers to keep competitive with foreign suppliers.

It may be objected that, in the context of given resource endowments, state of technology, and pattern of demand, the increment in efficiency which trade permits and enforces, once captured, cannot be repeated. That is, having reached a state of optimum resource allocation and exchange through trade, a country exhausts this source of economic growth, though it may continue indefinitely, of course, to enjoy the benefits of maximum efficiency.

While this observation is true in the context specified, it should be noted that in fact the bases of comparative advantage tend to shift more or less continually in response to changing relative factor endowments, technology, and patterns of demand at home and abroad. When these changes are favorable to a country's economy (which they not always are), trade permits their exploitation in the interest of the national economy and its development. In this sense, potential new benefits of trade are constantly appearing.

Dynamic Effects

Notwithstanding the last comments above, the effects of trade so far considered are largely once-over and static, hence, hardly the fuel to make trade a powerful "engine of growth." To qualify in the latter role, trade must release dynamic forces that go beyond merely increasing the efficient use of given productive capacity, to stimulating the creation of additional capacity. This point may be expressed in terms of the production transformation or possibilities curve which constitutes the production boundary of an economy: growth requires not only reaching the most efficient location on a given curve but an expansion of the curve in an upward and outward direction. Some of the possibilities of trade having this kind of expansionary impact on the production boundary will now be explored.

Increased Factor Utilization. By opening world markets to the products of a country, trade can lead to the utilization of resources previously dormant or only partly brought into the production process. Many countries during the 19th century—Canada, Argentina, Australia, among others—experienced such export-led growth as the result of an expanding world demand for their natural resources and grains. In more recent times, one thinks of the petroleum industry in the Middle East as an outstanding example of the opportunities afforded by world markets for the exploitation of natural resources and the development of the possessor countries.

Trade can lead to the fuller use of not only natural resources but of labor as well. It is a common observation that in many less developed countries there is large-scale underemployment of the labor force, especially in the dominant agricultural sector. The major potential source of increased employment in such cases is the creation or expansion of light industries. The absence of sufficient domestic markets to absorb a larger output of manufactures acts as a barrier to the development of industries; trade can remove this barrier, provided that costs are competitive in world markets.

Increased Factor Supplies. An obvious contribution of trade to growth is in providing access to resources and products not available domestically but essential for development. For example, to develop hydroelectric energy, it may be necessary to import most of the machinery and equipment.

Of more general importance is an increase in the supply of capital which foreign trade may stimulate. Trade can influence capital formation in several ways. First, because of the increased real income produced by the more efficient use of resources through trade, saving, which is a prerequisite of capital formation, tends to rise. Second, trade itself opens up profitable investment opportunities in potential export industries. Finally, the increase in the level of domestic economic activity and the potential of developing export industries associated with engagement in trade relations may attract an inflow of foreign capital (and, in the case of sparsely settled areas, of labor as well). The role of capital inflows will be examined below.

Skills and Technical Knowledge. A characteristic of most less developed countries is the scarcity of skilled labor and technical know-how, which is one of the principal barriers to economic development. Contacts and trade with more highly developed countries are conduits for the transmission from abroad of ideas and technical know-how which can be applied or adapted to the domestic economy. Besides these general indirect effects of trade contacts, more direct transferals of foreign technology and skills may be provided through licensing arrangements, the employment of foreign technicians, and the establishment of foreign subsidiary companies in the local economy.

Linkages and Spillovers. Trade obviously stimulates economic activity in export and import industries. However, unless the trade sector becomes an enclave largely insulated from the rest of the economy—a possibility discussed below—the stimulative effects of trade spread beyond the industries immediately involved. Production of goods for export may induce an expansion in the industries furnishing inputs to the export sector—so-called "backward linkages." Moreover, the output of export industries usually is not entirely exported but partly remains in the local economy. To the extent that the output is an input to other domestic industries—for example, a cotton export industry furnishing input to a domestic clothing industry—there are "forward linkages."

Other "spillovers" from the foreign trade sector are normally to be expected. Thus, the technical knowledge acquired and the skills developed as the result of trade are not necessarily, or usually, confined to the trade sector of the economy.

CAPITAL INFLOWS AND DEVELOPMENT

Foreign trade may contribute to a country's development, as we have seen, through increasing the efficiency of resource use and through releasing dynamic forces which encourage the growth of production. However, trade itself does not provide additional resources to a country. As long as a country is constrained to pay for its imports of goods and services with exports of equal value, the total flow of goods and services available to it is limited to its national product or income.

The only way a country can obtain a flow of goods and services greater than its national production is to receive an excess of imports over exports. This can be formally expressed in terms of the following equations:

$$Y = C + I + X - M \qquad (1)$$
$$A = C + I \qquad (2)$$

Equation (1) is the national income identity, familiar from an earlier discussion (see page 309 ff.), where Y represents income, C consumption, I investment, X exports, and M imports. Equation (2) shows the current flow of goods and services available to the domestic economy (A) for consumption (C) and investment (I). Clearly, A can exceed Y only if M is greater than X.

A principal constraint on growth in less developed economies is inadequate saving to finance the rate of investment required for an increase in per capita productivity. The problem is how to increase investment (I in the above equations) at a given level of national income and current volume of consumption. The solution is indicated by rewriting equation (1) as:

$$I = S + M - X \qquad (3)$$

This is equivalent to equation (1), since saving (S) is definitionally equal to income (Y) minus consumption (C).

From equation (3) it is clear that if investment is to exceed domestic saving, imports must exceed exports. We arrive, then, at the same result as before, except that now it is expressed in terms of the crucial saving-investment relationship rather than in terms of the overall availability of resources.

Since the typical less developed country is faced with the barrier to growth arising out of the insufficiency of domestic saving, it follows that one way of hurdling the barrier is to realize an import surplus over a period of some years. Provided that the extra resources thus rendered available are devoted to investment in productive capacity (rather than used to increase current consumption), an important contribution to development is made.

An obvious question now suggests itself: how is a country to finance an import surplus over an extended period? The answer is furnished by our earlier analysis of the balance of payments (see Chapter 14). To avoid balance-of-payments disequilibrium, an import surplus of goods and services must be accompanied by an autonomous inflow of capital. To put it the other way around, a net autonomous inflow of capital is transferred in the form of a net movement of goods and services into the capital-receiving country.

In the traditional view, private long-term capital movements perform a function parallel to that of trade in fostering the development of countries. In the absence of artificial impediments, developed countries tend to be net capital exporters, the less developed countries net capital importers. The mechanism bringing this about consists of differential rates of return on capital investment. Developed countries, almost by definition, are relatively capital-abundant, while less developed countries are relatively capital-scarce. As a consequence, marginal rates of return on investment and interest rates tend to be low in developed economies and high in less developed economies. In seeking maximum returns on their investible funds, private individuals and business firms are led to seek outlets in less developed areas. Not only are additional resources thus provided to the latter, but managerial skills and technical know-how are transmitted.

CRITIQUE OF THE CONVENTIONAL VIEW

The conventional analysis of the positive role of trade and capital flows in economic development presented above has been subjected to severe criticism by some economists and by many spokesmen of the LDCs.[1] The criticism varies in its nature and intensity, ranging from essentially political bases to technical economic considerations and from rejection of any positive contribution of trade and capital flows to acceptance of the latter but only under strongly controlled conditions.

The Dual Economy

The most radical critics of the conventional view is that free market trade, and even more so private capital flows, impose an imperialistic, colonial pattern on less developed countries. This conclusion is essentially Marxian and is held mainly by those ideologically attracted to that philosophy. A modified version popular especially among the newly emerging countries is that trade and foreign capital inflows threaten the security of recently won political and economic independence from colonial powers.

One of the characteristics of the "colonial pattern" objected to is the so-called "dual economy," with a relatively advanced, small export sector surrounded by a backward domestic sector. Foreign investment is held especially responsible for this unbalanced structure, with the capital invested mainly in means of exploiting natural re-

---

[1] Among the principal dissenters to the classical proposition are W. H. Singer (see his "The Distribution of Gains between Investing and Borrowing Countries"), *American Economic Review, Papers and Proceedings,* May 1950; Paul Prebisch (see his report, as Secretary-General of the United Nations Conference on Trade and Development, *Towards a New Policy for Development* [New York, 1964]); and Gunnar Myrdal (see his *Rich Lands and Poor* [New York: Harper & Row, 1957]).

sources that are exported, leaving practically untouched the sector producing for local consumption.

Apart from the relatively rare proposal to seek economic isolation from the world economy, the common response to the fear of developing a dual economy consists of programs of "balanced" growth that will be discussed below.

The Widening Gap

To support the charge that conventional theory of the role of trade and capital flows in development is defective, critics point to the widening economic gap between the LDCs and developed countries. The facts are not in dispute: the differential in per capita real income between developed and less developed countries has increased as trade and capital movements have expanded. What can be disputed is the allegation that conventional theory is thereby shown to be invalidated.

This allegation is apparently based on a misconception of the theory of factor price equalization discussed many pages ago (see p. 61 ff.). It will be recalled that the theory states that, *under certain rigid conditions,* free trade leads to the international equalization of the prices of productive factors—wages, interest, etc. The theory does *not* predict that in fact equalization will occur. Indeed, the theory is most useful in explaining why in reality equalization does *not* occur—because of the absence in reality of the required conditions.

A second misconception is that even if factor prices were equalized this would mean the disappearance of international differences in real income. Income is a function of the *quantity* of resources owned as well as of their prices, and the theory does not predict that trade will tend to equalize the amount of productive resources possessed by different countries.

A last misconception relates not to economic theory but to arithmetic. Unless one chooses to define progress in development to mean bringing real per capita income in the LDCs to the level prevailing in developed countries, there is no inconsistency between successful development and the "widening gap." Since the per capita income of developed countries is initially higher than of less developed countries, if both groups realize the same growth rate the absolute difference in their incomes increases over time.[2] For the LDCs to

---

2 For example, if income is $1,000 in *A* and $100 in *B* and each grows at a rate of 5 percent, the initial difference of $900 is increased at the end of one year's growth to $945.

catch up with developed countries in real per capita income their growth rate would have to be fantastically high in many cases.[3]

The Terms of Trade

A central thesis of the critics is that, for a variety of reasons, free international trade does not transmit to less developed countries their fair share of the fruits of progress enjoyed by developed countries. One of the principal reasons is the alleged secular deterioration in the terms of trade of the LDCs. This deterioration is attributed both to the nature of their export products and to institutions and policies of the developed countries.

The exports of LDCs consist chiefly of foodstuffs and raw materials, plus a few lightly manufactured goods. But these are products for which the income- (as well as price-) elasticity of demand is low. This means that demand does not keep pace with the growth in income. The situation is aggravated by the tendency in developed countries to create synthetic import substitutes for natural raw materials. In addition, the developed countries are accused of deliberately restricting their demand for the imported goods, of which the LDCs are the principal suppliers, through tariffs, quotas, and taxes. This charge will be discussed below.

On the other side of the coin, it is alleged that while export prices of primary products are determined by worldwide competitive forces and reflect cost conditions, the prices of manufactured goods exported by developed countries are set in monopolistic markets and do not respond to decreases in costs of production.

If the prices which a country's exports command in world markets fall relatively to the world prices that must be paid for imported goods, the country's terms of trade deteriorate. As will be recalled from a much earlier discussion (see p. 68 ff., above), the terms of trade determine the distribution of the gains from trade among countries. If it were true that the long-run trend in the terms of trade of LDCs is seriously unfavorable, this would be a potent argument against the view that free trade is a stimulant to growth. Indeed, it is possible in an extreme case for a deterioration in the terms of trade to be so severe that the gain from the effect of trade on the volume of output is more than offset by the loss from adverse terms of trade.

---

[3] Thus, to continue the example in the preceding footnote, for the initial difference in income merely to be held the same, at the end of a year, as *A* grows by 5 percent, *B* would have to grow by 50 percent!

Such a theoretical possibility has been dubbed "immiserizing growth" by its author.[4]

Although the terms of trade of LDCs—as for other countries—fluctuate, there is no established empirical basis for the sweeping generalization that, as a group, the LDCs suffer from a long-run adverse trend in their terms of trade. Because of the different types of products entering importantly into the exports of different countries, the experience of the LDCs is certainly not uniform.

It should also be noted that, apart from the case of "immiserizing growth"—which is probably of limited application to the real world—deteriorating terms of trade, when they occur, reduce the growth effects of trade but need not eliminate them. For example, suppose that productivity increases in export industries and that the increased output leads to a decrease in export prices. As long as the productivity increase is greater than the price decrease, real income rises notwithstanding the adverse effect on the terms of trade.

Instability of Export Earnings

Associated with the complaint of LDCs that their terms of trade are unfavorable is the charge that their export earnings are highly unstable. Because of low elasticities of demand and supply for primary products, relatively small shifts in demand or supply cause large price changes and accompanying fluctuations in the export earnings of LDCs. Vulnerability in this respect is greatest when the volume of output is subject to unpredictable variables, such as weather conditions. For example, if favorable growing conditions lead to a large increase in the output of coffee, an inelastic demand results in a sharp decrease in price and contraction in total receipts from the sale of the crop.

Severe, continuing fluctuations in export earnings must be counted as a handicap to realizing fully the growth effects of trade. To the extent that domestic investment plans are dependent upon a stable flow of income and of imports, periodic contractions in the flow interfere with the development process.

As in the case of the terms of trade, however, it is too facile a generalization to conclude that LDCs are peculiarly vulnerable to export instability and that such instability when present constitutes a serious impediment to development. Experience with export insta-

---

[4] Jagdish Bhagwati, "Immiserizing Growth: A Geometrical Note," *Review of Economic Studies,* June 1958, pp. 201–05.

bility varies widely among countries and not always in accordance with their status as developed or less developed.[5] Moreover, empirical investigations indicate that the adverse effects of export instability on development is quite weak.[6]

ISSUES IN DEVELOPMENT POLICIES

The objections to the conventional theory of the potential role of trade and capital flows in development lead naturally to certain policy conclusions which are quite different from those following upon acceptance of the conventional theory. This conflict in policy prescriptions has generated lively controversies, but actual experience has blunted the sharpness of earlier disagreements.

Balanced Growth versus Outward-Looking Policies

The thrust of earlier development policies pursued by the LDCs was in the direction of attempting to overcome what the critics of the conventional theory alleged to be the handicaps to development imposed by free trade and capital flows. If the latter result, as the critics charge, to the creation and perpetuation of a "dual economy," to a continually "widening gap," to declining terms of trade, and to instability in export earnings, the appropriate response would seem to be the adoption of policies to avoid these unfortunate effects.

The central theme guiding policies was achievement of "balanced growth" through fostering domestic manufacturing industry. Thereby the perpetuation of the dual economy would be broken, the fruits of industrialization reaped, and excessive dependence upon primary products eliminated. To achieve balanced growth, domestic resources would be directed into import-substitution industries, protected from the competition of lower cost foreign producers by high tariffs, exchange controls, and a variety of other restrictive devices, and directly subsidized through government-provided cheap credit, tax breaks, etc.

It is obvious that this approach to development is contrary to the prescriptions suggested by economic theory. The attempt to rationalize the program by appeals to the infant-industry argument and the

---

[5] See Joseph D. Coppock, *International Economic Instability: The Experience after World War II* (New York: McGraw-Hill, 1962).

[6] See A. I. MacBean, *Export Instability and Economic Development* (London: Allen & Unwin, 1966).

alleged presence of "disguised unemployment" had only a limited success with conventional economists.[7] The critical objection to import-substitution programs is that they are based on misconceived perceptions of their impact on development and impose extremely heavy costs on the economy.

The natural tendency to ascribe the failure of an economy to develop as hoped to the various alleged unfavorable effects of trade finds little objective support either theoretically or from experience.

Theory does *not* predict that trade will lead to development but only that it has the potential of contributing to development. Failure of the potential to be realized is not proof of the theory's invalidity; it is equally explainable in terms of the absence of the internal conditions and policies conducive to capturing the potential.

Perhaps more influential than theoretical reasoning is actual experience. Gradually it has become clear that the earlier pessimism as to the contributions of trade to development has proved to be unfounded. LDCs have grown more rapidly in recent years than was anticipated—with an average annual rate of growth in income of over 5 percent, the target rate set for the decade of the 60s—and for many of the most rapidly growing countries trade has played a leading role.[8]

As the high cost and disappointing results of import-substitution programs became evident and the pessimism with respect to export possibilities weakened, the LDCs shifted to more outward-looking policies. The shift in outlook can be dated with the first meeting of the United Nations Conference on Trade and Development (UNCTAD) held in 1964. At that conference, the emphasis changed from import-substitution policies to the promotion of exports, especially manufactures, and this emphasis continued to be expressed in subsequent meetings of UNCTAD. Concurrently, a new set of policy issues has emerged.

Trade Preferences

In our earlier discussion of commercial policies (see Chapter 10), we noted the significant movement toward a reduction in trade barriers, formally expressed in the General Agreement on Trade and Tariffs (GATT). However, the LDCs complain—and with a great

---

[7] See, for example, H. Myint, *The Economics of the Developing Countries* (London: Hutchinson & Co., 1973), pp. 127 ff.

[8] See Hollis B. Chenery and Helen Hughes, "Industrialization and Trade Trends: Some Issues for 1970's," *Prospects for Partnership* ed., Helen Hughes (Baltimore: Johns Hopkins University Press, 1973), chap. 1.

deal of justice—that the trade policies embodied in GATT are mainly directed toward and relevant to trade among the developed countries. Even though trade for the latter countries has been greatly liberalized in the postwar years, the exports of the LDCs remain severely handicapped by a variety of protectionist devices.

As for primary products—accounting for over four fifths of the export earnings of LDCs—import quotas on certain products are commonly imposed by developed countries as part of their programs of domestic price supports or, as in the case of petroleum for example, in pursuit of national security interests. Tariffs are also levied on certain primary products to protect domestic producers. Even in the case of commodities not produced at home—such as tropical foodstuffs—import demand is frequently limited by high consumption taxes.

Most primary products used as raw material inputs in making other products are subject to low or zero tariffs. On the surface, this would seem to suggest that importing countries are giving free rein to the export of such materials by the LDCs. Actually, however, from the standpoint of the total export earnings of LDCs, an accurate assessment of the effects of low duties on raw materials cannot be made without taking into account tariffs levied on the processing of the materials. Typically, the more highly processed a material is and the higher the stage reached in the production of the final output, the greater is the tariff imposed. As a consequence, low tariffs on raw materials increase the protective effect of the tariffs on products processed from the materials. (The point here is the distinction between nominal tariffs and effective rates of protection, discussed on pages 185–87.) For instance, if $1 of imported raw material, duty-free, is processed into a product worth $2 on which a 25 percent tariff is levied, the effective rate of protection on the value added by the processing is 50 percent. The net result is to reduce the import market for processed materials and prevent the less developed exporting countries from realizing potential export earnings from this source.

The fact that the tariffs of developed countries are generally higher on goods the more advanced are their stages of production, together with the significant difference that may exist between nominal and effective rates of protection, are also important considerations in determining the access of LDCs to the markets in developed countries for manufactured goods. The successive rounds of negotiations for lower tariffs under GATT, described in Chapter

10, have reduced the *average* nominal tariff on manufactures to a markedly lower level than previously prevailed. However, nominal tariffs on manufactured products which the LDCs have the greatest ability to export in particular, labor-intensive, light manufactures—tend to be considerably higher than the average, while the effective rates of protection are frequently a great deal higher than the nominal rates.

The difficulties encountered by LDCs in increasing their export of manufactured goods to developed countries are not limited to the tariffs of the latter. Whenever the import of particular goods into the developed countries appears to affect adversely domestic competing industries, additional restrictive measures are often taken or threatened to be taken. A prime example is cotton textiles, the prototype of manufactured products in which many LDCs have a comparative advantage and which they are able to export, even over tariff walls. As noted in an earlier discussion, the United States and other developed countries have responded to the increased inflow of foreign cotton textiles by threatening to impose quotas if the exporting countries do not "volunteer" to restrict the volume of their exports. The overt imposition of import quotas has been avoided so far (the possibility of their use in the future is always present) only through an international agreement severely limiting cotton textile exports to developed countries by the LDCs.

If developed countries wish to open the way for an expansion in the exports of less developed countries, a reduction in the trade barriers described above would be an obvious route to take. The conventional free-trade approach consists simply of removing tariffs and quantitative restrictions on all goods. In the framework of currently accepted rules of conduct as embodied in GATT, however, any reduction in tariffs is supposed to be on the basis of negotiated *reciprocity* and applied in a *nondiscriminatory* manner. On both counts, the less developed countries have other ideas.

The principle of reciprocity is opposed on the grounds that it would lead to the perpetuation of the traditional pattern of trade, with the LDCs continuing to produce and export mainly primary products and to import manufactured goods. The goal of industrialization would therefore be ill-served. The LDCs insist that trade concessions to them should be *unilateral* and extend in particular to manufactures and semimanufactures.

The principle of nondiscrimination is opposed on the grounds that what LDCs need to foster their industrialization is an initial period during which industries can have a chance to develop without the competition in export markets of already well-established industries in developed countries. The central idea here is mainly infant-industry protection but afforded by the developed countries rather than by the less developed countries themselves through their own tariffs or subsidies. Hence, the proposal is for developed countries to extend *preferential* treatment to the products of LDCs. For example, if the United States were to maintain a tariff of 20 percent on shoe imports from other developed countries, it might reduce the tariff to 10 percent or some other level less than 20 percent on shoes imported from LDCs.

From a theoretical point of view, most economists are opposed to preferential trade policies. The principal objection is the distortion they cause in price relationships, leading to a misallocation of resources. However, a vast amount of price distortion already exists, and it can be argued that the real issue, therefore, is whether trade preferences for less developed countries would be productive in stimulating development, rather than whether they would have ideal allocative effects.[9]

The alternative to preferential treatment for the manufactures of LDCs is removal of the hindrances to their export imposed by the developed countries. This approach has many advantages over trade preferences.

In the first place, it would obviate all the cumbersome, costly administrative machinery and possible conflicts in policies that preferences would entail. Second, it would avoid conflicting with the hard-won code of liberal conduct in international economic relations embodied in GATT. Third, it would encourage the development of those industries in LDCs in which they have or can acquire a genuine comparative advantage and which can survive free competition in world markets. (If infant-industry protection is justified, this can best be afforded through subsidies provided by the individual country concerned.) It is highly improbable that a preference system could be devised to yield a rational pattern of stimulation to the industries of the LDCs.

Notwithstanding the theoretical advantage of the trade liberalization approach over a preference system, it would be unfortunate if disputation over their relative merits were to result in no effective action of any kind being taken to expand the markets of the LDCs.

---

[9] This argument is supported by the theory of "second best," which shows that when ideal conditions do not prevail throughout an economy, the optimum policy with respect to any sector may require deviation from the ideal.

In comparison with the present situation, trade preferences for the LDCs would undoubtedly improve their prospect for development.

Commodity Price Stabilization

The second major proposal emanating from UNCTAD meetings relates to the problem of instability in export earnings discussed above. Various devices may be employed in an effort to stabilize commodity prices. One is the use of *buffer stocks*. An agency would buy and store commodities during periods of price decline and sell them during periods of price increase. Such a scheme is feasible only for products that are storable at a reasonable cost. More important, the procedure suffers from the serious weakness of tending to set prices that are either too low or too high. If the price is set below the long-run equilibrium level, stocks will become exhausted and therewith the ability to keep prices down. In the more probable case in practice, prices would be set above equilibrium levels, resulting in the accumulation of stocks and the eventual necessity of ceasing further acquisition.

A second variety of stabilization schemes is *production* or *export restriction* for the purpose of maintaining prices above their free-market levels. This can be done through production or export quotas for supplying countries, but to be effective it requires that major importing countries agree to enforce the quotas through their import policies.

Like buffer-stock programs, output or export restrictions suffer from the difficulty of projecting future equilibrium conditions, in the latter case demand conditions. Moreover, the supply side is likely to prove resistant to control, since there is always the temptation for individual producers to escape from the program and sell larger quantities than they are supposed to. Finally, restrictive measures protect inefficient producers and foster a misallocation of resources.

Other schemes, such as multilateral contracts between producing and consuming countries and price compensation arrangements have been used or proposed as methods of stabilizing prices or export earnings. The history of international commodity agreements, however, is replete with failures. Even if successful in stabilizing prices, moreover, this would not be tantamount to stabilizing *export earnings* of the LDCs. To the extent that price fluctuations arise from shifts in supply, stabilizing prices can have the effect of aggravating the instability of earnings.

An alternative approach to the problem of price instability for the exports of LDCs is *compensatory financing*. If a country suffers from a temporary decline in its export earnings, the impact on its economy could be softened by giving the country access to credits or outright grants. The former system is already in operation under arrangements introduced in 1963 by the International Monetary Fund. Under the IMF program, less developed members may borrow 50 percent of their IMF quotas if their export earnings fall short of the recent average.

Although as of April, 1974, over a half billion dollars of compensatory drawings on the Fund had been made, the arrangement is regarded by LCDs as inadequate. However, the plan for reforming the international monetary system adopted in June, 1974, envisages the creation of a new facility in the IMF under which developing countries would receive longer term finance to meet balance-of-payments problems.

Foreign Aid

Finally, we consider one of the most persistent and controversial issues in the international economics of development—foreign aid.

In an earlier part of this chapter the possible role of private capital flows in development was briefly considered. This role has been subject to even stronger dispute by the critics of conventional theory than that of trade. Private foreign investment is associated in the minds of many persons with imperialism and colonialism and with foreign-dominated enclaves surrounded by an undeveloped native sector. Moreover, it is charged that the gains in output produced by foreign investments are withdrawn from the local economy in the form of profits remitted to their foreign owners. Recent highly publicized activities of giant multinational corporations and the threat they allegedly pose to the political as well as economic independence of host countries has served to reenforce traditional antiforeign-investment sentiment on the part of many LCDs. Nevertheless, the hostility to foreign capital is not uniform, and the flow of private funds into the LDCs has been growing at a rapid pace.

Although most economists probably agree that the criticism of the role of private capital in development is highly overdrawn, it is generally acknowledged that in any event there is room for significant contributions to development from foreign publicly provided assistance.

Like private capital flows, foreign aid represents a transfer of resources to recipient countries which increases their ability to increase the stock of capital without reducing current consumption. The difference is that foreign aid is extended in the form of grants, repayment of which is not expected, or in the form of concessionary loans—that is, loans on terms less onerous than would be demanded by private investors—and is furnished on a bilateral governmental basis or multilaterally through international agencies. Consequently, foreign aid can provide capital for projects, such as infrastructure and "social overhead" investments, to which private investors are not attracted. Yet this type of investment—in roads, harbors, irrigation systems, hydroelectric plants, training schools, health institutes, and similar projects of a public utility nature—is frequently extremely fruitful in preparing the stage for more rapid growth generally.

The really significant issues with respect to foreign aid relate not to its potentiality for contributing to development but to a host of other aspects. Among the major issues are (*a*) how important aid is in the development process, (b) the kind of aid, and the conditions under which it is given, and (*c*) bilateral versus multilateral aid programs. Each of these issues will now be briefly considered.

The Importance of Aid in Development. Two extreme views are that development is not possible without foreign aid and that foreign aid contributes nothing net to development. The incorrectness of the first view is demonstrated by the historical experience of present developed countries which achieved this status without foreign aid and by the lack of correlation between the rate of growth in current developing countries and the amount of foreign aid received. The second view is less easily disproved, but the evidence is fairly clear that some countries at least have developed more rapidly as the result of having received external aid.

Nearly everyone agrees that foreign assistance does not necessarily contribute to development and that when it does the contribution is marginal. The success of development programs depends overwhelmingly upon the efforts of developing countries to use their own resources in the manner best suited to promote development. If these efforts are absent or misguided, foreign aid may serve to do no more than to disguise their failure. If domestic conditions and policies are favorable to growth, it will usually occur without external assistance but will be less rapid and more onerous than with aid.

Related to the question of the role of aid in development is whether it has been of appropriate magnitude. In gross terms the amount of external assistance flowing to less developed countries over the past several years is impressive. From 1960 through 1972, gross official financial flows from "free world" countries to less developed countries totaled in excess of $100 billion.[10] However, these flows fell far short of the target established several years ago, of assistance equal to 1 percent of the gross national product of the wealthier donor countries. Moreover, in real terms, the flow of assistance has been declining in recent years.

Disenchantment in donor countries with the apparent results produced by foreign aid accounts for the contraction in the amount provided. To some observers, however, aid has had a significant positive effect on development, with much of the disappointment attributable to unrealistic expectations and the illegitimate intrusion of political and military objectives. Essentially this is the assessment of the international group of experts assigned the task of studying the past and future of development assistance, as revealed in the "Pearson Report."[11] Accordingly, the Report recommends that the percentage of the gross national product of donor countries assigned to development assistance be roughly double the 1968 level (page 18 of the Report) .

Kinds and Conditions of Aid.   The effectiveness of foreign assistance is perhaps more importantly determined by its qualitative characteristics than by its gross quantity.

A significant portion of foreign assistance has not been directed toward economic development but rather toward political and military support. Whatever the merits or demerits of assistance for such purposes, it does not properly belong to the same category as development assistance. Hence, the actual amount of development assistance extended is overstated in the data on official capital flows and the basis for judging its effectiveness compromised.

It should also be noted that, dollar for dollar, aid in the forms of loans represents a smaller amount of real resources than aid in the form of grants, since the former must be repaid, with interest. In calculating the amount of foreign aid represented by a loan, the present discounted value of future interest and amortization payments must be deducted from the amount of the loan. On this basis, the "grant element" in loans to developing countries in recent years has been calculated to average only about one third of the face value

---

[10] *International Economic Report of the President* (Washington, D.C.: U.S. Government Printing Office, February 1974) , table 43, p. 105.

[11] *Partners in Progress,* Report of the Commission on International Development (New York: Praeger Publishers, 1969) .

of the loans.[12] Outright grants, plus the grant element of loans, together have amounted to less than half the total flow of resources.[13]

A third characteristic of aid programs which reduces its effectiveness is the practice of "tying" it in the case of bilateral assistance. This means requiring the receiving country to spend aid funds, in whole or in part, on the goods of the donor country. The practice is sometimes justified on balance-of-payments grounds, but we may suspect that a large element of subsidy to donor countries' industries is also involved. In any event, the effect of tying aid is to force recipient countries to purchase goods which frequently are not as suitable or as cheap as those available elsewhere.

Besides being tied to the donor country, aid may also be tied to specific projects. This means that a given loan or grant is designated for a particular use. One reason for such specification is that it allows the donor and recipient countries to observe the concrete results of aid, with attribution of the assistance properly identified. A second reason is the desire to prevent aid resources from being frittered away on useless projects or ending up in the pockets of corrupt politicians.

Project tying has as serious defects as country tying. It encourages "showcase" investments which may be politically attractive but not sensible from the point of view of the recipient country's development. More fundamental, it is fatuous to suppose that effective use of aid resources can be assured through directing them into specific projects. The amount of resources provided by aid is always a small fraction of the total resources of the recipient country. If the objective is general development, it is how total available resources are employed that matters. Moreover, it makes little sense to try to separate aid resources from domestic resources, for they are to a large extent substitutable for each other.

The above considerations strongly support aid being extended on a general program basis rather than on a specific project basis.

Bilateral versus Multilateral Assistance. Foreign assistance to the less developed countries is predominantly bilateral in character. Bilateral aid is given on the basis of an agreement between each donor and recipient country. Multilateral aid, on the other hand, is channeled through international organizations, avoiding the country-to-country relationship of bilateral programs.

One drawback of bilateral programs is the opportunity they offer for the interjection of national political considerations into the aid-

---

12 See World Bank/IDA, *Annual Report 1973,* table 9, p. 93.
13 Ibid.

giving process. While it is naïve to believe that political motives can be kept out of aid programs, the multilateral approach removes the opportunity for expression of the more virulent forms of nationalism and, moreover, reduces the fear of the LDCs of foreign domination.

The economic weaknesses of bilateral program stem first of all from the difficulties of rational development planning when aid is being received from numerous donor countries, each with its own demands as to the proper use of aid resources. These difficulties are compounded when, again as a characteristic of bilateral programs, aid is tied, by either country or by project, or both.

The surest way of avoiding the difficulties associated with bilateral programs, of course, is the provision of aid multilaterally through international organizations. Several such organizations have been created, with generally satisfactory records.

The prototype of international assistance institutions is the International Bank for Reconstruction and Development (IBRD), popularly known as the World Bank. Created at the Bretton Woods Conference in 1944 as a specialized agency of the United Nations, the Bank is a twin sister of the International Monetary Fund. While the IMF was designed to bring order and cooperation in international monetary relations, the IBRD was designed to help in reconstruction and development after World War II.

The central activity of the World Bank consists of making loans to less developed member countries.[14] The bulk of the loan funds of the IBRD is obtained through bond issues in private capital markets. To this extent, the Bank serves mainly as an intermediary between less developed countries and private investors in developed countries. The intermediation is necessary to acquire private capital at close to market rates of interest, for the credit standing of the Bank is high, its obligations being fully guaranteed by its member governments.

Two other institutions were later created to complement and extend the activities of the World Bank. These are the International Development Association (IDA) and the International Finance Corporation (IFC), which, together with the World Bank, form the triad known as the World Bank Group.

IDA was formed as a source of development assistance available on more favorable terms than required by the World Bank. Credits are

---

14 The original idea was for the Bank to stimulate *private* foreign capital movements through its powers to guarantee and participate in private loans and investments. As it turned out, the Bank has confined itself to making direct loans, while the role of participation with private investors has been assumed by the International Finance Corporation, discussed below.

extended for long periods (up to 50 years), are repayable in easy stages after a ten-year period of grace, and carry no interest except for a small service charge. Because of these concessionary terms, IDA loans contain a large element of grant aid. The financial resources of IDA are derived from capital subscriptions of its members, supplemented by grants from the World Bank.

The IFC operates on quite different principles from its sister members of the World Bank Group. Its central purpose is to stimulate private investment in the LDCs by providing directly to business firms part of the required capital. The IFC will not cover more than half the total investment cost of an enterprise and leaves the management and operation of the enterprise in the hands of the private owners. The funds which the IFC invests are obtained mainly from paid-in capital from member countries and the sale of equity stock and portions of loans acquired in its operations.

Numerous other multilateral agencies, regional in their operations, provide development assistance. The Inter-American Development Bank, the European Investment Bank, the African Development Bank, and the Asian Development Bank are the principal regional assistance institutions.

SUMMARY AND CONCLUSIONS

We have seen in this chapter that whereas conventional economic theory suggests that free market trade and private capital movements have the potential of stimulating development, critics of the theory assert that in reality the results are loss of national independence, the creation of a dual economy, a widening of the gap between LDCs and developed countries, a deterioration in the terms of trade, and instability in export earnings. In their early development policies, the LDCs generally heeded the voice of the critics and attempted to overcome the alleged unfavorable effects of free market trade through fostering the creation of domestic industries to substitute for imports. Experience, however, proved such policies to be unfruitful and costly, whereupon the emphasis turned from import substitution to the promotion of exports. Concomitantly, the issues of development policy turned to the role of trade preferences by developed countries for the products of the LCDs, measures to stabilize the world prices of primary products and the export earnings of LDCs, and foreign assistance programs.

Perhaps the clearest impression that emerges from our discussion is that the development process is highly complicated and fraught with unresolved issues. If one is inclined to adopt a somewhat optimistic outlook, gleams of hope can be found in the not insignificant progress in development that has occurred, notwithstanding formidable obstacles, and from some indications that important lessons have been learned as to the most fruitful policies to be pursued in the struggle to achieve development.

RECOMMENDED READINGS

BHAGWATI, JAGDISH. *The Economics of Underdeveloped Countries,* chap. xxv. New York: McGraw-Hill, 1966.

HUGHES, HELEN, ED. *Prospects for Partnership.* Baltimore: Johns Hopkins University Press, 1973.

INTERNATIONAL FINANCE CORPORATION. *Annual Reports.*

JOHNSON, HARRY G. *Economic Policies Toward Less Developed Countries,* chap. ii–vi. Washington, D.C.: Brookings Institution, 1967. By far the most extensive and balanced treatment of the topics considered in this chapter.

LITTLE, I. M. D. AND CLIFFORD, J. M. *International Aid.* Chicago: Aldine Publishing Co., 1966.

MEIER, GERALD M. *The International Economics of Development,* chaps. vii–ix. New York: Harper & Row, 1968.

MIKESELL, RAYMOND F. *The Economics of Foreign Aid.* Chicago: Aldine Publishing Co., 1968.

MYINT, H. *The Economics of the Developing Countries.* 4th ed. London: Hutchinson University Library, 1973.

Partners in Development. Report of the Commission on International Development. New York: Praeger Publishers, 1969.

WORLD BANK/IDA. *Annual Reports.*

STUDY QUESTIONS

1. Describe the various ways in which international trade may serve as an "engine of growth."
2. Distinguish between the static efficiency effects and the dynamic effects of trade.
3. How can trade increase factor utilization? Factor supplies?
4. Assess the role of trade as a conduit for the transmission of skills and technical knowledge.
5. What is meant by "linkages and spillovers" from trade? Cite some examples.

6. How do capital inflows provide additional resources to an economy?

7. What is meant by a "dual economy"? How is trade alleged to be responsible for its existence?

8. What is the basis of the allegation that the terms of trade of the LDCs tend to deteriorate over the long run? Is there any evidence that this is true?

9. Why is it highly improbable that most LCDs will ever achieve a level of per capita real income equal to that of the United States?

10. How does the factor price equalization theorem relate to the so-called "widening gap"?

11. Define "immiserizing growth" and explain the basis for it.

12. Describe and evaluate the policy of import substitution as a means of development.

13. What change in the outlook of LCDs occurred at the first UNCTAD meeting?

14. Evaluate trade preferences as a means of fostering development of the LCDs.

15. Describe buffer-stock and output restriction schemes for stabilizing commodity prices. What are the objections to them?

16. Summarize the major issues with respect to foreign aid.

Index

Index

This book has been set in 11 and 10 point Baskerville, leaded 2 points. Part numbers and titles are 24 point (small) Helvetica. Chapter numbers are 30 point Helvetica and chapter titles are 18 point Helvetica. The size of the type page is 27 x 46½ picas.